PENGUIN BOOKS

REAL BOYS' VOICES

William S. Pollack, Ph.D., a clinical psychologist, is
an assistant clinical professor of psychiatry at Harvard
Medical School, director of the Center for Men at
McLean Hospital, and a founding member and fellow
of the American Psychological Association's Society
for the Psychological Study of Men and Masculinity.
He and his family live in Massachusetts.

WILLIAM S. POLLACK, PH.D.

REAL BOYS' VOICES

WITH TODD SHUSTER

PENGUIN BOOKS

PENGUIN BOOKS
Published by the Penguin Group
Penguin Putnam Inc., 375 Hudson Street,
New York, New York 10014, U.S.A.
Penguin Books Ltd, 27 Wrights Lane,
London W8 5TZ, England
Penguin Books Australia Ltd, Ringwood,
Victoria, Australia
Penguin Books Canada Ltd, 10 Alcorn Avenue,
Toronto, Ontario, Canada M4V 3B2
Penguin Books (N.Z.) Ltd, 182-190 Wairau Road,
Auckland 10, New Zealand

Penguin Books Ltd, Registered Offices:
Harmondsworth, Middlesex, England

First published in the United States of America by Random House, 2000
Published in Penguin Books 2001

1 3 5 7 9 10 8 6 4 2

THE LIBRARY OF CONGRESS HAS CATALOGED
THE HARDCOVER EDITION AS FOLLOWS:
Pollack, William S.
Real boys' voices / William S. Pollack with Todd Shuster.
p.   cm.
ISBN 0-679-46299-6 (hc.)
ISBN 0 14 10.0294 8 (pbk.)
1. Boys—United States—Attitudes.   I. Shuster, Todd   II. Title.
HQ775.P66   2000
305.23'0973—dc21   00-035318

Printed in the United States of America
Set in Times

This book is dedicated to

Marsha and Sarah—

who have taught me how to genuinely listen

My parents and grandparents—

who heard this boy's voice

and

The boys themselves and all who love them—

they opened up their inner lives to us, courageously baring

their hearts and souls with genuine voices.

They await our response.

AUTHOR'S NOTE

All of the voices contained in this book are derived from my ongoing *Real Boys' Voices* research project. However, names, places, and other details contained in these materials have been altered to protect the privacy and anonymity of the individuals to whom they refer. Therefore, any similarity between the names and stories of individuals described in this book and those of individuals known to readers is inadvertent and purely coincidental. The one exception is the chapter discussing the courageous boys of Littleton, Colorado, whose names and stories have become public for the most tragic and unfortunate of reasons.

ACKNOWLEDGMENTS

Boys' voices, for all the reasons explored in this book, do not always easily find their way to expression. It is especially challenging to capture them on the page—particularly in a book that aims to uncover their deeper meaning and show their relevance to the lives of boys and all of us who care about and love them. Such a work, while ultimately the responsibility of one person, does not reach fruition without the sweat, tenacity, and intelligence of a team of dedicated people. As an author, one is buoyed by the toil and insight of a number of colleagues whose contributions to the work—both individually and collectively—help strengthen its messages and, in this case, create a forum in which those who have too long been silenced can finally have their voices heard and appreciated.

I would thus like to take this brief opportunity to offer my gratitude to some of the people who helped make *Real Boys' Voices* possible.

First, I would like to thank Kate Medina, my editor, whose wisdom, energy, and intellectual support were essential to the making of this book. From her earliest connection with my work through her guidance in the creation of this book's older sibling, *Real Boys: Rescuing Our Sons from the Myths of Boyhood,* Kate has helped to create an important difference in how we think about and raise boys in America and throughout the world. Her editorial suggestions are reflective of the highest order of professional excellence, and her magical eye in organizing, shaping, and polishing this book have had a profound impact. Her skill, sincere dedication to this enterprise, and faith in my work with boys cannot be praised too highly.

Other staff at Random House have also been unceasingly supportive. Most especially, I'd like to acknowledge the support of Meaghan Rady, Ms. Medina's former assistant, who from the earliest phases of my relationship with the publishing house always made everything happen. I would like to thank Frankie Jones, too, who ably stepped in to carry the ball when Meaghan made an important career move as we were nearing completion of the manuscript. Random House's remarkable publicists Carol Schneider, Liz Fogarty, and Tom Perry deserve my praise as well for bringing this work to the public's attention even before its pages were complete. Beth Pearson, Don McConnell, Karen Richardson, and Caroline Cunningham are also to be acknowledged for making the finished product as elegant as it is.

Next, I would like to convey my deep appreciation for the invaluable assistance and support I received from Todd Shuster. Todd devoted immense time and energy to helping me reach out to communities across the country, arranging interviews with boys, helping shape interview transcripts into prose, and honing my written commentary in a thoughtful, sensitive way. Todd has truly become a fellow traveler in the world of understanding boys. His literary skills are only outstripped by his indefatigable enthusiasm and depth of caring about the themes raised in this book. I am proud to have had him along with me on this adventure into the inner world of boys.

I would also like to convey my deep thanks to Lane Zachary, who worked closely with Todd in both improving the precision of this written document and adding her unique creative insights to the process. The book would not have been the same without her original touch.

My personal gratitude is also expressed for the assistance provided to me by Todd's colleagues at the Zachary Shuster Agency: Esmond Harmsworth, Kendra Lider-Johnson, and Jennifer Gates did a beautiful job helping me condense, transcribe, and edit numerous interview transcripts.

As part of my research team, I was particularly blessed to have the help of John Butman. John brings tremendous wit and creativity to everything he does. I am thankful for his fantastic job conducting research interviews at several schools, editing this material into essays, and offering his own perceptions about the results of this research. His personal understanding of boys as a loving and caring father only served to enhance the quality of this work. I appreciate the thoughtful assistance, too, of John's colleagues Charles Moore and Dorothy Crawford. I would also like to thank Susan Lawrence, who showed the wisdom of a master teacher and particular sensitivity in interviewing several of the younger boys whose voices appear in this book.

It would be most fitting to mention by specific reference to their respective institutions the educators, organizational leaders, and grass-roots organizers who on behalf of boys contributed so much to the success of this project. However, the need to maintain the privacy and confidentiality of the majority of the boys who participated requires that we merely list them in alphabetical order. This mundane approach does not begin to reflect the abundance of my gratitude, nor does it diminish the meaningfulness of their contribution. I would like to extend my heartiest thanks to: George Armstrong, Susan Batlin, Cindy Blinn, Diane Bohmer, Cindy Bouvier, Linda Cobbe, Jef Conor, John D'Auria, Denise Day, W. Brewster Ely IV, Dale Emme, Dar Emme, John Farber, Robin Finegan, Richard P. Fitzgerald, Krystan Flannigan, Larry Frey, Ronna Frick, Jeanie Goddard, Richard Hawley, Shari Hobson, Laurie Hoffner, Michael Jenkins, Brenda Keegan, Matthew King, Carleton Land, Armand LaSelva, Barbara Macgillivray, Carolyn Mack, Judy Malone-Neville, P. J. McDonald, Robert Meikle, Richard Melvoin, Rena Mirkin, Peter Nelson, Vivien Orlen, Margarita Otero Alvarez, Carol Palmer, Gary Porto, Ray Randonis, Gail Revis, Michael Riendeau, John Ritchie, Suzanne Schrader, Paul Stein, Pam Stinson, Vince Sussman, Elizabeth Twomey, Greg Ventre, Robert Vitalo, Glenn Williams, Ken Wilson, Carolyn Wyatt, and Jeffrey M. Young.

That said, there are some organizations that I feel compelled to acknowledge by name. The Yellow Ribbon suicide prevention program, founded by Dar and Dale Emme, literally saves boys' lives daily. Dar and Dale provided me with invaluable assistance in relation to my thinking about suicide in boys and introduced me to one of their most devoted teen leaders, Michael Hilterbrand, whose intelligence, honesty, and enthusiasm for this project hold special meaning for me.

Likewise, I am deeply indebted to the International Coalition of Boys' Schools. The coalition has long recognized the need for a new psychology of boys and always generously supported my work. I would like to thank John Farber, Brewster Ely, Richard Melvoin, Richard Hawley, Bradford Gioia, and Diane Hulse, as well as the other members of the board and research committee, for their unrelenting faith in my project.

Although this research project was carried out independently under the auspices of The Real Boys Education Program™, I would still like to acknowledge the support of my colleagues at Harvard Medical School and McLean Hospital, particularly Drs. Bruce Cohen, Joseph

Coyle, and Philip Levendusky. The encouragement of the Department of Continuing Education at McLean, and my coworkers (past and present) Carol Brown and Cathy Toon must not go unmentioned. I should also express my gratitude to Dr. Shervert Frazier, Psychiatrist in Chief (emeritus) of McLean Hospital, who has been an incredible mentor, helping me to develop my own voice in a field of psychological study that was once largely overlooked. Never before or since have I had the opportunity to absorb such sagacity about the inner lives of boys and men.

I would like to thank my associates at the Society for the Psychological Study of Men and Masculinity, Division 51 of the American Psychological Association, from whom I have learned so much about gender study, and my friends at the Threat Assessment Division of the United States Secret Service, including Bryan Vossekuil, its director, and Dr. Robert Fein, who have provided me with a wealth of thoughtful information about boys and violence.

Although my research derives from many years of work with boys and men, it is important to recognize the important influences that the "new" psychology of girls and women has had on this entire field. I would like to mention my particular appreciation of the seminal work of Carol Gilligan, whose insights on girls' voices provide an important inspiration for this work, and also that of the core faculty of the Wellesley Stone Center—Jean Baker Miller, Irene Stiver, Judith Jordan, et al.—all of whom have helped to shape a concept of a "connected self" in women that bears much relevance to my own theories of trauma in boys and the possibilities they have, throughout their lives, to heal from it. Dr. Judith Jordan, my colleague, collaborator, and friend, has had a tremendously positive impact on my thinking in this field. Her intelligence and inspiration may be felt throughout my work. Dr. Mary Pipher has generously shared her support for my endeavors. Together we have engaged in much stimulating conversation that I hope will continue to lead to greater collaboration and understanding between boys and girls, men and women.

Researching and writing this work would have been impossible without the love, understanding, and unyielding patience of my family. I am deeply indebted to my wife, Dr. Marsha Padwa, for her invaluable insights about children, adolescents, and their families, and her important critical input with earlier drafts of this work; and to both Marsha and my daughter Sarah Faye Pollack, for their unwavering love and support—juggling schedules, borrowing computers, and sustaining my spirits during times of distress.

To the boys who participated in the study, their parents, and my patients, who have opened their lives to us, and who have taught me so much through their struggles, I extend my personal gratitude and thanks. With the exception of a number of boys whose identities were unfortunately only too clear from the tragedy in Colorado, we have opted to keep the identities of authors of the other original pieces anonymous, to protect each boy's privacy. I would thus like to acknowledge their contributions, which collectively provided the heart and soul of this work. I hope the dissemination of their words will begin to make a difference in how we understand boys, and, in turn, ourselves.

Some of the boys who shared their voices with me in connection with this project opted (with the consent of their parents or guardians) to receive attribution. I am thus delighted to extend my heartfelt appreciation to: Sean Baird, Brian Barenberg, Austin Barrett, Michael Bell, Andrew Birnberg, Andrew Bisotti, Matt Botler, John L. Bujaci, Raheem Carr, Hervey Carvajal, Ken Case, Richard Castaldo, Andrew Clark, Patrick Clarke, Matthew David, Isaiah Davison-Weiss, Nicholas DeWilde, Michael Ferguson, Andrew Fraser, Adam Freedman, Johnny Fry, Mario Fuentes, Chris Gentel, Justin Golenbock, James Gombocz, Darryl Gordon II, Sean Graves, Gregory Greenway, Joe Grimm, Carrington Guzman, Ryan Haines, John Ham, Ben Hart, Jeff Harwin, Brad Hedrick, Matt Henry, Wilber Hernandez, José Herrera, Juan Herrera, David Hilson, Michael S. Hilterbrand, Christopher Hoffner, Gregory Jiminez, Jefferson Lee, Jonathan Kim, Jesse King, Jason Kowrach, Johnny LaSalle, Chris Lascelle, Robert Leary, Jake LeBlanc, Alexander Lee, Todd Lieberman, Michael Lopez, Tobias Loss-Eaton, George MacDonnell, Denny Majewski, Jr., Steven Marty, Irvin Matteo, Dave McCormack, Paul McKoy, Geoff McNally, Mark Merren, Joe Miller, Robert Scott Miller, Teague Mitchell, Milton Morel, Joseph Moya, Jake Murphy, Michael Neff, Chris Neimeyer, Derek Nelson, Chris Neuenfeldt, David Norton, Eric Obeng, Adam Occaso, Donal O'Ceallaigh, Eric Trilling O'Malley, Franklin Onuoha, Reggie Patterson, Carlos Puente, Bryan Purcell, Santosh Rasnet, Kyle Reed, Jordan Rhodes, Matt Richardson, Paul Risenmay, Joseph Rivard, Saul Saldarriaga, Jeremy Sandler, Christopher Schappert, Jeff Schram, Rand Semke, Nicholas E. Short, Rob Stanton, Harry Stanwood, Adam Sussman, Alex

Svoboda, Will Szabo, Kenny Talanian, David Tassone, Tyler Tolbert, Rafael Torres, Julian Turner, Chris Verillo, Paris Wallace, Jeremy Welsh-Loveman, Bryan White, George Williams, Michael Williams, Sam Willie, Michael Wilson, and Austin Woerner.

Real Boys' Voices has been a work of the heart, and I hope it will reveal the love boys themselves have been struggling to convey—along with their angst, loneliness, and longing to connect.

CONTENTS

INTRODUCTION

LISTENING TO BOYS' VOICES

"Boys are supposed to shut up and take it, to keep it all in. It's harder for them to release or vent without feeling girly. And that can drive them to shoot themselves."

—Scotty, 13, from a small town in northern New England

I N MY TRAVELS THROUGHOUT THIS COUNTRY—FROM THE inner-city neighborhoods of Boston, New York, and San Francisco to suburbs in Florida, Connecticut, and Rhode Island; from small, rural villages in New Hampshire, Kentucky, and Pennsylvania to the pain-filled classrooms of Littleton, Colorado—I have discovered a glaring truth: America's boys are absolutely desperate to talk about their lives. They long to talk about the things that are hurting them—their harassment from other boys, their troubled relationships with their fathers, their embarrassment around girls and confusion about sex, their disconnection from parents, the violence that haunts them at school and on the street, their constant fear that they might not be as masculine as other boys.

But this desperate coast-to-coast longing is silenced by the Boy Code—old rules that favor male stoicism and make boys feel ashamed about expressing weakness or vulnerability. Although our boys urgently want to talk about who they really are, they fear that they will be teased, bullied, humiliated, beaten up, and even murdered if they give voice to their truest feelings. Thus, our nation is home to millions of boys who feel they are navigating life alone—who on an emotional level *are* alone—and who are cast out to sea in separate lifeboats, and feel they are drowning in isolation, depression, loneliness, and despair.

Our sons, brothers, nephews, students are struggling. Our boy-friends are crying out to be understood. But many of them are afraid to talk. Scotty, a thirteen-year-old boy from a small town in northern New England, recently said to me, "Boys are supposed to shut up and take it, to keep it all in. It's harder for them to release or vent without feeling girly. And that can drive them to shoot themselves."

I am particularly concerned about the intense angst I see in so many of America's young men and teenaged boys. I saw this angst as I did research for *Real Boys,* and then again in talking with boys for this book. Boys from all walks of life, including boys who seem to have made it— the suburban high school football captain, the seventh-grade prep school class president, the small-town police chief's son, the inner-city student who is an outstanding cartoonist and son of a welfare mother— all were feeling so alone that I worried that they often seemed to channel their despair into rage not only toward others but toward themselves. An ordinary boy's sadness, his everyday feelings of disappointment and shame, push him not only to dislike himself and to feel private moments of anguish or self-doubt, but also, impulsively, to assault, wound, and kill. Forced to handle life's emotional ups and downs on their own, many boys and young men—many good, honest, caring boys—are silently allowing their lives to wither away, or explode.

We still live in a society in which our boys and young men are simply not receiving the consistent attention, empathy, and support they truly need and desire. We are only listening to parts of what our sons and brothers and boyfriends are telling us. Though our intentions are good, we've developed a culture in which too often boys only feel comfortable communicating a small portion of their feelings and experiences. And through no fault of our own, frequently we don't understand what they are saying to us when they do finally talk.

Boys are acutely aware of how society constrains them. They also notice how it holds back other boys and young men, including their peers, their male teachers, and their fathers. "When bad things happen in our family," Jesse, an astute twelve-year-old boy from a large middle-class suburb of Los Angeles, recently told me, "my father gets blocked. Like if he's upset about something that happened at work, he can't say anything and we have no idea what he's thinking. He just sits in front of the television, spends time on the Internet, or just goes off on his own. You can't get through to him at all. He just gets totally blocked." Of course, Jesse is learning to do the same. And if we don't allow, even teach boys like Jesse to express their emotion and cry tears, some will cry bullets instead.

A Nationwide Journey

I began a new nationwide journey to listen to boys' voices last summer in my native Massachusetts. In one of the very first interviews, I sat down with Clayton, a sixteen-year-old boy living in a modest apartment in Arlington, a medium-sized suburb of Boston. Clay introduced me to his mother and older sister, and then brought me to his attic hideaway, a small room with only two small wooden windows that allowed light into the room through a series of tiny slits. Clay decided to share some of his writing with me—poetry and prose he had written on leaves of white and yellow paper. His writings were deeply moving, but even more extraordinary were the charcoal sketches that, once he grew comfortable with my presence, he decided he would also share. His eyes downcast, his shoulders slumped inward, he opened his black sketchbook and flipped gently through the pages.

On each consecutive sheet of parchment, Clay had created a series of beautiful images in rich, multicolored charcoal and pastels. "You're a talented artist," I said, expressing my real enthusiasm.

"I haven't shown these to too many people," he said, blushing. "I don't think anyone would really be too interested."

Clay's pictures revealed his angst, and in graphic, brutal detail. There was a special series of drawings of "angels." They were half human, half creature, with beautiful wings, but their boyish faces were deeply pained. Soaring somewhere between earth and heaven, the angels seemed to be trying to free themselves from earthly repression, striving for expression, longing to reach the freedom of the skies. They evoked the mundane world where Clayton's psychological pain felt real and inescapable, yet they also evoked an imaginary place where he could feel safe, relaxed, and free.

In our conversation, Clayton revealed that his inner sense of loss and sadness had at times been so great that on at least one occasion he had seriously contemplated suicide.

"I never actually did anything to commit suicide. I was too afraid I'd end up in a permanent hell . . . but that's how bad I felt. I wanted to end it all."

I thought to myself that maybe that's what these tortured angels were about—a combination of heavenly hope mixed up with a boy's suppressed "voice" of pain.

Clayton then revealed "The Bound Angel," a breathtaking sketch of one of his winged, half-man creatures bent over in pain, eyes looking skyward, but trunk and legs bound like an animal awaiting slaughter.

Clayton explained, "His hands are tied, and his mouth is sealed so he cannot speak. He's in pain, but he has no way to run from it, to express it, or to get to heaven."

"Your angel wants to shout out his troubles to the high heavens, but he is bound and gagged. He wants to move toward someone, but he is frozen in space. He needs to release his voice, but he cannot, and fears he will not be heard. That's why he's so tortured."

"Yes, exactly," he said.

"I guess if he's tied up long enough," I responded, "and can't release that voice, he'll want to die, like you did."

"I think so," Clay said.

There is no reason we should wait until a boy like Clay feels hopeless, suicidal, or homicidal to address his inner experience. The time to listen to boys is now.

MOMENTS OF DOUBT

As devoted as our country is gradually becoming to changing things for boys, society remains ambivalent about giving boys permission to express their feelings. I was recently speaking at a Congregational church in a small New Hampshire town. It was a bright October Saturday morning and I was there to talk to boys and their parents about my Listening to Boys' Voices project. Gazing out at the rows and rows of boys and their parents, I explained that several research associates and I were going across the country to interview and capture the unique voices of adolescent males ranging in ages eleven through twenty. I told the audience, "I hope this project will be just the beginning, that we will all find a way to reconnect with boys, listen to them carefully, and get to know what's really happening inside their minds and hearts."

"That's not so easy," a young, well-dressed woman said from the pews. "I have four sons," she continued, "and, with all due respect, Dr. Pollack, let me tell you something. Number one: my husband is not so hot on my trying to sit down and get all emotional with our sons. I'm not so sure he's going to encourage me to do that. And number two: these days, I don't think our boys are capable of saying much about anything other than girls and sports, and girls and sports." People chuckled throughout the church.

"How old are your sons?" I asked.

"Eleven, thirteen, fourteen, and seventeen," the woman said.

"Do you wish you could reach inside them and get to what they're really feeling and thinking about? Is this something you would like to do?"

"If I could," she said intently, "I would." Looking around at the other boys and parents in the audience and shaking her head incredulously, she added, "I don't think many of the people in this room really feel in touch with their kids, especially not their boys. To be able to do that, we'd have to all decide we're going to give boys a break. Otherwise, nobody in this room is going to take the first step. Nobody wants his or her kid to be an outcast. So I'm not sure any of us are going to take that first step."

"I'm not so sure I agree with you," I said. "The fact that you showed up today to talk about boys is itself one of those first steps. In fact, everybody in this room decided to come here this morning because they care about boys and about making things better for boys. So everyone in this room actually is taking an important first step."

"I guess you're right," the woman said. "So thank you. Thank you for coming way out here to talk to us."

HELPING BOYS TO BE THEMSELVES

Ultimately, there is only one reasonable solution to this national dilemma: helping boys to tell us who they really are, and learning—in a new way—to listen and respond to this reality. Ophelia has been revived more and more. Ophelia speaks. Now we must find the opportunity to hear real boys' voices. That is a fundamental aspect of my work, an important theme in my book *Real Boys,* and the central concept of this book: to help us hear what boys say when they share their "real" voices, open their souls to us; help us recognize the impediments that have blocked this process; to help parents, teachers, coaches, girl-friends, and buddies—all of us who love boys—find a new way to listen to boys, and give America's sons a safe forum in which at last they may speak from more deeply inside themselves. Boys are inherently just as competent about their emotions as girls are, and they are as interested in, and yearning for, spiritual growth, close friendships, and connections.

When we use all our senses to perceive a boy's signals, we may discover that he is replete with emotion, and that he will find all sorts of ways, some direct and obvious, others covert or subtle, to voice his inner feelings and experience. He may blast us with anger. He may bluster with false pride. He may cloak disappointment or shame with utter silence. He may enact his sadness and his despair in gruesome acts of violence or self-destruction. He may drink away his pain and longing. These feelings, and many others, are constantly present inside of him. And yet in many schoolrooms across the country, and within many genuinely warm, loving families throughout the world, so many of these intense feelings seem never to be heard or understood. So the reality of a boy's life and inner world may go undetected or ignored.

On the surface, many boys may appear to satisfy traditional notions about boyhood—they may seem cheerful, confident, bold, and athletic. They may appear to be cool and in control, unaffected by the pain and difficulties that surround them. But when we look beneath the surface, and when boys and young men feel safe enough to let us go to that deeper place inside themselves, we discover that there is so much more that they are feeling and experiencing. Underneath the buoyant public persona of many boys like these, there is a wealth and breadth of feeling.

Whether we are a buddy, a parent, a girlfriend, or a teacher of boys, it can be a remarkably positive experience to discover the rich, sometimes hidden (or quiet) ways in which a boy's actions or words reflect his innermost thoughts and feelings. When we achieve this special understanding, we're able to develop powerful, meaningful connections with boys. We come to know and empathize with them deeply. We learn to see and appreciate not only what the boy shows on the surface—not only the here-and-now outer self he presents to the world—but also the more vulnerable self, the true person inside, his unique soul. It is a wonderful feeling when we genuinely come to know and understand somebody. And, for the boy, it is truly a special experience to feel as though he has been fully heard and understood. To a large extent, feeling heard and understood for who you really are is the very essence of love.

We must get behind the "mask of masculinity," a stance of male bravado and stoicism that many boys develop to cover their inner feelings of sadness, loneliness, and vulnerability. When life becomes too onerous for boys, sometimes the only pathway to safety is to hide the true self, and with it, the genuine voice beneath. This helps to explain why many girls may often use long, rich sentences to express a wide range of their feelings, while in stark contrast, boys seem to have a myriad of monosyllabic responses to questions about what appear to be their deepest experiences: "OK"; "I'm fine"; "No problem." This paradox leaves our boys and all of us who love them at a terrible disadvantage. They become cut off from their deepest voices of vulnerable and loving feeling, missing out, often for a lifetime, on an essential part of themselves. And we, in turn, lose touch with the "real boy" in our midst.

REACHING OUT AND LISTENING TO BOYS: A NEW APPROACH

Reaching out to young and adolescent boys, getting behind the mask of masculinity, and helping them discover and express their genuine voices is an exciting and rewarding process. It is a wonderful feeling to know you can learn to help a boy transcend the forces of repression I discussed above, shake free of society's straitjacket of gender, and speak their true hearts and minds. There are several steps that seem particularly important to this process: (1) creating a "safe space" for the boy; (2) giving him the time he needs to feel comfortable expressing himself; (3) seeking out and providing alternative pathways for expression, especially by engaging in "action talk"—i.e., talking and relating to the boy while you participate in action-oriented activity with him; (4) listening, without interrupting or judging, to everything he has to say; and (5) giving him affirmations and affection.

In an effort to facilitate this essential process, I have outlined, below, the reasons these steps are significant and offered suggestions about how they can be implemented:

Creating a safe space: the shame-free zone.   Before a boy will let you into his inner emotional world, before he will share his true thoughts and feelings, he must first be made to feel safe. He must trust that he is loved and cared for, that nothing he expresses will lead him to be judged, teased, or shamed in any way.

A safe space is one, above all, that protects the boy against further embarrassment or humiliation. It is a "shame-free zone," a place where the boy can talk about anything without fear that his peers, or others, will harass or bully him. As a practical matter, most boys will feel much more comfortable talking about their true thoughts and feelings in a space that is physically separate from, and outside the earshot of, his peer group. The boy needs to feel that he is speaking to you in confidence and that what he is sharing with you is his to bring up in the future. There are few people who enjoy sharing their deepest feelings and experiences with a listener who later "throws it back" at them. It is reassuring for the boy to be told by his listener, "I will not bring up whatever you tell me to anyone, even to you, unless you tell me to. We can talk about this now and you can let me know if you want to talk about it again in the future." Giving the boy control over the information he is sharing builds his confidence that he will not subsequently be shamed, or otherwise punished, for his candor.

A safe space is one that allows for physical and emotional closeness. While the space can be located virtually anywhere—a school, in the home, the car, outdoors—it needs to be somewhere the boy and his listener can achieve a sense of intimacy and connection. There should be few major distractions or interruptions—a blaring radio or television, visits from other people, phone calls. The listener must make it clear that he or she is giving the boy his or her undivided attention. The message to the boy must be: "There is nothing that feels more important to me right now than listening to you."

A safe space, too, is one in which a boy senses complete empathy. Even if he previously did or said something that might have offended or disappointed the listener—even if he concealed something important, acted irresponsibly, hurt or mistreated someone else, or behaved in some other way that seemed inappropriate or simply wrong—he needs to know that his listener is tolerant and forgiving, that he or she is now on the boy's side. He must feel loved. While we may express "zero tolerance" for the unacceptable act, we must always remain compassionate and fully committed to the boy himself.

Time.   Before a boy will allow us to listen to him, he often needs to take some time to think things through on his own. Once we signal to him that we are there for him, that he is free, whenever he would like, to talk with and confide in us, it's important to be patient and permit the boy to decide when he is ready for this. For most anybody, it would probably feel upsetting to be told when to express his or her feelings. But boys often face an additional challenge: the Boy Code tells them that aside from conveying anger, they should rarely if ever express their emotions, especially their vulnerable emotions. Instead they are taught that they should bottle them up and hide their pain behind the mask of masculinity. According to the Code, talking about emotions and exposing the real self are signs of weakness, being a "sissy" or "feminine," and therefore shameful steps to take.

So imagine what it must be like when a boy is told by a sibling, a parent, or his girlfriend, in effect: "Let's sit down right now and talk about what's going on." The boy, in such a case, doesn't simply feel a loss of control; he feels like he's being forced into a forbidden realm, that if he abides, he will surely fail to fulfill the Boy Code. He feels a profound sense of shame. But give him the chance to set his own schedule and take the time he needs to get comfortable—give him what I call "timed silence"—and he will virtually always return to you. He will almost always come back and seek connection.

When he reaches out again in this unique, boylike way, his signals may be subtle. He may ask you a mundane question, such as "Is lunch ready?" "What time is Dad coming home tonight?" or "What are we doing this weekend?" Or "Do you want to listen to the new CD I just bought?" But in almost all of these cases, although he may not be conscious of it, the boy is really saying, "OK. I'm ready. I've been able to shake off my feelings of shame. Now we can talk." Even more, he's truly telling us: "I need your help. I really need to connect—I need you to listen to me right now."

In sum, the trick is to let the boy know that you're available to talk to him whenever he would like. Then, after a time, keep an eye out for the subtle, often indirect ways in which he may signal that he is ready to take you up on your offer. When you notice this gesture, try to say something as simple (and nonthreatening) as "Hey, how about we go hang out in the living room and catch up on things?" Or "Say, what about going for a bike ride together?" By doing something together, the door for connection will be open.

Providing multiple avenues for expression: action talk. As the voices in this book reflect, not all boys express themselves in exactly the same way. Some boys are extremely comfortable talkers and find it relatively easy (in the right space and at the right time) to verbalize what they are feeling and experiencing. With these boys, we can forge a connection by engaging in thoughtful conversation and by listening closely to what they have to say to us.

Some boys express themselves more easily in writing. These boys can benefit enormously from being given the chance to draft poems, stories, essays, or entries in a journal or diary. What matters most in this context is not whether we have the chance to read what he has written, but simply that we encourage him to write, and to see writing as a viable outlet for self-expression. Tragically, too many boys are given the message that writing for yourself is something that mostly girls and women do. Conveying to boys that it is OK to express themselves through writing—that this does not make them any less masculine—is critically important both for their intellectual and emotional development.

Many boys, however, are best able to share themselves with others not by writing or speaking, but instead through action. Thus, as important as it is to encourage boys to talk to us, and to get their thoughts down on paper, it is also paramount to become aware of the ways that boys may communicate, and forge connections with others, through action. A boy who feels angry may whittle away at a twig with a knife, initiate boxing matches with friends, or punch holes in a paperboard wall. A lonely boy might draw a picture of a single fish exploring the deep blue sea, engage in a playful wrestling match with a peer, or knock on his parents' door. A boy who feels afraid or anxious may isolate himself in his bedroom, act silly or rambunctious, tug on his dad's coattails, or take an unusually long route on his daily walk to school. If we pay close attention to all of his behavior, we can discover many messages, some intentional and others completely subconscious, that indicate the boy's deepest thoughts, feelings, and moods.

Boys often express themselves too through the confluence of talking and acting—"action talk." Many boys feel far more comfortable opening themselves up to us if they are also busily engaged in some activity. If we simply ask a boy, in a nonactive setting, how he is feeling, his answer may be a disappointing "OK" or "great." But go for a walk with the same boy, play hoops with him, or take him out in the car for a quick drive or errand, and often you will find that he is far more comfortable talking with you. The mask will come off and he may pour out his feelings. The same person who was taciturn and self-protective in a passive, nonactive setting can become remarkably open and expressive when engaged in activity.

ZACH'S STORY

When I think about the effectiveness of "action talk," I remember Zachary, a fourteen-year-old boy from the Midwest whose parents and school recently asked me to meet with him. Zachary had been called to the principal's office for the third time in a month, and this time he and his parents were informed that he was being accused of sexual harassment. Zachary and his parents would need to attend an upcoming disciplinary hearing, during which Zachary might be expelled from school.

Zachary could speak up for himself neither in the office nor later when he was staring into the eyes of his anxious and angry parents. They settled for sending him off to his room as punishment. "If you can't talk about this," they told him in frustration, "maybe you should go think about it alone!" Understandably, Zachary and his parents were secretly terrified. Each of them quietly wondered what would happen next week during the hearing. They turned to me for advice.

Before I arrived at their home I heard an earful about this formerly "nice" boy who had become "willful," "sassy," and "sullen." I was told that Zachary was somebody whom no one could talk to. Given the seriousness of the charges and the negative descriptions, I confess that I, too, had begun to wonder whether we had a juvenile miscreant, perhaps even a budding criminal, on our hands.

But then I met Zach. He had short sandy hair, deep blue eyes, and the sad smile of a lonely fourteen-year-old boy. Zachary, I sensed, was in trouble way over his head. We spoke briefly about what had been happening with him at school—I gave him the lead in our conversation—and then I asked what activity he liked doing most. Zachary's favorite pastime was hunting for frogs in the local swamp. That, I thought to myself, would probably have both its good sides and bad sides. Yet off we went! The ground was wet and muddy, and mosquitoes were buzzing about us everywhere. My khakis quickly looked like spin art. But for Zach the swamp was a safe zone, away from peers and family, away from the specter of shame, a place where he could take control and lead the way. Since I was quite rusty at frog hunting (it had been awhile since I took a net to tadpoles), Zach was able to become the "senior" explorer.

Sloshing through the swamp, Zach with two frogs already in the net and me having only gotten covered with mud, I waited quietly for the right moment to talk. Quietly and casually, in as nonthreatening a manner as I could muster, I slowly opened up a conversation about the troubles Zach had been having at school. "So I hear things have been a bit rough at school lately," I offered.

Zach, who just an hour earlier had been as taciturn as he was uncooperative, now lay bare his soul. He spoke to me with what seemed not only ease but eagerness. The harassment, he explained in some detail, consisted of telling a girl peer, on about three occasions, that she was cute. The girl apparently rejected these "advances" and then complained to the teacher, who subsequently raised the issue with the principal. Zach, of course, had already been on the school administration's negative list for the "trouble" he'd been getting into lately.

"What sort of trouble have you been in? Doesn't sound like too much fun," I said, conveying my genuine empathy.

Zach explained that he felt so sad so much of the time that often he had to find a private spot on the playground where he could cry unnoticed. Often other boys would try to hassle him. When they wouldn't give him space—"They never leave me be," Zach told me—minor skirmishes broke out and Zach ended up getting blamed.

"I guess I'm just an angry kid, like they say," Zach said morosely, reaching for a squirming frog.

"Maybe," I replied. "But I doubt it. I think the frustration builds up because of your fear of shedding tears around your classmates."

"Oh, if anybody sees you crying, they just call you a fag," he responded instantly.

"Yeah, but it's important to deal with the sadness you're feeling. You shouldn't have to go through it alone. What do you think the sadness is all about?" I asked.

"Well, I'm not sure, but I have been lying awake at night worrying whether my mother's new diabetes treatment will work. Do you think she could die?"

Apparently neither Zach's parents nor the school had talked with him about this medical problem, seeing it as under control and finding no way to imagine that this "bad" boy was sad and acting out his pain. "Did anybody else ever talk with you about this?" I asked.

"Nope. They just gave me pink slips and told me to stop causing trouble."

"I don't think you're a bad kid," I told Zach directly. "I think you are sad but have no safe space to show it, no one to reach out to. So it builds into anger. When you finally do express your anger, when you do try to connect, it's misunderstood. Then you're punished—and then you feel bad about yourself, and that's not fair."

"Exactly."

"You know what, Zach? The grown-ups in your life need to know what you're afraid of, give you some answers and some extra time to go frog hunting."

"That would be good," Zach said, his face brightening.

"Can I tell them about your worries and make some suggestions?" I inquired.

"Sure, that'd be great."

After our meeting together in the safe zone of the swamp, I followed up with Zach's parents, telling them about Zach's underlying pain. We spoke about the action talk and shame-free approaches I had used to reconnect with their son. I suggested they try these approaches, and I also advised them about how to deal with the school.

Two weeks later, Zach sent me an e-mail, thanking me on behalf of the whole family. He told me that his mom was making his dad read my book and "it must be working," he wrote, because "now they spend more time in the swamp talking with me." Zach wrote that the folks at school were being nicer to him, and he asked whether I'd been practicing my frog-catching technique. I thought to myself that Zach had improved at connecting with people much more than I will ever improve at hunting frogs.

Genuine listening without judgment or interruption. When a boy takes the risk to share his vulnerable core self with the wider world, what is most important, more than any other thing, is that we stop what we are doing and listen to him.

When we put aside our own agendas and concerns, stop in our tracks, and turn our attention to the boy, when we listen to everything he is telling us without interrupting him, he gains confidence that we care about him, that we are invested in his fate, that we want things to go his way. We also show him that we take him seriously, that what he says really matters. I find there are four important components to listening: body language, facial expression, attitude, and tone.

When we listen to a boy, he notices everything we say to him, including our body language. If we truly wish to connect with him, our body language should communicate that: "I am here for you. I'm your friend. I care about you." Of course it's important to pay attention to him, but not to be overbearing, recognizing a boy's sensitivity to shame. We simply need to be there, so that he can come as close to us as he would like.

When a boy shares his feelings with us, he also notices how our facial expressions indicate how we are responding to what he is telling us. The best listeners use their faces to demonstrate that they fully understand what the boy is saying to them. This means that when a boy conveys his joy, we smile, our eyes widen, and we nod our heads. When he speaks about sadness and fear, our eyebrows join at the center; our foreheads wrinkle up, our lips and chin shift upward to show how concerned we are about what he has experienced. When he expresses his shock or anger at life's unfairness, we shake our heads in shared disbelief and allow our faces to reflect our dismay. Our expression should show that we have not missed a single beat, that we hear exactly what he's saying and know just what he means. Sometimes, too, boys may need moments to shift their eyes away from us. We should not interpret these moments as disgust or disinterest on their part. Rather, boys may simply need some time away from the intensity of our gaze. We should give them this space while continuing to use our facial expressions to show our patience and empathy, our unwavering desire to connect with them.

As listeners, our attitude must be encouraging and nonjudgmental. When our boys are baring their souls to us, we want to convey the feeling that "The more I listen to you, the better I understand you and the more I like you. Thank you for trusting me and sharing your feelings with me. You are a great person." Criticizing the boy, chastising him, even giving him well-intentioned armchair advice is almost always unhelpful. These things are the equivalent of physically pushing the boy away. Even if in your heart you feel you know what is right for the boy, even if you think you can put your finger on the solution to a boy's problems or provide the antidote to his pain, listening well means conveying that you understand him—not that you want to pass along your judgments and advice.

What may be helpful, if it is genuine, is sharing a similar problem from your own childhood or linking it with one in your adult life. This lets boys know they are not alone, or strange or odd. It also telegraphs the sense that by sharing their inner feelings with a listener, that listener, in turn, will feel more comfortable reflecting back on his or her own sources of pain and vulnerability. As critical as it is not to lecture the boy, sharing a quick story about your own painful experiences can help strengthen your bond to him.

Tone is the last important component of listening. When you share your thoughts with the boy and reflect back that you are indeed hearing him, the tone you use matters tremendously. Just as we can use our facial expressions to convey our empathy, we can use tone—the words we choose and the sounds we make with those words—to show that we understand exactly what he's feeling. So if he's angry we might say to him, using an emphatic tone, "Wow, that's just not right! How unfair!" If he's sad, we might offer in a gentle, soft voice, "That really sounds hard. I'm so sorry." What seems like just a simple shift in tone can go a long way toward displaying your empathy and compassion.

Giving recognition and affection.   When a boy decides to talk and tell you what he is feeling, often he is seeking not only your understanding, but also your capacity, as his friend, his mentor, his parent, or his loved one, to remind him that he is good, that he matters to you and to others, that the future is full of hope and possibility, that one person indeed can make a difference. He is seeking these affirmations and all of the love and affection you can muster.

The Boy Code comes down hard on boys and men who ask for help, who show their weakness, or who seem to need even a modicum of nurturing from others. Subconsciously boys fear that if they reveal they have these kinds of basic human emotional needs, they will betray how much they miss the "holding environment" they enjoyed as very young boys, the warm, protective, nurturing world that traditionally mothers (and increasing numbers of fathers) created for their sons. Boys feel as if they are failing at being "manly" when they ask for love or affection, or expose their fundamental emotional needs and desires. They feel ashamed of themselves for seeking out these supposedly "feminine" kinds of fulfillment.

But almost every boy craves to be recognized and to receive affection from others. Listening to what boys are saying is of fundamental importance. But they will return to us as listeners, and they themselves will learn how to listen to us, only if we make the experience of sharing their emotions a thoroughly positive one. We must make boys feel that they are good and special people. We must seize every opportunity we can to say, "Nice going." "Good job." "You're a great person." "I think you're cool." "I love you, friend!" "You're a real boy."

Here, in summary form, are steps to getting behind the mask of masculinity and to helping boys speak with and discover their true voices:

GETTING BEHIND THE MASK

ACTION TALK
- Honor a boy's need for "Timed Silence"—to choose when to talk.
- Find a safe place, a "shame-free zone."
- Connect through activity or play (an activity the boy likes).
- Avoid shaming—boys are shame-phobic.
- Make brief statements and wait—do not lecture.
- Share your own experiences (if relevant). It lets your boy know he's not alone.
- Be quiet and *listen*.
- Convey how much you admire and care about and love the boy.

ENCOURAGING BOYS' VOICES
- Give your boy regular periods of undivided attention and listening space.
- Don't prematurely push him to be "independent."
- Encourage the expression of a full and wide range of emotions.
- Let him know that "real boys" and "real men" do cry and speak.
- Express your love as openly as you would with a girl (although in different ways, at times).
- When you see aggressive or angry behavior, look for the pain behind it.
- Let him know he doesn't always have to be tough and strong.

THE *REAL BOYS' VOICES* PROJECT

The process of conducting this new phase of the *Real Boys' Voices* research project was itself a personally moving experience. I and several research associates met with boys from across the nation, sometimes in their schools, sometimes in their homes, and sometimes elsewhere, and gave them each the chance either to provide an oral story or craft a written piece—an essay, poem, or other piece of writing—to capture their unique voice as boys or young men. We met with boys as young as ten and with young men as old as twenty. We worked with school systems, clubs, grassroots organizations, and Internet family sites to recruit a wide range of boys. Most of the boys were in middle, junior, or high school. Some of the boys came from privileged backgrounds; others lived in some of our country's poorest communities. We spoke with boys and young men of many races and ethnic backgrounds—white, African-American, Asian, Dominican, Puerto Rican, Chicano. Some of the boys were in serious trouble, facing significant psychological or educational hurdles. Most were ostensibly ordinary boys—the "every boy," the "boy next door" I spoke of earlier.

In some cases, the boys created written compositions on their own. They worked alone, or with a mentor, to shape a written piece that they felt represented who they were or what was most important or relevant to them at the time. In other cases, we held one-on-one interviews with the boys, transcribed these interviews, and provided just the minor editing necessary to translate to the written page each boy's unique voice.

Many of the voices contained in this book are deeply personal. I would like to note that to protect the confidentiality of the boys and young men who contributed them, we felt it was appropriate in many instances to change the names of the contributors as well as other identifying details (such as their precise location or the names of the schools they attend). But the words, facts, message, and meaning of each and every entry contained in this book come directly from the boys. They are the proud authors of these poignant voices. With the consent of their parents and guardians, these courageous boys took the bold step of saying, in effect, "I am ready to be heard. Here is my voice. Here I am."

PART I

THE SECRET EMOTIONAL LIVES OF BOYS

1

THE SECRET EMOTIONAL LIVES OF AMERICA'S BOYS: WHAT THEY'RE REALLY TALKING ABOUT

As I listen to boys across America, I am struck by the depth, compassion, and cry of their voices. They reveal a hunger for connection, a longing to be themselves, and a powerful yearning for change. These voices are a gift to us and to our country because they hint at ways in which our society can not only become a more caring and safe environment for boys, but also a more open and humane place for everyone. Our sons are telling us that the tremendous pressure they experience every day has become unendurable: they constantly feel prone to flunking out of school, becoming addicted to drugs, falling into depression, and to "snapping" with such intensity that at any moment their rage could spill over into violence. They feel lonely and disconnected, forced to fit into rigid and cruel school cliques, to accept lives of quiet desperation. They can never show weakness, they are constantly bullied, they live in a world in which violence can erupt at a moment's notice, they have to prove themselves in classrooms, on playing fields, and in physical fights, and they must always appear strong. Their parents, particularly their fathers, and their teachers, coaches, and other mentors are often much too hard on them. Although they have friends, they can't truly talk to them. And yet they are eager to talk, eager to connect with all of us.

The Boy Code, which restricts a boy's expression of emotion and his cries for help, has silenced the souls of our sons and paralyzed our natural instincts to reach out to them. Our boys are exceedingly isolated. And unwittingly, we—their parents, teachers, adult mentors, buddies, and girlfriends—are still leaving them out in the cold.

The most resounding message I hear is just how alone and disconnected these boys are and how pressured they feel to keep their true feelings secret, to hide huge parts of themselves from peers and family. Boys are telling us that instead of trying to appreciate them for who they really are and giving them "shame-free zones," where they can go to voice their fears, confusion, and angst, society imposes upon them an impossible test of masculinity that they feel they will never be able to win. Whether the biggest bully in the school, the strongest wrestler on the team, or the boy with 1600 on his SAT scores—each, in some way, feels that he does not measure up, that he is a failure. A boy might win football or hockey trophies but have no friends in whom he can confide his embarrassment about being overweight. He might get A's in science and history but secretly feel devastated about being teased for being short. The pressure to constantly appear tough and in control—and the pressure to keep those true feelings secret—have a cumulative negative effect. These pressures cause boys to have sex prematurely; to reject all things considered feminine, including the sharing of fear, sorrow, and sadness; to be overly concerned about the fitness and prowess of their bodies; to participate in bullying and violence; to abuse drugs and alcohol; to maintain a cool, impenetrable veneer that says, "I am on top; I need no help; nothing can hurt me." And finally, these pressures lead to depression, suicide, serious violence in our schools and neighborhoods, even murder.

I am particularly struck by how many of America's boys today are talking about Columbine and all of the implications that tragedy has had for them as young males in this world. The recent spate of school shootings, culminating in the tragic massacre of a teacher and students in Littleton, Colorado, has left our nation frustrated and confused about the threat of extreme violence and its connection, in particular, with boys. The shock of these crimes has been substantial, the repercussions pervasive. It has led to a syndrome whereby students, parents, and teachers have become extremely apprehensive about which boys among them are violent, who the next perpetrators might be, and who their victims will become. The consequence is that boys themselves are becoming increasingly anxious and afraid.

Perhaps more than ever before, America's boys are terrified not only of being victimized by violence but of being misunderstood, or falsely accused, of having what it takes to perpetrate such deeds of destruction. Moreover, many boys themselves are beginning to worry if maybe, just maybe their own anger—and their own feelings of sadness and pain, which have been pushed underground by the Boy Code— could in fact cause them to lash out and seriously harm themselves or others.

The voices of the boys to whom I spoke carry a profound underlying message of alienation and despair: society is pushing them to be just one kind of person, nudging them at a very young age to disconnect from their loved ones and to sacrifice that part within themselves that is genuinely loving, caring, and affectionate. We are still allowing boys to be shamed for their sweet side, to go to school every day worrying when they will next be teased, assaulted, or even shot to death. But America's boys are finally saying "Enough." They want to be let back in. They want it to be okay to laugh, cry, cheer, and tremble. They want it to be acceptable to have bodies that are short, tall, round, or thin. They want to be able to show intellectual curiosity, show their fragility, discover beauty in words, images, tastes, and sounds. They want to find adults with whom they can honestly share and connect. They want to have close friendships and relationships with girls and with other boys based on emotional authenticity and intimacy rather than on bravado and disconnection. America's boys want to be their real selves. America's boys want change.

Glenn, an eighteen-year-old-boy from the Midwest who loves music, describes the male armor he has to put on every day: "You can never flinch. Like when you are heading to school and you are getting into that mind-set—now it's time to be *on* for school—you start thinking to yourself 'Do this, don't do that.' I'm always thinking, *Don't let your feelings show.*"

Seventeen-year-old Terry, a devout Baptist from the Midwest, expresses the fear that he will be laughed at by other boys if he doesn't fit into the mold of acceptable male behavior. "Just being in a certain clique, being with your friends and making sure they like you and stuff, can be stressful. If you know that every day you are going to be made fun of, you might get pushed over the edge."

Finally, Michael, a seventeen-year-old from a small town in the

Midwest, claims that after fulfilling all the demands of the Boy Code, he no longer knows who he truly is. "In some ways, I feel like I don't have a personality. I feel like who I am is just school and soccer and music, just whatever I do. I don't have any time to just be myself. Sometimes, I want to be who I really am, instead of just a collection of all the things I do. . . . Sometimes I just wish I had more time to myself. But I don't really feel in charge of making that happen. There's all this external pressure and internal pressure. And sometimes I keep myself so busy that I don't even think about it. I guess part of being busy may be to avoid feeling so terrible."

Boys have told me that one of the biggest tests of their masculinity is sex: Given the macho boy culture, they are swiftly ostracized and made to feel unmanly if they disclose how confused they really are about when to become sexually active and when (or if) to lose their virginity. Many feel that society forces them to have sex before they truly want to. Jeff, a sixteen-year-old in the Northeast, describes this relentless pressure. "Your virginity is what determines whether you're a man or a boy in the eyes of every teenage male. Teenage men see sex as a race: the first one to the finish line wins. Your virginity is the single most important thing that determines your social status in the eyes of almost every teenage male. In high school, virginity is a self-demeaning label that you want nothing more than to get rid of. It is almost inconceivable to think that your virginity, your one and only innocence, could be your worst enemy. I will never forget the first time I was asked if I was a virgin. I still remember the fear that the question struck in me—the fear of not being accepted by my friends, the fear of not being able to get with girls."

Winston, a seventeen-year-old Southerner, told me, "I'm a virgin and I try to stay pure because of my religious beliefs, but there is a lot of pressure on guys to have sex with girls. If you haven't had sex yet, there's something wrong with you."

Although having sex with girls is a crucial test of masculinity, many boys say that appearing vulnerable—and thereby, by definition, "feminine"—is the biggest taboo of the Boy Code. The worst insult a boy can experience is to be called "wimp," "fag," "homo," or "wuss." Interestingly enough, these words are as much an expression of homophobia as they are a fear of or repulsion toward any display of dependency or need—so-called female traits. This taboo places even more restraints on how a boy can present himself to the world, thereby pushing him into deeper fear and isolation.

Jacob, a seventeen-year-old living in a suburb outside of Boston, says, "Guys have this notion that if you like reading and don't like wrestling and you'd rather go to an art museum than play football, then that means you are gay. And that's just wrong." Jacob's schoolmate Carlos, a twelve-year-old who is an excellent student and loves sports, explains why boys are barred from showing any emotional display. "If I was upset by something at school, I might not cry there because the other boys will stare at me. Or they might call me 'girly.' So boys will save their crying for home." Seventeen-year-old Brett, from the South, states that boys can't form close friendships for fear of seeming feminine. "You can never get close with another guy because it'll look like you're gay, you're feminine. And it's not acceptable to be at all feminine when you're a guy. At school they would call you fag and stuff like that."

"I don't cry in front of people," said Teddy, a sixteen-year-old from Tennessee. "I'll do it sometimes when I'm in my own room or talking to one of my good friends on the phone. But not in front of the guys. I feel really embarrassed when I cry in front of guys. They look at you as a wimp. It comes off as physically weak. You just don't amount to much as a guy if you cry in front of others. When I get upset about things, I usually just go to my room and isolate myself."

Because they want to ensure that they never appear weak and that others never shame or reject them, boys are very conscious of their body image. Jason, an eighth grader at an inner-city public school in the Northeast, says, "When I was little, I was a chubby kid. In third and fourth grades, I weighed almost as much as I do now that I'm in eighth. I was a big kid. I ate a ton of food. I'd always have third and fourth helpings of food. I got teased a lot, bullies called me names. Name-calling and picking on me in the hall, and making fun of me. It would bring tears to my eyes but I really wouldn't let them watch me cry because I didn't want to further embarrass myself. In gym class, if we did running or anything, I'd always be the one trailing behind. Everyone would be saying, 'Why do we have to wait for Jason, he's so slow.' I couldn't put up with that. I just had to be up with those kids. So, in fourth grade I decided, 'I've got to shape up. I can't go on like this." Across America many boys like Jason are spending countless hours dieting, pumping iron, and doing aerobic exercise, all in an effort to transform the size and shape of their bodies.

Another way for boys to adhere to the Boy Code and protect against vulnerability is to cruelly tease, bully, and fight, exhibiting physical strength and force over other boys. Sixteen-year-old Vinny from Massachusetts says, "I don't think of the fights I've had as violence. For me, fighting is about trying to establish authority for myself." Twelve-year-old Eric, from an affluent town in the Northeast, explains it this way: "It's fun to tackle people. It's not bullying. You're going out there and you know you will get hit. And even if you're pumped up and then you get hit or tackled, then you're mad, so you get even more pumped up until you just nail somebody." Brad, an eighth grader living in a suburb in the Northeast who wants to be a Navy SEAL, says: "One time in gym, we were playing basketball. A kid whacks my ball over to the corner so I have to run over and get it, and I lost, so I wanted to do something to that kid. I wanted to pound the kid into the wall."

But most of the boys to whom I spoke don't want to exert their physical strength over other boys. They simply do not want to appear weak. A top football player in his school explains: "People see me as a big person, an aggressive football player, and then when they see me shed a tear, they're like, 'Whoa, is that Cedric?' It's like I'm a different person just because I shed a tear and I cry. People look at boys as rough and tough. They don't want us to cry, they don't want us to be sad, they expect us to take things as they are. Boys are human, too, boys have feelings, we should be able to express ourselves like girls can. It's destructive to bottle stuff up inside."

In addition to the pressure boys experience always to appear masculine and strong, they feel an incredible pressure from adults, often their parents, to work hard and perform well at school and in sports. Many spoke about how much they disappoint their mothers and fathers, and about how much their parents' disappointment hurts them. Mo, a senior at a prestigious high school in New England who attends a church youth group and gets very good grades, says, "I played basketball in fifth and sixth grades, and my dad coached the team. We'd talk about how I did after the game, and we'd always end up in an argument. He thought I played poorly. I was the tallest kid on the team and he'd tell me that I should have been handling the ball more or getting more rebounds. It always seemed there was one aspect of my game that I didn't do right. He'd say, 'You did good shooting free throws,' or something like that. Then he'd say, 'But you should have gotten more rebounds.' I just didn't want to hear it. I'd say something like 'What game were you watching?' Then he'd yell at me."

Tony, age sixteen, from a city in the Northeast, says, "My mom raised me and I can't talk to her at all. She's very tough and we don't really get along. Mostly, I don't deal with her anymore. Instead of facing the problem, I just don't bring up the problem. She's unhappy with everything I do. She just walks up to me, takes me by my neck, and starts telling me that everything's wrong with me. Then she just throws me on the ground and walks away."

Sixteen-year-old Eamon, from the Midwest, describes it this way: "It's hell on earth trying to deal with my dad. I mean, when I want to talk to him, it feels like there's a cage around me. And I can't get away from those expectations and him being constantly angry with me. I always try to do better and when he is still mad I think, What's it worth?"

Boys have described to me how every day of their lives they receive covert and overt messages that they do not measure up, and yet they feel that they must cover up their sadness and confusion about their plummeting self-esteem. Forced into this gender straitjacket—and pushed to mask their feelings—so many boys I met experience depression, loneliness, and suicidal ideation. Arthur, an eighteen-year-old from New Hampshire, describes his depression this way: "There are some days when I feel totally alone and helpless to do anything about it. I never told many people what I am going to say now. There was one day back in middle school when I came home to an empty, dark house; my parents were not home. I looked in the mirror and realized that I hated myself. I hated myself because I hated the place I was in and I hated the fact that I was not respected, to say the least. I found myself going for a kitchen knife to slit my wrists with."

Seventeen-year-old Kirk, from the Midwest, told me: "If you see me around school, you'll think I'm a fucking popular kid. . . . But I don't really connect with anyone. I just feel depressed. I feel like I'm not up to doing all the things that I love to do. I feel like shutting myself off from the world."

"I've been treated for slight depression," explains seventeen-year-old Thomas, from a Southern resort town. "But I get around it with help from friends. Sometimes, though, it just catches up to you and you can't do anything about it. Depression just hits you and hits you. Sadness just comes over you and you can't stop thinking of the time you failed that class, or how you could have done things better if you just got off your lazy butt. I get self-critical and think about the thing I could have done that I didn't. I've even gone so far as to make a mental plan of how I would want to die: jumping off a building."

Tony explains, "I hurt myself. I scratch myself. I'll be sitting at home thinking of everything that's happening, and it starts building up in my head. All of a sudden I just burst, and I'll punch the wall or scratch myself with a knife until I'm bleeding, and then that's it. Then I just sit and I calm down. I throw a fit and it's over in five seconds. Sometimes I just want to end it all. When something really good happens in school I don't think about it, but most other days I come home from school and I picture it in my head. I picture me, holding a gun to my head, and I start thinking, What if I didn't do it, what difference would it make? I don't cry, though. The last time I remember crying was in junior high school."

Unlike girls, boys don't know how to get the help and empathy they need and deserve. They are too afraid to reveal any chink in their male armor. Fifteen-year-old Henry from suburban Rhode Island, who loves to play soccer, told us, "If I were to go for help, I'm afraid I just wouldn't know what to say. I've had very little practice in being able to tell people how I feel. I've had a lot of practice in the opposite, in how to hide it."

"I'm concerned about how people would feel if I told them I was down," seventeen-year-old Michael, from the Midwest, told me. "They would see me as a guy with problems. It's not a cool thing; it's just not cool to say 'I've got problems. I'm depressed.' They wouldn't tease me, but they would see me differently. They would start seeing me as somebody who's having emotional problems. And I would see myself as being less than I am now. . . . Also, if I said to my parents, 'You know, Mom and Dad, this is a lot of pressure I'm under and I'd like to go talk to somebody,' they would get too worried. I need to protect them from that."

"I always have and probably always will hold things in," said Lars, a popular seventeen-year-old from New England. "I know that this is not the best thing to do, and I know that I can talk about it whenever I would like to, but I don't. I don't really know why I don't and after a while of holding things in, I sometimes erupt, whether it be in anger or sadness. When I erupt, which is not very often, I will yell or hit a wall and hurt my own knuckles. I may also cry, which I am not afraid to admit. I feel hurt or a little sad for what I did, afterward."

Sixteen-year-old Grant, from the South, quietly told me, "I think that other boys, like me, hold emotions in. I think they also have difficulty talking about things that bother them. Boys are expected to be tough. They are told to shake it off when they are hurt. They are thought of as being weak when they cry. . . . Most boys don't talk a lot about feelings, or try to help each other when they are having hard times. Most boys are afraid to let other people know their real feelings, so they hide their anger and sadness. They don't want to risk having other people make fun of them."

The affection boys have for their mothers is overwhelming. Fourteen-year-old Hector, from the Midwest, told me, "I love my mom so much. When I need her, she's always there for me. She's always taking care of me. She always tells me, 'Even if you grow up to be twenty-six, you'll always be my baby.' We go to the mall together. We go to the science museum and we just walk around. We talk about school. Every day she asks me, 'How was school?' and I tell her how it was."

"I go to my mother about everything," Warren, a successful high school athlete from the Northeast, told me cheerfully. "Some people are scared to go to their mothers with some things, but I can tell my mother anything and she won't get mad. She'll talk to me about it, just tell me the consequences and rewards. Some days, when I'm moping around the house, she notices and asks what's wrong. If I don't feel like telling her right then, I'll write parts of it down to highlight what I'm feeling, so she can understand what's going on."

"I talk to my mom because I can't hold it in me, it's impossible," said twelve-year-old Nick, from a suburb in the Northeast. "I have to talk to my mom; I have to talk. She loves it because she likes to know what's going on with me. I talk to her about everyday stuff because she can give me advice. Often I give myself advice and my mom agrees with me."

"My mother and I are so close," eighteen-year-old Dwayne, from the Northeast, told me. "She is such a lovely lady. She's wonderful. She supports me in every possible way. I mean, she kind of spoils me. But who cares? She's one of my role models. She's intelligent, smart, hardworking. I look up to her in every way."

I was also tremendously encouraged to hear stories about how boys can reveal their feelings to girls in the context of platonic as well as romantic relationships: "My closest friends are girls," said sixteen-year-old Eugene, from the South. "Girls are a lot better listeners than guys are. You can be yourself when you are around them because when you have good friends that are girls, they have accepted you for who you are."

"Girls are understanding," Shaun, a ninth grader from a working-class town outside of Boston, said. "They say, 'Oh, I know you're in pain. It'll be okay.' So in school, I hang out mostly with girls. Some of my best friends are girls."

"One of many special people in my life stands out more than the others," eighteen-year-old Nicholas, from New York, told me. "She is there through thick and thin, rain or shine, heaven or hell. Elisa will always be there. Whether it's just listening, giving me advice, forcing me to do the right thing, she's always there."

Many boys also seem to find outlets for expression and channels of self-discovery through their participation in the arts. I was thrilled when they told me about how they are able to express their true feelings through music, photography, drawing, and writing.

"I've been a drummer for almost five years," blond-haired, sixteen-year-old Rubin, from New England, told me. "Doing original songs allows you to express yourself. You can't really express yourself at school like you can through music. I can almost feel I'm expressing myself through drums. I'm not really saying anything, but there's a strange feeling that I am getting my feelings across."

"When I dance, I feel like I can do anything," Dwayne told me in an animated voice. "When I get up on stage, it's all about having fun and being positive and being able to think that you can do what you want up there. It's just a nice feeling. Not everybody gets the chance to have that feeling about himself. . . . It really does make you feel positive. It makes you feel strong."

"One of my favorite hobbies is playing the guitar," seventeen-year-old Trevor, from Florida, explained. "It's kind of like an outlet for my emotions. When I play, a lot of aggression and frustration with school and stuff comes out."

Thirteen-year-old Scott, from an affluent suburb of Boston, described how he finds joy and release in the written word. "I like writing. At night, I'll jot my feelings down and if something happens, I'll write it down. It really helps me if I write my feelings down because that gets it out of my mind. I can clear it out, put it away, whatever; save it for later, save it for a song or something like that."

Many boys seeking deeper meaning and a safe place to show their feelings do not only turn to friends or family or to artistic exploration, they also immerse themselves in religious or spiritual practice. I was deeply struck by how many boys seek inner truth through *spirituality.* Cedric, fourteen, from a city in the Northeast, told me with confidence, "God is the person who is there when nobody else is. There's my uncle and people like that, but God is the one person who's always going to listen. Even though he can't talk back, I can let him know my feelings. When I pray, I ask God for good health, and to protect my family."

Brendan, eighteen, from the South, said to me, "I consider myself a spiritual person. I feel protected by God. I pray to God about everything. I feel close to God. I feel like I can talk to him openly about who I really am, and about the problems I have. There are some things that I tell God that I wouldn't want anyone to know because they are very private, they are personal to me. . . . The one sort of male figure boys have to talk to, whom we can trust, with whom we can completely be ourselves, is God. God never says 'Oh, you are such a jerk' or 'You are a wimp' or 'Why aren't you doing better in school?' God is always there. And I always wonder what it would be like if we felt the same thing toward other guys, or toward our fathers."

From a city in the Northeast, seventeen-year-old Antonio spoke passionately about his philosophy: "I'm a spiritual person, but I'm not really religious. I believe in . . . someone out there. I just don't give him the title of God. I just try to prove to him that I deserve to live the way I want to. . . . I figure my next life will be great if I'm a good person in this life."

In my travels across America, boys spoke to me about so many things. Although it was clear to me that many felt a distinct emptiness and pain, I heard a new chord during this trip that caused me to be hopeful. Boys are ready to be released from their straitjackets. They are no longer willing to see gender as destiny. Although they don't know how to do it alone and they don't want to be the first one to do it, they desire to be more expressive, to be closer to other human beings, and to be allowed more flexibility and tolerance in how they reveal themselves to the world. They want the doors to open.

Eighteen-year-old Glenn, from a small town in the Midwest, summed it up for me: "If I were president," he began, "and I could change everything and make things just the way I wanted to, I would make it so guys would not need to be ashamed of their feelings. They would be able to express them and that would not be considered wrong, or looked down upon. I think it's okay for guys to express themselves or to have emotion. I think it is normal. It is human."

When asked what advice they would give younger boys in a world often hostile to young males, most older boys responded with astounding regularity, "Be yourself." I hope that in genuinely listening to their voices, we will feel ready to step up to the plate for all the boys we love. Here are heroic boys letting us into their secret worlds, revealing their inner emotional lives, and speaking frankly about their whole and their true selves. Instead of waiting passively for yet another wake-up call— an unwanted pregnancy, a suicide attempt, a schoolroom mass murder—I am hopeful that we can make the necessary changes to give America's boys complete emotional freedom, to offer them the deep human understanding they desire and so richly deserve.

2

TAKING OFF THE GENDER
STRAITJACKET

"I think my parents loved my brother more than me. . . . He was captain of the soccer team and the lacrosse team. My parents loved it—that's what parents want when they have boys."
—Lars, 17, from a suburb in New England

"I'm always thinking: Don't let your feelings show."
—Glenn, 18, from a small town in the Midwest

TERRIFIED
Ethan, 17, from a suburb in the West

I definitely think male roles are changing. I'm lucky that I did not grow up hearing some of the messages other guys hear all the time. My dad never told me that I shouldn't talk about my feelings or that being emotional was effeminate. I hope that guys will eventually find it much easier to talk about feelings.

Society as a whole, though, is still pretty restrictive on guys. I'm comfortable talking about my feelings with other guys. Some people, though, might think because of that I'm gay. Now, I couldn't care less because I know I'm not gay. But I honestly think that many guys are so afraid of that accusation that they just don't ever feel comfortable opening up to another guy. I think guys are terrified of being called gay, because they don't really understand it, and are also terrified of being called feminine. Maybe it's the same fear: many guys think gay men are feminine, and their worries about being called gay might be the same as their worries about being thought feminine.

It would be better if everyone was just treated the same regardless of their race or their sexuality and we could just get over this sort of thing. It would also be better if we just stopped poking fun at people for who they are or what they do. It's another thing that led to Columbine: those kids were just completely made fun of all the time. And it's hard to deal with that, especially if you can't talk to somebody about it. And until people can accept other people for who they are, no matter what they do, then society won't change.

It's just a small group of guys who think that I'm gay. I know myself well and I know I'm not gay—I have a girlfriend now—so it doesn't bother me when they say things or try to harass me. In the peer counseling program last semester we talked with a guy who came out during high school and told people that he was gay. And it was really difficult for him. He had things written on his locker, on his car, notes written to him. And I don't know how I would react to the things the guys say if I really was gay. I think I would be actually afraid that people knew.

It was especially painful last year, because a lot of my best friends were girls. I was really close to them. And then I'd get harassed in school and go home, thinking, "Why does anyone think I'm gay?" I'm lucky in that I have Craig, my best friend, whom I tell everything to. He was a real support. And now I just say to the guys who say things to me: "You know what—I'm *not*. Just get your facts straight. If you want to keep calling me that, it's okay, but I'm straight and everyone else knows it. And that's all that matters to me."

I didn't tell my parents about how bothered I was about all this. I haven't talked to them about personal things for a while and I really never discuss my friends with them. I used to have a very close friend who thought it was really uncool to talk about personal things with your parents, and I guess his opinion really influenced me because I stopped talking with them. I used to only share things with my sister: she's in middle school and I can relate to her and her friends better than I can to my parents.

It's still hard to really open up to them. I want my parents to think I'm successful and that I'm doing well in school and going to get good grades. I get concerned that, if I really tell them my problems, they will worry that I won't have a good year at school. I also think that most guys don't want their parents, ever, to think they're weak. We all want our parents to think we're independent and strong. It's funny, but our fears about our parents are kind of the same as the fears we have at school. We want our friends at school to think we're strong, independent, and masculine. The same is true at home.

It's best if parents don't ask too many questions. Before, when I wasn't talking to them about personal stuff, they would sometimes ask me if I had a girlfriend, or how I was doing emotionally. Those questions made me instantly put up a wall. They pushed me farther and farther away. You see, before someone will talk to you or answer your questions, you have to put them at ease. That can't be done by just asking very direct questions. Parents need to get their kids comfortable with them first, and the best way to do that is to show the kids that they will always be there for them, no matter what. So, instead of interrogating me every day, my parents should have waited for me to make the first move, to tell them I wasn't having a good day. The only thing they should have said to me to make me comfortable enough to make that move—and they should have said this again and again—is that they would be there for me no matter what. No matter what I'd done and no matter what I might tell them.

I think a good parent should even say to their kid that they will always be there for them, no matter what the problem is, even if it's sex, sexual preference, bullying, bad school problems or whatever. Then their kid will be able to really talk with them.

GUYS AREN'T SUPPOSED TO BE . . .

Brad, 14, from a suburb in the Northwest

Guys aren't supposed to be weak or vulnerable. Guys aren't supposed to be sweet. A friend of mine died in the hospital and I was surprised. His wife was there, and she's a really good friend of mine. I knew that, as a guy, I was supposed to be strong and I wasn't supposed to show any emotion, and it was really hard to do, but I had to do it. In that situation, I was supposed to be tough, so I pretended that I wasn't hurt as deeply as I was. Then when I went home, I just sat by myself and let myself cry. I let myself show the emotion that I couldn't show before.

I think guys feel ashamed to show their emotions in public. We're not supposed to show emotion. We have to be strong and tough. If we show our feelings, we're gay. I don't even see the problem with that in the first place. Take women, for example—women have always been considered weak, or not as tough or as strong as men, and because gays like men, they're like women. They're supposed to be weak and not strong. People are prejudiced against gays. Gays were singled out and, eventually, being gay was considered a bad thing. We're correcting that now, but it's slow. Eventually people won't be homophobic, but for now some people still are, so for now, being gay can still be considered a bad thing. I know gay people and it doesn't bother me. What another person does is his own business, but in general, society is still fairly homophobic. Time is what will fix that. With each generation, it will get better. Education is important, but as far as teaching it in schools goes, I'm not sure. What are you going to say? Are schools going to teach that there's nothing wrong with being gay? That's an opinion. You can't make an entire class accept your opinion. If parents teach their children that everyone is equal and that, in society, some people are heterosexual and others are homosexual, then being gay won't seem so foreign. When any group is unfamiliar, it becomes an oddity or is considered different.

If I become a parent someday, I would teach my children that it doesn't matter how other people live their lives. If they are good people, treat them well. If they are bad people, ignore them. If they try to hurt you, then you can react.

If children were taught by their parents that being gay was fine, then boys wouldn't worry so much about seeming gay, or feminine. Guys wouldn't worry so much about missing a ball or crying when someone dies.

America's boys are crying out for a new gender revolution that does for them what the last forty years of feminism has tried to do for girls and women. As you listen to the voices in this chapter, you'll discover that too often society as a whole continues to stress an outmoded Boy Code—old rules that force boys into the stereotype of the stoic, unfeeling little hero, rules that exhort boys not to cry but to "act like men," to "fight it out," and to "stand up on your own two feet." This Boy Code severely limits what boys can say and do, and thus limits their development; instead, each individual boy needs to be encouraged to express his whole, wide range of emotions, and to fulfill his own dreams and destiny. Under the Boy Code, there is often only a very narrow band of acceptable male or masculine behavior, and boys are teased and shamed when they try to break free from these harmful stereotypes and strictures—when they try to be the real boys that they are.

A related problem is that the Boy Code contributes to boys being afraid to be and express who they fully are for fear of being teased as being gay or a sissy. Robert, an eighteen-year-old from a Colorado school that is less than an hour away from Littleton, speaks poignantly about what happens when a guy steps over the Boy Code line. Robert had begun to express his enthusiasm for sports as a basketball player when he was drawn into the gymnastics of cheerleading. He and the other guys on the cheerleading squad initially faced a mountain of peer resistance. Teased ruthlessly by classmates, Robert realized that things had changed from when he was much younger and the Boy Code was enforced less stringently: "Some guys don't do the things they really want to do—like cheerleading—because those are 'girls' things.' But younger kids don't feel like that. There are no boundaries for them . . . no hatred between them, no judgment of one another. No one says: 'Oh, he's playing with a doll. He must be weird, so we can't hang out with him.' "

"When does that change happen?" we asked Robert.

"I think society starts to change us when we're seven or so," he answered. "That's when boys start separating from girls and vice versa. That's when sports teams are all boys or all girls. Somehow that sends a message to the kids."

"And what is that message?"

"Guys don't like things they're not familiar with," explained Robert. "They don't like it when guys do things that they think only girls do. Their instant reaction is that a guy who does that must be gay."

Our culture underestimates and at times actively discourages boys' human need for connection, these natural, normal parts of themselves that yearn for nurturance from others and a safe place where they can talk and shed tears. As a culture we restrict how much open affection boys can show, especially to one another, and often look askance upon young males' displays of empathy and affection as inappropriate. "Sometimes I wish that things were different," says eighteen-year-old Glenn, from a small town in the Midwest, "because it would be a whole lot easier if we could break down the barrier between guys."

One of the most traumatic aspects of this boy culture is that very early on, boys are told to separate from their mothers and therefore from everything we consider emotionally open or caring and thus "feminine." Boys are prematurely pushed to overcome their "dependence" upon their loved ones, especially their mothers, in the mistaken belief that learning to live without this protection is the only true pathway to healthy masculinity. When any boy, especially a sensitive one, runs crying back to reconnect with this warm nest of love and support—or when any boy acts in any way that appears even remotely vulnerable or needy—he encounters swift discouragement and rejection.

When I first began my research, I asked boys if they ever felt sexually harassed. At first they said no. I then changed my question to "Have you ever been called a 'wuss,' 'wimp,' or 'fag'?" "Oh, *that*," one boy said. "That happens every day. I thought it was just a part of being a boy!" Eleven-year-old Jake from rural Massachusetts recounted how he was teased for crying on the baseball field when hit in the shin with a ball: "I'll probably be teased for the whole season, and into the summer, because a 'real' guy isn't supposed to cry when he feels pain. I feel like boys are just as sensitive as girls are, but we're not allowed to show our feelings. We're put in this narrow *box* and if we try to break out, we're made fun of, or threatened."

Such daily repression not only puts a boy like Jake at a great disadvantage in today's world of change—cutting off his passions before he can even begin to realize them—but it also traumatizes him into avoiding a wide range of personal growth. Boys constantly live in the fear that they will somehow be perceived through their normal yearning as moving into a world reserved for only girls and women.

Sadly, many members of society still attack boys who seek connection with this feeling realm. So many adolescent boys, it seems, spend huge amounts of time and energy doing everything they possibly can to avoid the humiliation of being perceived as either "feminine" or homosexual.

THE LAST HURDLE: THE CRUELTY OF HOMOPHOBIA

No matter what their sexual orientation actually is, adolescent boys often feel forced to hide their true thoughts and feelings, put aside their first interests and passions, and disguise the very essence of who they are. To protect themselves from the painful accusation that they are not masculine enough, boys feel forced to become extremely watchful, carefully monitoring how other boys act and expending huge amounts of time and energy desperately trying to fit in and pass muster.

Some boys recognize how fundamentally misguided this really is. "The way you act does not really in any way determine your sexual preference," says seventeen-year-old David. "Just because a guy is sensitive and doesn't want to get into fights doesn't make him gay." As boys like David will tell you, the question is not—and should not be— whether they are homosexual. Instead, the real question is whether boys will ever be allowed to be themselves, to be free, to be *real*. America's boys are calling out for the love, acceptance, and encouragement that will enable them to move beyond the old rules of masculinity, discover their whole selves, including those sides of themselves that are weak, creative, vulnerable, humorous, gentle, or sweet. And they're asking us to allow them to be perfectly honest and to feel good about loving and caring for others, including other boys. Boys want it to be all right to shout, whisper, giggle, or cry. They want to be able to pursue all of their personal interests—reading, dancing, participating in sports, hunting, helping out at home, collecting things, fishing, sailing, playing with dolls. They want to be allowed to hug and love one another in contexts other than sports or funeral parlors. They want their friends, siblings, girlfriends, parents, and society in general to say, "We love you just the way you really are!" Listen to the voices on these pages and you will hear boys facing the same kinds of prejudices and anxieties that women encountered when they sought to vote, Jews experienced as they fought their way into the mainstream, and African Americans struggled against for equal access to the rights and privileges of white Americans. I was deeply moved by the great number of boys, boys as young as eleven years old, who hadn't even hit puberty yet, who told me that homophobia— the fear of being, or being perceived as, gay—is the greatest obstacle to their development into healthy, happy boys.

This is not an academic matter. It is a matter of truth versus falsehood, a matter of life and death itself. We must put all of our energy into helping boys break free from the strictures of the straitjacket and be their true selves. We must dismantle the Boy Code as we have our outmoded definitions of girlhood, and take on homophobia as another form of bias and prejudice, eradicating it in the same manner we address anti-

Semitism, attacks against people of color, and the hurtful discrimination against women in our society. This is not just a political agenda, for if we listen to the voices of our boys, it is inherent in their hopes for healthy emotional growth and central to their survival.

It's Not Always Easy

Glenn, 18, from a small town in the Midwest

I have always liked music, it's kind of a way to express myself and help others by bringing them enjoyment. At school I am in the choir and orchestra. I play the violin and the piano. I am also the choir director and organist at my church, about half an hour away from here.

In some ways I might be considered different because I am so involved in music. I like sports but I just don't really have time to play them. My brother does. My brother is a coach, and so I kind of follow sports through him and what he does.

It's not always easy being a guy, always trying to be successful and look good in other people's eyes. There is a lot of pressure not to screw things up, to be good at what you do. You have to follow the rules of what boys are supposed to be, and how a guy is supposed to act. It has to do with the way you've been brought up, the way society kind of looks at guys, the way guys are always supposed to seem—macho, kind of cool, on top of things, and always knowing what's going on.

You can never flinch. Like when you are heading to school and you are getting into that mind-set—now it's time to be "on" for school—you start thinking to yourself, "Do this, don't do that." I'm always thinking, *Don't let your feelings show.*

It's tough to become part of the group. You have to conform or people wonder what's wrong with you. Even teachers expect you to act a certain way. They are an extension of society and of what you are supposed to be like. And if you don't fit in with everybody else, you get teased.

When I was younger, other kids made fun of me. But they have gotten over it now. After a while people begin to look up to you as long as you don't let go of the truth. If you hold on to it, if you stick to what you believe in, people will come around. My advice to other boys is to stick to your guns. It's not easy. I mean, people can be really hard on you for a while. But as they mature, they kind of grow out of things and loosen up.

It's really hard because boys don't have much confidence. Like you might start out with confidence, and as soon as somebody says something negative, it just tears you down right away. And you might go in the next day feeling good again, and then it just starts all over again. I mean, it doesn't take much. It just depends on how you started out on any particular day. Sometimes just one negative remark can put you down for the rest of the day. Other people's attitudes can be really dumb—not just the way they look at things, but also about what they think is "normal." I think each person has a unique personality, with his or her own qualities. Everyone is special in their own way. I think you should respect that.

In elementary school it's usually not so bad. You are just kind of starting out. In middle school, when everybody starts kind of hitting puberty and doing their own thing, you are still the way you are, but people start to notice the differences more then.

From the time boys are, say eleven or twelve until they are seventeen or eighteen, they are hard on each other, teasing each other all the time. They are saying, "You're a fag." I'm not sure why they do it then. Just before they are about to go to college they realize, like, "Oh, yes, actually, maybe it would have been good if I tried to be good at what I really love doing, and not just try to fit in." I'm not sure why society is teaching boys to do this. Maybe society wants boys to try to impress girls, kind of like a male peacock showing off its feathers to a female one.

Maybe when a boy becomes sexual and wants to court girls, he is competing. He tries to look as good as he can in comparison to the other boys. That makes him start to insult other boys, try to strip them down, make them look less masculine and make himself look better compared to the other boys.

When I was becoming an adolescent I felt like other people were doing that to me, putting me down that way. I didn't pay attention to them. I tried to ignore them. I just kind of went on, and they looked more stupid by the stuff they said anyway. I just tried not to let it bother me, look past it, and understand where they were coming from.

If girls insult each other, normally what would they do? They would go and cry. They would talk to their friends about it. They would tell their parents. They would be very upset. Boys often just say, "Oh, I just got beyond it." Boys feel pain but they don't let it show, or at least they try not to let it show. They bottle it up.

I always waited until I got home to deal with things. However bad I felt, I just lay there and thought about my feelings and tried to get over them. I'd go to my room, lay on the bed and just think. If it was really bad, maybe I'd talk with my mom. She is a person with whom I can talk openly.

I don't talk to my dad so much. He is kind of quiet. I mean, I *could* talk to him, but I just wouldn't feel as comfortable as with my mom. My mom and I have always been closer, I guess. My dad is more into sports. My mom likes music, and I feel like I have more in common with her. My dad usually has a lot to deal with anyway, his own problems from work and stuff like that. It's not that he doesn't care or wouldn't have anything to say. I just don't feel like I should bother him.

I'm not sure why so many guys talk to their moms instead of their dads. I guess it's for the same reason why guys don't always talk that much to other guys. You don't really feel embarrassed, but you feel less of a man or something. You feel like you are letting too much of yourself go, like you are showing too much of yourself. And dads don't connect with their sons the way moms do because the dads themselves have gone through the same thing that their sons are going through now. So they can't get in touch with their feelings either.

Sometimes I wish that things were different because it would be a whole lot easier if we could break down the barrier between guys. I would like to be able to talk to another guy, especially my dad, because he has been through everything I've been through and knows more. But it's just so hard to even start the conversation.

I've only had long talks with another guy about this stuff maybe once or twice. In a long car ride, me and one of my best friends were talking, and just kind of went over everything. But it's hard to do, it's hard to find that kind of friend. It wasn't as hard with him because he's a cool guy and keeps in touch with his feelings. Sometimes I imagine things might have been different if my dad and I could talk more, be open and share all of our feelings.

If I were president, and I could change everything and make things just the way I wanted to, I would make it so guys wouldn't need to be ashamed of their feelings. They would be able to express them and that would not be considered wrong, or looked down upon. I think it's okay for guys to express themselves or to have emotion. I think it's normal. It's human.

I have a couple of close friends, all of whom are involved with me in music. I have one friend who is also an organist, and he is away at college in New York. I miss him. He is two years older so for nearly two years we haven't been able to hang out. I like him but I guess he would be an example of someone who for a long time couldn't let his feelings out.

After he went away to college, when he came back to see us, he told me that he was gay. He had gone all through high school and never told me that, never told anyone that. It was very surprising for me. I felt bad that he felt like he could not tell me. I mean, it didn't bother me—he was still the same person!

I'm not certain what made him so afraid to tell me. Embarrassment, I guess.

As soon as he came back here, everyone started saying things. And his parents were the same way. They weren't accepting of it, especially not his dad.

But I was there for him and now he is still my friend. It's kind of sad. All that time he had to pretend to be somebody he wasn't because he was afraid that I would judge him negatively. I felt betrayed somehow. I wish he had trusted me with this earlier. And he probably feels like he wished he could have told me earlier, too.

I think a lot of this goes on. A lot of times people aren't honest about who they really are, and they miss out on each other. Maybe my friend knew that he was gay three years ago, four years ago, whatever. He could have confided in me, and I could have been there to support him and be his friend. But he missed out on that. And I missed out on being able to support him in that way.

The good part of this experience is that I have learned to be more accepting of gay people and to kind of let my feelings show a little bit more. When I saw all the people in my town kind of turning against him, or judging him or his parents—and his father being so hard on him—I felt like they were small people.

I understand that the Bible says that being gay is wrong. But I think that there is more to your life than just that one part. You know, it's OK for people to drink and get drunk. People don't talk about them forever. But if a guy is gay, people say things like "Don't be around him" or "Don't talk to him—if you do you might become gay, too." It's hypocritical. In other words, the message that it's immoral to be gay seems sort of silly, at least if it's coming from people who themselves get drunk, can't stay in their own relationships, cheat on each other, whatever.

My friend helped me to see that he is still the same person. It's hard to think that he is a bad person—I still care so much about him. I used to look up to him. And I still do. He is a good guy, a real quality person.

I'm Against Stereotypes

John, 16, from a suburb in the Northeast

I'm against stereotypes. I like football, but I also like art and reading. My way is not the traditional way to be a guy. I think stereotypes are bland and stupid. Let's just get together and throw them away. They come from everyone trying to fit one norm.

I hope boys can feel good about not just being athletic, but being smart and artistic, too.

Boys Don't Cry

Carlos, 12, from a suburb in the Northeast

I think a boy should be strong and fast. He should know all about men's stuff, know how to fix a car. Boys should be stronger than girls, and boys should be faster. Boys should be fast because if a girl was having problems, he could run real fast and save her.

Girls want to do lots of things. I'm not stopping them; I think they should do whatever they want. Some mothers are faster than fathers. Some fathers make food, and some mothers don't. You can't tell your future. There might be a girl smarter than you, or stronger than you. You don't know.

The good thing for boys is that we are going to be growing up. Everything is fun about a boy. But boys get in more trouble than girls. There is this kid in our school who always talks back to the teacher. He never does his homework. If his pencil is broken, he comes in without his homework and he'll say, "It's because my pencil broke." The teacher will say, "But you could have used a pen." He'll say, "I didn't want to." He tries to act tough.

Boys don't cry as much as girls. But let's just say this: You had a son, and you were the father. Your son died in front of your face. What would you do? Just stay there, not crying? I would cry because my son died in front of me. So would a girl.

But sometimes boys won't show it when they're sad. Girls will, because they don't care. If I was upset by something at school, I might not cry there because the other boys will stare at me. Or they might call me "girly." So boys will save their crying for home. At home, I will cry in my own room. Then my mom will come in and say, "What's the problem? Don't worry. Take a nap. You will get over it." At home, you only have to hold your crying for a second because no one will tease you there. But in school you can't do that. You have to live with it. At school, there will be a rumor that "He cried. He cried for this stupid little thing."

I'm a Cheerleader

Robert, 18, from a suburb in the West

I'm a cheerleader and I love it. At first I wasn't serious about it. My counselor suggested it to me and I thought it sounded like fun, and I took it up casually. I'm much more serious about it now, because now I'm in a cheerleading league. I have a summer job this year traveling across the U.S., teaching kids how to be cheerleaders. I may even get to go to Japan to teach cheerleading there. That's my goal.

Some guys don't do the things they really want to do—like cheerleading—because those things are "girls' things." But younger kids don't feel like that. There are no boundaries for them. They play with each other and there's no hatred between them, no judgment of one another. No one says: "Oh, he's playing with a doll. He must be weird, so we can't hang out with him."

I think society starts to change us when we're seven or so, in first grade. That's when boys start separating from girls and vice versa. That's when sports teams are all boys or all girls. Somehow that sends a message to the kids.

You have to do a lot of lifting and training to be a cheerleader. Many of the moves involve picking up the girls, throwing them up in the air and catching them. Cheerleading also takes a lot of teamwork. If someone forgets a move, or the group doesn't act like a team, it can be really dangerous. The team members have to be able to really count on one another. This summer one of the girls dislocated her shoulder because she fell out of a stunt—and it could have been much worse. We do a lot of partner stunts. The chemistry between the two partners and their mutual trust level has to be very high. My partner and I are like brother and sister. We get along great and we trust each other.

Before cheerleading I played basketball, but one day I realized I just wasn't enjoying it anymore, and I stopped. My other teammates didn't appreciate some of the things I was doing. It's not that I wasn't taking things seriously—maybe I took them a bit too seriously. I worked really hard during practice and I always tried to impress the coach so I could get a better position in the team. The other players liked to goof off more during practice.

Now, cheerleading has become a passion for me. I feel that there is always more to learn, always new, harder stunts to practice. Cheerleading makes me grow.

When we started, we got teased a lot. The other kids accused us either of being gay or of being sex maniacs, getting into cheerleading just so we could touch the girls. But then we did a half-time show and we got a standing ovation from everyone at the game. I guess they thought that cheerleading was just for girls, but then we knocked their socks off with our show and they changed their minds. Since then, we've been well respected because people realize that we are skilled at what we do. The first year was hard to deal with because of the teasing, but I'm used to it. . . . I let it roll off my back. I started cheerleading to have fun, and that's what I decided to do.

Guys don't like things they're not familiar with. They don't like it when guys do things that they think only girls do. Their instant reaction is that a guy who does that must be gay. I mean, by now, in the new millennium, it's not so unacceptable to be gay.

One friend of mine, Jason, told me that he was gay. I think he was pretty scared to tell me. And at first I was like, "Whoa, hold on a second." I was shocked when he first told me. He always had girls around him. At first I got really self-conscious, worried he'd misinterpret things I said to him. I didn't want him to feel I was rejecting him and I didn't want him to think I was gay, too, and interested in him. Because he is a cheerleader as well, it was tough. I worried people would say we were gay if we did a cheer together. I'm very glad I was careful with what I said. I would not want to ruin a good friendship because of saying something rash. I'm glad he didn't try to hug me or kiss me, because I am a little bit homophobic. I was apprehensive at first about that, but now that I've been able to get past that, I've learned to respect him and our friendship has been much richer.

I think homophobia is based on lack of understanding. Straight guys don't understand why another guy would want to have sex or relationships with a man. And, for me, my church does not allow homosexuality. I'm fairly OK with it in the outside world, because I know that society is OK with it. Though it's hard to feel comfortable with it in my church. I think that if you are religious you apply the Bible to your own life but you let your friends be your friends.

I'm not going to do anything to make Jason not be what he wants to be. It's his life, so he can live it.

A "Guy" Just Means "Male"

Jacob, 17, from a suburb in the Northeast

Guys have this notion that if you like reading and you don't like wrestling and you'd rather go to an art museum than play football, then that means that you are gay. And that's just wrong. A lot of people call me "gay." But I know I'm not gay. It used to really tick me off, but it stopped getting to me, and then they sort of stopped calling me gay.

Smart kids are called gay. What some people think it means to be a real guy is that you play football, watch wrestling, and get in fights. Intellectuals are fruity. But I don't think that's right.

A "guy" just means "male." I'm a guy. I've got a cock. What do you want? Machismo isn't what makes somebody a real man. Physical strength doesn't mean anything.

My mom is an academic and there are a lot of academics who are homosexual; I've met quite a few. Something I've noticed is that the way you act, behaviorwise, does not really in any way determine your sexual preference. Just because a guy is sensitive and doesn't want to get into fights doesn't make him gay.

There's this whole thing with modern psychology about getting in touch with your feminine side. As far as I can gather, your feminine side is your sensitive side. Does that mean that women are sensitive and guys are arrogant and football players? I don't believe that that's true.

I'm a guy. I don't play football. I have no interest in playing football.

Actually, I feel unconfident in gym class. When I'm not as good as everybody else, I try to be like "Yeah, whatever. My fault, my fault. I'm sorry for missing that ball." I try not to let it get to me, but you can't really stop it. It's hard because you want to be accepted. But you don't know if they're going to accept you.

There are cliques, popular people, and the jocks are in that category and they wear certain clothes. Polo shirts that are tucked in are sort of nerdy; that was how I dressed last year. I made a decision to change the way I dressed because the stuff I was interested in had switched. Before, I had been "must do good in school." Now I do well in school, but what's more important to me is music and having a good time. Loose shirts and wallet chains are punky and sort of skaterish. The thing that makes my shirt sort of punky and not nerdy is that it's really loose. I'm more comfortable, because fewer people make fun of me. If I was wearing a crisp, ironed, buttoned-down shirt, tucked in, that would be nerdy.

BEING MEN

Edward, 16, from a city in the Northeast

My dad's family is into being men. He comes from a family of six kids, four brothers and a sister. They all like to be tough guys.

I don't know if I've ever seen my father cry. It's something we talk about in my family. Even at a recent family funeral, I don't think he cried. He was visibly upset. But his family believes it's important for the man to be the strong one in the family and for everyone to look up to the man of the house.

My mom was really sick two years ago. It was my first year in high school, a lot of stuff going on for me, so they didn't tell me everything when it was happening. I found out later that my mom was within hours of dying. My sister skipped out of school and was with my mom at the hospital and she said that she saw my father cry then. I'm sure when he was alone with my mom, he was very emotional, too. But when he came home, he had to run the house. It was important for the family that my dad be the strength and not show emotion. My dad's like a lot of guys. He doesn't cook much and doesn't clean much, but he tried to set an example and keep things running normally. My mom's OK now.

My parents love to run. They run four miles a day four or five times a week. But Dad's getting older and his knees are giving out. So, sometimes he'll ride a bike instead of running and we'll call him Sally or some other girl's name. He hates it. He really has a problem with it. He can't laugh with his boys about it. If I tell him, "Hey, Dad, take your skirt off," he just can't deal. He wants to be manly and macho.

In fact, we had some big fights about it. He got really angry. I said, "Dad, you know, I'm not really putting you down. I just want to joke around with my dad and have a fun relationship with you. I know you're a tough guy and that you're much bigger than me. You could wrestle me to the ground any day."

My mom almost splits a gut when Dad does something goofy. I'll say something about it and she has to bite her tongue. She knows if we all laugh, he'll get really mad. Being really manly is big for him. My uncles are very traditional, strong men, too. They're all stiffs, in fact. None of them has a sense of humor. I guess you'd say I'm a tough guy, too. No guy wants to be labeled a wimp. But I've got a sense of humor. I can dish it out, so I've got to take it, too.

I Don't Know
David, 17, from a suburb in New England

I was talking to my old girlfriend recently, and we were talking about stuff from the past, and all of a sudden she said, "When I first came to this school, everybody told me that you were gay." That comment shocked me.

At school I did a study on masculinity, about how people prove their masculinity in different ways, and how it can be really harmful to their health and to society. For example, a lot of kids will wrestle and do "manly" things. There's one group of about eight guys at school who wrestle at each other's house and watch WWF matches. And that's all they're into. I don't partake in that behavior. Yes, I'll do it sometimes, but I'm not really into it. So that kind of puts me on the outside. And then everybody makes judgments about you based on the fact that you're not into wrestling and behavior like that—if you're not into that, then you might be gay.

Macho Stuff
Sam, 16, from a city in New England

I think most of the macho stuff guys do is stupid. I make fun of the kids who are very macho, like the kids who do wrestling moves in the hall. At the same time, there are things that I wouldn't do because I'm a guy. I've never gone to a guy friend, for example, and said, "I'm feeling hurt right now and let's talk about it." I have said that to some of my friends who are girls, but I'm less comfortable doing that with guys.

I think girls have much more of an outlet for expressing their emotions than guys do. I don't know too many guys who go to their parents and say, "I'm emotionally distraught right now" and "I just got shafted by my friend" or "I just got humiliated socially" or "I'm feeling very depressed" and really talk about it.

Girls will come home and talk about that stuff with their parents, and even more with their friends. It's more accepted for them, but with guys it's not really accepted. If you get shafted or humiliated, you just suck it up and don't say anything. Girls seem, at least from my experience, to be much more comfortable talking with other girls, even if they're not really tight. It's okay for them to run to the bathroom crying. Other girls who don't know them well, but happen to be in the class, will get up and follow them. You know, kind of console them and say, "What's the problem?"

A guy would never get up and run out crying. That would never happen. Even if it did, or even if a guy who was in the bathroom was really upset, the response would be "Look out, dude. He's freaking out." You're supposed to go be alone with it.

There have been times when I felt like I got socially humiliated and I won't want to say anything about it, because it feels like it's more of an embarrassment to guys than to girls. For some girls, it can even be an attention-getting device. "Oh, I've run to the bathroom crying and then, look, everyone follows me, and we can have this big consoling group therapy!" It's kind of an attention-getting thing, even about something that isn't a big deal. But for guys it seems very embarrassing to admit to real grief.

3

THE MASK OF MASCULINITY
AND THE DOUBLE LIFE:
SUPPRESSION AND BRAVADO

"Sometimes people say there are two me's, that I have a dual personality. . . . The public persona is not really who I am; it's a tool . . . to be who everyone wants me to be."

—Raphael, 17, from a city in the West

WHEN BOYS SPEAK ABOUT "BEING THEMSELVES," MANY describe a double life in which they are one person in public—a cool guy who plays fast and lives by the rules of the Boy Code—and somebody completely different in his private life, often a much more creative, gentle, caring sort of guy. Others say they can "be themselves" only after they go home, go to their own rooms, and shut out the outside world. What just about every boy says he knows all too well is what I call the mask of masculinity, a stance of male bravado and stoicism boys learn to use to cover over their inner feelings of sadness, loneliness, and vulnerability, to act cool, and to protect themselves from being shamed by their peers. When boys wear this mask, they completely repress their inner emotional lives and instead act tough, composed, daring, unflappable, laughing off their pain. They may wax strong and silent or lash out with fists and fighting words. They may strike to injure others or, more often, simply take things out on themselves. As eighteen-year-old Walt from a suburb in New England puts it,

"How many guys do I know who have broken hands punching inanimate objects?"

When life within the Boy Code becomes too much for boys, sometimes the only pathway to safety for a boy is to hide his true self under a mask, and with that self, his genuine voice as well. This helps to explain why many girls may often use rich language to express a wide range of their feelings, while most boys seem to have a myriad of monosyllabic responses to questions about their deepest experiences: "OK"; "I'm fine"; "Leave me alone." This paradox leaves our boys and all of us who love them at a terrible disadvantage. Beginning in early childhood, they become cut off from their vulnerability and their loving feelings, missing out, often for a lifetime, on an essential part of themselves. We, in turn, lose touch with the "real" boys in our midst. As eighteen-year-old Brendan, from the South, laments: "I think guys have a lot of secrets inside of them. . . . They are keeping secrets about who they really are, what they want to be, what they feel, what they think is right or wrong."

As a society, we tolerate, indeed collude in creating the mask boys wear, allowing them to keep their emotional lives secret from us, permitting only one stereotypical, "masculine" feeling to continue to be openly expressed—the "OK" male emotion of anger. When you listen to the voices in this chapter and throughout this book, you'll hear boys say they are "frustrated," "annoyed," "moody," or "pissed off." Most apt, perhaps, is that they say they are "beside myself." These are their words for the OK male emotion of anger, the rage society tolerates in lieu of exploring the angst, anxiety, or depression that lie just beneath the anger.

Sadly, boys know that the mask is off-putting to friends and family, and that repressing all of their emotions is a heavy burden to carry alone. "I know that this shield I have frustrates people sometimes," explains seventeen-year-old Allan, from a suburb in the West, who lost his father as a toddler and lives with a disabled mom. "Sometimes it's just too much, though, and I've had times where I get down in the dumps. I try to work around it, try to get myself out of it. I've been so independent my entire life that I don't like to have to go to other people for help." But boys wear this mask, or "shield," as Allan calls it, not just to defend themselves from their inner pain, but also because they have the distinct impression that this is what society actually wants them to do.

As seventeen-year-old Robert explains, "Men are not supposed to show sadness or fear." Or as eighteen-year-old Brian, from a city in the South, puts it, "Guys close themselves off, or shut themselves down, and put on a disguise for other guys. They do it for girls, too." Put simply, boys wear the mask because all their buddies, girlfriends, parents, and teachers still expect them to "stand tall," "take it" quietly, be "strong," and "tough it out." Some boys still say this is what they think girls and women find attractive in them. Still others boast of physical injuries they've suffered and talk about how they've learned to endure the pain and live with the scars without crying, complaining, or "tattling" about these things.

In essence, the mask is how boys both cope and defend themselves as they try to fulfill what I think of as the Impossible Test of Masculinity. David Gilmore, the cultural anthropologist, has written about a Native-American tribe whose ritual rite for boys approaching manhood translates roughly into "the big impossible." As boys enter adolescence, they speak often of this constant pressure and impossible quest to prove to themselves and others that they are meeting society's traditional expectations of them as males. Many of these tests involve engaging in reckless or hurtful acts of bravado, or showing that they can handle physical or emotional trauma without uttering a word or conveying a single emotion.

The Impossible Test requires boys not only to cut off their emotions and shut off their relationship skills, but also, especially during adolescence, to succeed at sports, work hard, make money, seduce women, and produce children. "It seems like there's a score card," Pierce, a senior in a large Chicago high school, explained to me. "How good are you at sports? Are you 'down' with the other guys—are you cool with them? Do you get the best-looking girls? Can you fight if someone starts messing with you? How many fights have you won?"

For the young boy trying to forge his own path and discover his own unique voice, this pressure to fulfill traditional rules about masculinity can often feel overwhelming. It can lead him to tease, bully, or abuse others. It can cause him to make mistakes in how he treats girls and young women and become compulsive about seeking out sex. It can push him to drink alcohol or take drugs. It can prod him toward depression. And as we've seen, it may even lead him to frightful, sometimes lethal acts of aggression and violence. In almost all cases, it makes him want to limit the range of his personal expression or silence his genuine, inner voice entirely.

As twelve-year-old Benson in Dallas, Texas, told me, "If you don't say anything, nobody will bother you. Just keep it bottled inside of you and don't say a thing. Then they know you're cool. If you rank high, they'll leave you be."

The boys in this chapter show us just how impossible and constant society's tests of masculinity still remain. They show us the mask, sometimes by describing their acts of bravado and the injuries they've been able to withstand. Other times they explain how they have challenged the rules by removing the veil that surrounds their feelings, facing down the Impossible Test. In allowing us into their private, hidden worlds, these boys are taking a heroic risk, perhaps with the hope, as seventeen-year-old Laurence, from the South, puts it, that boys will be able to become "more themselves . . . more available." But for this to happen, we must help boys recognize that bravado is a defense against shame. We must let them know that what we too often mistake for "badness" is really covert sadness and frustration about having to fulfill an impossible test of self. When we help the boys we love to remove the mask, we open up the gates for new possibilities within them, helping them forge relationships with their friends, girlfriends, mothers, and fathers that are far more honest, deep, loving, and peaceful.

THIS SHIELD I HAVE

Allan, 17, from a suburb in the West

When I was young, my mom was in and out of the hospital with lupus and I missed a lot of my kindergarten year. I really didn't pay that much attention to school to begin with, so I fell way behind in reading skills. But I got better at it, and now I'm all caught up. I like to find areas that are challenging for me and then push myself to do better in them. My mom has told me a lot about my dad, and says I got that quality from him.

My dad got bullied around a lot when he was in high school because he was kind of a skinny guy. People would tell him that he was not able to do things, and his parents weren't all that supportive either. They would tell him, "No, you can't do this. You're not good enough." But he worked to pay his own way through college. He decided to prove them all wrong. I've taken that approach in my own life.

I learned from a very young age that you have to deal with whatever you're given. My dad died from a stroke when I was two; he was only thirty-three when he died. Basically it was my mom who raised me, but I spent a lot of time with other family, my aunts and uncles and grandparents, when she was in the hospital. My mom lost her kidneys when I was three, and she was in the hospital eight months out of every year until I was probably thirteen. It started one night when I heard my mom get up to go to the bathroom in the middle of the night. When she didn't come out for a while, I went and checked on her, and she had passed out and hit her head and knocked herself out on the toilet. That's how it was with my father, too: he had a stroke and I found him in the garage.

I guess I've kind of desensitized myself to everything, with my dad dying when I was so young and my mom going to the hospital for my entire childhood. I remember one time when we were in Pennsylvania right after she lost the function of her kidneys and was in a coma. I had always thought the hospital was like this big maze, and I would just run around and have fun. I was small enough that as long as I didn't cause any trouble, nobody ever paid attention to me or cared. I remember going around the corner one time, coming back to my mom's room, and hearing the doctor say that she wasn't going to make it—that she wasn't going to come out of the coma, or if she did, that she would probably be brain dead or a paraplegic. I was only three years old. Since then, I've desensitized myself to a lot of it. It's just my way of defending against the pain. I don't know if I would recommend it to other people, but I don't know that I would not recommend it either.

I know that this shield I have frustrates people sometimes. I've had teachers tell me that. And my mom has told me repeatedly, but it's just my way of dealing with it and I don't want to change. I like that part about myself. I like that I can take all this pressure and everything that's around me, and I can take that and turn it into momentum and just continue on and do more things. If I'm sad or if I'm depressed, I'd rather not think about it. I'd rather go out and do something else to change my mood, something fun. I'll go work out, or I'll go draw. Just something to take my mind off it. If my mood's not changing on its own, I'll make it change.

Sometimes it's just too much, though, and I've had times where I get down in the dumps. I try to work around it, try to get myself out of it. Sometimes it's hard, but I try to do it on my own. I've been so independent my entire life that I don't like to have to go to other people for help. I think that, stereotypically, guys are expected to be independent like that. It doesn't have to be that way, but I do feel it has to be that way for me. I try not to go to people for help or to show my depression, although sometimes I can't help it. I usually end up getting angry at myself and I'll go to the gym and work that off, take it out on the weights. That will bring me out of it. Sometimes it's taken a while, but I get over it by turning my depression into anger and turning my anger into action.

TWO ME'S

Raphael, 17, from a city in the West

I live at home with my mom and my nine-year-old brother. My mom does volunteer work but she doesn't work. She is disabled from a bone infection she had from when she was a baby. She is pretty mobile, and she does everything that everyone else does. It's tough tying her shoe every once in a while, and lifting and carrying stuff. She's had several fake hips put in, but none of them wound up working. So they just cut off the ball of the femur.

I don't really remember my dad very well. He is out there somewhere, but I'm not really in touch with him. I know bits and pieces about him from his parents, and we have occasional contact. He calls once in a blue moon. But I don't really think about him very much. He was never really a very big part of my life. There are things about me, though, that are hard-wired into my system because of him, and they've really come back to haunt me. Things that I didn't really see as being attributed to him until recently. Like I remember when I was a really little kid, he would say he would come by and then he just wouldn't show up. So now, every time someone says that they are going to come over, I am at the door waiting. I am tapping my feet and getting up and making calls, and my mom is always asking me why I get so antsy. Well, we just figured it out a year ago. I think that my mom has been really supportive of the "healing process." She recognized the issues early, all the manifestations of him leaving, and really helped me with those before they became a problem.

I don't think a lot of guys have the skills to express their feelings. A lot of people are taught by their parents not to express themselves and to buy the whole American hero thing. The all-American football player who gets hurt and doesn't say it, and then goes out for the team and makes the touchdown. I think that has really percolated down through the generations, and so people feel that they have to be like that. If you look at all the real role models, who do you have? You have war heroes who got shot fifteen times and dragged everybody back to the line. You have football heroes and basketball heroes. You don't really have any poets or anyone representing other perspectives or ways to live.

Sometimes people say there are two me's, that I have a dual personality. One side is quick to make a joke, charismatic, the life of the party, and the other side is more introspective and honest, deeper. There is definitely much more depth to my character when I am talking to someone I trust. The public persona is not really who I am; it's a tool to make friends, to be who everyone wants me to be. Like people come up to me all the time and say, "Say something funny." What am I supposed to do? That's just what people want.

I like being able to make people happy and to help people through hard times, and being liked by everyone on a fairly superficial level. I think I am a natural thespian. Like superficially, I can have a connection with whomever, and they think that we're good buddies. But then, it would be hard if I didn't have those close friends that I could really express myself with and share how I felt. It's really hard for me to make actual emotional bonds; it's hard for me to trust people because of the way my father disappointed me by leaving me and my mother when I was so young. The way he withdrew and never came back has really affected my ability to have relationships with people.

NEVER REALLY CARED
Ronny, 12, from a city in the West

My mom is always amazed. I don't know why, but I've always kind of been picked on, and I've never cared.

There was one time, I think it was second grade, where these kids invited every single kid in the class, and they went to an amusement park and they had a great time, but they didn't invite me. I never really cared about it.

And then just a couple of months ago, the Greenberg family had a bar mitzvah for their son, and they didn't invite three kids in the class, and I was one of them. I didn't care. I mean, you can't really take it all that seriously, and for crying out loud, it's seventh grade. I mean, you can't really let it get to you that much. I've always had kind of a thick skin for that kind of stuff.

It does hurt sometimes. One time I was sitting at lunch, and the whole table started to pick on me, and I had to move. It gets to you sometimes. I try never to resort to telling a teacher. That's just the worst. For one thing, you don't like it when kids tell on you for doing something, and having a reputation as a tattletale is not the greatest thing in the world either, because then kids don't want to be your friend. So you just sort of have to take it, but it hurts inside.

Athletics have always been something I could fall back on. I started growing really early and becoming athletic in third grade, so I've always been able to outrun kids and outthrow kids, and been able just to back up on that. I was never "in." Never. Until the last year or so. I've been hanging out with girls a lot. I had a girlfriend for like four months or something, and now I'm kind of changing and getting into a different crowd, but I've never been really popular. Sort of on the outside.

When I get angry, a lot of times I don't really notice it, but sometimes I take it out on my mom or on my brother. I'll be angry the rest of the day. My dad does that, too. My mom hates Sundays now because the players on the team my dad likes really suck. I mean, they just suck, and so my dad will be mad all day, and I'll just go into my little shell and I just won't talk with anybody. I'll just stay with myself. Sometimes it comes out as anger, but usually I just bottle it all up, and usually it just kind of eases its way out, and by the next day or the day after, I'll be OK. Sometimes when I get really mad at school, I'll hit my locker really hard.

I don't know if I've ever really wanted to cry. I know some people say that crying helps and that bottling up really doesn't, but it's just my way of dealing with my pain. Sometimes when I get really, really scared, I'll cry, like when my mom and I were in Africa on vacation and she broke her back. She wasn't paralyzed but she had a compression fracture. She was on a runaway horse, and all I saw was her fall off the horse and bang her head really hard against the fence post, and I just started to cry because I didn't know what the heck was going to happen. I was really scared.

Maybe sometimes that's the way guys kind of protect ourselves—usually we can just brush it off, or laugh it off, or go inside our shell and just deal with it, but sometimes it's too much, and you can't control it anymore. I've hardly ever resorted to crying—usually when I cry, it's more a fake cry to get someone in trouble, like if some kid pushed me down, I might start crying. When my mom broke her back, that was really a healthy cry, because it was just eighteen of us, all of our family, like nine cousins and my grandpa and my grandma and my great-uncles. No one cared that I was crying. My brother was crying, too. It was funny, because the people who worked the corral there ran over and tried to pick her up, but with a back injury, you're supposed to let the victim see if they can move their legs, so my dad had to run over and push them off, because they were trying to pick her up. We didn't know what happened to her back. We were in a rural part of Africa.

We've been discussing in school whether or not guys should cry more often and kind of just be themselves. It's been a big topic. We have really cool discussion groups, and we talk about whatever we want, and it came up once that it's okay for girls to cry and it's okay for girls to stay around the home, but it's not cool for guys to cry, and that guys need to be more independent than girls. I don't know if it would be okay if guys could cry. It's kind of like a macho thing, it really is, not to cry. It's not like anybody is going to laugh at you for crying if you really get hurt, but emotional crying is different, like if someone gets picked on they start crying—that's not a good thing in middle school. If someone starts picking on you and you start to cry, you're just a wuss.

I don't really like the macho thing. People should be able to do what they want and not be affected by other people, but they can't. I don't like that factor. It's not for me. I don't need to cry, because the way I deal with pain and anger is just my way, and I like it my way. My way is holding it inside. I'm okay with that. I can go the rest of the day and still be happy. There's still this part of me that's angry, but that's the way I have always done it. It eats me up a little bit but usually it goes away. I don't know what happens.

A FRONT
Teddy, 16, from a town in the Midwest

When I look around, it seems like most guys put on a front, worrying what everyone else thinks and trying to be someone they are not. It's like they have to be a "bad boy" to fit in. They have to get in trouble, not care about grades, back-talk everybody. Most of the people that are considered the macho guys, outside of school are actually not that macho. They might be some of the nicest people that you've ever talked to, but in school, when there are lots of kids around, they act like rebels, like they don't really care what goes on.

TV shows and society give a mixed message about how guys are supposed to act. One show will have the cool guy who is always rebellious, who doesn't care what everybody says about him. He is going to do what he wants to, talk back to people. Stuff like that just gets into people's minds. "Hey, I've got to act like that. I have to be cool." But then on the next show, the cool guy will be the one that is caring, listening, crying, everything like that.

Most guys don't feel like they can be their own person. They're afraid of being called a wimp or a crybaby, maybe, or of being embarrassed by the way they really are. I don't really know why that is, since most people like you more if you act like yourself. I try not to put on a front myself, but sometimes it happens. I know it's bad, but sometimes I make fun of people, because it seems like the thing to do. I'll tell someone that they're ditzy or something. When I'm mean like that to people, it hurts inside and I feel bad for doing it. But I do it sometimes just to be cool, to be big and bad. I'll tell them I'm just joking afterward, but not around the other guys. They would probably say I was a wimp. It takes a lot to say, "Oh, I am going to be my own person, and I am not going to try to impress anybody. They can accept me for who I am, and if they don't, then that's their loss."

I don't cry in front of people, but I'll do it sometimes when I'm in my own room or talking to one of my good friends on the phone. But not in front of guys. I feel really embarrassed when I cry in front of guys. It comes off as physically weak. You just don't amount to much as a guy if you cry in front of others. When I get upset about things, usually I just go to my room and isolate myself. I feel like I can't talk to my parents about it, and I can't talk to my brother about it. My parents would think something is wrong, like I am going to kill myself or something. And my brother, I can't really go crying to him because he's a guy, and the whole wimp thing comes into play again.

A lot of guys make stuff up just to form that macho picture of themselves. "I could beat you in a fight. I have been with this girl and that girl. I go out and get drunk every weekend. I had run-ins with the cops."

I don't think it's cool. I think it's cool when a guy can act like himself, be himself, and not have to worry about impressing anybody or letting their opinions get to him. Being cool is being yourself.

I NEVER REALLY WANT TO HURT ANYONE
Drew, 15, from a suburb in New England

I used to be a really violent kid. I used to get into fights and I was always in the principal's office. I was known as hot-tempered. I went to a psychiatrist and that didn't do much. All he did was diagnose me with ADD.

I'm taking medication now. I don't want to take it, but I get easily distracted in school, and I'm very stubborn. So, I just said, "What the hell, I'll take it." Now I'm a lot more focused. But reading doesn't interest me. There's not really much to follow, so I just think about other things.

Skateboarding is one of those things where you just grab your skateboard and go. I have to wear a helmet at school, and it bothers me because I feel so confined. At skateboard camp, I have to wear a bunch of pads.

I haven't taken that many falls. Most of them were on my shoulder or my hand. I wrecked my thumb because I got stuck on the step and I came down on it. There's not much you can do about that, except learn to fall properly. I've had plenty of times when I've landed almost upside down but haven't hit my head.

I'm not against helmets. If I felt there was a need for me to wear a helmet, if I was prone to hitting my head, I'd wear one. A friend of a friend of mine died when he was hit by a car. The doctor said if he was wearing a helmet, he'd still be alive. Not in very good shape, probably, because he got hit pretty hard. So my friend wears a helmet now.

Another friend wears a helmet because a basketball hoop fell on his head and fractured his skull and he came pretty close to dying. He gets afraid and that's why he doesn't snowboard or jump on the trampoline. He's really cautious with his head.

My parents know that skateboarding has a bad rep. They don't like all the ramps I have in the yard and driveway. The first year of skateboarding, they were kind of strict about it, but not anymore. My dad would much rather have me skateboarding than hanging out on the streets or causing trouble. I think it's good because it keeps me going, and gives me something to do.

I also play hockey. That's where I get to take out all my aggression. In hockey, some kids just deserve to get hit. You want to hit them really hard.

I'm learning how to flip people. A guy hits me on the boards, and I take him down. I'm on my hands and knees and he's kind of laid across my shoulders and I pick him up and flip him. I don't know where I get all that strength.

The last game, there were a couple of fights. Usually I stand there and let the kid hit me, because I want to play. But a kid almost really hurt me. He came from behind and hit me and I went face first into the boards. If I hadn't had my face up I could have broken my neck. So I got up and I punched him to the ground.

One of my friends had already gotten hurt in that game, and I wasn't going to tolerate any more. I try not to be violent, but . . .

I never really want to hurt anyone, unless they deserve it. For example, in fourth grade there was a kid named Tom and he was pretty much psycho. He punched my girlfriend. I came over from behind him, tackled him and started punching him in the face. That got me in trouble. I didn't want to break his nose; I hit him mostly on the cheeks.

My dad has a pretty bad temper, too. He sees where I'm coming from. He knows that I don't fight unless I need to.

I was talking to my dad's mom once and she said he got beat up every day at school when he was a kid, and he'd come home all bloody and he'd get grounded. My grandmother said, "Hit them back. Don't let them do that."

So one day the kids came up to him, and he punched the lead kid in the face. And he got sent home all bloody and everything, but his mom was proud of him because he stood up for himself. I guess that's what my dad believes in.

I don't do it to make myself look better or bigger. I know a lot of guys do things just to make themselves look better. I'm not really with that.

One time last year I felt kind of lost. Everything was building up inside and I couldn't really hold anything in. My mom was being a real bitch. She was attacking me and I don't know why. I had the stress of school, too. And I didn't really have a girlfriend, someone I could love.

That puts a lot of stress on me. I felt really depressive. I wouldn't say much, just look at the floor, thinking about things.

One night, I threw a fit. I ran downstairs and punched a hole through the wall. I ran to the punching bag, and ended up ripping it off the ceiling and throwing it into the wall. Then I said, "I'm going for a walk."

I went for a walk and ended up in a cornfield. I just wanted to sit down, to calm myself. I fell asleep. It was late at night. I woke up the next morning in the field. I don't remember much about it.

MEN CRY
Walt, 18, from a suburb in New England

I was twelve. I was in the basement. Building a solid-food structure for a school program called "Odyssey of the Mind." Ducked under a clothesline and ran into a door. My head went through the area where a window should have been. Lucky for me there was no window, but the sharp right angle of the wood caused a peeling-tomato effect on my scalp, a semicircular cut on my head.

Fell on the ground. My friends came over. They said, "Walt, you're bleeding."

"No, I'm not."

"Walt, you're bleeding."

"No, I'm not."

"Get up off the floor."

I looked at the blood all over my hand. "Oh, I'm bleeding." Put my hand back on top of my head. Walk upstairs. Go to my mother and my father, who are having a conversation. In my father's office.

"Mom, I cut my head open. I need to go to the hospital." I feel logical. No time to panic and not be able to say anything. Now is the time to get help. Later, if I still felt like crying, cry then.

"Mom, I cut my head open and I need to go to the hospital."

"Walt, go wash off that red paint right now."

"It wasn't from painting."

I've always been one for practical jokes and playing around.

"Mom, I cut my head open."

"Walt, I'm having a conversation with your father right now. Go wash your head."

It went on like this for a good couple of minutes.

"Cut my head open."

"Wash off the red paint."

"Cut my head open."

"Wash off the red paint."

Finally my father got angry. He got up, grabbed me by the back of the neck. Walked me into the kitchen. Shoved my head in the sink, turned on the water.

Then he said, "Oh! Which one of us is going to take Walt to the hospital?"

Mom said, "I don't want to be around these damn kids. I'll do it."

My mother drove to the hospital with one hand on my head. That would be fine in an automatic, but we were in a standard, and she refused to take that hand off my head. We drove to the hospital, and she would overcorrect, careening into traffic. She'd let go of the wheel as the car started swerving back in the other direction. Slammed her foot onto the clutch, shift the car into the next gear. Grab the wheel and again correct so we didn't run off the road, and then do it again. I never thought I was going to make it to the hospital. I thought I was doomed.

I think as long as women are brought up to be women and men are brought up to be men, they will always have the communication problem that they have today. It's just continually passed on. Girls are brought up and treated like girls and are treated differently because they're girls and they, indeed, are different. But I'm not sure. Are they actually different? Do they actually think at all differently? Is there some scientific proof yet? I'm curious.

Anyway, they're brought up with this set of female ideals, just as men are brought up with the male baseball ideals. Women are supposed to be pretty. Which is a horrible, horrible thing. They're all pretty, for the most part.

Women cry. That's cool. Men cry, and that's not cool. I cried once and I'm sure someone made fun of it.

Emotion versus aggression. Women suppress aggression, feel emotion. Men suppress feelings, yet express aggression fairly well. How often do you see women break out in bar fights? Yet how many guys do I know who have broken hands punching inanimate objects?

What is wrong with people who think, I'm not going to hurt someone else, so I'm going to hurt myself? Can't you at least take the time to find a pillow? Go to the gym. They've got lots of punching bags. Put on some boxing gloves. Then beat up a tree.

A kid I know punched a refrigerator. Broke his wrist and finger. I can understand so much anger welling up in someone that they want to release it yet don't know how. But where'd the logic go? Can you not maintain logic? It's one thing I try to do at all times. Stay logical about situations.

The thing that's been on my mind most lately is self-improvement. And how to go about it. How to really live life to the fullest. How to get my life orchestrated so I can get it all in line and then just go about enjoying it.

ADVICE TO A TEN-YEAR-OLD BOY
Laurence, 17, from a city in the South

If I were to give advice to a ten-year-old boy on how to make it through and succeed in this world, I'd tell him that he could do what he wanted, as long as he had an open mind and an open line of communication to the rest of the world.

I think there are a lot of guys who shut themselves off. They get into this punk thing or dress differently and they cut themselves off. They're not going to be involved with the majority of people in the school. And there's nothing inherently wrong with that, but when you sever that line of communication, you miss out on a lot. My advice would be to do what you want to do, but keep that line intact somehow.

I'd also tell someone younger than me to reach out and get to know people. I think a lot of people are hard to talk to, and if you don't know them, if you're not on a personal level with them, they're hard to communicate with.

Friendships come when you can open yourself up. I think guys close themselves off, or shut themselves down, and put on a disguise for other people. They need to just be more themselves, be honest, and make themselves a little bit more available.

4

THE ANGST OF BECOMING A MAN:

COMING OF AGE

"I just don't want to become a man, at least not the kind of man I have known far too often."

—Gordon, 18, from a small town in the South

MY OWN DESTINY

David, 17, from a small town in southern New England

My parents were divorced when I was in the fifth grade, which changed the course of how I would be raised. Instead of having the Marine Corps influence as my two older brothers had, I would be without that strict discipline and without the attitude that we were representing our father in our actions wherever we went. So, my mother and my brothers and I returned to our hometown to start a new life without him.

Things in our home changed. There wasn't any harsh penalty for wrongdoing, and the realization of my father's hypocrisy started to bleed through. First there was the wedding that I was never invited to, where my father married a woman who was more concerned that he wore a Rolex watch than that he check on his three sons in their new lives. Although he chose to marry this woman, he continued to preach to us about caring who people are inside and not worrying about their status.

I carried on through my junior high years still heeding his advice on my troubles. Even though he was well over two thousand miles away from every situation, I still believed that he knew exactly where I was coming from. Seeing him on occasion was enough to make me believe that he not only knew best, but that he knew better than my mother, too, though she was the one raising me.

I pushed on into high school, where "the beginning of the rest of your life is to be built." Sure, I played sports because he said so. I was prodded into doing whatever he thought was best for me. This was the case through my first two years of high school, until my brothers finally felt that I was old enough to hear the truth that took them so long to figure out for themselves. The truth was that Dad really was a hypocrite: he had cheated on my mom for years. My brothers told me, "David, you don't have to do what he says all the time." On and on they talked until they were sure I understood.

I used to have a dad and I still do have a father, but as I've grown up and away from him, I feel that our relationship has become the biggest concern I've ever had to deal with on an adult level. I've especially realized this now that I'm finishing high school and it's the "big decision" time about where to go next. Overcoming hardships throughout my younger years has helped me to establish how I want my later years to flow. I'm trying to uproot the fallacies that have been crammed into my brain so that I can hit the road and move on, hopefully to the place that will build my character to the utmost. Meanwhile, my father is still full of the advice that he sees fit for me. His main concerns seem to be that I check out the schools near him and that I don't sell myself short. But pushing myself away from him is what I need to do so I can fulfill my own destiny, not just his. This may not seem to put me in dire straits, but it is the only thing that troubles me. I worry that I'm not strong enough to break the heart of the man who made me by telling him the truth of how it really is.

GROWING INTO MEN, FOR MANY OF AMERICA'S BOYS, IS A profoundly ambivalent experience. So many of the boys I talked with say they treasure the new autonomy that comes with manhood, yet fear that becoming an adult could make their lives even more lonely, restricted, and oppressive. For Gordon, quoted above, who's growing up in a small, isolated Southern town with a troubled father, a scarcity of positive adult male role models causes him to doubt his willingness to grow into manhood: "I am scared to become a man," Gordon went on, "for all the men in my family . . . have been the epitome of negativity. Some have become wrapped up in infidelity, some abuse, some alcoholism. I don't want to become a man, because I don't want to become this."

Throughout childhood, boys are constantly reminded of society's rigid expectations of men: men should be more aggressive than caring, more macho than emotionally expansive, more dispassionate and adventurous than nurturing and socially connected. From infancy, boys are forced into a gender straitjacket from which they find it nearly impossible to break free. As the caring, loving, sometimes fearful voices of the boys on these pages illustrate, becoming men who can break out of this male-gendered "box" feels as daunting and painful to them as penetrating the "glass ceiling" has felt to girls. As they make the transition into manhood, boys' resistance increases because they don't always like what they see ahead. Many boys don't want to have to act like strong and silent men. They don't want to become alienated or learn to "get by on their own." And they don't want to have to work as hard in such an unsatisfying way as they sometimes see the adults around them doing. Even boys with the most gentle, loving fathers comment on how the daily grind of work—a grind that society still sees as essential to stereotypical male "success"—seriously compromises their dads' emotional presence and availability. Few boys see a burned-out man as the type of adult they would dream of becoming. "My dad's life is no fun," one seventeen-year-old boy from the Midwest told us. "He has no friends. He works all the time and when he gets home, all he does is read magazines and watch television until he falls asleep. I'm in no rush to grow up."

Becoming a man is also painful for many boys because it means leaving home and the emotionally nurturing "holding environment" that home often represents. For many boys, home may be the one and only place where they have been able to go to escape society's harsh expectations of them as males, a safety zone in which it is okay for them to buck gender rules, relax, give and receive affection, and be their real selves. Many boys-becoming-men, as they head off into the world, feel gloomy about a future where finding such safety zones may be far more difficult. Thus, when their parents begin to sever ties with them and urge them to separate, many boys become anxious about the loneliness and disconnection that may lie just ahead. "Parents seem to abandon boys . . . because we're supposed to be independent and manly and things like that," explains Daryn, sixteen, from a suburb in the South. "It really hurts when that change happens, but I think people are unaware of it because boys are so busy trying not to show it. We try to be big and tough and stand tall. But it hurts. . . . Part of that might have to do with me, but part of it has to do with the way society says, Be a guy . . . do it all on your own."

Coming of age is also particularly confusing to boys because of the mixed messages they receive about what society wants from today's men. While the Boy Code, with all of its various rules about masculinity, still tells this generation of boys that they must act in the traditionally masculine ways described above, society is also constantly broadcasting messages today about all the ways men should reform their behavior and attitudes so that they will be more emotionally appealing and better attuned to the needs of girls and women. Society seeks men who are more sensitive, men willing to help perform housework and become involved in child care, men who are more socially adept, nurturing, and empathic. These conflicting outlooks produce much soul searching and, at times, a great deal of personal pain for boys. Indeed, who wants to grow into a man if society is not clear about what a man should be?

Society still sometimes misunderstands boys' hesitation to grow up as being the "narcissism" of young men unwilling to embrace adult responsibilities. Yet as the poignant voices here reflect, far from being selfish, misguided, or unrealistic Peter Pans, most boys are simply terrified to embark on the uncharted territory of manhood. They are anxious about whether, in making that journey, they will satisfy not only their own dreams and expectations, but also those of friends, family, and society at large. "I'm trying to uproot the fallacies that have been crammed into my brain so that I can hit the road and move on," David, seventeen, tells us. "My father is still full of the advice that he sees fit for me. But pushing myself away from him is what I need to do so I can fulfill my own destiny, not just his. I worry that I'm not strong enough to break the heart of the man who made me by telling him the truth of how it really is."

A BACKWARD VIEW

Gordon, 18, from a small town in the South

As Sherwood Anderson once said in *Winesburg, Ohio,* "There is a time in every boy's life when, for the first time, he takes a backward view." I guess that this is my problem right now.

I live in a small rural town. Some people stay here forever, but I know that I need to get out of this place. One of my favorite books of all time is *The Catcher in the Rye,* by J. D. Salinger. I love that book because the main character, Holden Caulfield, did what probably every disgruntled teenager has ever wanted to do—he left. After a lot of reflection, I've decided that now it is my turn to leave. I'm ready to move on.

But looking back and looking forward are both difficult for me. By turning eighteen, society has deemed me something that I have always profoundly disliked—a man. I have had practically nothing but bad experiences with males, except for my grandfather, who I called Paw. I always say that all that I am or ever will become in some way has a link to that man's knee (me sitting on his knee and he discussing things with me). Paw is one of the only positive male role models that I have ever had as a boy in this world.

Paw received little more than an eight-year formal education and lived his life illiterate. But Paw was the wisest person I have ever had the chance to meet. In life, with a little luck, one is blessed with a person who always knows what to say in any given situation, who seems to know everything about everything. This is my grandfather.

I can still remember his deep, baritone voice, his hearty Southern laughter and the way it would make his big belly shake, the way he smelled. To me, English Leather is probably one of the most horrific-smelling aftershaves you could ever buy, but on Paw it smelled good. I can still see him in the kitchen, which was his home, frying some of his famous chicken or whipping up his other notable delicacy, chili sauce, whistling a made-up song he would adamantly refuse to admit he had invented. Everyone loved his fried chicken and chili sauce and I was a big fan of the songs that came out of him.

The side I remember best is his giving side. Though it has been nearly four years since his death, I still meet up with old friends of his who recount stories about his generosity—about a child who received presents for Christmas for the first time through my grandfather's anonymous donation; about how Paw had braved a deep snowstorm to go to the grocery store for a homebound elderly woman; about how he had cooked a dinner from scratch for our church's entire five-hundred-member congregation, yet refused payment for his labors.

Paw taught me the basics of life: how to treat other people, how to conduct myself in public, the importance of charity. The lessons I received while firmly planted on his knee stay with me until this day. Many of them I still use as my life guidelines. It is by my grandfather that I try to measure my manhood.

Unfortunately, my father wasn't the nicest person to my mother and me when I was growing up. He hit and punched me. I have burn marks on my stomach. I had to get stitches on the back of my head. Scars are there to prove that, and you can physically see them. But those aren't the ones that I'm worried about. It's the emotional scars that hurt. For regardless how much vitamin E may be applied to them, they will never, ever go away. It has been almost ten years since my last encounter with physical abuse at his hands. But I still live with the memories. They will never go away.

These days, when I see a parent in Wal-Mart haul off and smack a crying child, the wounds are reopened. I just want to rush up and beat the shit out of the parent, to give that parent a taste of his or her own medicine because I know what it feels like. I know the feelings of degradation and self-unworthiness that come with having your ears boxed in a public place. It hurts then, and even more, later on in life, when an isolated event is unexpectedly played out in all its vivid splendor in the middle of the night. You're asleep and then a dream wakes you up, sweat mixing with the tears that roll down your face.

But, as I was saying, I am scared to become a man. For all the men in my family, except for Paw, have been the epitome of negativity. Some have become wrapped up in infidelity, some abuse, some alcoholism. I don't want to become a man, because I don't want to become this. I guess you could say that in my heart I know that I won't. But how many times can you remember being able to get your heart and brain to work in synchronization? It doesn't happen easily. It isn't that I'm scared of responsibility. I love having that. I just don't want to become a man, at least not the kind of man I have known far too often.

I Just Want to Stay Young

Asa, 14, from a city in the Northeast

I don't want to get old. I mean old like thirty. Once you hit thirty, your life ends. I don't want to die. I've got a horrible, horrible fear of dying. It's not that I go around afraid that something is going to fall on me or anything like that; I mean I don't want to stop existing. I think it goes back to a dream I had when I was two years old that I died. I got really scared. I don't cope well with death.

I don't want to get frail. I don't want my body to disintegrate. I don't want my mind to disintegrate. I don't want the people around me to die. I don't want to change. I just want to stay young like Peter Pan. I want to live in never-never land and be young forever.

A typical teenage thing to say, isn't it? At the same time, I really want to get older, because I want to grow up and travel the world. Turning eighteen would be good, if I could be eighteen forever. I really don't want to get older than that.

Actually, I don't even like being young that much, I just don't want to get old. I don't love the situation I'm in now, because I am pretty sad.

I think John Lennon was the most brilliant man that ever lived. When I was in sixth grade, I thought I was him. I thought I was his reincarnation. It all goes back to my fear of dying. Lennon is going to be remembered forever, because he was so brilliant and so wonderful. Everyone loves him. I want that so much. God, that would be beautiful!

Apparently I'm a repressed adolescent, or whatever you want to call it, because a lot of times I act like I'm a two-year-old. It really pisses off my dad. One night, I was acting like a two-year-old; I was singing and generally being annoying. I had made a graph as part of my homework. I showed my dad the graph. He said, "It's nice." I said, "Don't you think it's beautiful?" He says, "It's nice." And I ask him again, "Don't you think it's beautiful?" He says, "It's all right." I ask him again, "Don't you think it's beautiful?" I kept on badgering him to say it was really pretty. He refused to say it. So I got really exasperated. I kept after him, "Please say it's pretty. Please say it's pretty." He just refused, and then got really annoyed. So I stopped for about twenty minutes, but then I did it again about something else. I felt really angry. I kept on acting like that the whole night. I sang a lot of really silly songs. I was jumping up and down, and dancing.

I bugged my dad so much that he chased me around the house. He was ordering me, "Asa, go to your room." And I said, "No, what the hell are you talking about?" He's like "Go to your room. I'm going to count to three." He counts to three, and he gets up, and I run away. You know those movie or television scenes where there is a table and the two people are on either side of the table and they're going around it, one trying to catch the other? That's what we did. My dad would push the table and I'd run away. I was laughing the whole time, but it wasn't funny to him.

Finally, he caught me and pushed me into my room and shut the door. It was really weird; it was just what he did when I was two. I would wait a little while, and then I would try to open the door and come out, but he would be holding the door closed. He'd say, "Get away from the door." I wouldn't move, but I'd say, "OK, I am away from the door now." He knew I was still there, so he'd say, "Get away from the door, Asa." "I *am* away from the door," I'd tell him. Then he'd repeat it, "Asa, I said get away from the door!"

You know that feeling you get when you want to jump out of your skin, and run around and smash things? Well, that is the feeling I had that night. There was a real antsiness. A whole lot of energy. My bones felt like they were going to explode. Then I got really sad. It's a weird dichotomy of feelings. At one point, it's like I want to take something, smash it and destroy it. At the other point, there is this feeling like I want to hold on to something really tightly. Just be clutching to it for dear life. Then I just want to rip it apart again. It goes back and forth. It creates an emptiness in my stomach that is cold and weird. It is such an awful feeling. That's why I act like a two-year-old.

I have this terrible teen-angst bullshit. If you see me around school, you'll think I'm a popular kid. There are people around me most of the time who I am chitchatting with. Most of the time you see me, you'd say, "Look at that happy little boy." But I don't think that people like me. They don't hate me; they don't go around saying, "Oh, look, there is Asa, let's all make fun of him!" But I don't really connect with any-one, and no one really connects with me. I've got people who I can be around, but I don't have any good friends.

There are so many conflicting ideas going through my head. All of this stuff makes me very sad, and when I get sad I sulk, then I play music.

I'M READY TO MOVE ON
Taylor, 17, from a city in the South

I'm seventeen now, I'm growing up, and I'm ready to move on.

It would take like an act of God for me to be close emotionally with my parents, but I actually don't mind much. There's something inside me that doesn't want to get close to them or open up to them. When I'm with them, I get embarrassed about who I am. I don't mind talking about school and work and stuff like that, but I avoid anything that requires personal knowledge. I don't like talking about problems I'm having, or relationships, or sex, anything like that. The only thing I ever opened up to my parents about was a breakup with a girlfriend, and that ended up being an interesting conversation, and both of them took turns telling me stories. They're pretty good parents, they're "nice to have around," but right now it's just tough to be close to them. I'd like to get out and move out, but I think we'll be closer one day. I'm not sure we'll ever get deep-down, emotionally close, because right now, it's emotionally dead between us.

When I was younger we were a lot closer. My mom's a teacher, so in elementary school she was always around. Then I got thrust into middle school, and that's when it hit. I felt abandoned, I guess. Parents seem to abandon boys at that age because we're supposed to be independent and manly and things like that. It really hurts when that change happens, but I think people are unaware of it because boys are so busy trying not to show it. We try to be big and tough and stand tall. But it hurts.

Before the fifth grade, I used to cry when I had to go to my uncle's house for the summer. I used to cry because I didn't want to be away from my mom and my dad. But now I pine to get away, I cherish the time away. There isn't any attachment anymore. I needed them then but I don't anymore. They're like a fixture in the house. They're there, but you don't feel it. It's kind of empty. And it's been empty since middle school.

Part of that might have to do with me, but part of it has to do with the way society says: Be a guy, go have sex, do it all on your own. I'm ready to move on.

THE AMERICAN DREAM
Francis, 18, from a suburb in the Northwest

My dad has been very successful and he epitomizes the American dream. Subconsciously, his success probably does rub off on me a bit.

But I don't go to school thinking, "Oh God, I have to get into a top college so I can fill my dad's shoes." Actually, I think how it affects me is by making me want to distance myself from him. I wouldn't want to follow his career footsteps or have to live up to his image. I want a sense of accomplishment that is completely independent of him.

I am closer to my mom because she is almost always there when I get home from school. My dad tends to be out of town on the weekdays. I get along with my dad and can talk to him, but I think my mom is just there more often. By my age, it's not really hard anymore that my father is gone so much. I definitely remember when I was younger, being disappointed when he missed my basketball or baseball games. I still remember the times he had to leave early for a business trip, or work late in the office and not get home until after 8:30. I would have to go to bed at 8:30. I can remember it would have been nice if he had been there.

We all made sacrifices and part of the reason that I go to a great private school is the sacrifices my dad made, and the sacrifices I made in terms of my time with him. It's part of life, and I don't hold it against him. All the same, I am not quite sure I want to make the same choices for myself. Knowing how nice it would have been for me if my dad were home more, I don't know if it's necessarily worth it. Because he travels so much, I have noticed that I don't like traveling myself. It reminds me of what it was like when my dad wasn't there for me, and I would rather just stay home.

I think part of all this goes back to Darwinism, something that was genetically bred into us over the millennia. The male's position is to provide for the family, to have the best cave, the best meat, whatever. The male is supposed to make sure that his family is protected and adequately provided for. And my dad was disappointed that he couldn't come to my games, but at the same time he felt that he had to provide. That was his job, and he couldn't fail at it. I don't hold it against him because something in me realizes that that was the role the man had to play for so long. I am just not sure it will be the path I will take.

When I have a family I want to have more time with my children, more of a human connection. I think you can find a way for both your career and your family. By prioritizing things, there is room for both. Whenever you can, you make that sacrifice to be there at that sporting event or at that parent conference. You just have to evaluate what is really important and what really matters in life. I want to be able to look back on my life and say, "I'm proud of what I did, I'm proud of how I raised my children, I'm proud of what I meant as a person." My advice to people is to just make sure that you are proud of what you decide to do, so that you can look back and say with sincerity, "I made the right decisions."

5

OF TWO MINDS:

HAVING SEX WITH GIRLS

"Guys are worried about being virgins."

—Rocky, 15, from a city in the Northeast

"There's certainly a lot of pressure not to be a virgin, but I've resisted it and I'm proud to be a virgin."

—Tyrone, 17, from New York City

IT'S BEEN EMOTIONAL
Rocky, 15, from a city in the Northeast

I have a girlfriend named Laura. She's a senior at a private school near where I live. I met her on the train. We've been going out since October. You know, we do stuff, the usual stuff, like make out. I am close to her.

I try my best to talk to Laura. But I can't talk to her about everything (like about other girls and stuff). I couldn't tell her about that because she'd dump me. Honesty just doesn't work with girls. If you tell them about other girls they're gonna get mad no matter what.

The rules are different for girls and guys. Guys are worried about being virgins. When they have sex with a girl, well, with their friends, you know, it's just another X on the card. You get with the girl and you're done. It's cool for a guy if you can have a lot of X's on your card. Guys don't want to get into the details; that's more of what the girls do. Girls will go and call up all their girlfriends and talk about it. Like what it was like, the experience. Guys just say, "Yeah, I fucked her." And that's all the other guys really want to know. They don't want to get into details about anything. They just want to brag.

But if you brag to the other guys, they may think the girl's a whore or something. They'll tell your other friends, and those guys get the wrong impression about the girl. So you know, you kind of keep that quiet. A girl is not supposed to brag, but she can tell her other girl-friends. Because if she tells the guys, she'll be considered a "ho." A guy can brag to all of his friends, or to other girls, and he is not considered a "ho." If you tell your friends what you did, they give you a high five, like "way to go!"

I think it's hard for guys to be on the level, to be straightforward with each other. Sometimes you have to play a different role. Like when I'm around different groups of people, I know I have to act different with them. When you're out with the players, you know, with the guys, you gotta act like a player so they can say, "Yeah, he's cool!"

Like I said, it's like having a scorecard and there's a little X for each girl. Guys don't really say exactly how many X's they have. One friend of mine has a lot of X's, but all with the same girl. Yeah, he's a player!

I don't have an X yet. I'm a virgin, in a modern sense. I've done some sexual stuff. But I haven't had intercourse yet. I want to. But, you know, sometimes when I think about wanting to do it, I think I'd like to wait and find the right person to do it with. Other times I just want to do it! I'll know I met the right person when I love that person a lot.

I don't feel pressure from my girlfriend to have sex. But I do feel pressure from other guys, with all their scorecards. They will be like "You've been going out with her for a month and you still haven't done it yet! What's going on? You didn't hit that yet?"

I really don't say much about my girlfriend around school. I'm afraid that guys will give me a hard time and ridicule me. Even though they probably never did anything with their girlfriends either! Guys lie to make themselves look cool with other guys. They're trying to get re-spect. They're afraid that if they didn't brag about having sex, if they told the truth and said, "Well, I've kissed, but I've never had sex," other guys would make fun of them.

Some guys are afraid of relationships. So they might distance them-selves to be playboy-type guys. That's cool for now, I guess, but when you're thirty-five or something, you have to settle down. Because if you're a Mac daddy and you're fifty-five years old—unless you have a lot of money like Hugh Hefner—it's not gonna work out.

But I don't think guys should have to be worried about what other guys think. I mean, girls will appreciate a guy who takes things slow and is honest about it. Girls will say, "He's a virgin . . . so what?" A nice girl wants a guy who's actually understanding and who's not a big mouth about what he does. Girls have a different kind of scorecard. It's not about what they've done. It's about how it was. For some guys maybe it's just physical. For girls it's emotional *and* physical.

Sometimes for me it's just physical. But it's been emotional for me, too.

A Real Commitment
Brad, 16, from a suburb in New England

Girls have generally come on to me, rather than the other way around. I don't have a whole lot of confidence in that regard—I'm not confident enough to approach a strange woman at the mall or something. I won't try a pickup line; I think that's kind of lame. I might make eye contact across the room, but I probably wouldn't approach her and introduce myself. I wouldn't feel comfortable doing that.

I have a girlfriend now, but the relationship is kind of vague and am-biguous. We're not telling other people that we're going out. But we are at the point where if either of us screwed around with anyone else, there'd be trouble. Her friends would be pissed if I did that and vice versa.

To be honest, I'm kind of stalling with this "maybe" girlfriend. From what I've heard from her friends, she wants a real commitment and I don't know about that. We haven't had a frank discussion about "this is where we're going." We'll just see how things unfold. And her friends have said, "So, she really likes you." And I'm like "Mmm, good."

A real commitment would be when you "officially" become a cou-ple and you're recognized as such by everyone else. I'm just not sure I like her that much, and that kind of commitment binds you to the rela-tionship. If you become a steady thing then you can't decide in two weeks "I've had enough of this." I couldn't extricate myself without looking like an asshole.

I think this need for commitment is more common with girls than guys, but I have a lot of guy friends who are in relationships with girls that they're very committed to. It's neither cool nor uncool. And it's not something that people think, "You should strive for this."

Right now, there's no girl I want to have sex with. Having sex, again, feels like making a commitment. My little brother says, "Do it! What are you waiting for?" Some friends just say, "Get laid as quickly as possible." I don't think there necessarily has to be true love for sex. But I think a lot of guys have sex without really thinking about it. They just do it because it is expected. Guys don't necessarily think, "I've succumbed to pressure by having sex with her." It's more like, "I did it and that's cool." And then you go tell your friends about it and it's a respect thing.

T HOUGH MUCH OF SOCIETY MAY THINK THAT A BOY'S DWELL-ing on sex is about as American as apple pie, teenage boys across our nation actually feel deeply conflicted about sex and about how to make smart decisions in their romantic lives. The myth still exists that as they reach the preteen years and their hormones begin to run amuck, most boys will have difficulty managing their natural impulses, luring girls and young women into sex before they are ready, and possibly exposing themselves, and their mates, to sexually transmitted diseases and unwanted pregnancies. While there's little question that many, if not most, teenagers in America are experimenting with premarital sex, boys across the country, if we listen to them carefully, seem to be telling us that they are hardly certain or single-minded about becoming sexual and seeking out sex. In reality, boys are just as anxious and confused about sex as girls are.

Many of the boys we spoke with told us they are not at all sure when they should begin their sexual lives with girls. Some feel confident that they would prefer to wait until they are in love, or until they are married, before engaging in sexual contact. Many speak of the tremendous pressure they feel being placed on them by other boys, and by girls, siblings, the media, and others to set aside their scruples and move more quickly toward intercourse. Others told us that they feel ready to explore their sexuality, but are completely confounded by what girls expect and desire.

Much of the confusion boys experience stems from the mixed messages about sex and masculinity that society continues to set forth. On the one hand, boys are told that they should be a new kind of young man—responsible, respectful, abstinent. This message resonates with traditional and revisionist thinkers alike—traditionalists like it because it implies that boys will refrain from sex before marriage; revisionists favor it because it means that boys will defer thoughtfully to what girls and young women feel about becoming sexually involved. On the other hand, boys are also being told that masculine men have intercourse as much as they can, and don't need to love women to have sex. They are told that they should take any opportunity that presents itself for dispassionate, biological discharge. Being a man, many boys told us, requires them to "score." By contrast, being a virgin, according to many boys, is considered anathema. Listen to Jeff, a sixteen-year-old from a small town in New England:

> Your virginity is what determines whether you're a man or a boy in the eyes of every teenage male. Teenage men see sex as a race: the first one to the finish line wins. Your virginity is the single most important thing that determines your social status in the eyes of almost every teenage male. In high school, virginity is a self-demeaning label that you want nothing more than to get rid of. It is almost inconceivable to think that your virginity, your one and only innocence, could be your worst enemy.

In a society in which we preach equality and growing gender mutuality, it is striking how old attitudes toward boys and their sexuality die hard, even as the boys themselves struggle for a different type of relationship. When it comes to sex, the old-fashioned Boy Code does not seem to be working. Within one breath, the Code tells them to "stop," in the next to "go." It's no wonder, then, that boys act out their confusion in how they go about pursuing and having sex.

The picture that emerges is one in which young men project macho bravado on the outside, but underneath they are frightened and concerned as they encounter their sexuality for the first time. They are also sensitive to the medical and psychological complexities of sexuality. Many boys speak about how worried they are about AIDS, about the importance of using condoms. They speak about abstaining from sex altogether.

Some boys feel that as "difficult" as it might be, they would like to wait until marriage—or at least until they are older and in a committed relationship—to engage in sexual intercourse. "It's important to me to be a virgin," says Scott, seventeen, from Florida. "I want to wait until I find someone I really like [so] that it will mean something that's more than just some high school kid having a relationship just because he wants to let out his hormones. I want to wait till I find a girl who's important to me. There's no rush."

But the Boy Code comes down hard on these boys, pushing them to chastise one another as "wimps" or "faggots" if they aren't able to talk about their successful sexual conquests. Many boys notice the bragging or boasting about girls and sex that dominates conversation among their peers. But many of them notice, too, that much of this is mere puffery, designed to be a shield against peer ridicule, bullying, and hazing.

Tyrone speaks eloquently of these themes:

There's a lot of pressure from other guys . . . not to be a virgin, but I've resisted it and I'm proud to be a virgin. Everyone at school knows I am and some of them think it's a joke. I think most other guys lie about sex anyway, and pretend not to be virgins when they are. I thing virginity is something so sacred, so beautiful and holy that you should only lose it when your feelings for your girlfriend are real. I have to wait for that special someone before I lose my virginity.

Despite his personal decision to wait to have sex, Tyrone and so many others like him still feel forced to accept locker-room bravado. This atavistic model of sex—encased in the old, unhelpful Boy Code—not only raises serious physical and emotional risks for girls and women, it also causes significant angst and quite similar physical and emotional risks for boys themselves.

Of course, the Boy Code is not only enforced by boys. Girls, too, sometimes help to refortify its strictures. Many boys spoke to us, in a hesitant although genuine way, about the fact that girls have sexual urges as well, and that it is not at all uncommon for the young woman to be the initiator, indeed the prime mover in a premature or risky sexual encounter. Seventeen-year-old Winston, from a city in the South, spoke of his regret:

My former girlfriend told me about her other boyfriends and then I felt like I had to . . . become better than them, even outdo them. It has to do with masculinity. I felt as though I had to be more of the guy, be more "the man," be more the masculine, aggressive-type guy. Then you do that, try to fulfill her. And then, you still are left not knowing whether you satisfied her and she's kind of like, "Well . . ." And then it feels senseless. It feels like "What did I just do?" I've done things I wish I hadn't done. I kind of regret a lot of that. It's empty afterward, it's not like anything's there.

Like Winston, many boys wonder whether they are satisfying their girlfriends, or if they are doing the right thing by having sex. Many, too, are not exactly sure where they stand with their girlfriends. Some have solid friend relationships that turn into "girlfriend" relationships involving sexual activity. Sometimes these relationships revert to friend status. Some boys want to have a "real" girlfriend, but have no idea how to go about it. A few boys have strong girlfriend relationships, but aren't sure where they are headed or how the girl views the situation.

In general, boys feel they have little control or power or even equality in the relationship; from their perspective it is the girls who are calling the shots. The girls decide whether to go out, to have sex, and when to end the relationship. Often, when a relationship does end, the girl won't talk about why. This is in contradiction to the view that girls are always the ones who want to talk about relationships. In many cases, boys say that they wanted to talk, but the girl seemed to have little interest in doing so. This leaves the boy feeling extremely confused. He also feels ashamed, and more timid about the possibility of his next encounter with a girl.

I have found in my work that boys long for understanding and love in a sexual encounter, just as girls do. As Rohan, a seventeen-year-old who lives in New York City, puts it, "I want to make love, not just have sex in the park." But we continue to treat boys unfairly by tarring the majority with the brush of the very few who may be genuinely compulsive, uncaring, or dangerous. The media still portray boys as emotionally disconnected sexual predators who have little interest in love and mutual sharing with the opposite sex. They are painted as men up to "no good" sexually, always having the upper hand and being in the "driver's seat." The stories in this chapter belie these messages, laying bare boys' fears of as well as their respect for the girls they are attracted to. These voices also illustrate how "weird" the whole situation frequently feels to them.

In some ways, making decisions about sex, for America's boys, indeed *is* "weird" simply because so few people help them sort through all the confusing messages and figure out what they really want and how to honor it. No matter what our political or religious beliefs are, boys seem to be telling us that they need to hear more than just "no" or "yes" or "stop" or "go." The bafflement adolescent boys feel about sex, in reality, is perfectly normal. But perhaps it's our job, as those who love and care about boys, to help them, as best we can, to see things more clearly. We now have an opportunity to push beyond the stereotype of the boy who only wishes to prey on girls, and create a balance between the sexes based on mutual respect and understanding.

JUST ANOTHER KIND OF FRIEND
Austin, 17, from a suburb in the South

As a guy there is big pressure to have a girlfriend, and a lot of guys are looked up to because they have had all these girlfriends, or they've scored a lot of times. But relationships with girls shouldn't be viewed as scoring or as a possession. Girls should be treated with respect and not just as objects; they are just another kind of friend that you can get close to. I don't have a girlfriend now but I have girls that are friends, and it's different from guy friends.

I think sex should be saved for marriage. There are a lot of acts that are clearly sexual that should wait. Even holding hands can be sexual; it's more the thoughts behind the acts that could be dangerous. Giving yourself to someone sexually is probably the most intimate thing you can do with another person, and I think that it's a onetime thing that should be saved for one person. It demotes that act to just a pleasurable experience if you are always doing it with multiple people. Plus, I've seen people get close sexually and then it doesn't work out. And that's really hard.

I think in high school a lot of relationships between guys and girls often just produce heartache in the end. They're not going to be permanent most of the time, and breaking up is devastating for some. The closer you get, the harder it is, and you can either completely put up walls around yourself so you'll never be hurt, or you can open yourself up to other people and risk the pain that can come.

Some guys brag to get attention, or to try and get another girl. When I hear them talking about scoring with this girl or that girl, at the time I might have a twinge when I think, "Why can't I do that?" or "That is really cool." I've had desires, definitely, but I think God has protected me from falling to that temptation. And it's hard not to submit to the peer pressure. It takes real strength to stick to the choices that you feel are right for you. But I think that you are stronger for having held on to your lifestyle. Keep that integrity, because once it's gone, it's gone forever.

I've had a girlfriend before, but it was always kind of a gray matter with us. It doesn't have to be "Will you go out with me? Will you be my girlfriend?" There's that nonverbal kind of communication that goes on, like certain types of eye contact that can say, "Yes, you are my girlfriend." You don't always have to have that discussion where you say you are formally going out. She and I got close just by doing things together, activities in school and out. Talking on the phone and at school, glancing at each other and stuff like that. I think all that strengthened the relationship to a point. But then when she realized that I didn't want to pursue the relationship physically, I think that definitely stopped the romantic part of it. She would have gone with me if I had pursued a physical relationship, and when I didn't, we both started to pull back. And since then, we rarely talk anymore. I miss it. Not necessarily her, but having that closeness with someone.

Now when I'm attracted to a girl, I have to make sure that she wants the same thing that I do out of the relationship, that she will not be pushing to have sex before marriage. Because if that's the case, then the relationship isn't going to work out. Having that standard kind of rules me out for a lot of girls. But that's okay, because I can still relate to them as friends.

So Sacred, So Beautiful and Holy

Tyrone, 17, from New York City

Sometimes I'm with my friends and they will just go up and start talking to girls we don't know, talking with them and asking them out. I'll then feel like I have to go talk to the girls, too, or else I'll look weak, like I don't have enough heart. I'm lucky—I'm not shy around girls. Even if a girl is really pretty and intimidating, I'll go up to her, put on a smile, show her my personality and I bet I'll have a good chance with her. I love to flirt with girls, and I do it so much other guys at school call me a little play-boy. I don't just talk to them to try to pick them up, I try to be a friend to girls. I think it's great to be sweet to a girl, to respect her and treat her like a princess. I write my girlfriends poems. Sometimes they don't take what I'm doing at face value and sometimes they don't understand me, and then I know the right thing to do is to break up with them.

I like many different kinds of girls. I don't just talk to the most beautiful girls, or to the girls with the best bodies or most makeup on. My favorite girls are the ones who are the sweetest. My girlfriends need to dedicate a lot of time to our relationship and give me a lot of atten-tion. I like girls who really want to do things with me, not just go on dates and go to movies. I'd like to wake up early, call up my girlfriend, and get her out on the basketball court. After a great game of basketball, we'd all go to McDonald's. And we'd go dutch—I like a girl who pays for herself.

The best way to be successful with girls is just to be yourself. If they don't like you, then you are just not the right person for them. It's silly to try to impress girls by acting tough, wearing different clothes, or being very sensitive. You shouldn't have to change yourself for any-body.

There's a lot of pressure from other guys that makes us do these things. There's certainly a lot of pressure not to be a virgin, but I've re-sisted it and I'm proud to be a virgin. Everyone at school knows I am and some of them think it's a joke. I think most other guys lie about sex anyway, and pretend not to be virgins when they are. I think virginity is something so sacred, so beautiful and holy that you should only lose it when your feelings for your girlfriend are real. I have to wait for that special someone before I lose my virginity.

Society is tough on boys. Many people see us as worthless and they treat us like scapegoats. I think they blame us for a lot of things that happen in our society. But we can't help it if we've grown up in a really bad environment. Some boys have parents who don't love them and mistreat them. The way parents treat you is so important. The only foundation you get for life is the love of your parents. If you don't get that sort of love and nurturing, sometimes you go looking for it in sex, drugs, or violence.

THE FINISH LINE

Jeff, 16, from a small town in New England

Your virginity is what determines whether you're a man or a boy in the eyes of every teenage male. Teenage men see sex as a race: the first one to the finish line wins. Your virginity is the single most important thing that determines your social status in the eyes of almost every teenage male. In high school, virginity is a self-demeaning label that you want nothing more than to get rid of. It is almost inconceivable to think that your virginity, your one and only innocence, could be your worst enemy. Sex is something that every teenager thinks about every minute of every day.

The pressure of being a virgin in high school has been one of the hardest things I have had to deal with as a teenager. I will never forget the first time I was asked if I was a virgin. I still remember the fear that the question struck in me—the fear of not being accepted by my friends, the fear of not being able to get with girls. I would lie in bed awake at night wondering if I was ever going to have sex.

It is much tougher for women to deal with sex in high school then in any other environment. Men are more critical of women who have sex than men who have sex. A woman who has lots of sex at a young age is considered a slut. Women who don't have sex at all are considered prudes—and this is a remark usually thrown at a woman when she will not easily agree to having sex. Men use it as a defense mechanism so they don't look weak for not getting any.

The double standard is a trap for females. Society encourages a man to get with a woman while at the same time discouraging females to have sex. Women live in a society in which they are looked down upon if and when they have sex. Ironically, men, the sexual aggressors and the voice behind our society, forbid women to have sex before marriage. If a man can get with a woman, society says that he is more of a man. I have thought that if you were able to take a woman's virginity, then all your other male friends would consider you great. This might be a reason why it is considered a goal for men to get women in bed. You would think that this male-dominated society of ours would encourage women to have sex so that men could have more partners.

It is always a goal for a man to take away a woman's virginity. Taking a woman's virginity gives a man a feeling of power, of being the first one to break through a forbidden barrier. As a young teenager it is very important for me to be able to take away a woman's virginity.

Men and women are going to always struggle as young adults. High school is a very insecure time for men and women. I think that society influences young adults to act in stereotypical ways with each other. We can only stop this problem by opening up our eyes and realizing that women should be treated with just as much respect as men.

A Simple Relationship

Winston, 17, from a city in the South

I had a girlfriend for about a year and a half. She was very creative and spunky and all over the place. She had a very outrageous personality; she was very strong and passionate about certain things. We met at our church, through friends in the youth group. For a guy and a girl these days, there's pressure, pressure, and very little pleasure. It's hard trying to be yourself and keep them happy at the same time. When you meet a girl, you're not necessarily being yourself, because you're busy flirting and trying to impress her. Then you're afraid if you open up and she gets to know the real you, you're not going to be as enticing. When I first met Amber, I thought, "This is interesting, this is somebody I want to be around." So I acted a certain way so she would think I'm fun and would want to be with me.

A lot of girls give a confusing message about what they want. They dress a certain way and act real flirtatious, and then when it comes to the next level of relationships they're standoffish. It's like they don't want to deal with a serious relationship. For most guys, if they get close to a girl, the sexual attraction is going to happen. Girls like to be close to somebody, but they aren't really up front about sexual things. It's kind of confusing to a guy, because when he is able to have a close relationship with a woman, he kind of expects it to become sexual. And when it doesn't, he's confused and upset. A flat-out answer—Do you want to have a relationship or not?—can be so helpful.

I'm a virgin and I try to stay pure because of my religious beliefs, but there is a lot of pressure on guys to have sex with girls. If you haven't had sex yet, there's something wrong with you. I've broken some rules myself, and I've done some sexual things that I regret now. It's like some kind of emptiness afterward. But I heard things about

Amber's past boyfriends, and I felt like I had to meet that level, to outdo them. Be more masculine, be more the man. So I would do something because of that, but after I would be left not knowing whether either one of us was satisfied. I still feel a little guilty about it.

Because of my religious beliefs, before I get in a relationship I try to find out what a girl's perspective is on sex; if she's very loose in her sexual behavior, I tend not to care for that. But girls never admit to anything; they are doing it, but they're not talking about it. For guys, though, it's all about bragging rights. It's a manhood kind of thing. Spread the fruit of your loins or something, I don't know. In general, once you're sixteen it's a thing you need to do, like getting a car. Get the car, get the girl, get laid. It's like a rite of passage. Guys talk about it in class, but they're not even telling the truth! They just make stories up to get attention from other guys and from girls, too. I tend to have less respect for guys who go around sleeping with whoever.

What kind of relationship do I want? A simple relationship. No pressure about sex or anything like that; if it happens, it happens. Looks are second to me. Then there are the qualities I look for in a woman: kind of off the main, a little alternative, something new.

REAL LOVE
Rohan, 17, from New York City

A lot of people give me advice about my love life. On the weekends, I work in the city at a flower shop. I am one of the youngest ones there. And a lot of people tell me, "Rohan, this is wrong, you shouldn't do that." "Rohan, why don't you do this? Why don't you think about that?"

There was a girl, she works in the supermarket around where I work. I used to pass by every day and notice this girl always looking at me. And I used to look at her. She is nineteen and very good-looking. So then one day she gives me her number, and her friend gives me her number. They live in the same house. And they were trying to put a joke on me, like "Wait up, you came to the wrong house." So anyway, I left.

The next day I went by to her house again and I said, "Hey, I forgot to call you."

She goes, "Oh, yes. Come in."

So I go in and there's this guy sitting next to her. She goes, "This is my husband."

I'm like, "What?"

"It's my husband." I shook his hand or whatever.

Then we spoke again on the phone. "You have a husband? You're married?"

She's like, "I have two kids."

I am like "Oh my God." I'm thinking, "This girl wants to mess with me."

That's a big problem, me getting into somebody else's marriage. I am not going to do that. It could cause me problems, and my friends at work are like "Yo—I went through what you are going through. It's not worth it, man. What if he comes back? He could kill you. He could kill both of you."

I've thought about it. I don't think I want to lose my life for some-one who's not available. Getting into that is not even worth it, do you know what I'm saying?

She was still saying, "Oh no, but I am going to leave him."

I told her, "That's not my problem. You leave him if you want to. That's not up to me. We could be friends." I couldn't get into that. Never with married women. No way.

Anyway, I just told myself, "You don't know what disease she might have. You don't know who she has been with." In my opinion, un-less you like another person for a very, very long time, and you go check yourselves by getting a test, having sex can be dangerous.

At our school we had an AIDS class two weeks ago where people from outside the school came to talk to us. One of the guys had AIDS. And he had been living with the disease for a very long while, but he didn't know that. And he was saying how it's very hard, how he's got to take thirty pills a day. If he doesn't take them, one day the disease could come back. Even if he takes them, his body could get used to it and then the disease will return.

I mean, it's incredible. Why not think about things? Why not take the slow way? Why has it got to be fast? Why has it got to be rushed? Do you know what I'm saying? That girl I met, she told me, "I want to have sex with you in the hotel. And that's the only place where we are going to do it."

I said, "We are not going to go to a hotel, I am not going to go be-hind other people's backs." At first I went along with it. I said, "Oh yes, we are going to go to a hotel, this and that." But then I thought, "This is not right." She is married. She has two kids. I don't think I have to get in there and start messing things up. That's where problems start. So I didn't take things any further. I didn't call her back. I haven't spoken to her ever since. It's not worth it.

When I make love, I want it to be very special. I want it with candlelight. And I want to pour chocolate on top of her and just start eating her everywhere. That's what I want to do. That's when it's making love. But when it's just what we call "ghetto fucking," it's wrong. Do you know what I am saying? We just go to the park, we get naked, and we just start doing it. But making love is making love. It's different. When you are making love, you feel it. When you are just ghetto fucking, you don't. It's just like "Yeah, we did it, we did it." We put on our clothes, and that's it. It didn't mean anything. But making love, it has a meaning. And that's important.

I have experienced the difference. I have had sex in the park. It's not the same when you're in the park, and when you are making love at home. In the park, you are afraid that somebody is watching you. It's a very big difference when you are making love to someone you like, and all that. It's cool, very cool. It is something God created which people shouldn't take as a joke. That's what real love is.

I'm Afraid to Lose It

Grant, 17, from a suburb in the Northeast

I have a girlfriend. We've been going out for about two months. I think we really are a good match in a lot of ways, in terms of being able to support each other and help each other out. That is the most important part of a relationship. That's what people really want when they're interested in a girl, even if they think it's not the real reason. That is my theory.

We try to see each other, hang out during lunch. She is a very hardworking girl, so she is always doing her work when I am just wandering and not wanting to distract her. She is very organized, unlike me.

Sometimes if I'm doing my work I think, "She is going to be so proud of me." It's goofy.

She and I have a lot of compulsive and silly qualities in common. But I don't think I could ever influence her to be less meticulous about her work. She has to dot every "i" and cross every "t" and write incredibly neatly. She is one of those neat girls. All through elementary school I was jealous of the neat girls, who could make any poster about Christopher Columbus, or whatever it was supposed to be, put no effort into it at all, and it would be dazzling.

I am confused about when I should lose my virginity. How important it is to lose your virginity or not. Whether it's something that I should be regarding as a big deal, or whether it is something I should just let happen when it happens.

Most of my friends are virgins. We talk about "Yeah, I can't wait to lose it." We also say, "But I'm afraid to lose it."

My fear of losing my virginity is that it's the only piece of innocence I have left. I haven't been in wars, starvation, or famine, but I have been through a lot. I have been through suicidal feelings, and friends and enemies, death in the family. I feel like I have been through a lot and it has hardened me in some ways. I want to hang on to my childhood just a little more.

CONFUSED
Evan, 18, from a suburb in New England

I met a girl recently who lives close to me. I really like her. She's beautiful. She's sweet. We met and displayed the fact that we had affection for each other, and she expressed the fact that she also had affection for this other guy at school. She felt an obligation to pursue that relationship first because she met him first.

I said, "Well, what do you want to do?" And she said, "It's not really what I want, it's what is morally right."

So she started going out with him and she started to find out how much she really didn't like this guy. Wonderful. Ever since then, she doesn't have much positive to say about this guy. She's finally admitted that she wants to break up with him. But she won't do it. And it pains me. There's no reason she should continue to go out with someone she doesn't like.

It's not fair to her. It's not fair to him. Especially not fair to me.

My feeling now is confused. I'm not quite sure what to do. I still lust after her. She's gorgeous. There's no way around that. I can't make her ugly. I feel like maybe I don't want to go out with her but I know I still want her to break up with the other guy. He's a bastard to her. I don't like him. He doesn't return the affection in any manner. He treats her like a trophy. With people around, he's somewhat affectionate. If people aren't around, he blows her off.

She doesn't say much. That's one amazing talent she has. Shutting me out. "Nope. Not going to talk about it." Finding any way out of the conversation. Changing the subject. If another call comes on the other line, no matter who it is, she all of a sudden has this great feeling of wanting to talk with them. Just because it gets her out of whatever predicament she's in.

I'm not in love yet. And when I'm in love, I should hope I'll know I'm in love. Wholeheartedly, no questions asked. Nothing but love. And if that comes, great. I'll be absolutely thrilled. I don't think I'll ever know a better feeling than that.

DO WHAT YOU WANT, WHEN YOU'RE READY

Ben, 13, from a suburb in New England

I'm going out with a girl now, and the stuff that I think about when I masturbate and the stuff that I think about when I'm with her are about as far apart as things go. Later on in my relationship with her, maybe two years down the line.

I don't agree with abstinence at all, another idea thought up by wandering nomads three thousand years ago. Be careful, really careful, but do what you want, when you're ready.

I don't feel yet that I want to have that kind of physical relationship with the girl I hang out with now. She's smart. She's interested in me because of my thoughts. She's nice. She's fun to be around. We go to movies, go out to lunch, and hang out downtown. She lives pretty close to me and we walk home three or four times a week. The relationship I have with her started with us being really good friends. People spread rumors that we were going out.

Maybe if I'm still going out with her in another six months, things will get slightly physical. I don't think that people should rush to do physical stuff. You should just do what you're comfortable with. I've never really been in a physical situation. If I kissed a girl, that would be a big deal.

Guys lie about everything. I've heard guys say they've been to third base six times, with ten different girls. Obviously they're lying, but they're trying to impress you. They're usually joking around, and you don't say, "You're lying." That's not OK. You say, "Yeah, whatever," because they're obviously not telling you the truth. It's like that joke: Snow White is walking down the street and she sees Pinocchio. So she pushes him down, sits on his head, and says, "Lie to me, lie to me."

6

THE PRESSURE TO WORK
AND SUCCEED

*"It's like running a race . . . but not being able to look behind you
and see the people closing in on you."*

—Ivan, 11, from a small town in northern New England

ALTHOUGH WE PLACE INCREASING PRESSURES ON GIRLS
to perform in today's fast-paced, work-intensive world, boys are
telling us that as males in that world, they still feel obliged to toil too
long and too hard, compete zealously against peers—indeed to do
everything possible to rise to the top. More than fulfilling the old Hora-
tio Alger ideal of pulling oneself up by one's bootstraps or satisfying a
healthy contemporary work ethic, many boys report a grueling, grinding pressure, a millstone of unrealistic expectations that saps their spirits and wears away at their bodies and health. By engaging in these
superhuman feats of work, school, sports, and chores at a pace that
would probably do in even the most courageous and energetic among
us, unwittingly boys are striving to pass the Impossible Test of Masculinity, to appear ever strong, resilient, and successful.

Many boys' psyches are deeply ingrained with society's notion that
working hard is what a boy must do to become a "real man." Work not
only yields products of which a boy can feel proud, but it distracts him
from an emotional life that society still isn't quite ready for him to lead.
Being able to "take it" and "proving oneself" through work are still considered reliable signs of manliness, safe currency among boys of all
ages. These are pursuits that help boys feel they are meeting the Impos-

sible Test, even as they anesthetize themselves against their own sadness and disappointment. Work, for boys, is both a cause and result of
the pain they're constantly attempting to bury and hide. Much of the depression we see in boys, as well as much of the acting out—teasing,
fighting, drinking, and drugging—seem to be linked to an intense fear of
letting down their peers and their parents. "My dad," fifteen-year-old
Denzel said, "is a great guy, but he's always on my back to do more. I
know how important it is to succeed, but after a while it just wears you
down . . . it's just too much."

This pressure to work and achieve is pervasive within our culture,
sparing few. While some boys told us they must work long hours at paying jobs for practical, monetary reasons, most, no matter what their
background or resources, attested to being overworked and overbur-
dened with endless responsibility. In this era of moral lectures about
lazy males and the importance of increased boyhood responsibility, I
have encountered quite the opposite reality—a boy-based Cinderella
Syndrome by which boys unnecessarily toil away at endless tasks in a
society that gives them little empathy and no magical hero or heroine
who will come to the rescue.

Boys will be quick to tell you, too, that as grueling as these competitive work pressures may be, they do not feel free to complain about
them. To protest would be to admit defeat and appear vulnerable. As we
probe beneath their stoic, workaholic exteriors, we discover that they
are not just tired, overwrought, even seriously depressed, they are also
tremendously insecure about whether they are doing a good enough job
at the tasks they're expected to complete. They also wonder whether
they are achieving anything at all. Striving to fit into their fathers' shoe
size prematurely, boys often feel like puny failures. Among those we interviewed, many seemed on the outside to be doing quite well—varsity
athletes with B-plus averages, steady after-school jobs, and multiple
college offers. But they explained to us that, if the truth be told, they
were actually feeling incompetent and unsuccessful, as well as fatigued,
enervated, and unable to press on.

I believe it is our responsibility to rescue boys from the overly intense pressure of success. We must reframe society, our schools, and
our homes into places where boys are loved for who they are and not for
what they do. We've had enough of this old-fashioned moral "virtue"
talk, which is merely a prettified version of boy servitude. Eventually, it

leads to our greatest nightmare: boys dropping out, doing drugs, collapsing under the unbearable burden. Girls, too, can help out by conveying the lessons they've learned through their own liberation. They can affirm and support those boys who resist the false ideals of manhood, boys who can be helped to focus on human relationships and forge their own paths toward unique selfhood.

I CAN'T TAKE IT ANYMORE

Allan, 17, from a city in southern New England

I am not a machine. I can only handle so much. I know I've screwed up, but making my life miserable will not teach me a lesson. I'm trying hard to regain my grades. But I'm not going to spend every second out of school doing what you want me to do. I need a life of my own.

"Allan, do you have any homework? Did you do your dishes? When was the last time you washed laundry? Is your room clean? Can you work on my truck?"

This is what I look forward to after I get home from school. "Allan, do you have any studying to do?"

"No, Pop, I had a test today."

"That doesn't mean you can't study that material anymore."

I can't take it anymore.

I'm stressed out enough. I can't seem to get a girlfriend, our football team has dropped from second in the state to fifth, I can't play football this season because of an injury. I might not be able to live out my dream of being a United States Army soldier because of the same injury. Then I'll have to put up with my father nagging me. I seem to be the only one with any brains in our family. My parents are so hard on me.

I go to school every day thinking it's one day closer to joining the Army, one day closer to turning and leaving everything behind. But in the meantime I wonder, "What's it going to be today?"

I AM JUST HER SON

Victor, 17, New York City

I've been living in the United States for about nine years. Before that, I lived in the Dominican Republic, where I only spoke Spanish. It was really hard coming here, being just eight years old and knowing only Spanish.

These days, things are challenging because I have a full schedule with a lot of work. I have a big load of homework from school, plus I work part-time as an usher at a Broadway theater. After school, in the afternoons and evenings, and on the weekends, I work at the theater where the show *Kiss Me, Kate* is playing. I usher and clean, clean and usher. I go there every day except Mondays. Most days I wake up at 7:00 A.M., get to school at 8:30, go to my classes, and then usually hang out after school and by 4:30 go to my job. I don't get home till about 10:00 P.M. and then I have to do my homework.

When it comes to work, you've just got to do it. Why?

My mom works with disabled people and other people who have problems and can't work anymore. So my mom helps them eat and go to the bathroom, things like that. She pays a lot of rent, I think about $900 each month. I live with my mother, my grandmother, my grandfather, my brother, and my uncle. So we all help my mother. We all try to chip in.

I am close to my mom. She is a good person. But sometimes she blames me for most of the things that happen, and that's not always fair. Usually she's upset about something having to do with chores. She will write notes that say, "Wash the dishes after you eat" or "Clean the bathroom." And then if we leave rice on the sink, she will come to me and ask me why I didn't clean better.

Sometimes I come home tired and I don't want to hear these things. I just want to take a shower and go to sleep.

I know my mother has been through a lot. Maybe sometimes when she is getting upset and stuff, it's because of her experience, that she has had a hard time, so she is taking that out on me. But I don't think she is doing the right thing, because I don't have anything to do with what she went through. I am just her son.

HEAVEN WOULD BE WHERE YOU'RE FREE

Eamon, 16, from a town in the Midwest

Money is pretty tight in my family, and my dad is always threatened with layoffs. A drought usually means a lot of people will lose their jobs, and my dad tells us that he is always first on the list to go. We've moved a lot for him to find another job. It's really hard because I can't keep in touch with many of the friends that I make. But at the same time I am always making new ones, so it kind of balances out.

My parents have high expectations for me, because I have to get scholarships if I want to go to college. They can't afford to put me through themselves. My mom is more lenient with her expectations and says stuff to build me up, but my dad is always so hard on me. I mean, he sees that his job could always be on the line, and he doesn't want me to go through the same thing. He doesn't want to see me fail; he wants me to have a good job, be able to support my family by myself. I try to remember where he's coming from, but it's hard because he is constantly, constantly on my back about something that I'm doing wrong. Every now and then he will talk to me about something good that I did, but to him the bad things outnumber the good by a wide margin.

My dad and I don't usually get along, because we both have somewhat bad tempers. In general I don't get angry too easily, but at home I get mad just from being around him. He expects so much out of me around the house, like chores and whatnot, yet he sits around and doesn't do any of it himself and doesn't help out at all. It makes me mad that he thinks that the children should do it all. And in school he expects so much out of me, and I try my hardest, and he just says, "You've got to do better." He will get on me about having a B on my report card, which I think is perfectly good, especially in the classes that I'm taking. Honors English is really hard, and I've got a bunch of other stuff going on, too. It's hard to keep up with everything.

Heaven would be where you are free from people's expectations, where you could just do whatever makes you happy. I feel free like that when I play sports. But it's hell on earth trying to deal with my dad. I mean, when I want to talk to him, it feels like there is a cage around me. And I can't get away from those expectations and him being constantly angry with me. I always try to do better, and when he is still mad, I think, "Oh, well, what's it worth? I am trying, and he's still on my back about it." So sometimes I do something to make my dad mad on purpose. I go out and do something that I shouldn't, and hope that he finds out about it, just to get him off the grades or whatever and on to something new. It's pretty desperate measures, but it seems to work.

If I could say anything I wanted to my dad, I would probably ask him to just let me do what I'm doing now. I'm sixteen and I consider myself very successful so far, so I would want him to just give me some space. It's really hard to not have him rallying behind me when I feel like I'm doing a pretty good job. He is just so hard on me it makes me feel really low and bad about myself. When I do try to ask him to leave me alone, he gets mad. He says, "I am your dad. I am supposed to be like this." But I just want him to be a little nicer about it, so we won't end up getting in a big fight.

I get depressed about it sometimes, especially this last fight we had. It was over a phone bill, and I was grounded from using the phone and the Internet. But I got on the Internet anyway, because I needed it to finish some schoolwork, and he flew off the handle. He said that I need to start acting like a member of the family, and that I was ten times worse than my brother Kent ever was.

Kent is perfect; he got all these straight A's in school, he does all this great stuff, and it seems like he never gets in trouble. Dad thinks I need to be that way, too. It's hard to live up to those expectations, because, really, I am nothing like Kent. Plus, it doesn't seem like Dad cracks down on him like he does me. I mean, if I do the littlest thing he will get on me, but Kent gets away with a lot more.

Even teachers expect more out of me, because they had my brother in class before. It hurts, because I am my own person and they are thinking that I have to be the same as my brother. And it's not going to happen. I just do what I'm doing and try to earn the grades that I get and keep them consistent. I can't be exactly like him and I don't want to be. I don't have to get the perfect grade and be the good kid. I don't have to be perfect to be liked. I've got to be my own person.

I TRY AND I TRY

Conrad, 16, from a city in New England

I live at home with my mother, my father, my fifteen-year-old brother, Byron, and my ten-year-old sister, Elyse. We also have a dog and a fish. We're a very religious family and traditional. We go by the Bible, which is mostly patriarchal. The partnership between my parents is pretty equal, but if there had to be a very last word it would come from my father.

I can't really talk to my father because we're too much alike. The only difference between us is that I'm more open to new ideas, and he's basically very tunnel-minded. Sometimes I think I'm more intelligent than him because of this. There are things I can comprehend and understand that he won't even consider or pay attention to. His way, straight ahead, is the only way; there are no turns in his sight.

The last four years of my life have been so depressing and stressful that a lot of times I'll just cry that I try and I try and I try, and nothing's happening. I try to do what my father says, I'm trying to do what people say to improve my grades, but it just doesn't work. My father just doesn't understand what's going on.

I'm in the ninth grade, and my school is like hell on earth. It stresses out the students too much, by overworking them without giving them a chance to adapt to what is basically a college environment. I was forced to mature. In middle school I didn't have to worry about a thing: I had friends, my grades were good, I could care less who looked at me. Then I got to my high school, and I had to quickly mature. The students walk around looking like college graduates, and the work that the teachers throw on is just incredible. So it was a big jump and I didn't do very well. I was forced to mature socially and I've learned a lot about life, but my grades weren't showing it. It got to be a pattern where I would go home with a couple of D's on my report card and I would know right away that I couldn't expect any support or encouragement from my father. He would tell me that I was gonna fail, and then I wouldn't be motivated to do better, so of course my grades didn't ever improve.

I know he still loves me. When things are going good, I do get support from him, but when things are not going so good . . . If he can understand right away, he can help me find a solution to the problem, but if he doesn't understand and he has no idea of what is going on, there's no point in even talking to him. He just gets blocks, and that makes me feel alone. He wouldn't listen if I were to try to talk to him about it. If I said, "Dad, I feel that you don't listen to me," or "I feel sad about what goes on," he would find some way to turn it around and make it my fault. He would tell me that maybe if my grades were good, I wouldn't be going through these problems.

What I do to get by is I try to block it out, him and all that criticism. Luckily I have a head on my shoulders so I can pretty much make good decisions; if I didn't, I don't know where I would be. If I know I'm wrong—which is kind of hard to tell sometimes because I'm still young—I do try to listen. But a lot of times I'll block off the wrong criticism; you block out so much of the bad stuff that you block out some of the good stuff, too.

I'm pretty much my own man, and I've had to learn for myself how to deal with stress and people and emotions. I ask myself, Am I happy now? How should I deal with this when I get home? I just try to aim for my goals and move forward the best way I can.

OK, OK, OK!
Chip, 13, from a suburb in New England

My dad says, "Chip, you can do anything. You've just got to do everything you can in school. Chip, just whatever you do, do not start a Columbine incident, and you'll be all right." With all the gun talk, I think it's at the very back of his mind, buried in some pile of junk or something. He's as worried about that as he is about all of the dirt under the stove.

My dad does special projects. He puts bids on buildings. He bosses about five guys. My mom does daycare for kids in our house, so they're all running around. We're starting twins next month, so it's going to boost up her salary a bit. She might call me down to watch the kids while she does the laundry or something like that.

But what I really hate is all her work, the insurance, legal stuff for having the kids, and she also does a lot of volunteer work, which I hate. I find volunteer work pointless slavery. She's been given a small pot of flowers once. She trains the kids who do altar serving at our church. She helps out with the family Mass, too. If nobody else is going to do it, who's going to do it?

My dad scares the crap out of me: "If you want to be a pilot, if you're not going to collect garbage, if you're not going to flip burgers at McDonald's and you want to fly planes making $300,000 a year, if you're going to invest, if you're going to have children, if you're going to have a humongous house, if you're going to have a pool, if you're going to have a car, if you're going to have your own plane, if you're going to have a boat, you're going to do good in math!"

I'm like, "OK, OK, OK."

THE RACE
Ivan, 11, from a small town in northern New England

I live in a rural town. I have a mom and a dad, a sister and a brother. I am the oldest of our trio. We have two horses and a cat. People who live in the city would consider where I live country. My mom has always stayed home to look after us, and that's a tough job! My family and I eat a home-cooked dinner together almost every night. At the dinner table we talk about how our day has been.

I help my father work around the house. For instance, we are building a barn right now, and the new house that we built ourselves is still unfinished, so I am expected to help him build. I don't know very many other kids who know how to swing a hammer. My dad has a forestry degree, so we cut down trees to make our own lumber. I drive the tractor and help haul the trees out of our woods. There's also firewood to be cut and split to keep us warm in the winter. Helping my dad is not just a chore—being around him is enjoyable. He has taught me a lot of things.

It's not easy being an eleven-year-old boy these days. Especially when I'm just beginning to move from class to class with different teachers, instead of one teacher that teaches everything. It is not as easy as it looks. Keeping organized is a challenge. I am one of the more advanced kids in my class, which is also not easy. They expect more from me than they do from an average student.

Sometimes your classmates don't accept you or get mad at you because you are smarter than them. It's only happened once or twice and it doesn't really bother me because I know that person was just jealous. Ever since I've been given letter grades I have gotten straight A's. It's been hard to start at the top and stay there. It's like running a race and being in the lead, but not being able to look behind you and see the people closing in on you. It's easier to start off being in the middle of the race and work your way to first place. So the road that I have chosen to take is definitely a challenging one.

This year will not be the easiest. But I will still try my hardest to succeed.

7

SPIRITUALITY AND
RENEWAL

"God is the person who is there when nobody else is."
—Cedric, 14, from a city in the Northeast

ONE OF THE MOST INSPIRATIONAL EXPERIENCES I HAD IN my recent trek across the country, listening to and learning from America's boys and young men, is the large number of them—individuals from all walks of life—who feel a meaningful connection with a *spiritual* or religious force, an all-powerful presence outside themselves, a deeply caring being who is always there to listen to, love, and protect them. Some boys, based on their traditional practices and beliefs, speak eloquently of a central relationship with God, Jesus Christ, or Buddha. Others evoke a being without a name, someone or something "out there" they can't identify in a specific way, but who can and must be trusted to nurture and look after them. From dealing with sparring parents or managing a neighborhood bully, to handling abuse, coping with depression, resisting addiction, or trying desperately to feel good about who they are as people, scores of boys emphasize just how important a spiritual being is to their happiness and their survival.

A few years back, thirteen-year-old Julio emigrated with his mother to the United States. He lives without his father, who remains thousands of miles away in South America. Julio gave words to this soulful power: "With the help of God," Julio explained in a robust and cheerful tone, "you can do everything."

Despite conventional wisdom that says today's boys tend to shun the strictures of traditional religions, that they may frequently prefer the athletic field or the television set to church, I have found that many of them, much like Julio, put spirituality first. These are boys who have an unshakable faith in a supreme and powerful being separate from themselves. In our materialistic, technology-driven world, boys are often portrayed as being compelled more by the fast-paced action and energy that surrounds their lives than by the far more interior and contemplative offerings of most spiritual and religious practices. One still thinks of Mark Twain's *Huckleberry Finn,* in which little Huck wriggles in his seat at church, desperate to escape to his playmates and a sense of unfettered male autonomy.

Yet it seems boys and young men are a much more spiritual group than many of us might have ever imagined. Their belief—whether in God or an organized religion, or in a spiritual wellspring beyond themselves—is widespread and pronounced. For many boys, such a spiritual core is not only profoundly meaningful but also emotionally sustaining, leading to hopefulness and renewal when perhaps all other avenues and possibilities seemed compromised or lost. Even after my many years of close work with young men, I was struck, and indeed deeply moved, by the depth of the spiritual thread that ran through so many of their stories.

In the realm of God and spirituality, many boys seem to be seeking, and finding, a source of unconditional love and empathy. Especially for boys who struggle with some of life's most searing kinds of emotional pain—loneliness, depression, abuse, sickness, death, and loss—turning to a caring and loving God for support often feels like their sole salvation. As the voices that appear throughout this book consistently reflect, many boys do not feel capable of removing the shackles of the Boy Code. They don't feel that they can "be themselves"; they don't always sense that it is safe to talk to parents, siblings, teachers, or friends about their sadness, fear, and longing. As we have seen, their pain often grows more acute, turns inward, or simply explodes. Believing in God, or believing in an unnamed spiritual force, enables many boys to open up their pain outward and to be heard in a positive, peaceful, and constructive way. Whether they practice their spirituality independently or within a religious community, whether they speak of their spiritual experiences or keep them to themselves, so many boys and young men routinely depend on a spiritual relationship to see them through difficult situations.

For some boys, sadly, God seems to be the only male-identified force to whom they can turn for comfort and understanding. While many boys do not believe in a specific god (or believe in God but don't identify God as being either male or female), others unequivocally perceive God as male, as "he." Especially among boys who live in the absence of their biological fathers or who have fathers who are emotionally distant or unavailable, God often seems to provide them with a sense that there is a male force, separate from themselves. They perceive God as someone who, in addition to their mothers, will attend to their deepest fears and their most soulful yearnings. God listens, he is there for them, he understands.

Fourteen-year-old Cedric, whose father left his mother when he was very young, explains, "I had a lot of problems when my dad left the family. I thought, 'Why did he leave? Was it me?' My aunt told me to pray to God, to ask God what happened. It didn't really give me an answer, but it helped just to ask. Some way or another the answer will come to me. It won't come to me directly . . . but somewhere down the road, it'll come."

"What is God for you?"

"God," Cedric said eloquently, "is the person who is there when nobody else is. There's my uncle and people like that, but God is the one person who's always going to listen. Even though he can't talk back, I can let him know my feelings. When I prayed about my father, I got the feeling that I would be okay without him. I got this far being OK."

Boys like Cedric are not putting forth a "politically uninformed" view of religion, one that needs to be revised or updated. Rather, Cedric, like so many of our nation's sons, may be calling from the depths of his soul for the warmth and affection of a loving, fatherly spirit, one to whom he can turn for higher guidance, for answers to life's tough questions.

As we think about these inspiring voices, the challenge for us all is to figure out what we can do to apply religious and spiritual practice proactively to help boys. Can the kind of opening up and sharing of the genuine self that happens in a religious setting somehow be transferred to or applied in other contexts? How can we get boys to tell us—their friends and loved ones—what they need and who they really are in the same way that they would do when praying to God? What other positive aspects of this spiritual "crucible" can be brought into their everyday secular lives?

In addition to our skepticism about boys' enthusiasm for religious and spiritual practices, there is a worry that such practices could be exploited by religious leaders and other adults with negative agendas.

Even as we steer our boys toward good friends, and institutions and meeting places where they can relax, be themselves, and speak honestly about their inner experiences, we must protect them from the people and the places whose belief systems are not loving, tolerant, and inclusive. We must steer our boys away from the people and places that will make young males in our society feel more shame, more self-hatred, and more anger toward themselves and others. "There's something I believe in and I pray to it," explains seventeen-year-old Antonio from a city in the Northeast. But, he says, "I'm not into religion, because I think it's filled with a lot of hypocrisy and hatred and stuff."

Antonio teaches us a valuable lesson: he tells us to go to a spiritual place that is loving rather than hateful, one grounded in connection rather than disconnection, one that does not injure the human spirit but instead allows us to come together to heal.

I will always remember the town meeting I attended in Littleton, Colorado, only four days after the heinous school shootings at Columbine High School. I had been called in to help search for answers. As I listened to the testimony of students, teachers, and parents, I was impressed particularly with the courageous teenagers in the audience who had had direct contact with the perpetrators of this horrifying crime. Deeply grieving and still in profound shock, a whole community came together to mourn, pray, and seek the solace of their loved ones. Several boys were among those who spoke. Many of them called upon a higher power not only to help them tolerate their own personal pain, but also to heal the suffering of family, neighbors, and an entire nation torn apart by hatred and violence.

At one point in the meeting, one of the town's important politicians directed a question to me about my research, inquiring about the importance of putting God in boys' lives. He asked whether parents in places like Littleton were to blame for not doing their proper job in this regard. It was a difficult question to answer, especially among an audience of parents who had just experienced a terrible trauma and were especially vulnerable to feelings of guilt, shame, and confusion.

A young man named Tad, a junior at the high school, rescued me. A few minutes earlier, Tad had poured his heart out about just how painful bullying, teasing, and shame can be and the self-hatred it can breed. "Mr. Johnston," he began, addressing this well-meaning town official, "God is a powerful force in my life. But you've got to be careful when you ask that question." The room became very quiet.

Tad continued, "I know we can't explain what happened to us just by talking about discipline, gun control, teasing, and peer pressure. But if we focus on God just in a way that's gonna make people feel even more at fault, that's going to be just like the teasing and isolation that probably caused Eric and Dylan to shoot at us."

One boy started to weep openly. Tad put his arm around his shoulder in an act of spiritual healing without words. The local politician looked almost dumbfounded. We had all learned something special that evening. Religion and spirituality can bring us together for prayer, healing, and a sense of community, helping individuals place things in perspective, commune with a force outside themselves. Both can teach people to look outward and feel hope. But as Tad pointed out, religion and spirituality, if used to make people feel guilty or ashamed, can also separate people, even amplify feelings of isolation and pain.

For many boys, relating to a loving, forgiving, understanding spiritual force can help sustain their sense of self, create a confidence and a strength that may be difficult to find elsewhere and may offer unique opportunities for renewal. When boys seek this special connection and understanding, we must support the wide range of ways they can find it. In so doing, we help them to stop worrying about whether they are "real" enough boys, to put aside the hurtful codes of manhood. We help them, at last, to heal their wounds, allowing them to find fulfillment in who they genuinely are.

IN THIS LIFE
Antonio, 17, from a city in the Northeast

I'm a spiritual person, but I'm not really religious. I believe in reincarnation and I believe in someone out there—I just don't give him the title of God. I don't know what to call him. I just try to prove to him that I deserve to live the way I want to. I hope that when I die he'll put me in another incarnation where I can live the way I deserve to based on my actions in this life. I figure my next life will be great if I'm a good person in this life.

My pen and paper are my shelter—they're where I go when I need to think about something and talk about it. When things don't work out the way you want, you've just got to relax, be patient, and look on the brighter side of life. So I write things down in poetry and in lyrics for the songs that I compose.

I'm a firm believer in destiny. That's why I try to make the most of every single day that I live. When I was nine years old, one time I was over playing bingo with my friend at his apartment and three guys came over in hoods and masks to rob the place. One of them put a gun to my head and they searched the whole apartment. It felt like it went on for two hours. At first I thought they were cops, and I just played along. But then after the third hour, I got really scared and I realized they were bad people and that I might get killed. When my mom came to get me, the guy opened the door and tried to pull her inside the apartment. She just started screaming, "Oh my God, they're gonna kill my baby." Everybody heard and people started opening the doors and getting out of their apartments. The thieves just got scared and ran. I was so terrified. Some days, I still feel scared.

One place I find comfort is in prayer. I don't believe in "God," but I believe there's a spirit out there and I talk to him. I do pray. I start out by just telling him how my day went. I tell him the things I did that were wrong. And, I just thank him for being alive, for having healthy parents, for giving me the opportunity to be alive another day. Because to me, the most beautiful gift I can have is just being alive another day, to prove myself to him, or her, whatever it is. I don't see it like a person, I see it like a force, an energy, like a green ray of light floating around that nobody can see except me sometimes. It's the same energy which started the first single organism, which ignited life.

I love to put my words and prayers into music. Music is great because it gives me a way to speak to other people who share my culture and experiences. People in the inner city like to hear about other people going through the same things they go through. It helps them relate to other people. I love to watch people listen to my words—it makes me feel important.

I want to have beautiful memories so at the time I go, whether it's early in my life, whether in my mid-twenties or my mid-forties, I'll never regret anything I've done and always be happy.

PRAYER FOR ANOTHER DAY
Isaiah, 18, New York City

How did the universe get here? Science says a ball exploded in space. But how did a ball get there? Nobody can explain it, and I think God put it there. He wanted the universe to be created, so he put a ball there filled with energy and it exploded.

When I pray, I ask God to make sure my family stays all right. I worry because around where I live in the Bronx, it's crazy: you walk down the street and see somebody selling drugs in one place, then cross the street and see somebody fighting. I hear gunfire more than once a week. I've had family die.

Kenny was my best friend and I loved him like family. We played sports, we wrote music together, he helped me with my schoolwork. I remember one time I brought home a bad report card. He told me he didn't want to see grades like that from me anymore. Really, he was like an older brother in that way. He told me to always strive for the best, to do the best that you can. I admired him for the way he took care of his daughter, Crystal. He loved his daughter to death, he did anything for her. Even though he and Crystal's mother separated, he spent as much time as he possibly could with her. That's one thing that I loved about him. He always looked after his daughter.

Kenny was in the wrong place at the wrong time. My mother sat me down after I came home from school and told me Kenny had been in an accident and was in the hospital. He'd been mistaken for somebody else and got beat in the head with a bat. From there on I was in tears. I just put my head down. I was hoping that he would make it, but I couldn't go to the hospital to see him because I was too young. He was in the hospital for three days and then he died. I didn't get to see him at all.

Why did it have to happen? I can't think of anything he'd done to deserve that. He was not a violent person; he was taking care of his kid. He'd been at my house hanging out the night it happened, and he could have just stayed over. None of this would have happened. He would have still been here today. But he went out.

My dad lives out on Long Island, and we don't really communicate. We speak from time to time, but he's really not in the picture right now. I do miss him, because we used to do a lot of great things together. What reason could you have to leave without saying nothing? Without calling or nothing? You're not supposed to desert your kids.

I definitely want to have children of my own, I want to have a family. When I do, I want to make sure it's at the right time, when I'm financially ready and ready inside to make that kind of commitment. Because I know that when I have a child, I want to be there for her at all times. When you've brought a child into the world, you don't just care for it. You really care for it, you stop thinking about yourself and put all your love into the child. You devote yourself to it with your heart and soul, all of it.

I believe in God and I know he is looking over me all the time. He is there to help me better myself and guide me down the path of my life. When I pray to God, I ask him to see another day.

ONE STARRY NIGHT
Matthew, 18, from a small town in the Midwest

Situated directly below the ladle of the Big Dipper is a small, dim star. In seventeen years, this star and I have been through an astonishing number of hells together: a painful childhood, divorce, death, depression, alcoholism, drug addiction, suicide. I can still remember when he first came, offering his services as my wishing star. It was the night that my mother, no longer being able to withstand the abuse inflicted upon her and me alike by my father, departed, leaving me alone with the monster. My eight-year-old body had taken both mine and my mother's beating that night, and under the G.I. Joe bedspread I laid, a crying, tiny ball of bruises.

Consumed by anguish, confusion, and loneliness, it was then that the star came to me, twinkling so bright and happy, saying, "I'm here, you can talk to me. I can't promise that I'll be able to help, but I'll try."

On black, starry nights, I still go outside and talk to my friend; and with an ever constant and loving ear, he still listens. Sometimes we like to reminisce on the obstacles that we together have overcome, the progress that we have made. We laugh about how he probably would have never come to me if he had known just how hard times would be, and sometimes we talk about my depression, my suicide attempt, and he reminds me that he was there that night, watching over me, protecting me, giving my family strength, the paramedics swift, deft hands, and the doctors a clear mind for quick decision making. But then our conversation becomes drowned in the chirruping of the crickets and the deafening silence of the still, clear night, and I am left with my thoughts.

When I met Kathy, I made her my sun. My life became the planets that would revolve around the orb. Unlike the girls that had preceded her, Kathy intimately understood my deepest thoughts, dreams, and fears. All of my life, I had battled with the insecurities that come with an excruciating childhood. I had always felt, in some way, inadequate. But with her acceptance and understanding, her kind words, her affirmations, I became strong, self-confident, proud. But soon after Valentine's Day, around our nine-month anniversary, I discovered that Kathy was seeing someone behind my back. I was crushed. Until then, my life had felt like a tent, and she had been the poles that gave it structure and shape. Her unfaithfulness made me feel like the poles had been ruthlessly ripped from the tent, leaving it a shapeless, lifeless piece of plastic. Once her decision had been unearthed, the relationship was over, ending my life, or so I thought.

With the philosophy that I had neither nothing to look back on with pride nor anything to look forward to with hope, I decided what had to be done. Procuring from my dresser drawer an Altoid mint tin stocked with various forms of pills, I began to cry uncontrollably. Why did things have to turn out like this? Why couldn't I have led a nice, normal, happy life? Why had I been put through so many hells? Why was I left with no other alternative but suicide? I didn't want to die; I didn't want to be a loser. As my last words, I wrote a short poem saying that I had fought and lost too many battles, that I was weary, and that I wanted rest. It stated that though I was only sixteen years old, I could not help but feeling that my time on earth was complete. Placing this letter in a conspicuous place, I then knelt down to pray.

Laboriously and hopelessly, I prayed to God for his forgiveness as I prepared to commit the only unforgivable sin. I prayed that he would take into consideration all of the tribulations that I had suffered through in such a short period of time. I confessed that this time he had trusted me too much by putting so weighty a burden on my spare shoulders. With this done, I took a deep breath and, in one gulp, swallowed thirty pills and washed them down with a pint of gin.

To end my story is futile, for my fight continues, it is endless. My dealings with two monsters—depression and suicide—sliced my soul to its quick, and the emotional pain, no matter how much I talk about it and no matter how much time elapses, will probably be there for the rest of my life.

I once heard that within every adversity, there lies a slumbering possibility. It took quite some time for me to realize just how blessed I was to have been able to experience such a profound depression and such a close suicide attempt. I have been given a new lease on life. Having been shown just how horrible it can be and how quickly it can be taken away, now I take advantage of life, squeezing every last drop of fun from each new day. It took almost losing my life to start living it.

With an army of friends by my side, I fight to slay the dragon every day, and I know that I am winning. And on that black, starry night, when my time is up, I'll make a detour on my way up to heaven and personally thank my star.

PERSPECTIVE

Chip, 17, from a small town in the Midwest

When it comes to basketball, I turn to God for some help here and there. This year the coach hasn't played me as often as I would like. But that's OK with me, because I know I can play pretty well, so I try to be patient.

Of course, you get disappointed when you go to a game and you have to sit there on the bench and wait. At a recent basketball game I made a turnover from the sidelines. It wasn't so much that I turned the ball over, it was the fact that I made a jump pass and the coach doesn't particularly like that. And as a result I didn't get another chance. If it had been one of the other players, a couple of minutes on the bench, and he would have given them another opportunity. I really don't know why he is putting so much pressure on me. For some reason, I'm just not the guy for him on the basketball court. Maybe I just need to loosen up and ignore him. Just play ball.

And then there's losing. I don't like losing. At this level in high school, they kind of forget about the idea that "winning isn't everything." You've grown up with these people for a long time and you've been playing every year. You've been working to win the state championship. Sometimes your coaches, if they are not successful, lose their jobs. It is real competitive. And it's real intense.

When things get rough, I bring my spiritual faith to my game. I don't pray for things that make me score twenty points. I don't pray that he will let me and our team win. I just pray for strength, courage to play, and a safe trip to and from the game, things of that nature. And if I have a tough night or whatever, I just talk to God for comfort.

God is a more magnificent power than anything that you are going to face on a basketball court. And when you know that reassurance is there, then you don't worry about making a turnover or something like that. I mean, when it happens you do, but after it's over you let it go, and you come back to practice the next day. God actually helps give you perspective, so that you are not so focused on the game and on how well you did. In the moment of playing the game, if you don't do something as well as you would have wished, you might get upset. But afterward, you can put your disappointment in perspective because you know that there is something else out there that is bigger and more important.

So I don't focus too much on what mistakes I might make during a game. Even if I play well, I give God thanks because he gave me the ability to play. I try not to take too much credit for the victory. Anyway, when you have a strong faith in God, the wins and the losses aren't what matter quite as much because you still have another day to look forward to.

THE ONE WHO IS THERE
Cedric, 14, from a city in the Northeast

God is the person who is there when nobody else is. There's my uncle and people like that, but God is the one person who's *always* going to listen. Even though he can't talk back, I can let him know my feelings. When I pray, I ask God for good health, and to protect my family. When my grandmother had a mini-stroke, I prayed for like ten minutes that she wouldn't die. I asked God to please take care of her, take care of my family, help get me through the day, things like that.

When I have painful thoughts or get angry, sometimes I just try to zone it out. I try to do anything to get my mind off it. I play sports, or sometimes I read a book. I also write things down in a journal at home. My teachers told me it's bad to keep things locked inside of you, because it will just come back in your mind, over and over again. So if you have feelings and thoughts, write them down. Every day I write "Dear Cedric," I write a letter to myself and I sign it, I write the date. And every Friday I read my entries from the week, so I can remember what went on during the week and how I felt about things.

Guys have different ways of getting out their feelings. Some write poems or raps. Some play sports to let out their aggression. I usually write things down in my journal.

Girls deal with their feelings verbally—they're more expressive than boys are. Girls are more sensitive, too, so they let it out to other people, let them know how they really feel.

But boys can't really do that. People look at us as tough and rough. They don't want us to cry, they don't want us to be sad, they expect us to take things as they are. Boys worry, "If I say this, people might look at me like I'm a punk, or I'm soft."

It's destructive to bottle stuff up inside so I try to let it out. People see me as a big person, an aggressive football player, and then when they see me shed a tear, they're like, "Whoa, is that Cedric?" It's like I'm a different person just because I shed a tear. I feel like saying to them: "Boys are human, too, boys have feelings." After all, we should be able to express ourselves just like girls can.

My father left me and my mother when I was only seven years old. I haven't seen much of him since. If I need to talk about something, I can go to my mother. But I don't always tell her everything about my troubles because I don't want her to feel ashamed or sad, like it's her fault if I'm failing in a class or something. I want her to be happy, because she gave me my happiness. I'm not an adult yet, but I'm old enough to care for myself more, so now is my time to show her how I appreciate her bringing me up to be responsible. I want to give back to her and do good. She taught me when I was young what was good and bad, so when I do good, she knows that it got through to me.

I go to church maybe twice a month, but I wouldn't call myself a very religious person. I'm Baptist and I believe that God is my savior, but I don't follow the Bible by heart. I don't think anybody really follows the Bible word by word. But I do consider myself a believer.

When I was young I had a lot of problems when my dad left the family. I thought, "Why did he leave? Was it me?" My aunt told me to pray to God, to ask God what happened. It didn't really give me an answer, but it helped just to ask. Some way or another the answer will come to me. It won't come to me directly or right there and then, but somewhere down the road it'll come.

When I pray about my father, I get the feeling that I will be OK without him. God gave me the talents to help me forget about my father, like playing football and writing in my journal, and also a personality that lets me make friends who have what I need to replace that father figure.

I got this far being OK—I'm not a bad person—so I don't really need my father at the moment. Who knows what might happen to me in the future? Anything can happen, so I live for the day, for the time I am in right now.

DAVID AND GOLIATH
Julio, 13, from a suburb in the Northeast

I have scoliosis of the spine, which makes me very short. You may not believe me, but I love being short. It's fun. People say, "Oh, you're so cute." And all the girls hug you and everything. Even though I'm short, I'm thinking of trying out for the basketball team. I'm a great passer.

I got teased when I was in the fourth and fifth grades. The other kids called me short. It hurt sometimes. I'm very sensitive. I told the teachers and the principal. I left them to handle it, and they punished the people who teased me.

I believe in God. I go to church every Sunday with my mother and my uncles. In church, first we sing and then they say prayers and then they collect the offering. And then I go upstairs to the class.

My favorite Bible story is David and Goliath. The short guy. He was small, and with the help of God, he defeated Goliath. The Hebrews were fighting the bad people, and so they sent David out to challenge Goliath. They fought each other and David threw a stone with his slingshot. He hit Goliath right between the eyes and killed him. That story means that, with the help of God, you can do everything. Even if you're short.

I look up to Stephen Hawking and Albert Einstein. I admire Dr. Hawking because even though he has a disability, he goes on and doesn't stop. Einstein is my hero because he was really smart. Even though he dropped out of high school, he still studied and he went on. He wasn't even that good in math, but he came up with the theory of relativity.

I'm like Hawking and Einstein. They had obstacles, and being short is an obstacle for me. But I just keep on going.

DEEP INSIDE YOURSELF
Martin, 17, from a city in New England

It's so important to have people you can talk to about serious things. My immediate friends, we definitely have deep conversations about religion, things that are going on, and creative ideas we have. And that's essential for us. That's also something that I had growing up with my father. We would just sit down and talk for hours about these sorts of things. When I have kids, I'll do the same thing because I think it's important to be able to talk about anything.

I live with my mother and my father. I'm into all types of music, but I'm especially into hip-hop. I perform in a group, and we've been all over the New England area. I love it. I also play basketball for fun.

For some reason, I feel like I'm at a point in my life right now where I don't know what to think about religion. As soon as I came out of the womb I was Christian, because my parents were Christian. I've gone to a Methodist church all my life. At a young age you go to church because it's just that's the way things are, but now I'm at an age where I'm questioning religion and the faith I've always grown up with. I don't really have any problems with the church, but that's the only thing I've been exposed to and I think there's something more. I don't think the Bible is the only place where the truth is. I think I should try to look into other things and not be too closed-minded. Just because I grew up with these certain beliefs and my parents are that way doesn't mean I should stay that way.

A few days ago, the police near where I live found this girl's body. She was seven months pregnant and had been missing for about a month. She was buried three feet deep and she had multiple stab wounds. It was just a sick, sick crime. I don't know how somebody could do that. I mean, you couldn't be yourself to do it. And it's even crazier to me because I know him, the kid who's been accused. He was allegedly the father of the unborn child. I went to school with him. I hung out with him and dealt with him and it makes me wonder, how much do you really know a person? I thought he was a real cool kid, and when he came to school he was a smart kid, so I saw the potential in him. I would have never thought he could do something like that.

The shooting at Columbine affected me, but this one really hit home 'cause I've sat next to the kid in class. It makes me wonder, what if we had gotten into a deep conversation? Could I have seen that he could do something like this? Could I have had an impact on his life? We all chitchat in school, we see each other every day and say, "Hey, what's up, man, what's going on?" But I wonder whether if we'd had a conversation, I could have had any impact on his life. Could the man in the hallway or the person who lived upstairs have had any impact on his

life? Maybe if we had gotten the chance to talk about something important, it would have made a difference.

The truth is everywhere. I've been reading different books, talking
to people who have other religious faiths. I find things interesting in different faiths that I can apply to my life. And then I find things in the religion that I grew up with that I can't apply to my life. I think you pick
and pull from everything.

For example, I've spoken to people that have Islamic beliefs, people that are part of the Nation of Islam. Here in the United States, it's an
all-black religion, and I kind of like that, how it's dealing with black
people and black people's issues and empowering black people eco-
nomically. Then there are students here at school who are from Africa
who believe in Islam, and for them the religion seems to be more about
peace, about being at peace with yourself.

I believe there's a God, and that's important to me as a motivational
force. My belief is that God is within each and every one of us. It's not
like you say, "Hey, God, give me motivation." If you really look deep
inside yourself, that's where you'll find God and that's what will help
you do whatever you want to do in life. It's this kind of spiritual thing,
like praying.

Going to church doesn't make one person more spiritual or religious
than the next person, so even though not as many men go to church as
women, that doesn't mean many guys aren't praying and living spiritual
lives. For instance, I just spoke to an old friend of mine—he wasn't trouble, but maybe he was doing things he shouldn't have been doing—and
he told me he just got saved, baptized. I was proud to hear that, because
he was a kid who I would have predicted that in ten years he would probably be into something he shouldn't be into. Prison, for example, or even
dead on the street. But he made that big step and accepted God and religion. It may be surprising to a lot of adults and people in general, but a
lot of young guys are definitely deeply involved in their religion or have
a sense of who God is and what God means to them.

SOMEONE TO LOVE

Brendan, 18, from a town in the South

I consider myself a spiritual person. I can pray about most of my problems, or talk to God about them, or read what the Bible says about them.

I also get close to God through music, by singing hymns, playing the organ and conducting the church choir. I let God handle things, and then I usually don't have to worry about them. I feel protected by God. I pray to God about everything. I mean, I pray about the whole day, what is going to go on that day, whatever problems I may be facing. I pray about anything. I pray in the morning before I go to school and at night in my room just before going to bed. When I think of God, I sense that he's in control of everything, and he wants all people to know him, and know Jesus Christ; that's his goal, his desire. But not everyone accepts Jesus as their God. And I believe he truly cares for everyone. I know that since he is in control of my life, I don't have as many worries. And that's one thing that I appreciate. If you truly trust in him, there is not that much to worry about. I mean, it's not always that easy to believe, but after a while it becomes easier, I guess.

You see more things happen that he has taken care of—problems at school, problems with other people. You see people change for the better. I feel close to God. I feel like I can talk to him openly about who I really am, and about the problems I have. There are some things that I tell God that I wouldn't want anyone to know because they are very private, they are personal to me.

But sometimes I wish I could talk to my dad the way I talk to God, openly, telling him my real problems. It would be easier if I could tell my dad about friends of mine at school who I am upset with, or what I am worried about each day. Then I would have my mom, my dad, and God to talk to.

The one sort of male figure boys have to talk to, whom we can trust, with whom we can be completely ourselves, is God. God never says, "Oh, you are such a jerk," or "You are a wimp," or "Why aren't you doing better in school?" God is always there. And I always wonder, what would it be like if we felt the same thing toward other guys, or toward our fathers? Because girls, I think, generally feel they can talk to their mom, their dad, anybody in that kind of way. But for guys, often the only male kind of energy and force they can go to for that kind of comfort is God.

In any friendship, I am looking for somebody who shares the same feelings I do about life—the same view of God, of Christianity. We would probably also share an interest in music. I guess the relationship would probably be with someone who would love me back as much as I love them. And that's kind of the tough part, I guess.

Some people are ashamed to show their love. Or they are afraid to let go of their feelings. All it would take is a big hug. And maybe for them to do it first, instead of me always initiating. I wish the world were different sometimes, that all of us could be more open, accepting, more loving and affectionate. If I could give a message to people who are religious to hear, it would be that everybody makes mistakes, that we are all sinners, that God loves us anyway, that we can't do anything that will make God love us any less, or any more, that he loves us the same, and that we should love each other in that same way. And to show that love, to be accepting and to be loving toward others, and to be there for others. And to just accept others and the special things that are in their life that make them different. And to see these differences as good instead of bad.

True love is giving yourself up, being willing to give the person everything you have without wanting anything in return. Kind of the image of Christ giving up his life for us. I am someone who loves people and loves being around people. I love music and like to make others feel better through it. I make mistakes just like everybody else, and it's not always easy not to make them. I guess I am just trying to live the life that God would have wanted me to lead.

THE CLOSEST FRIEND

William, 16, from a city in the South

Probably the hardest thing for a guy in high school these days is to keep a clear focus. It's a transition time, you're obviously growing up, looking ahead to college and decisions you have to make. Relationships with family, friends, girlfriends. I think that takes a big toll on some people. Just changing relationships, finding out which are good and which aren't. Sports. Just the future in general. There are lots of big decisions. Plus, you've got a lot of peer pressure to do things like drugs and smoking; fitting in is a big part of high school. It can be a stressful time.

I have a very supportive family, though, and I think they've brought me up very well. Since a child I've been brought up in a Christian family, and that's a big part of our lives. To us, God is Jesus Christ and the Trinity, meaning God the Father; the Holy Spirit, who works in my life; and Jesus, who sacrificed himself to forgive me of my sins. My parents are probably strict by some standards, but it's to encourage a Christian lifestyle. And because of their example, that has become a part of who I am. They do punish me at times, but I think they want it to be a lifestyle that I choose to live, not just a lifestyle they choose for me. So I don't think they're strict in that way.

I've been encouraged to have a relationship of my own with God, so I've learned to trust in him to help me get through things. And that has helped me get through a lot of hard times. Because of my dad's work, we've moved four times, and that's been hard. I was born in Oregon, then we moved to Vermont, to Charleston, back to Vermont, and down here to Florida just this past summer. Making those transitions is hard, and they have gotten harder as I've gotten older. In high school I think you are more connected with friends and school, you're more involved in everything.

I had a really close group of friends in Vermont, and I liked the school I was going to. It was a small private school of only about five hundred. I keep in touch with them by phone and e-mail. Actually, my best friend Jake moved to Hong Kong while I was still up in Vermont, and this past summer I was able to go visit him. We keep in touch a lot, and we tell each other pretty much everything. He is the person in my life that I've felt closest to. We would talk about anything. Spiritual struggles like sins, or when you're not seeing in your life what God wants, or it seems like he's just silent up there and does he even exist? Also just daily things that you share together, small things that strengthen a friendship. Girls, definitely. And also we pray for each other. That's a big part. We were very comfortable in being ourselves around each other, and I think that put us at a deep level.

I still have a friendship with him, we keep in touch, but knowing that I'm not on that level with anybody now . . . I'm not disappointed, because that was unique. But it has definitely left a hole, and every day I feel it. It has been hard not having those close friends here. I'm optimistic about the future, though. Fortunately, it hasn't been too hard for me to make new friends. It was definitely hard to leave my old ones; it's not so much that *here* is bad, but that *there* was so good.

I think in order to be in a good relationship you have to be able to confidently be yourself. You don't have to try and change who you are to fit the other person's standards, and if it is a true friendship, the other person will accept that. Some people, though, have trouble acting like

themselves. Maybe it's from trying to impress the other person, or trying to put yourself ahead of the person. I think everyone to a certain extent wants to elevate themselves, and I think that stifles a lot of
friendships.

Having a relationship with God is like having the closest friend. I
can always talk to God. Some people say that it's not really two-way,
but I really do get encouragement knowing that he is caring for me and
working in my life, that he actually does orchestrate my life through his
will. So it has been comforting. And you know, I can pray to God and I
know that he loves me as a person and that he will work his will through
my life. So I can almost give up to him the things that I'm struggling
with. I mean, I can plan the future as much as I want, but he's going to
make his will happen, so I have to be able to let myself fall back and just
trust that he will work his way. That takes a lot of courage at times, and
it's not easy to do, because as humans we want to hang on to every part
of our life and be in control all the time. And you can't be. Moving to
Florida this summer felt the most out of control for me, but I had God
to fall back on and he brought me through it.

When I pray to God, at times I may ask him for specifically the
health of a family member or to work out a personal struggle I might be
going through with a friend. College and the future, that he would make
those decisions clear. And then just day-to-day things, like schoolwork
that I'm struggling with. It's not like he's going to throw down a piece
of paper with an A-plus on it, but he can provide encouragement for me
to complete the everyday things as well as the big things.

Not submitting to peer pressure is a struggle I pray about. I have
different values—I don't drink or smoke or do drugs—and when I'm
with friends who do those things, it's hard. There's kind of a wall between the two of us when I say, "No, I'm not going to do that." We can't
relate on that issue, which leaves me with mixed feelings. I'm glad that
I didn't give in to it, but also sad that I can't relate to that friend. In some
ways it's almost impossible to get to that most intimate point of a
friendship with them, because there's always going to be that difference
unless one of you changes. It's hard, because I would want to be closer
to that friend, but as far as personal integrity goes, I couldn't.

The particular sins I worry about are lying or having bad thoughts
about other people, but also it's on a big scale, because I think that as
much as we try, there's no way we can be perfect, because we're sinful.

That's hard to deal with, but on the other hand, because Jesus Christ paid for our sins by dying for us, I have been freed from the burden that everybody has, Christian and non-Christian, of knowing that they are sinful. I think a personal relationship with Christ is the only way to get over sin.

Prayer is how you can have a personal relationship with God, and that doesn't mean you have to stop and bow your head or go to church to pray. You can be thinking of God just as you walk through the halls: "Just help me be able to talk to this person nicely," or "I want to do your will in this decision. Let me know what that is." He doesn't always specifically say something, but a lot of times he'll make a decision clear. And just like a regular friendship, the more trials you go through together, the closer you become. Going through difficult moments in your life in a relationship with God brings you closer to God.

God has helped me deal with the loss of friends and with moving so much. When you move, your whole life is just basically blown away, because if every aspect of your life changes, you have nothing to keep you who you are. You might lose all your values, because there's a barrage of new and different things that are open to you now. You have to have some kind of constant in your life, and for me, that's God. He keeps you together as your whole life changes.

8

BULLYING AND TEASING:

FITTING IN

AND BEING LEFT OUT

"What I hate about this school is that I'm being picked on in the halls and just about everywhere else."

—Cody, 14, from a suburb in New England

"My philosophy is, a could-be *will never be. There's a difference between a* could-be *and an* is. *A* could-be *will never be because it could have been but you never did. It will never be. And* is *is right now. Is* is yourself."

—Brandon, 17, from a suburb in the Midwest

O F ALL THE THINGS BOYS ACROSS AMERICA ARE TALKING about, teasing, bullying, and the need to "fit in" figure at the top of the list.

Ricky, a senior in high school, showed a sadness in his eyes as he talked about the endless teasing he suffered at school. It began when he was eleven years old and it was just now subsiding. A brilliant trombone player, but not athletically inclined, Ricky did not fit in and he had been subjected day after day to ruthless taunts: "You wuss . . . you little band fag." Once, a group of boys from the football team, just before a home game, smashed the bell of his trombone on the pavement of his high school parking lot, punched his stomach repeatedly, and then spat on him. Warned that they would kill him if he told anybody about the incident, Ricky went home, where, too afraid and ashamed to tell his parents, he fibbed about dropping his new trombone on the ground. Having previously had numerous conversations with Ricky about the importance of protecting his new trombone against just such "accidents," and without the benefit of knowing Ricky's true experience and inner feelings, his parents chastised him for having been so irresponsible and promptly forbade him to watch television for a month. As painful as the situation might have been, Ricky preferred to endure his parents' punishment rather than face a possible reprisal of his peers' vicious attack.

"Boys will be boys," some might say, dismissing teasing, bullying, and peer pressure as inevitable behavior among many adolescent and preadolescent boys. But we now know that this painful set of relentless practices sanctioned by the boy culture and laughed off by many well-meaning parents and teachers falls along a continuum of boys abusing each other, a slippery slope that ranges from verbal taunts to physical threats to sheer (and sometimes lethal) violence. It is not a minor predicament worrying a small subset of boys, but a constant and widespread problem that is insidiously eating away at the quality of life of so many of America's boys. As one young man explained, prevalent bullying demands that boys live in perpetual fear and carefully comply with "the rules of what boys are supposed to be," making sure that they always "act macho, cool [and] on top of things." Boys describe it as a life where you cannot let your feelings show and dare not flinch, for fear of ending up humiliated, seriously injured, or dead.

The predominance of dangerous bullying, and the fact that we tolerate it, is nothing less than a national disgrace. Millions of boys around America live within this painful gender straitjacket every day. Daily they go to school bracing themselves against expectations of harassment, terrified that with one small slip in their Boy Code performance they'll end up attacked or condemned. Even the smallest breach can lead to being ostracized, teased to the breaking point of depression or violence, or becoming the next victim of vicious physical assaults that we continue to minimize with the term "bullying." One seventh grader told us, "I [got] bullied by kids. They've hit me . . . ruined my bike. I wish they would understand but they don't!"

Do *we*? According to a report from the National Association of School Psychologists, every single day in America over 160,000 children miss school because of fears—or acts—of bullying. In a recent study sponsored by the Centers for Disease Control, 81 percent of students surveyed admitted to bullying their classmates in one form or another. These staggering figures support other research showing that 75 percent of adolescents nationally had been bullied during their teen years. This is not a question of isolated boyish pranks, but rather a pervasive high-risk public health problem that is quickly gaining force across the nation.

If you ask them, boys will tell you that bullying seems to happen as part of a vicious circle. "In the case of guys," explains sixteen-year-old Owen, from a suburb in the West, who gets teased because he likes swimming more than football, "I think bullying is a circle that begins with homophobia. It starts there and then it goes to being made fun of. Then it goes to repressing your anger, and then it goes to acting out." Owen sees the truth: that bullying is a cycle that begins and ends with the Boy Code, the strict rules of masculinity that punish boys who seem feminine, weak, or gay to their peers. Boys who worry that they're not fulfilling the Code lash out. *They* bully. Their victims, often the ones who outwardly seem to be breaking conventional rules about masculinity, absorb the insults and the hits. They harden themselves against the blows, suppress their sadness and shame, and contain their pain and anger. When it all becomes too much, when they can no longer mask their pain, they explode, sometimes violently, taking out their pent-up frustration and rage on themselves or others. Their behavior, tragically, looks frighteningly similar to the bullying that first provoked the cycle.

Wise beyond his seventeen years, Andrew Fraser from Littleton, Colorado, understands all too well how teasing and bullying can lead to violence. "I wouldn't say that teasing was the sole thing that affected Eric and Dylan. I'm sure they had a lot of other problems in life already. But I think in the long run that was the biggest factor, the spark that ended up setting off the fuse."

As we've seen, many boys, just like many girls, are suffering from low self-esteem and a fragile sense of self, doubting their place in society, becoming sad or depressed and then lashing out at their peers. Thus the same set of concerns—of being seen as unmanly, of being rejected and isolated by peers, of feeling that there's no one to turn to for help—is what leads boys to become both the victims and the perpetrators of these destructive bullying behaviors. The great majority of boys we

spoke to—boys of all shapes and sizes, with all different kinds of interests, persuasions, and personalities—testified that to escape an on-
slaught of teasing and bullying they must act tough, succeed at sports,
hide their emotions, and avoid things traditionally thought of as "girly"
or feminine. They also said that they must periodically tease and bully
other boys to avoid being victimized by those same behaviors. Indeed,
our most recent science shows that a significant subgroup of boys who
routinely tease and bully, far from being some small group of ruffians,
are actually among the most popular members of their classes! "Some
people only care about popularity, and the well-being of others just
doesn't matter to them," says thirteen-year-old Vinny, from a small
town in northern New England. "I have seen popular kids make fun of
people without being funny."

Though some people may stereotype them as being cocky, malicious, hyperaggressive individuals, most boy bullies, in reality, are insecure, isolated, and exceedingly unhappy. Many of them, statistics show,
are actually the most depressed of their peers, putting them at risk for
both suicide and violence toward others. One of the young men you will
hear from gets the point of both the fragile self-esteem that fuels this boy
behavior and the negative effects it's bound to have on other boys: "It's
really hard because boys don't have much confidence . . . and as soon
as somebody says something negative, it just tears you down right
away. . . . It doesn't take much."

Beginning with the Boy Code and continuing with the push in early
adolescence to pass the Impossible Test of Masculinity, to bully is both
to protect and survive—to show you are a man when you doubt it yourself. It causes tremendous, at times irreparable harm. In addition to the
shame it feeds off of, and the self-confidence it drains, teasing and bullying create an everyday boyhood culture of hurtfulness and hostility,
one in which it is more important to fit in than to care or understand.

Fitting in seems to entail a push not just to conform and belong, but
to abide by a caste system that ranks boys according to individual differences among them. Boys from minority groups or lower socioeconomic
classes and boys with certain body types and personality traits or styles
all become targeted for not hitting the mark or fulfilling the most common standards. "I don't feel safe in my school at all," explains thirteen-
year-old Brad, from Massachusetts. "There are clique kids."

Twelve-year-old Lucas, from a small town in northern New England, agrees: "In my opinion, people should not be categorized. Someday I hope this will change." Sam, thirteen, from a city on the West Coast, echoes the same sentiment: "There's three kinds of social classes. There are the top kids, the middle kids, and the bottom kids. I don't always hang out with the cool kids and I have a lot of friends who are not exactly 'with it.' So I'm kind of in the middle."

Boys throughout the country, urban boys as well as suburban and rural ones, tell us that by age fifteen you're pigeonholed into a subgroup: you're categorized emphatically as one of the "jocks" or the "players," the "preppies," the "brains," the "goths," the "nerds," or the "geeks" or the "freaks," with jocks at the top and freaks at the bottom of the social ladder. The pressure is extreme, we will hear, to be part of a group and compete for a rank within it. Otherwise, you're all alone. You're an outsider and a loser, an undesirable misfit who's likely to be mercilessly teased and pushed to the fringe, just like the highly troubled boys we've recently seen who snap and then commit brutal, hate-filled shootings.

Once classified, each boy's individuality and sense of self seem to become almost permanently eclipsed. I still remember Kevin, a handsome, strapping, apparently successful football captain, bemoaning the fact that all anyone sees him as or calls him is a jock; and while powerful on campus, jocks are seen as shallow and unintelligent. "I'm not dumb," Kevin pleaded. "I love to read, but no one will recognize that in me." And so Kevin evokes another tremendous loss that comes with the boy culture of fitting in and teasing: the loss of the adolescent boy's real self—perhaps his most precious commodity during these developing years.

When asked what advice they could offer to adolescent boys struggling with this oppressive boyhood culture, so many of the young males we spoke with implored their peers, and younger boys dealing with this perilous journey, to do just one thing. Be yourself, they insisted. Be yourself!

This is excellent advice, to be sure, but it is given within a society that makes it nearly impossible for a young male to have a true self, to be a "real boy."

The voices of pain and insight you will read below testify to the fact that we can no longer allow a culture of unbridled boyhood bullying. To tolerate it is to look the other way at what is in fact a serious form of violence, and one that breeds even more overt, news-making forms of violence. But I maintain that we must develop empathy both for the bullies and the bullied. Quick-fix, so-called zero tolerance strategies in which we blame, punish, and banish the boy offenders are not only unfair but doomed to fail. For while we have a responsibility as a society, as parents, as friends, and as girlfriends to say "No!" to such violence, we must do so without saying "No!" to loving boys.

As I described earlier, the boys that bully are not just aggressive, they are most often depressed—their inner selves hollowed out by pressure to act manly and fit in. Bullies are often not bad boys; they are *sad* boys. We owe it to our boys, and to ourselves, to propose something better than ultimatums. I do not believe we should be soft on teasing terror, but I do reject the idea of being hard on boys. Because being hard on boys is the problem it all begins with, and so it seems extremely unlikely that more of the same will yield the solution that is so sorely needed. The pressure on boys to fit in, to tease and bully must be seen as part of an outdated Boy Code, which we now have every reason, and an opportunity, to replace. We need to construct a new code of masculinity that encourages boys to be their true selves, instead of perpetuating the old system that punished or inhibited boys for being honest. As many of the voices that follow reflect, if we leave the old Boy Code in place, we will see boys from all walks of life facing psychic and physical destruction. "Be yourself," boys are telling one another. The time has come for us to do all that it takes to allow them to accomplish just that.

THREE CATEGORIES, NINE FRIENDS
Lucas, 12, from a small town in northern New England

One thing about having friends is that they are hard to choose. I have only about nine friends because not many kids fit the criteria I have; I want my friends to be nice, reliable, and trustworthy.

In the middle school where I go, kids are divided into three categories. The biggest category is the "popular" category, which is made up of the kids who are supposedly "cool" and get B's and C's for grades, and sometimes F's. They think they're cool. Some of them don't care about school at all.

The middle category is the "average" category. This group contains almost all the people in the school who get mostly B's and some A's. This is the category I am in, along with all of my friends.

Finally, the smallest category is the "smart" category, where everybody gets mostly A's and sometimes a couple B's. There are about twelve people in my school who are in the smart category. They are really smart.

Out of all of these categories you may run into a couple smaller, separate, private ones every now and then. During lunch, each category separates in the cafeteria. The smart kids sit with the smart kids, the average kids sit with the average kids, and the popular kids sit with other popular kids.

Not one of my good friends is in the popular group, mainly because I don't like the way they act. I do talk with some of the smart kids.

I dress differently from the popular kids. I wear mostly cargo pants or shorts and T-shirts. The popular kids wear oversized pants and big shirts. The smart kids wear what they want to wear. In class, the popular kids talk to each other, and sometimes ignore the teacher. I act differently in class. I listen to the teacher and do my homework. The smart kids do this, too.

In my opinion, people should not be categorized, and someday I hope this will change.

Don't Trap Yourself

Thomas, 16, from a suburb in the Northeast

My little brother and I are really tight, probably tighter than any of my friends. We're pretty different, but we recognize our differences. He's more of a jock than I am and he plays sports and he can get into more traditional guy roles. At the same time, I feel like he's not just a stereotype. He's a good kid.

My advice to him, or to any boy, is don't trap yourself in anything. It's easy, out of insecurity, for a guy to hang out with a group he thinks will make him cooler or with a group that he feels he should be part of. When I was in seventh and eighth grade, I went through one group of stoners and the hooligans and I thought, "Wow, those kids are pretty cool. I should try and hang out with them." But it didn't work at all. It really wasn't me, and they were just dumb. So I stopped and thought, "What am I doing? I don't even like these kids, what am I thinking?" So don't trap yourself out of insecurity.

Think about things prior to doing them. If you've thought about it, you still think, Well, it *might* be dumb, but the potential benefits outweigh its stupidity and so you still do it, that's one thing. But if you're just doing it because everyone else is doing it, you really are dumb; that's ridiculous.

I wouldn't call myself that nonconformist, and I certainly do my share of stupid things, but at least I try to be conscious of them. Self-reflection is a good habit and a good habit to start early. I think it would save you a lot of screwups and a lot of unpleasantness when you're younger—particularly in junior high, where you're trying to define yourself. It's important to define yourself as *you* want to be defined, and not as other people want you to be.

HATE BEGETS HATE
Leo, 18, from a suburb in the West

School has always been really hard for me, literally from the first day I started elementary school. People saw me as a victim, as a good target. They just started picking on me for next to no reason, and they usually started in on me because of my name. If your last name is "Stone," you're easy to pick on.

Up until I was twelve, they made fun of my name. Then, they made fun of me when I started gaining weight. And once more when I got glasses. In high school, at first I didn't have many friends. But toward the end I started getting more and more popular, and school became much easier. Senior year has been the only year I really enjoyed. I'm still going through a lot of self-esteem issues because of the eleven years I was a target.

I think people who bully do it because of their own problems with self-esteem. Most bullies pick on people so they can feel better. They want to separate out a group of people, pick on them and regard them as inferior because, deep down, they feel inferior. They just want there to be some people who are inferior even to them. Sometimes it's homophobia, sometimes envy. They know that somewhere inside of them there's a possibility that they're like these people, and they don't want to be, but they don't know how to express that part of themselves. They don't know what it is and they're afraid of it. So they make fun of it. If you think you're weak, you pick on someone else who appears weak. If you think you might be gay, you pick on someone else who acts very much like they are gay.

A lot of the time the problems bullies have come from their parents. Parents can put unhealthy thoughts into the minds of their children. Thoughts about how some types of people are inferior. This makes the children grow up and ridicule the people their parents criticized. For instance, if a six-year-old kid hears his dad say that homosexuals are evil and against the Bible and God, when he grows up he may reflect the thoughts of his father onto any gay person he meets and bully them because of it. If he's gay himself, and can't deal with it, he may project that hatred onto other gay people and pick them as his targets for bullying.

So, it can all operate like a big vicious circle. High school makes it worse, because in high school everyone divides up into little cliques or groups. The guys who like sports are automatically the jocks, and the guys who are artistic and emotional automatically end up being thought of as freaks and don't join any of the popular cliques. The freaks and jocks constantly make fun of one another. And it never gets any better. Neither side can ever understand the other. The same rivalry and misunderstanding happens between the wealthy kids who don't like or understand the middle-class kids. Hate just begets hate and misunderstanding begets misunderstanding.

There are still times when I think I'm worthless, that I don't deserve to take care of myself. But I've gotten to the point where I can view myself as a good person and consider myself attractive. I know now that people don't hate me.

If I knew someone else was being bullied or mistreated, I'd tell them, "Try not to let it get to you." Of course it will, but it's important to remember that the people bullying you in school are people who have their own demons. They are probably reacting to their own self-esteem problems. But if you accept who you are and ignore them, someday you will do something great.

PEOPLE ARE PEOPLE
Brett, 17, from a city in the South

At seventeen, the thing I enjoy most is music. One of my favorite hobbies is playing the guitar. I play electric and acoustic, and my dad plays a twelve-string. He does two things in his life: play baseball and play guitar. My brother got baseball and I got the guitar, so it worked out. I've been playing since I was ten, and pretty much when I'm not eating, sleeping, or doing schoolwork, I'm practicing guitar. It's kind of an out-let for my emotions.

When I play, lots of aggression and frustration with school and stuff comes out. Mostly it's frustration that things aren't happening fast enough. I get really bored in class; teachers sometimes take so long to do something that I get upset with it all. It's just like "Come on, get to the point!" Sometimes it doesn't seem worth going.

My brother is three years younger than me, and we don't really click that well as people. We've taken different paths, I guess. We grew up differently, with different influences even though we have the same parents. I had more of my dad's attention before my brother came along, but by the time he was eight, he was more athletic and my parents got more involved with him. Me and my dad play guitar together sometimes, but we don't do anything else together that often. He coaches my brother's team, so during the season they're not ever home till probably eleven o'clock each night. Meanwhile I'll be by myself for hours on end.

I miss that time with my dad, but over time I just scarred over emo-tionally. You just kind of get used to it. I don't care anymore if they go to baseball and are gone for six hours. There's not much you can do about it, really. I can mention it to my dad, and he'll say that he'll do something about it, but then it's just back to how it was. There's not much I say to change things. I wish I could tell him that I'm here, that I'm not invisible. I walk through the house sometimes and no one even pays attention to me.

I used to be real close to my mom, but that changed when I hit pu-berty. I think I was afraid to be close to her. I don't like the risk, emo-tionally. You put stock in people, you trust them, and then you get screwed over somehow. I've been burned before.

In fifth grade, a group of kids used to do things to me like throw me in the Dumpster or hang me by my belt loops from a coat hook in the locker room and just leave me there. Those experiences had a big im-pact on me, and these days, I'm kind of like the Lone Ranger.

I never have any close guy friends. You can't, really. There's always the buddy relationship, but you can never get close with another guy be-cause it'll look like you're gay, you're feminine. And it's not acceptable to be at all feminine when you're a guy. At school they would call you "fag" and stuff like that. I think it's the way boys grow up; it's just a fundamental thing. I've spent time in elementary schools, and even boys that age are always joking about someone being gay. I think they hear older ones say it, and they might not even know what it means, but they start using it and they just keep using it.

I think most guys are kind of isolated because it's thought of as weird if you have any really close guy friends. To get around it, guys will go fishing or hunting or bowling or something else "masculine," and then talk about personal or serious things while they're doing that activity. It's a way that they can connect and get closer. It's just the way they've grown up and what they understand to be a masculine thing to do. So, if they were taught it's masculine to sit together and talk about their feelings and listen to music together and to share, they would, and it would probably be better. I don't think there should be such a difference between feminine and masculine. People are people.

But we follow what we've been taught over the centuries. Our grandparents teach our parents, who then teach us. My dad's not very close to his dad on any kind of emotional level, and so I'm not close with my dad either. It gets passed down from generation to generation. It's a nonstopping change of events.

These days, your experience as a typical American high school guy really depends on what kind of crowd you follow. The preppy kind of group seems to have a lot more friends, and maybe a lot more opportunities come up for things to happen, socially. Like drinking and that sort of stuff. I hear stories about it constantly. "Oh, I got so trashed on the weekend," and all that stuff, but I don't do that. I'm not a part of that group, and I don't want to be. It's kind of frustrating sometimes to be the only person not in the group, but I like my own little creative path.

There are a lot of pressures to fit in at school. Right now at school I don't feel like I have a lot of things in common with people. It's kind of disheartening. There's definitely like an in-school and an out-of-school kind of thing. At school I don't hang out with many people. I have a lot more friends in Arkansas than I do here, and I'm only there in the summer, to visit my mom's family. My cousin and I had a band there for a while, but not anymore.

More often than not, though, I'll just go home and hang out by myself. My younger brother might be around, but we don't usually talk. I mean, we play video games together, we get along that way, but other than that, we don't really do much together. He's more in the preppy group.

There was a while there I was pretty lonely in the afternoons, from middle school till a few years ago. It was hard and I moped a lot. I used to have these little tantrums in the morning, where I didn't want to go to school because I felt bad, and my parents got mad at me. I just watched a lot of TV, and then I ended up getting more into the guitar. Music kind of helped, like a little bit of therapy. Now it makes it easier for me to come to school and deal with people that I don't necessarily like.

Down with Us

Julio, 16, from New York City

Last year just after I graduated from the eighth grade, I got hit by a car. I was supposed to meet my friend Josh and then go see a movie together. I was running across this big two-lane street, saw an oncoming car but thought I could beat it. The next thing I knew, I was on the street, flat on my back.

I had passed out. I'm looking up, then I asked the people for help. I didn't cry, but I was in a lot of pain. This one guy stopped and asked if I had been hit by a car. The ambulance came and I gave my dad's and my friend's numbers so someone would call and tell them so they wouldn't worry.

I had to spend the night at the hospital. I still have scars and abrasions on my head and some on my abdomen. I don't have to worry about looking grotesque or anything. You can't see them too much.

After the accident, the whole summer was blown. I had to start physical therapy and I didn't get to do anything I wanted to. Although I'm usually a happy person, I get depressed sometimes. I really don't have many friends in my neighborhood. I'm by myself because there's no one to be around with. The neighborhood I live in is bad. You go on the block, and you see the drug dealers right there in front of your building. You know who they are. They go downstairs into the basement, and when they come out, they reek of weed. You know, you just smell it. I don't want to be messing with those drug dealers down there because if I do, I'm gonna get caught.

Sometimes I feel like I have to act different around different people. I'm Puerto Rican and when I'm around white people—no offense or anything—but they listen to rock and roll. So when I'm around them, I listen to rock. Nine Inch Nails, Manson a little bit, Stag X, Fear Factory. But to be cool with black people, to feel like you have things in common with them, you have to listen to rap and just learn to blend in with them, to be down with them. Yesterday, I was hanging out with my friends on the street and we were listening to music. This white guy, an older guy, he was into rap. I'm sure my friends were probably laughing inside about this guy because he wanted to be down with us.

We were listening to Eve, a gangster rap artist, and he was saying, "Oh, this is hard-core, listening to Eve." He goes, "When you kids were three, four, I was listening to Public Enemy!"

He was trying to be down with the black kids and I was like "You crack me up with this." Here was this older white guy who really seemed to be into rap. My friends thought he was "whack."

At school, there are mostly Dominicans and black people. The Dominicans listen to salsa and they like to cut on the black kids who hang out with each other. I'm one of the only Puerto Rican guys. I don't fit in anywhere, because I listen to rock, and then they call me "white." People used to think I was kind of white, so I used to mess with their heads and say I was Jewish! So no one really knew who I was. I would probably fit in better if I went to a school that was all white. Maybe then I'd be perceived as the norm.

At my school I don't hang out with black people or Dominicans. I don't hang out at lunchtime, I just kind of walk around. Sometimes I hang out with this girl, her name's Ellen. I can talk to her. And sometimes I hang out with this other kid, Pedro. He's half Puerto Rican and half white. There's also another friend of mine, this pothead named Sean. And then there's another pothead girl I know, her name's Charisse, but she doesn't really come to school that often.

I guess I fit in best with the potheads. Sometimes I want to smoke pot but I really don't consider myself a pothead. My father doesn't know that I smoke. There was one time—actually it was kind of a close call—I was smoking on the roof of my building, then I came downstairs and he was right there, and I'm like "How you doing, Dad?" I didn't want to look at him, because my eyes were red. Two of my friends got me into smoking pot. But I've gotten smarter about it and now don't do it too often.

I guess that if you're different from other people, you have to just try to be yourself. You don't have to let yourself be assimilated into their culture. You don't have to like what they like or do what they do. If you don't like rap, you don't have to spend your time listening to it. If you don't want to smoke pot or do drugs, you don't have to.

I want to try to be myself. You know what? I'm just going to keep on listening to my rock and roll.

You Can Be Funny in Other Ways

Nick, 12, from a small town in New England

My parents are really mad at my brother because he never talks to them about anything. Not even about school, like what projects are due the next week. He's a senior in high school. My mom complains that he doesn't talk to her. But I talk to my mom, because I can't hold it in me, it's impossible. I have to talk.

My mom loves it, because she likes to know what's going on with me.

I talk to Mom about everyday stuff, because she can give me advice. Often I give myself advice and my mom agrees with me. She says that she's proud of me because she thinks I'm really smart to figure out what to do.

I'll tell my mom when I'm mad at my friends. We're studying bullying right now as a topic in school, and how to deal with it. I get mad at my friends because sometimes they're followers. They are afraid that they will be made fun of, too, if they don't follow what the person with all the power does. I really don't care what other people think of me, but it makes me mad when my friends just sit there, not standing up for me. It makes me feel like they're not being the best friends. They should stand up and say, "No, I don't know why you're saying that about Nick."

I've always been bullied at school for being short. Sometimes in the halls, people will say, "Shut up, Shorty." Usually I know they're just joking and I joke back with them. And then there's bullying, serious ganging up on someone, poking him around. When I was really bullied, it was really annoying.

I remember in the third grade, every day at the bus stop I'd be made fun of by the older kids because I was short. My friends just sat there and they made fun of me, too, and that was really frustrating. I would just ignore them. And eventually they stopped because they weren't getting any fun out of it. That's why people bully, because they see somebody suffering, and that's what makes them keep going, to make the person even more frustrated. But if you just sit there and ignore them, it's like talking to a wall and that's no fun for the bully.

They do it for attention. They're blocking out that they're bullying someone. They think that they're funny and that's why a lot of people like them. When kids are laughing, it gives them a kind of power, so they keep doing it. And I just think it's stupid that they're bullying. They should get attention by making jokes about other things. That's why I like my friends, because they make jokes that are not based on bullying somebody. You can be funny in other ways.

At the bus stop, they didn't really make a circle, but they were all ganging up on me, joke after joke after joke. That was bullying. That was serious. The thing that made me mad the most is the parents sitting there, watching. That was the one thing that got me mad at my mom. I brought it up two times, and she didn't believe me that it was serious. So I just stayed at the bus stop and ignored them, and eventually it went away.

That was really frustrating when my mom didn't believe me. I wanted her just to come and see it once. She thought she was solving the problem by calling one of the parents. And they said, "No, I haven't noticed anything happen." That's because they were too busy ignoring everything and talking to other parents and hadn't even observed it going on. So my mom thought I was just making this up, to get attention.

I don't think she had as much respect for me then as she does now. Mom thought I was just being a dumb little third grader. Now it's different, because she knows that I'm not going to kid around if I'm telling her this. I'm not going to lie about it.

If I ever had a family, I'd want my kids to talk to me. And I would probably talk to them a lot.

I WAS BULLIED

Bruce, 11, from a small town in northern New England

I was bullied during first, second, and third grades. I think it was just because I was one of the younger kids. In sixth grade, just about all the kids looked up to me. When I left the school I was back in the same position I was at the beginning. I was getting made fun of and I wasn't sure why.

I am not really sure why the older kids bullied me. I guess it was because I was fresh meat, someone new to pick on. I really don't think bullying somebody serves any purpose. I guess bullies do it because it makes them feel tough. After a while, I realized I was picked on because of the clothes I wore in the sixth grade. At that time, my mother bought my clothes because back then I didn't see the difference. This went on until I reached the age of eleven. At this age, I didn't think she really had the best taste in clothes. So, when I reached the seventh grade, I picked out my own clothing and since then things have changed. I am not bullied anymore and things are much better.

I don't think bullies realize what they do to somebody's self-esteem. They really can ruin someone's self-image and make them feel bad about themselves. I hope that bullies realize it's wrong and stop. Maybe they could even apologize!

My conclusion to bullying or being bullied is that there is no purpose to it. People shouldn't make fun of other people to make themselves feel better, especially when it only hurts people.

A "COULD-BE" WILL NEVER BE
Brandon, 17, from a suburb in the Midwest

When I was young I lived in Little Hong Kong, in a restaurant that my parents used to own. By the time I was in middle school, I started to be picked on because I was Asian. This one Hispanic guy used to pick on me all the time, calling me "Chink" and saying "Ching! Chow! Chay!" in my face. When he teased me, I'd just take it. I'm a passive person, so I just let it happen. I was raised that way by my parents.

My friends tried to stop that guy from teasing me, but the teacher never noticed it. I never told the teacher because I didn't want to start trouble. I just lived with it for a little bit, until the other boy got expelled for something else. He was just a bully in general.

These days I'm in the advanced-placement program and things are somewhat better for me. There's been some stuff in the school newspaper saying that at the beginning of the program, some people were making fun of the AP kids, probably because the AP program kind of wrecks the curve for the rest of the students. AP is graded on the highest scale, where you get a 5.0 for an A, and I think that some students have animosity over that. Maybe they're jealous because if they're not in this program, they can't be valedictorian.

I like to think of myself as original. I never fit into any of the cliques. I have this free-floating perspective of everyone, without being too biased toward one group or another group. I've seen the cliques. There's a prep-type clique, the richer, more popular kids, and a little AP clique, where all the AP students huddle together. Band students always huddle together, and that's weird because I was in band for two years and I never sat down with any of the band members. I'm mostly part of the gaming clique, the people who play card games, RPGs, video games, that type of stuff. I fit pretty well in that one. There are jocks, but that was a bigger thing in middle school and junior high. Of course all the football players stay with the football guys, the soccer players with the soccer guys, and the basketball players with the basketball guys. There's also a little cheerleading group, and a pom-pom group.

Sometimes I get real angry because I've had to hold everything in for all these years. All those things that happened, like that thing in middle school. I've had to watch passively as people make fun of other people behind their backs. It builds up, and then I usually express this anger by going into my room, going to sleep, and then waking up, screaming into my pillow, and getting ready for school. I also punch things, inanimate things, for no reason, like a pillow or a wall. I don't talk to anyone about it. I can vent it and deal with it myself most of the time.

My philosophy is, a *could-be* will never be. There's a difference between a *could-be* and an *is*. A *could-be* will never be because it could have been but you never did. It will never be. And *is* is right now. *Is* is yourself. *Is* is your individuality. You are the individual, so be happy that you are what you are and never go back or think, I could have done this, because you didn't. And all it did was make you stronger. Don't fall into the trap where you have to be like this person or like that person, because you are who you are. You make your own decisions. Just be yourself. Be an individual. Otherwise you're not going to get too far. Well, you might get far, but you'll never satisfy your soul—never satisfy that little inkling.

Cliques

Wayne, 16, from a suburb in the West

Cliques are very important. There are all kinds of cliques, like the jocks, stoners. Our school newspaper had an article about cliques that said, "Oh, all the jocks do is go to parties and have sex every weekend." In terms of drugs, they are really popular among the stoner and the gangster cliques. To be a stoner, you have to do drugs. In general, there is a lot of drinking and drugs. At basketball games and football games, I see people wobbling by and I can smell it. So if I can see it and smell it, the coaches, teachers, and the principal can, too. Some kids come to class and their eyes are bloodshot and they can't even talk right. The teachers do nothing. They realize what's going on but they don't want to confront the kid and do anything about it. So I know the school knows about it, but they can't really do anything.

We all kind of stay in our own little group but there are always friends between cliques. Everyone tries to get along. I think of my clique as being somewhat "jocky" and a lot of people say our clique is rich kids, but I don't see it that way.

I can't think of any one person that everybody truly picks on. But I did see teasing and bullying going through school. It was a big thing in elementary and middle school. In middle school the bully was usually the biggest kid, the older or the stronger kid. They'd push you and get other people against you. Usually, they were a grade higher. In elementary school, you'll see the fifth grader picking on the kindergartner. The school knew what was going on but they weren't going to do anything about it. It happens everywhere. I remember when I was in third or fourth grade walking down the street and seeing a high school student skateboarding and thinking, "Wow." But then the kid would snub his nose at me, because I was little.

Now that I'm older, I catch myself doing the same thing. I'll be with my friends and we'll see a little kid and stare at him or give him a look. Then I feel bad and I try to correct myself. But I slip sometimes. It just happens.

When I was in elementary school the way you dressed didn't really matter but in high school, it definitely does. Actually, I think it's worse for girls, because girls are a lot more worried about their appearance, whether they're skinny or fat. Guys worry more about whether they're geeky or weak. If you're part of a group, your friends will try to help you out and make suggestions about what to wear: "Hey, you should try this." But if people from other groups don't like what you're wearing, they'll put you down. They'll call you "faggot."

It's wrong to use that slang word but it happens. It's a really big thing. A lot of it is just joking around, but it's not good. It's just a slang word people use. I think they use it because it's degrading. So they'll call a guy a faggot to degrade him or to make him look stupid. Or just to see what he'll say.

Some guys who get picked on can feel so depressed that they might get suicidal. We learned in health class how the suicide rates are high and we learned about the symptoms. A major factor is being picked on.

I think that parenting, the way your parents teach you to be, is the only way to change anything. If the parents were bullies, they're going to teach their own children to be bullies. Parenting is the most important influence in a person's life. Kids take after their parents. You follow the way your parents brought you up. Some kids rebel against it, but I think, more or less, you become your parents. So doing something to help parents be better parents, like a parenting class, would be great. I think better parenting would stop the bullying and the violence.

If I had to give advice to another guy growing up, I'd tell him: Don't be too hard on yourself, have as many friends as you possibly can, and always make sure there's someone in your life you can fall back on so in hard times you'll have a shoulder to cry on.

CHANGING PEOPLE, ONE PERSON AT A TIME

Bart, 16, from a suburb in the West

It's part of our evolution as human beings to analyze a bully, and say there's an inferiority complex or a superiority complex, or his mother didn't give him enough love, or his mother gave him too much love, or his dad ran out, or his parents got divorced, or his dad killed himself. There's just a whole slew of things that can make you a bully.

Going to school day after day takes its toll on you eventually. I can't say that that can be changed, because school is essentially just to make sure that we understand this craziness we've created as human beings. I think that the key lies in finding your own way in all the conformity, finding your own outlets and making sure you're OK with yourself and with your friends. That's absolutely the most crucial thing.

Tolerance is a big part of this—being able to admit when you're wrong, and to have the common sense not to do things like punch people because you're angry at them, being able to tolerate people who are different from you. You don't have to like everyone. So I guess the only true way to a better society is self-improvement. That's all there is. People have been trying to change the world for so long, and it's never gotten us anywhere. They just keep trying to change other people, and it's like a domino effect, people trying to change other people when truly the problem lies in themselves.

I think the most crucial step in making the world a better place is just changing people, one person at a time, changing people's attitudes. That's really what most of the dysfunction in the world is based on, people's thinking and their attitudes toward their lives and the people around them and the cities they live in. And if you're the only person you can change, even that's a step. If you can think freely and be more tolerant and not judge, that's a pretty big step to take, a step in the right direction for the entire world.

I'm not one to be real idealistic and think of this utopia where everyone is happy and everyone gets along, because it's really not going to happen. The real toxic ideals are the ones that can physically affect people, the scapegoating and the propaganda and the spreading of these vitriolic messages of hate to other people, influencing people who are less educated or who need someone to blame. That's really how hatreds get started, with people sitting around bouncing ideas off each other until they find someone to blame. We can see so many examples in history, like after the Civil War, the poor whites scapegoating the blacks just because they were freed, or the Germans scapegoating the Jews after World War I, which eventually led to World War II. That's how problems get started, people influencing other people in a negative manner. It's still happening.

Maybe the most prominent example I can think of is Louis Farrakhan. He's influencing a great number of black Americans into believing that the way of the black Muslim man is to hate the Jewish man. I think a lot of black Muslims are feeling that they have to hate Jews and blame Jews as part of their religion because of what he's saying, because he's the leader of the Nation of Islam at present. There are countless other examples, too, beyond Farrakhan. David Duke is a very scary man. He has that unique ability that so many Southerners have as an excellent orator—it's kind of been their downfall in the past. He can influence people very easily, and he can make arguments that make sense, unlike other prominent racist figures in the past. He can influence people. He really can, and not just the lowest of the low either; not just the dumbest, and not just the poorest. He really has that charismatic effect on a lot of Southerners who are angry and looking for someone to blame. I think he's a very dangerous man. There are countless other examples of hatred but those are probably the two biggest ones in America right now. In the world, there's countless more examples.

I just try to keep a really open mind for myself. I try not to judge. I try to talk to other people, and to get some of their ideas and thoughts, because essentially the only way to defeat hatred is through tolerance and unlearning. Unlearning hatred. It's good just to talk to people and realize when you're wrong, and realize when other people have something to say, and to share your ideas with them. That's really the only way that change can be brought about—one person at a time.

IT'S OK TO BE SCARED

Bobby, 12, from a city in the West

Last year at school we had a problem with some kids who were just being really mean, saying these mean things. Like with fads; if someone was copying their style, they'd say, "You can't copy me. You are such a poser. I started this. Why are you copying me?" But I can't think of anything too bad. It's just being a little mean if you just say little things. And I don't think most kids are being mean, they are just joking around. I don't take it really seriously.

I like being a unique person. I want to act different from other people. I am not going to go around saying all of these mean things. I don't want anyone to think of me as a negative type of person. I don't get into fights and I hate violence. And I don't want to be the type of kid who comes to school and just takes out a gun and starts shooting. That school shooting last year at Columbine I think happened because they were not treated respectfully. People thought they were weird. They got teased a lot and then they got really angry and just wanted to get back at people.

Sometimes I really want to get someone back, but I can't because I know it's wrong. I don't want to hurt anyone so I just ignore them. Some people, though, if you say something, they just get really mad and start throwing out fists. Things like wrestling, I think, teach boys to be violent. Kids start saying all those things that the wrestlers say to each other to imitate them.

There is this one kid at our school who can be a little weird and a little violent. I am really scared that he is going to come up one day and be "Bang! Bang!" It's okay to be scared, though. I think some of the younger ones at our school get scared, too. Grown-ups just need to sit down and say violence is wrong: "You shouldn't be doing this and it's wrong." The violence, the acts of rudeness, the tone, the attitude, the behavior. I think that some people just aren't taking out the time that they should be, and they are letting kids get away with bullying. We need to have a sharper eye on things.

If You Just Were Yourself
Russ, 12, from a city in the West

At home I have a little brother, my mom and dad, and our housekeeper. My older sister and older brother are out of the house. My parents are pretty busy but they still have time to see me. I see them every morning and every night and on weekends, and to tell you the truth, I think that's enough.

At my school, the boys don't usually have as good a sense of humor as girls. That's because the boys are trying too hard to act cool. To look cool, you have to skateboard, listen to punk music and that sort of thing. I don't think it's always a bad thing, though, because acting cool can help people find out who they really are.

If you just were yourself for the rest of your life you would never find out how great it is to be yourself, but if you try to act cool for a little while and it doesn't work out, you figure out who you are. It's easier to figure out who you are if you try to be someone else for a bit. So if you act cool for a while when you're young, you can kind of try on different ways of being, and then find out who you really are.

I think there are some boys my age who are really comfortable with who they are, but then there are others who don't understand that being themselves is probably the best thing. Although if you are a really annoying person, you might want to change yourself a little so that you are just a little nicer, and then that can be you. There is this kid who is a really great person, but sometimes he tries to act cool. I think he's being stupid, because I like him better as himself and I think everyone else does, too. Personally, I have never really liked the thought of being cool. I prefer to be unique, the only one who does something.

People say that kids do a lot of teasing and bullying at my school, but it's not really that bad. Some people can't find a flaw in themselves and they won't accept that they are not perfect, so whenever someone says anything remotely bad about them, they get extremely mad. They get pissed off completely. I think people overreact. I am never really teased except in fun, and I just try to find a retort. I've never really gotten dissed that badly. I try to make up with the people that I tease, and people do the same with me.

I have a new really good friend that just came to our school last year. His name is Mike and I think he is going to be an inventor when he grows up because he is really good at making things. We were at his house once and his sisters kept trying to get into the room, so he kept making things that would prevent them from getting in. We also tricked my little brother Lucas into believing that we could make things levitate in the air. It was pretty funny.

The saddest thing that ever happened to me was when I lost one of my good friends. Toward the end of fifth grade, he started hanging out with these other kids and he stopped being my friend. I think he thought those other kids were cooler, so he thought it gave him a better image. I think he is trying to act cool, but I think he already is really cool naturally. He invited me over to his house once, but that is pretty much it. I was pretty sad because he's been my friend since kindergarten. He would probably say he was still my friend, but I know he's not anymore. I still get to talk to him, but he is just not the same around me anymore. He isn't being mean, but he acts like he doesn't know me as well as he does. He is acting distant, and I miss him.

BASKETBALL SEASON
Sam, 13, from a city in the West

Right now it's basketball season at our school, and I really want to play but I can't because I can't do the games and the practices and still play tennis. So I'm stuck with the kids who aren't playing basketball, which is for the most part like the geeky kind of kids. But then you also notice that I'm with all the popular kids like Dave and Martin and Jake and Tommy and Andrew who are completely nonathletic but completely popular.

There's kind of three social classes at my school. There are the top kids, the middle kids, and the bottom kids. I don't always hang out with the cool kids and I have a lot of friends who are not exactly "with it." So

I'm kind of in the middle. At the top are probably Andrew, Dave, Martin, maybe Tommy, and Jake. They're just always with everybody, and going to girls' schools and stuff like that. They're popular and successful with girls. The middle kids are like Matt and Jefferson and Anton and Baxter and Ron. Most of them are athletic, and school comes first for them, and then comes athletics, not social life, and then they hang out. At the bottom are the kind of kids who go homework, homework, homework. Kids who don't really play sports and just hang out at home.

It's hard for all of them. All of them have their ups and downs. You can't be at the top and be really, really good at school, or really, really good at sports because you have to dedicate all your time to it. In the middle, everything is kind of balanced, but then when you're at the bottom, everybody is always picking on you and teasing you. Kids make jokes and stuff.

The nerdiest kid who always got picked on the most just left. He went to England to go to school. They were picking on him because he was just so easy and vulnerable. I even caught myself sometimes picking on him because he was a complete nerd and it was so easy to make him mad, and he was really small and skinny, so if you made him mad it would just be fun to watch him lose control of himself, so all the kids would just completely taunt him and make him explode. Sometimes you get caught in a group with other kids and just one kid starts to do it and you think, Oh, that kid is doing it so why shouldn't I do it?

I think peer pressure kind of gets into it, like it happened to me once where I had this really good friend, but I got caught in a group with kids who were picking on him, and I even started picking on him. We would have discussion groups in school and we watched movies on peer pressure, and it's exactly what happened. You don't want to look like you are the wimp so you participate, but afterward, it doesn't feel good. Last week it happened once and I ended up calling my friend Isaac and telling him I was sorry, because I didn't feel good about it. He said it was OK, because it's happened before a couple of times, and I've always apologized because he got mad at me. We still hang out and stuff.

LAUGH IT OFF

Drew, 14, from a city in the Northwest

I'm a fairly serious artist. I do a lot of paintings and drawings. I like to do still lifes, animals, and people. When I was a little kid I used to draw superheroes. I've drawn so many now that my drawings are almost as good as the ones in the comic books. My painting hasn't come quite as far, but I'm working on it. It's getting there. It's a very important hobby for me. I draw and paint in my room. I work with charcoals, pastels, and acrylics, and I also have some drafting pencils that I use. I look around the room and when I find something I like, I draw it, or else I just use my imagination. Sometimes, I draw people at school.

When I was smaller and younger, I got teased a lot and I would take it to heart. People would laugh at me when I messed up in a sport. When I couldn't compete as well as everyone else, the problems started. They called me names. It hurt. I had to fight through it until I reached the point where I learned to laugh it off, but before I was able to do that, I used to get really upset. My parents were there and they helped out. They'd console me with a couple of words of encouragement and make sure I didn't lose perspective and think it was the end of the world.

I still get sad sometimes. There are times when the feeling pushes me over the edge. I think, "Screw this, I don't need to be here, I'm just so sick of this." A kid gets harassed for what other people think his flaws are. If someone is overweight, they'll be picked on for that. That wasn't much of a problem for me but I know people who were teased for being fat. It's almost guaranteed. Or, if you're too quiet.

You just have to forget about it. People will do what they're going to do, but if all they can do in life is harass other people, they won't get too far. Sometimes you take so much teasing that it puts you in a bad mood, and you feel out of sorts. When that happens, I ignore everyone and let everyone be. If they want to harass me, they can harass me, but I'm not going to listen. I only take in what's necessary to get through the day. I draw, and I only hang out with people who aren't against me. If you get a group of people ticked off at you, it can be overwhelming, and you need somebody to back you up. That's when you need your friends.

I've had a best friend since kindergarten and I really look out for him. He wasn't tall, so being strong wasn't going to do a whole lot for him. I think if he learned to express himself, to talk more and show people his personality, things would be different. He gets harassed a lot more than I do, so I look out for him, and being able to stick up for him gives me a little boost. I know I can always turn to him.

My best friend is very quiet and not athletic at all. He's a genius. He is one of the smartest people I know. He gets straight A-pluses in every class. If he scores anything below a 98, he's ticked off. He is a very smart guy, but schoolwork is his life. I try to get him involved in other things.

We'll go to the movies. Sometimes we'll play basketball with our other friends. We go bowling. If I'm going somewhere with a girl, I'll usually try to get him to come along just to get him involved with people. I think kids harass him because they figure he's gay. They say the same things to him that they said to me, but I grew physically and he didn't. I worked to improve myself physically, and I started to learn to laugh it off, but my best friend did the opposite. He didn't grow, he didn't improve athletically, and he cuts himself off socially and isolates himself. He's so quiet now, even around me. Sometimes, I can help him but other times, he's got to do it himself.

I don't know if we'll end up at the same high school. If we don't, he might have to look out for himself. It would be pretty bad if he started depending on one person. I try to help out but I also want him to look out for himself. He's not gay. He's just so quiet and he has never gone out with a girl. He should be able to be himself.

My advice to a younger guy who's getting teased because he isn't athletic and is feeling bad about himself would be "You've got to laugh it off." No matter what somebody says, it's just a word. They can't really harm you with a name. The worst that could happen is that they hurt your reputation, but at that age you'll be in high school soon, in a new school, with new people, where it should be different. A lot of times it's not even meant to be hurtful, but the pain is probably still somewhere inside. One thing you can do that I did is to improve physically. So I'd tell him, practice at a sport. If you want to get stronger, lift weights.

The way I chose to overcome the harassment is not necessarily the right way. It fit me. I was taller than everybody so I knew that if I got stronger, I'd be set.

CHICKEN

Gabriel, 13, from a suburb in New England

The only things I'm afraid of are spiders and heights. I try to confront my fear of heights in gym class. We have an exercise they call the "high element." You have to climb up really high and do something. When I got up there I was really scared, but I jumped off anyway. One time, a girl got really scared and she just sat up there for a long time, then decided to climb back down. That happened to me once, too.

I'm also afraid of roller coasters. My dad took us to Six Flags and he wanted me to go on a roller coaster, but I was too scared. He got mad at me, because my sister went on this ride with him, but I wouldn't. I wanted to go on a different ride, but my dad just left. He just kept calling me a chicken. When we came out, he got angry at me. He said, "Look at all the money we spent to take you to Six Flags and you didn't even get on a roller coaster!" I didn't feel anything about what he said because my mom's scared of roller coasters, too, so she knows how I feel and she wouldn't send me on one of those.

My dad also calls me chicken whenever I'm playing a video game. I'm a huge fan of video games. If I come home and don't have any homework, I eat, do my reading, and then play video games. I used to play video games for six hours at a time. But not straight—I had to go to the bathroom or eat sometimes. One time I was playing my video games and my eyes started to hurt so I stopped. I didn't play video games for a long time.

Sometimes when I'm playing video games, my dad comes in and annoys me. He says, "You wanna fight?" You know, fake, playing fighting. And I say, "No, I want to finish this game." And he says, "Chicken! *Bok bok bok bok!*" One time I got up and put the controller down and we started fighting. He doesn't like that because I always beat him up. But I enjoy it.

Once, the fighting got carried away. I always tickle him when I fight, and that's what makes him give up. He says, "Stop! Stop!" Even when I beat him, he always says that he wins, and that's when I get carried away and start punching him more.

OVERCOMING BULLYING

Overcoming teasing and bullying in our communities requires us to resolve that these behaviors are absolutely unacceptable, that they have serious negative consequences for all of society, which should no longer be tolerated. As the voices in this chapter reflect, boys who are bullied can become socially isolated, depressed, and suicidal. If pushed too far, they can become violent themselves, lashing out at peers or family members. Together we need to challenge the old Boy Code myths that say teasing and bullying are "child's play" or that these behaviors are somehow a necessary or healthy "hardening experience" that will prepare boys to become men. Nothing could be farther from the truth. Bullying is serious business. The destruction it may cause ranges from psychological trauma to physical injury to death.

To overcome bullying we must address not only the victims and perpetrators, but the whole boy culture that still allows (and sometimes encourages) the behavior to exist. We must put an end to Boy Code teasing, fighting, and killing. Together we must establish prominent ongoing antibullying programs that protect young and adolescent children wherever they go. While there are many measures we can—and must— implement to safeguard children in our schools, neighborhoods, and communities, here are some basic steps I believe are urgently required to begin this long-overdue process of social change:

Educate yourself and your community about the reality of bullying. The first step to eliminating bullying is to convince people in your community that it is a major problem. Experts currently estimate that up to 75 percent of children in our nation's schools are bullied. Make sure that the teachers and administrators in your schools and other important child-based organizations and the adults in your neighborhood and throughout your community are fully aware of the magnitude of the problem. Don't let them shrug it off as "natural" or "normal." Bullying can not only destroy the quality of a child's life, it can actually take away that life. You must convince people in your community that safety and life must come before old-fashioned ideas about masculine power and success, that ensuring children's health and happiness is much more valuable than pushing boys to prove their masculinity by harassing other children.

Educate your community about the pitfalls of the Boy Code.   Perhaps the most important way to help create a climate of bully-proof safety in schools and other community institutions and organizations is to educate your friends and family members about the pitfalls of the Boy Code. Teach them about how harmful it can be to resign oneself to the falsehood that "boys will be boys." Tell them what you know about how the Boy Code pushes boys to feel they need to be tough, act strong, and lash out at one another to defend their male honor. Talk to them about homophobia and the gender straitjacket. Explain to them that no matter how well boys seem to "take it," they, too, have profound feelings of sadness, fear, and loneliness. Read to them the voices in this chapter, and get the boys in your community to share their stories about bullying and being bullied. Without being alarmist, talk to them openly about the Matthew Shepard case and the school shootings that have occurred across our nation. Don't wait until it's too late to get the dialogue going. The earlier the better. If schools begin in kindergarten to teach ways of overcoming the Boy Code and of encouraging children to be real, the premise of much of the teasing and bullying we now observe will eventually be eliminated.

Learn the warning signs of bullying.   To stop bullying, you must learn to know it when you see it. Sometimes it may be tricky to know when a boy is being teased or bullied because he may feel too ashamed to bring it up with you directly. To avoid the feelings of shame and embarrassment, he may even try actively to hide the fact that he is being mistreated by peers. Also, boys often wait to bully until they find settings where there are few other people around to observe them (the school bus, in hallways between class periods, after school). It is thus especially important to learn some of the most common warning signs of bullying. Specifically, a boy who is being teased or bullied may: (1) stop talking about school or about a particular class or activity at school; (2) try to go to school late each day, take alternative walking routes or transportation methods to get there, miss classes, or make excuses to miss school entirely (for instance, by routinely getting "sick"); (3) make sudden or radical changes in his group of friends or appear to have few or no friends at all; (4) become moody or act irritable, aggravated, or frustrated; (5) act tired, withdrawn, or sullen; (6) become aggressive with peers, friends, or at home; (7) begin to act like a bully himself, often by teasing or physically taunting younger siblings or children; or (8) show classic signs of depression (see the list of these, page 167) such as social isolation, irritability, or low self-esteem.

Show boys that you take the problem seriously but avoid shaming them. When you think a boy is being teased or bullied, it is important to let him know you think there may be a problem and that you take it seriously. But you must do so in a way that is sensitive to how ashamed boys can easily be made to feel. Use the listening techniques described in the introduction to this book. Give boys "timed silence" and try to get them talking by engaging in action-oriented activities with them. If you show a boy how much you care about him and how much you enjoy doing things with him, he will begin to feel the emotional safety and trust to tell you about who is teasing or bullying him and what it is like for him. Don't become hysterical or retaliatory in your response. Just firmly and calmly show your resolve to help him find a solution.

Create safe, "shame-free" zones to which the boy can retreat. In the epilogue of this book, I explore how we can establish safe, "shame-free" zones, where boys can go to talk about their feelings, discuss the ways in which they are being teased or bullied, and find people with whom it is OK to be their real selves without fearing any further mistreatment. When boys know they can go to these safety zones, it helps give them strength to handle the teasing and bullying that may occur outside of them. Ideally these zones should also give boys opportunities to report bullying to responsible adults without fearing that asking for help will lead to further risk of harm.

Remind boys of the things you like about them. When a boy is getting barraged with mean comments and physical abuse, his self-esteem often plunges. He often begins to believe that he is "bad" or "unlikable" or "friendless." In this setting what he needs most, besides our empathy and physical protection, is a renewed sense of his own goodness and of how much we value him as a person. Although he may not always find it easy to say so, he desperately needs us to tell him what we like about him, what we think his strengths are, and why we would like to be close to him. So when you see a boy being teased or bullied, go out of your way to give him as much sincere encouragement as you can. Remind him of the things you admire in him. Show him, as often as is possible, that you love him and would like to spend time with him.

Solve the problem together. Rather than taking it upon yourself to solve the problem of teasing or bullying, first build an alliance with the boy and discuss with him how he thinks it might best be resolved. Rushing to talk with the boy's teacher, his peer group, or the bully himself— especially if you have not first consulted with the boy who is being bullied—may not only make the boy feel more ashamed, but in the wrong circumstances, it could inflame the problem. Initially the most important thing to do is simply to listen to the boy and be there for him. Talk to him about the fact that bullying is a widespread, national problem, that he is not alone, and that the danger inherent in bullying requires you to take action with him. Assuming you believe that there is no immediate danger to the boy, you can propose several approaches to solving the problem. These may include: (1) trying to ignore the behavior and see if the bully stops on his own volition (since many bullies are merely seeking attention); (2) confronting the bully in a nonviolent way by telling him that the bullying is "silly" or "foolish" and must stop; or (3) approaching an adult in a supervisory role and asking that person to help solve the problem; or (4) developing an alliance of people who will help protect the boy and bring an end to the bullying. Explain to the boy that you do not expect him to stop the bullying alone, that he should not feel compelled to have to "tough it out" himself. Stress to him that going to adults to help solve the problem, if done thoughtfully, can be positive and helpful. It is not "tattling." Of course, if a boy tells you that he is being bullied and you feel that he may be in immediate danger, you must take immediate action and see to it that the problem is addressed swiftly and effectively through appropriate channels within your community. Whatever you do, make sure that you never leave a boy to struggle with bullying all alone.

Help the boy to develop a group of allies.　Although a bully may stop mistreating others when confronted (or when simply ignored for a period of time), many bullies are persistent in their behavior, especially if other peers cheer them on. Overcoming teasing and bullying often requires building consensus and developing groups of like-minded people who are willing to become allies to the targeted boy and help him bring an end to the behavior. The allies can be adults or peers. Adults (and, if necessary, the proper authorities) can be particularly helpful in assessing the most appropriate way to stop the bullying. In addition, a buddy system—when a group of the boy's friends stand with him to face the bully—can go a long way to help boost a boy's morale and potentially put an end to the harassment. Thus when you discover that a boy is being teased or bullied—once you have his permission to do so—try to help him create a special group of people—adults and children—who are willing to help him conquer the problem. Work at this gradually by helping him approach potential allies or "buddies" one at a time. Help him to look first for loving kids and adults who you sense care about the way human beings are treated. Stay calm. Hold out to the boy and his friends and allies that you take the problem seriously and that you care. Stress that you are not comfortable allowing *anyone* to be mistreated.

Stay connected to the boy. When a boy is teased or bullied, in addition to feeling bad about himself, he generally feels incredibly alone. As important as it is to help him put a stop to the teasing and bullying, it is also critical to stay closely connected to him; otherwise, the bully has succeeded. Check in with the boy regularly. Offer to spend time with him doing things he enjoys. Encourage him to bring other friends along. Do everything you can to help him create a positive circle of friends who support him in a loving, genuine way.

Be cautious about contacting the bully's parents. While in some cases it may be a wise idea to contact the bully's parents to address the problem, this can be a risky approach because it is difficult to predict how the parents may respond. Before taking this risk, it's generally a better idea to work on developing the boy's support network. Helping boys to find a set of adults and peers upon whom they can rely must come first. Then, a representative of that group—perhaps you, perhaps somebody else who already has a relationship with the bully's parents and judges this to be a wise approach—might contact them and solicit their help to reform the bully's behavior.

Advocate for the boy at school. Since a large amount of teasing and bullying occurs at school, once you have discussed the matter with the boy, it may be important to contact the school (or the other organization where the behavior is happening) and request proper mediation. It is important that the school or other organization use smart, empathic, emotionally sensitive approaches to help change the bully's behavior. Punitive, so-called zero tolerance programs may only further spur on children prone to teasing and bullying their peers. If the school is not taking this seriously enough, or instead is being overly harsh, try to educate them about bully-proofing programs. If this is not effective (and even if it is), reach out to other parents for their help in bringing about the kinds of changes that will make the school a more peaceful, supportive place.

Rarely does bullying happen to just one child. There is power and strength of moral persuasion in numbers: use this to inspire teachers and administrators to adopt proactive measures against bullying.

Get support for yourself, too.   If you are a parent or adult helping a boy with bullying, it is important that you get the support that you need so you do not feel isolated or powerless yourself. When dealing with such a difficult situation, you, too, should not be left feeling alone.

WHAT IF YOUR CHILD IS BULLYING?

Look behind the mask and try to understand the bully's perspective. Although it is often difficult to empathize with a bully, it is critical that we try to develop close relationships with bullies so that we can understand their interior emotional lives and help them resolve the inner conflicts prodding them to become violent. If we do not probe under the mask of masculinity and try to understand a bully's motivations, if we simply take punitive approaches with him or her, we end up making that bully feel even more despondent and isolated, pushing him toward further rebellion. Most bullies, in reality, are simply boys in pain. So rather than rushing to discipline the bully, tell him you know that bullying usually happens because a boy feels down about life and that you wonder whether he might feel such distress. Explain that you would far prefer to help him end his pain than allow him to inflict pain on others.

Watch for the signs of depression.   With the exception of a very small number of sociopathic delinquents, most boys who bully have been hurt or abused themselves. Research now shows, too, that many of them are seriously depressed. Violence is never acceptable, and teasing and bullying must be stopped in their tracks. But, again, try to get to the emotional root of the bully's behavior rather than just addressing the outward behavior. Remember: bullying—not bullies—is the true nemesis.

Teach the bully alternative ways of expressing his pain.   As the voices in this book reflect, many boys cope with emotional difficulties and express their deepest pain and longing by playing sports, doing activities with friends and family, helping other people, getting involved in music, writing, or art, or by seeking connection with a spiritual other.

Many bullies are acting out because they do not feel connected to any-body or anything. They feel as though they have nothing going for them. Sometimes the quickest way of getting them to stop the teasing and bullying is to help them find an activity that comes easily to them and which they enjoy, and then doing that activity with them. Bullies need friends as much as the bullied. Of course, not all bullies are friend-less. Recent research reflects that many bullies are ordinary boys, even boys who are "popular" among their peers, who bully because they are caught in the net of the Boy Code and are trying to find a way out.

Do not tolerate the violence, but show appropriate empathy for the boy behind it.   So-called zero-tolerance programs often fail because they teach people to become hateful toward and intolerant of bullies instead of giving them the skills to help bullies make real changes in their lives. While it's wise to have zero tolerance for violence, it is critical to have abundant tolerance for the boy himself. Even if he has turned to teasing and bullying as a solution to his problems, try to show him your love and caring. Connect with him. Go for walks together. Listen to his voice. With few exceptions, you will discover a human being who is longing to make friends and find better solutions to cope with his inner angst and disappointment.

Give the bully opportunities to succeed at something.   Many bullies not only feel sad and lonely but suffer dismally low self-esteem. Some may struggle to achieve at school, do well at sports, or make close friends. Some may feel like total "losers," like there is nothing they are particu-larly good at. When trying to help a bully, ask him about what he thinks his strengths and weaknesses are. Help him to find at least one activity at which he excels and give him as much support and encouragement as possible to pursue it. Thus if he enjoys skateboarding, get him set up with a skateboard instructor. If he is talented with his hands, find an art teacher to give him sculpting lessons or a carpenter to teach him how to make things out of wood. If he likes roughhousing, set up a wrestling league and make him captain.

Set firm guidelines and if a bully persists in breaking them, place him in a new environment.   While zero-tolerance programs are not a solution I advocate, in our schools and communities we need to establish firm guidelines designed to curb bullying but that give bullies at least one second chance before formally disciplining him. Assuming he has been given appropriate help along the lines described above but still persists in bullying, for the psychological and physical safety of his peers, he must be moved out of the setting in which he is bullying and be placed in a new setting where he can be closely supervised and given the special, additional support he needs to work through the problems causing the violence. Most important, do not separate the bully and then leave him to deal with his problems alone. You must stay connected to him, stand by him despite his so-called bad behavior, and get him the help he needs.

WHAT SHOULD BOYS WHO ARE BULLIED KNOW?

There is nothing wrong with the boy who is targeted.   Boys who are targeted for teasing and bullying have nothing wrong with them. In some cases they are boys who are courageous in challenging society's old rules of masculinity. They are boys who take risks. When you discover that a boy is being bullied, tell him that he does not deserve the teasing and bullying he is currently suffering. Explain to him that it is not his fault that some boys become violent. And tell him that you will help him make things better, that life will go smoother for him in the future. Help to give him hope.

Help the boy to understand the psychology of the bully.   While the boy may not be able easily to forgive the bully, he will feel much better about himself if he is able to understand what makes people tease and bully one another. Explain to him that bullies often feel bad about themselves. Talk about the Boy Code and how bullies are often trying to act tough and aggressive to win their peers' approval. Point out to him that many boys who bully have themselves been bullied or abused. Most of them are hurting inside and are desperately looking for a way to make friends and be respected by peers. Even if the boy you are helping is not able to empathize with the bully, he will feel better if he can grasp what motivates a bully to act out.

Avoid the bully but stay connected to peers.   Tell the boy that it's wise to avoid the bully. It's OK to ask to be switched out of the same class, to take a different route on the way home to steer clear of the bully. But a boy targeted by a bully should not allow himself to become socially isolated. Encourage him to stay connected to peers, to seek out new friends, and to develop relationships with people outside of school—in other towns or through extracurricular activities with kids from other areas—so that he can enjoy some time free of the anxiety of coping with teasing and bullying.

Give him a sense of power.   It is no fun to feel like a victim. Encourage the boy to adopt the stance that the bully will not be allowed to have power over him. The bully may be physically stronger or have the temporary support of peers. But by adopting the attitude that the bully will never win, that the bully will not be able to "hook" the boy through aggression, the boy can prevent the bully from getting the best of him.

In the end, it is important for all of us to remember that overcoming bullying is a process in which we all must participate. It is not something that can be solved by a single intervention. It takes time, organization, and a lot of work. It entails changing our entire boy culture and gradually dismantling the old Boy Code. Sometimes, our efforts to eliminate bullying may not succeed immediately. For a time there may even be a bit more bullying. But if we all work diligently together, we can help boys to discover that embracing hatred and engaging in violence do little to advance them socially and nothing to help them become happier or more successful men. Eventually we can help them see that the most powerful currency of manhood is love.

9

SADNESS, DEPRESSION, AND SUICIDE: SAD BOYS OR BAD BOYS?

"Depression and anger are such close cousins. Anger is just depression pointed outward. [And depression is anger pointed inward.]"

—Xavier, 17, from a suburb in the Northeast

"A lot of people use words like 'psycho' or 'wacko' to refer to people who are feeling glum or think they might want to take their own life. I think these sorts of slang terms create further isolation in a teen, and that's not what you want to do to a teen who already feels alone."

—Alexander, 18, from a small town in the South

THE BEST THING I CAN DO IS GO ON AND LIVE
Thomas, 15, from a suburb in the South

Two years ago, when I was thirteen, my mom passed away. She had Hodgkin's disease when she was a young adult; she was one of the first people to be treated with chemotherapy, and it was successful. The doctors had said she would die in weeks, but she managed to live years. But anytime she caught a cold or something, she would get really sick and need two or three weeks just to get better. So when this cold came, we weren't too worried. We paid attention to her, but personally I was thinking, "All right, well, she's got another cold, she'll get through it again." But she just got sicker and sicker, and we finally admitted her into the hospital. They said she had pneumonia and that she wasn't getting enough oxygen. And so she just got worse.

After seeing her go into the hospital, I went out of town with one of my best friends. I wasn't too worried, but I called to check up on her one day, and the nurse said she was in intensive care and that she was not able to talk. I flew home the next day. I was there when she passed on, about two or three days later. I hadn't been able to talk to her because she was being given drugs the whole time and had a breathing tube down her throat. That was very upsetting.

The feelings when I lost my mother were unimaginable. You just couldn't describe it, you thought it was just a dream, you couldn't do anything about it. And knowing that you were just . . . you felt like you were almost dying with her, like a piece of you was just going with her. And she had been the closest person to me.

My mom was very sweet, kind, and loving. I could talk to her about anything. She was the one who always helped me out with things. She was very patient. She helped me out with all my subjects in school, and she did a great job. When she died, I tried to put it off, that sadness, as much as possible. It was too much, so I tried to keep busy, to push it out of the way. I would keep myself active in other things, especially with the family. Everybody was down—her brother and my aunt and her parents—and so I was dealing with all of them.

I still try to be the major caretaker in my family. My older brother and I do a lot of work around the house. Our father has a brain tumor, and he's legally blind. He's got tunnel vision right now, and he's probably going to go fully blind in the next two years. And there's nothing they can do about it. Taking care of him can be a chore in a way, but we've become much closer now that my mom's passed away. When he had more of his eyesight and didn't know about the brain tumor, he was mostly at the office, which was fine. But he was so busy back then that I couldn't do normal stuff with him.

I like having my dad around more, but I don't really want to get emotional with him. I'm not a very emotional type of guy; at least, I don't show it. I like to keep it all in, which I know is not very good. The one person I can just sit and talk to about how I feel is my brother. I have some great friends, but I don't usually like to put them in that situation of helping me with all my problems. Sometimes I sit down with one of my friends and talk. But that friend can't do anything about my problems. All he can do is say, "Yes, there's a pain." That's nice and all, but you want something else, you want something to be *done*. But nothing can be done.

When I feel like talking I just go to my brother. He tells me a lot of things to help me get along with our father. Sometimes I distract myself by doing other things, like making people around me laugh. That's one of the things I really love, making people laugh. It's a way for me to give back to people who care for me, and it helps me forget about my sadness for a little while.

I've been treated for slight depression, but I get around it with help from friends and family. Sometimes, though, it just catches up to you and you can't do anything about it. Depression just hits you and hits you. Sadness just comes over you, and you can't stop thinking of the time you failed that class, or how you could have done better if you just got off your lazy butt. I get self-critical and think about the things I could have done that I didn't. I've even gone as far as to make a mental plan of how I would want to die: jump off a building. But then I think, What would my dad do? What would my brother do? How would my friends react? I would be letting them down so much. I've discussed these suicidal thoughts with some of my friends, and they look at me and say, "If you ever have thoughts like that again, I want you to come and talk to me." Most of all, though, I think about my mom. As soon as I got up to heaven, she would kick my butt. She would want me to live, so I think the best thing I can do is to go on and live.

I went to a therapist for a while, but he didn't do too much; we were pretty much repeating the same stuff every week. I got out of some things that I needed to get out of, but I wasn't expecting too much to be done. I just didn't want to be there; I didn't feel comfortable telling all my feelings to a person I didn't know. I could tell that it was his job and he didn't care for me: he just wanted to get me in and get me out, so he could make some more money. He would look on his chart and then ask, "So, have you had any depression?" I'd go, "No, I don't think so," and he would answer, "Well, let's talk about your father again." Well, we'd already talked about that. He just wouldn't know where to start.

I've tried an antidepressant medication, too, but it made it difficult for me to focus on anything, so I stopped. Plus, I like to take care of things on my own. I like the feeling that I'm in control, that if I want to go left, I can go left. We all need other people, and I do have a lot of friends who help me through everyday situations by being there to get my mind away from some of my troubles. But I don't talk to them about how I feel. I don't like to go too deep into my depression. It might come back up again, and I would just rather have it stay back down there. I don't want to have to worry about it right now; I want to get along with my life. I like to live life to the fullest. I don't need to deal with that pain right now. It's been a tough two years. But you learn to adapt. Life gets a little easier every day.

SUICIDE AMONG ADOLESCENT BOYS IN OUR COUNTRY IS nothing other than a major national crisis. As painful as it may be for our nation to face, over the last fifty years the number of completed suicides among boys ages ten through nineteen has risen dramatically to alarmingly high levels; and for adolescent boys ages fifteen to nineteen, the suicide rate has tripled since 1970. The most recent statistics on suicide issued by the Centers for Disease Control and Prevention indicate that about 75 percent of all suicides committed by children ages ten to fourteen are committed by boys, and that among teens ages fifteen to nineteen, the number increases to approximately 83 percent. Stated simply, adolescent boys in America are completing suicides between four to six times more often than girls.

Putting aside gender and age, the statistics also reveal that in our country more people die from suicide than from homicide. In other words, from year to year, we are killing ourselves more often than we are killing others. We are also increasingly thinking about committing suicide, even if we do not immediately complete the act. This frightening phenomenon is particularly pronounced among teenagers. According to a nationwide study recently conducted by the American Association of Suicidology, more than 20 percent of high school students surveyed said that they had seriously considered attempting suicide in the preceding twelve months. The line between suicidal ideation and completed self-murder is, regrettably, a fine one. The bottom line? For every 100,000 American adolescents between the ages of fifteen and nineteen, somewhere between eight and ten of them will take their own lives, and at least three-quarters of them will be boys or young men.

There are probably many reasons why teenage boys are taking their lives in such great numbers. As the voices in this book reflect, boys in America are talking about all sorts of painful experiences that can become the apparent "proximate cause" for suicidal thoughts or for attempting suicide, including teasing, bullying, social rejection, failure at school or in sports, a broken romantic relationship, physical abuse at the hands of parents or other family members, addiction to drugs or alcohol, or the death of a loved one.

But after listening to many of the boys whose voices are heard in this book, I strongly believe that one of the most common causes of suicide is the predominant depression that plagues so many of our young sons. This "boy" depression is a result of accumulated hopelessness, loneliness, and troubled self-esteem. From a young age, boys are not allowed to express any of their confusion and vulnerability about themselves, so they hide who they are and develop a strong sense of isolation. In addition, they are constantly being told that they are not as masculine, strong, athletic, or good as the next boy. Thus, their sense of self is challenged brutally on a daily basis. These feelings accumulate over the years so that by the time boys become teenagers, especially if they haven't found outlets in which to release their pain—through sports, music, religion, or other activities that connect them meaningfully to family or friends—they come to experience a dullness, darkness, and powerlessness, a deep sadness that is profound, insidious, and paralyzing. Sensing that as boys they are forbidden to seek out help, they become prisoners of their sadness and depression, and see no possibility for change on the horizon, no way out.

Indeed, among psychologists across the country there is a growing consensus that depression in boys plays a huge role in attempted and completed suicides. There is little disagreement that younger boys are as likely to become depressed as girls are, and a number of new research projects have begun to indicate that lowered self-esteem is equally as important a problem for young males as it is for females. My own work suggests that despite society's misconception that girls are more often depressed than boys, when we look closely at boys' inner experiences, feelings, and writings—and learn the *boy-specific* signs for depression—teenage boys, in reality, are as, or almost as likely to fall prey to depression as teenage girls. In other words, there is probably not such a great difference in the incidence of depression in teenage boys and girls—but as a society we still seem more inclined to notice and treat depression in girls than we are apt to notice depression in boys and young men.

The deep sadness and often immobilizing depression that many boys experience so frequently go unnoticed because of the restrictive Boy Code. Whether we intend it or not, society continues to shame boys when they attempt to express weakness, desperation, or despair. Listen to the voice of Carlos, who at the age of twelve is just at the cusp of adolescence and manhood:

> [S]ometimes boys won't show it when they're sad. Girls will, because they don't care. If I was upset by something at school, I might not cry there because the other boys will stare at me [or] call me "girly." At home, I will cry in my own room. Then my mom will come in and say, "What's the problem? Don't worry. Take a nap. You will get over it." At home, you only have to hold your crying for a second because no one will tease you there. But in school you can't do that. You have to live with it. At school, there will be a rumor that "He cried. He cried for this stupid little thing."

Boys who show their vulnerability, especially if they do so in public spaces, are shamed, scolded, and punished or simply discouraged or ignored by adults; and they are teased, bullied, and even killed by their peers. To protect themselves, boys try to become numb and eradicate any outward sign of their true needs or feelings. If we ask how they are, often they will deny that they are upset or unwell. "I'm not depressed," many boys emphatically say to parents or friends, attempting to seem strong, self-composed, and "masculine" even as they begin to plot their own suicide.

IS HE BAD OR IS HE SAD?

When containing the pain becomes too much, many boys lose control, and their sadness turns to anger. "We don't tell people that we're sad," explained Tony, sixteen, who was recently suspended from his high school for fighting with other boys. "We tell people that we're angry or we really don't care." Or as Michael, seventeen, a talented and well-liked athlete at the top of his high school class told me—after explaining that though he really feels very sad, his family and friends tend to perceive him as having a bad temper—"I haven't done anything drastic when I'm in these moods, but they still scare me. They can't be good for me and sometimes I really feel like I could kill someone."

Over time, boys learn to channel what might have been words or thoughts or tears into anger, rage, and impulsive, often violent action. Instead of manifesting their sadness in genuine cries for help and receiving the love and support they truly crave, boys put on the mask of masculinity to hide their true feelings from friends and family. They either withdraw into isolation or lash out with dangerous acts of bravado. Many take drugs or drink away their feelings in a vain attempt at self-soothing or self-medication. Some become irritable, feisty, "rebellious," or "annoying," and others reach a critical breaking point—they *snap,* lose control and explode into fits of rage or acts of violence. All these behaviors reflect attempts to hide their vulnerability, cover over hopelessly lowered self-esteem, increasing sadness, the onset of depression, and the growing possibility of enacted suicide.

In so many cases, what in the teenage years may look like a *bad* boy is really a *sad* boy, whose underground pain may lead him to become extremely dangerous to others or, much more likely, to himself. Tragically, boys rarely "attempt" suicide; when they reach out for a knife, a rope, or a gun, generally they are not crying for help. Rather, they are very much trying to get the job done. Statistics clearly show that the means and methods boys choose (most often firearms) are much more likely to lead to death than those selected by their female counterparts (most often pills). When boys commit suicide, they are committing nothing other than what I've come to describe as "self-murder." They are annihilating their selves, killing the one person they can't stand living with anymore. They are finally bringing an end to the painful sense that they just can't live up to the Boy Code or that they will never be able to fulfill the Impossible Test of Masculinity. Boys who want to take their own lives are desperate not to fail at this last-gasp effort to prove their masculine selves. Committing suicide for boys demands no failure, no cries for help, but only a swift, stoic, inevitable death. Boys, tragically, are exceedingly adept at killing themselves.

Depression and suicide do not spare boys with any particular personality type—boys who may seem happy on the surface, athletic boys, popular boys, or boys who are of one race or another. All boys are susceptible. If the Boy Code is at the root of the problem, it's our job to make sure we do what we can to dismantle that code and figure out ways we can help boys get beyond it *now*. There isn't a moment to lose. As eighteen-year-old Alexander told me, a boy who himself was once only a few breaths away from death, only to be rescued from his recent suicide attempt by local paramedics, "One of the most common myths about suicide . . . is that [it] affects one certain type of person—one race, one gender, one color, one class. But depression and suicide are much like cancer—they can affect *anybody* at any time."

Indeed, one widespread myth is that black Americans are less susceptible to suicide. Research now shows that the suicide rate among African-American boys ten to fourteen years old (although the figure is lower than that for white boys within the same age range and has fluctuated) has increased overall by a staggering 146 percent since the 1950s. Another group of young people, to whom we must especially show our compassion and concern, is the huge number of gay teenagers who attempt or complete suicides each year. Extrapolating from one study, we can now conclude that at least one-third and as much as one-half of all male teen suicides in our nation are currently committed by boys who identify themselves as being gay.

Listen to the boys' stories in this chapter and see if some of the experiences they lay bare might match those of some of the boys whom you yourself know, teach, or love. Reflected in these poignant narratives is the hope that perhaps slowly but surely, many boys themselves are beginning to understand the problem more clearly, and are taking independent steps to make things better for themselves as well as for others. Across America, boys are starting to reject the Boy Code, taking risks by talking about their real feelings and their real selves, and reaching out to help save the lives of their buddies.

In many ways, it is now up to us to affirm what our sons, brothers, and boyfriends are starting to achieve. It's up to us to encourage boys and tell them that yes, it is okay to need help and that it's also okay to give it. When it comes to suicide, sometimes all it takes to put an end to the impulse is one phone call, one thoughtful word of reassurance, one loving hug. As a society, we cannot leave this critically important work to girls and women. All of us—boys and girls, men and women—need to become keenly aware of how boys demonstrate their unique signs of suicidal pain. And we must all become better at learning how to tell people when we need their love and to give others that love when they need it from us, despite the Boy Code and society's other shaming rules and messages.

While we were in the midst of collecting these voices, the boys at one school came to confide in us that they were worried about Michael: "Michael seems to be acting strange lately," they told me just before I sat down to interview their friend.

As I listened to Michael, he showed all the classic "boy signs" of depression, which no adult in his highly educated family nor in his so-phisticated school had noticed. He was angry, abusing alcohol, irritable, withdrawn, tempestuous, and engaging in reckless acts of bravado. He felt tired a lot of the time and was losing interest in his schoolwork. Michael, of course, denied any "depressive" feelings, because that was not how he experienced his pain. But as we spoke further, all the signs emerged. Carefully, in a manner sensitive to his fear and shame, I in-quired as to whether he had begun to think about dying, about taking his own life.

Thinking quietly for a moment, without confirming my worries di-rectly, Michael replied by wondering how I seemed to know about this preoccupation. I explained the different ways that boys and girls show their sadness and how he had many of the signs of depression—even though neither he nor the adults he trusted had recognized or spoken to him about them.

For the first time during our encounter, some sense of relief—or its potential—entered the room, and Michael asked for my advice. Since suicide was a danger, but not an immediate one, I explained that while I could talk to his parents, it would probably be best, if at all possible, if *he* were the one who could broach the issue with his mom and dad.

At first Michael was hesitant, as he explained that his parents would probably overreact and worry too much. But he agreed to stay in con-tact with me, and allowed me to speak to others if his own trials failed. Yet Michael's story ends well. Just several days after we had met, one of my research associates received a call from Kyle, another boy we had interviewed in the same community. Kyle told us that Michael had come to him, and to some other boys in town, and told them of his sadness. Kyle and his friends gave Michael the support and encouragement he needed to tell his parents how he was really feeling.

Kyle reported to us that Michael's parents, far from being angry or "overreacting," as Michael had anticipated, were instead actually "thrilled." Together, as a family, they had begun to see a psychologist who was helping them work through the feelings of pain that had been bottled up for so long inside of Michael.

With just one small but very significant gesture of love and caring from his friends, Michael was able to overcome feelings that could have spiraled into acts of destruction against others or himself. If we learn one thing from this story, and from the other voices that appear within these pages, it is that boys need to know and genuinely believe that it's all right to ask for our help. They need to know that if they come to us, we will not do anything to shame them. Ideally, before we detect the first signs of boylike depression—in fact, as often as possible—we need to let boys and young men know that no matter what they tell us and what they reveal about their inner feelings and experiences, we will continue to love and care for them with all our heart and all our soul.

THE PETALS OF A ROSE

Alexander, 18, from a small town in the South

As a survivor of a suicide attempt, I am always on the lookout for other kids who may be suffering and need help. I study people. In fact, I'm one of those guys who will go to a mall, find a place to sit, and just watch people go by. I'm fascinated with people in general and am particularly interested in those closest to me. I've become pretty good at noticing when somebody is hurting. Sometimes I'll see somebody at school, it could even be someone to whom I've never said a word in my entire life, and I can definitely recognize a shift in their personality, habits, or actions. I notice when they're down, when they need help. Sometimes I detect extreme withdrawal, people totally pulling inside of themselves. But sometimes it's just the opposite: I see other kids acting out in extreme ways. Boys are especially prone to this. They'll act rowdy or have discipline problems not because they are "troublemakers" but actually because they're depressed. Maybe because I am a guy, it's easier for me to see depression in other boys.

People have a lot of ignorant ideas about suicide. One of the most common myths about suicide, which people in society actually consider a truth, is that suicide affects one certain type of person—one race, one gender, one color, one class. But depression and suicide are much like cancer—they can affect *anybody* at any time. Another myth is that suicidal people are "crazy." I'm involved in a suicide prevention program called Yellow Ribbon, in which teenagers help other teenagers overcome feelings of depression and suicide impulses. When I meet with teens about participating in the program, some of them are kind of leery about helping teens who are depressed and suicidal because they think of people with these problems as being like characters from *One Flew Over the Cuckoo's Nest*. They get this image of really weird people running around and blurting out stuff. I really try to dispel these sorts of myths because I don't think feelings of depression and suicide should be classified as psychotic. A lot of people use words like "psycho" or "wacko" to refer to people who are feeling glum or think they might want to take their own life. I think these sorts of slang terms create further isolation in a teen, and that's *not* what you want to do to a teen who already feels alone.

I'm not sure why so many teenagers feel suicidal. I guess some of it may have to do with the biological shift that one experiences as a teen. But it also has to do with your early experiences as a child, and how well things go for you as a teenager. I grew up with an abusive, alcoholic father, and early on I suffered through several deaths of people who were really close to me. I also have had some rocky experiences in my love life. These things can add up and before you know it, you're feeling like you want to put an end to it all.

I think it's important for teenagers who themselves have felt depressed or suicidal to reach out and try to help other teens in the same position. The painful experiences I have had have given me an opportunity to understand other people and how their minds work. One thing I really don't like about psychologists and psychiatrists is that they can sit behind a desk in a plush chair and tell you that they "know how you feel." It's hard to trust that person, because he or she actually might *not* know how you feel. But another teen who really has recently felt very similar feelings can be tremendously helpful.

Unfortunately, I think most people have a hard time spotting depression. Like anything else, you're not going to see something that you don't want to see. Especially with boys, parents don't want to see things in their sons that seem harmful. They have this general idea about the right way to raise a boy—you don't want him to cry and pout around. You expect him to be strong, happy, and upbeat. I live in a small town. Around here, we feel out of touch with the rest of the world. People here don't believe that in such a small place suicide could be a problem, especially not in boys. They say things like: "You're not depressed"; "It's just that your hormones are all out of whack." How many times did I hear that? Or they would say, "You're just going through a rough time," or "You're in the midst of puberty." How many times did I hear those things? It's a lot of denial. It's like they're saying: "We don't really understand it; we don't know how to handle it; so let's just act like it's not there."

I'm trying to do everything I can to let people in my town know that depression and suicide are just reality, that they happen to people everywhere. That is one of my big labors. I try to get out to PTA meetings, city counsel meetings, and local parenting classes. I go to those places and say, "It's here, guys, it's happening right here." I mean, I'm living proof! It's been a year since I brought the Yellow Ribbon program to our small town and we've already aided thirty-two people when they were feeling suicidal.

As for myself, I can notice when I'm feeling a little bit down, or even feeling suicidal again. I'm not gonna lie, I still deal with depression. Sometimes I sit back and think about just how much I've matured in the past three or four months, let alone how much I've matured since I was sixteen years old. Through the work that I do with crisis intervention, I've learned a lot about myself and about how to cope with life. These days, I am much better able to notice the early signs of sadness and depression in myself. This gives me a one up, a way to try to handle it that I didn't have before.

Above all, I've learned that it is so important to pick the right people and the right friendships. I look for people with whom I can be honest, people I can trust. Being a teen is hard sometimes because it seems like you're always under the scrutiny of adults. You feel like they're thinking, "Yup, he's still an obnoxious teenage boy." So your friends become important to you. I guess in some ways, it doesn't really matter if you're a toddler, a teenager, or forty-five years old; it's always crucial to choose your friends wisely. You've got to select people who you can go to when you have a problem, who think it's okay to ask for help, and who let you know that the kind of help you're looking for is very much there. Your parents may not be there, or won't listen. Your school counselor may not be there and maybe he doesn't understand either. But your good friends, they love you, that's their job; they love you, they care about you, and they can talk to you.

As a guy, you have an overload of emotions. But by the time you're a teenager it's been so imprinted on your mind that you shouldn't ask for help. Guys get so confused; they're like, "Well, I have all these emotions, and I have all these thoughts running through my mind; what should I do?" I'm not sure it's very healthy during adolescence to live in a society that doesn't allow you to emote and be honest about who you are. Because adolescence is just the period when your body, both physically and emotionally, is *so* ready to do these things.

Actually, I see adolescence as a very inspirational time, because you get a lot of new insights on life; you are actually seeing life for the first time. For teens who have just entered adolescence or are in the middle of adolescence, that's the time when they should get to express their feelings and emotions, because for the first time in their life they're really feeling every emotion to its full capacity.

Being a teenager or hitting puberty isn't a disease that makes you unable to have feelings. If society were different, being a teenager would actually be an exciting time. Sure, there would be dangers and concerns, but there would be so much energy to talk about everything you are experiencing in life. The fact that teenage boys who get depressed don't talk about it isn't really a normal part of being a teenager. Actually, it's the opposite of what teenage life could be like for them if society were just a little bit different.

When you're a young kid, like age eight or eleven, it can be hard to be a boy and you start thinking to yourself, "Wow, I can't wait to hit thirteen and be older." When you become a teenager, it's almost like you have a second chance to remake your life the way you want it. But then society comes back in and tells you to control yourself, to act cool and tough and everything. Then that second chance is gone. You're back where you started. In some way, I wish I could do my adolescence all over again. I would do it differently if I could do it again. I mean, it's like we keep knocking boys down and down and down, and then we're surprised when they get depressed.

There's sort of a way that society robs boys my age of a lot of wonderful experiences. But because we're not supposed to act certain ways, and we're not supposed to ask for help when we're in pain, the excitement and energy we could be experiencing are lost. It's like, just at the moment a rose is going to bloom, you cut off the top of its bud and then it just kind of falls down.

LIFE IS HARD

Michael, 17, from a suburb in the Midwest

Life is hard. I really don't know where to start. I guess I'll start with school. It already takes up about eight hours of each of my weekdays.

I guess the school in itself is really not that bad, but it takes up so much time. I like going and seeing my friends and stuff. I just wish it weren't so early. The part I absolutely hate about school is homework. School has already taken up about one-third of my day. And I have a lot of other things to do and sleep to get. I will come home from school some nights with four hours of homework. Sometimes I just don't have enough time for it. And then my grades fall.

I know I am an above-average student, but sometimes I just can't get the time for homework, and then I get average grades. I wish my teachers would understand that I have other things to do. I mean, I already don't get enough sleep. I always have some kind of rehearsal after school. Lately, our orchestra has been working on the annual Christmas gala. I have been stuck at school rehearsing every day for the past week, and then when I get home, I have to call my girlfriend, Cindy. I mean I love her and everything, but she lives out of town. So I don't get to talk to her during the day and she expects me to talk to her on the phone for at least an hour every night. I don't even get started on my homework until about ten or eleven o'clock. If I don't call Cindy, for some reason she thinks that I don't like her anymore. I enjoy talking to her but it's just that some nights—like if I've only had three hours of sleep the night before—when I get home I'm just dead tired. All I want to do is go to sleep.

My life is like this all year round. In fall, I have soccer all day. In winter, it's the music gala and winter track and basketball. In spring, it's spring track and spring soccer. There's always an activity after school that I have to go to. Along with these activities, I also try to keep a social life. I like doing things with my friends and going to parties, but it is hard to keep up.

In some ways, I feel like I don't have a personality. I feel like who I am is just school and soccer and music—just whatever I do. I don't have any time just to be myself. Sometimes I just want to be who I really am, instead of just a collection of all the things I do.

All this work and pressure make me feel different sometimes. I don't get suicidal or anything, I just feel depressed. I feel like I'm not up to doing all the things that I love to do. I feel like shutting myself off from the world. The way I usually get out of these moods is by thinking to myself that I will be able to take it easy in the summer, that I should just get all this work over with now.

I haven't done anything drastic when I'm in these moods, but they still scare me. They can't be good for me and sometimes I really feel like I could kill someone. I just wish I had more time so I could relax and get more than five hours of sleep every night.

I get really pissed off when I have so much stuff to do and my parents put even more pressure on me. They expect me to do well at school. Then, when I get home, they want me to clean my room and do the dishes. They say "do this" or "do that." I don't really think my parents understand my frustration. I don't really talk to them very much.

I have two close friends whom I can talk to about these things, but usually I just kind of keep to myself. It's a lot to have to swallow sometimes. I just get so overwhelmed that I don't want to do anything. I just sit there and don't move. When I get really mad, I go on a jog because it helps me think. But lately my bad moods have sometimes gone on for about a week. The pain doesn't last for very long, though. It passes.

I have an older brother and sister, Scott and Sarah, who are both at college. It's tough because Sarah was really smart, a good student, and did well in math. She was also a big athlete and sports star at school, and my parents expect me to be better, and it's kind of hard to do. There's this legacy that I have to live up to.

I was pretty close to Scott because we used to play soccer together. But I was never really close with Sarah. Anyway, now they are both far away at school out in Oregon. I miss them, but I'm kind of used to them being gone. They are not as much a part of my life anymore.

Timmy, my younger brother, he's the closest one to me. I can talk to him better than I can talk to Luke and Max, because Luke and Max are still just little kids. Timmy, at least, he's starting to get a little older. I mean I love Luke and Max but they really annoy me sometimes. I just get really angry and then my temper flares up.

My parents can tell when I'm in a bad mood because I'm not very nice to them, and they just think that the best thing to do is leave me alone. A lot of the time they say it's just a teenage thing, a typical boy thing.

I don't get to see my dad very often because he's a busy lawyer. Ever since several of the other partners at his firm retired, he's been having to carry all their cases. He's been gone a lot; and anyway, I'm only home to eat, sleep, and do homework. Sometimes the two of us are like ships passing in the night.

My mom is a school guidance counselor and she kind of knows how to talk to people like me a little better, but she tries not to be too pushy, and tries to have these conversations that she thinks a mother and son should have. She likes to pick away and find out what I've been up to and ask questions about my girlfriend like "How's Cindy doing?" or "What are you guys up to lately?" She asks about how my friends are and who my best friend is—things like that.

I mean, it doesn't really bother me to tell my mom about what I've been doing, it just kind of annoys me how she's always trying to get into my social life. Part of me thinks it's a good thing for her to know who I like and what I'm up to. I'm sort of on the cusp: on the one hand, I think it's good to talk to her; on the other hand, maybe I'd like to keep my personal life to myself.

Sometimes my parents really try to talk to me, but I kind of brush them off. I don't know. I'm just not always in the mood to talk to anyone. It gets frustrating and it's hard to know what to do about it. So I just wait for it to pass and try to hope for the best.

Sometimes I feel like I should drop something I do. But I really wouldn't want to because there isn't anything that I don't like doing. I don't want to give up what I've got, yet what I've got is part of what makes me feel so overcommitted and pressured. I try to live with it. I do what I can. Sometimes I wish I weren't living this kind of life. I just wish I had more time to myself, but I don't really feel in charge of making that happen. There's all this external pressure and internal pressure. And sometimes I keep myself so busy that I don't even think about it. I guess part of being busy may be to avoid feeling so terrible.

Other people don't seem to quite recognize how disturbing this is to me. They notice my temper, but they don't know what causes it. I keep things to myself. I don't know—it's not embarrassing or anything like that—I just don't like talking about it. I just feel like the more I talk about it, the worse it gets.

When things get hard I don't have a sense that anyone else could help. I don't like talking about things. I guess I feel lonely. It just feels like something's missing, you know?

I guess all of this is something I have to go through. I always figured it would be like this during high school. Then I would go to college and do whatever you do there, and then I'd kind of take it slow after I got a job and a family. I would live through this pressure during high school and college. Maybe after that, I would get some relief.

I don't think anybody really knows how I feel because I can kind of easily mask how I'm feeling. I'll just go to school and even if I'm not feeling that great, I'll just act like I'm having fun and smile. I'll keep a happy face and people buy it.

So on the outside, I'm fun and joking, while on the inside I feel sad, frustrated, and alone. Maybe I'm worried that by acting unhappy it would make me feel worse.

Sometimes I've thought about going to see a professional, but I guess I think that the only people who need to talk to social workers or psychiatrists are people who are really having problems. I've never looked at my problems as if they were that bad; I mean, not as bad as some people who I've seen who are pretty disturbed. But my problems are bad enough to frustrate me and stop me from getting the grades I want. And they make me feel alone.

If I were to go for help, I'm afraid I just wouldn't know what to say. I've had very little practice in being able to tell people how I feel. I've had a lot of practice in the opposite, in how to hide it. Sometimes when I write things down I can describe how I feel. Then I can explain the kind of pain and frustration I have. So I guess in the right context I actually can talk about how I feel fairly well.

There must be something about this frame of mind that I feel isn't right, because if I thought it was right, I wouldn't have to try to cover it up. I am concerned about how people would feel if I told them I was down. They would see me as a guy with problems. It's not a cool thing; it's just not cool to say, "I've got problems. I'm depressed." They wouldn't tease me—I don't know if they'd lose respect for me—but they would see me differently. They would start seeing me as somebody who's having emotional problems. And I would see myself as being less than I am now.

Maybe if things were different, though, I wouldn't talk to people about it all the time. I also wouldn't walk around trying to make believe that I'm fine when I really am not. I would show that, yes, I am sad and I am down. The fact that I make believe that I'm happy shows that there's something that's not right.

Like I said, I have two friends whom I could really trust and talk to who wouldn't tell anybody else and who would try to help me as best as they could. I guess if I were ever to talk about my problems, I would go to them first. That would feel more comfortable then seeing a social worker or counselor or psychologist.

I guess it would help me emotionally to talk to somebody, but it's not like it's going to give me a couple of more hours in a day to get some sleep or something.

I just feel like by now I'm already in this so far. When I'm in a bad mood, if I started showing people how I really felt, they would think that there's something very seriously wrong because I've never really acted that way before.

If I said to my parents, "You know, Mom and Dad, this is a lot of pressure I'm under and I'd like to go see and talk to somebody," they would get too worried. I need to protect them from that.

They couldn't just say, "Oh, we didn't know things were so hard for you. Sure, we'll help you out." They'd say, "Oh my God! What's the matter?"

So that's what stops me from saying too much to them about how I really feel.

This one guy, Toby, he and I are best friends. He's real busy, too. Maybe I should talk to him.

AN EMPTY, DARK HOUSE
Arthur, 18, from a suburb in the Northeast

I would like to tell you about my life and the way family, friends, and neighbors have affected my life.

I was born in Dallas, Texas, at 11:45 at night on September 10,

1981. My parents adopted me five days after I was born, and brought me to live in a small house in Hudson, New York. The house was a nice size for two people just starting out and maybe a small kid. But as I got bigger, space became more demanding. When I was two and a half, my parents bought this beautiful house in Brewster, New York. That was when I began to meet kids and was the first step to hanging out with other kids my own age. That was something I did not have at the old house because the people who lived there were too old to play with. The neighbors at the new house in Brewster treated each other like family and helped each other by baby-sitting or helping out with moving furniture, even doing yard work for each other.

In Brewster I made many friends, and many remain good friends today, whom I see on occasion. Many of my friends enjoy going to the movies and playing video games. We like horror movies like *The Blob, Friday the 13th,* and *Halloween.* I love hanging out with friends and being able to scare people who walk by. We make them jump and run for their lives.

These days, I don't really get the chance to see all my family because they are very spread out. The last time I saw my cousins in New Mexico was almost one year ago. It kind of disappoints me because they are some of my favorite family members. We have so much in common with each other. Being an only child, I enjoy the company. They are older than I am, so I look up to them and respect their opinions. Since they are family, I feel a sense of comfort with them that I don't feel with everyone. I can talk about things with them that I can't with others.

My life in high school can be very stressful at times. I'm at boarding school, and the longest I have been alone was about one hour—and that was an all-time record. I feel too compacted with authority. I feel like I am in a prison sometimes because we are constantly being monitored.

There are some days when I feel totally alone and helpless to do anything about it. I have had so many days of debating whether or not to talk to a shrink. I never told many people what I am going to say now. There was one day back in middle school when I came home to an empty, dark house; my parents were not home. I looked in the mirror and realized that I hated myself. I hated myself because I hated the place I was in and I hated the fact that I was not respected, to say the least. I found myself going for a kitchen knife to slit my wrist with. I stopped and thought about my family and how much love and respect they give me, and I put the knife away and never brought it up to my parents. I never brought it up with my parents because I was afraid they would think I'm crazy and send me to a home for people with intentions similar to mine.

I have dealt with so much depression and anxiety that it was difficult to control how I felt. I only spoke to my best friend, Paul, about what I was going through. He knew exactly what I was talking about because he, too, had problems with depression. The two of us would get together at a café, smoke a cigarette, and talk about our problems. We still do this on weekends. Sometimes we talk about our problems together for almost three hours at a time.

I feel that depression is the biggest problem among teen groups because we all deal with rejection and anguish and hate. I find it is easier to talk to somebody who has had similar feelings of depression. We kind of share advice with each other. This is a very good relationship for me to have. These types of friendships are very important because there are not too many friends you can really trust.

But it all comes down to one thing: who you are and if you are proud of it.

A Threat to Myself

Tony, 16, from a city in the Northeast

I didn't grow up with a father. He left when I was four; now I'm sixteen. I only remember him a little and I don't know where he is now. I can't miss him because I don't remember that much. What do I miss?

A lot of parents are separated and the kid usually stays with the mother. It's easier for girls then, because they don't need the father as much. Something the father would give, they find it in a boyfriend or in a friend. How am I going to find my father in a friend? It can't happen. I don't know how I'm supposed to approach a guy to talk about things like feelings. My dad is supposed to be the guy I'm comfortable talking to, the only guy, and he's not there. So I have to deal with things myself. Even my mom taught me that: since I don't have a father, I gotta be tougher than most kids who do have a father. But some things you can't go on dealing with by yourself; you need somebody to talk to.

My mom raised me and I can't talk to her at all. She's very tough and we don't really get along. Mostly I don't deal with her anymore. Instead of facing the problem, I just don't bring up the problem. She's unhappy with everything I do. She just walks up to me, takes me by my neck, and starts telling me that everything's wrong with me. Then she just throws me on the ground and walks away. I have no idea how to deal with it.

Everybody at home just ignores me. When I come home looking sad, no one comes up to me at all. When I was young, all my mom's attention went to my sister and to my little brother, so I didn't get any attention. And I didn't get any encouragement for anything. I remember coming home one day with a perfect score on a test. I didn't even tell her, because I knew it wouldn't matter. I can't remember hugging my mom, ever.

If I could tell her whatever I wanted, I would say first of all that anything she doesn't like about me right now, one part is me, but the other part is something she did wrong when I was younger. I'm tired of blaming myself for everything. I don't think it's my fault, but I also don't ever want to be a parent myself because I'm afraid I'll do the same thing without realizing it.

People back away from me sometimes. I think they're afraid of the way I am, the way I act around school. I don't act up, I don't go around and insult the teachers or stuff like that. But I like to be upfront about things, and I don't like to tell people a bunch of stuff that's not true. So when we're discussing something in class, I bring something up and just stick with it. Even if nobody else is on my side, I stick with it, and so they think my thoughts are wrong and they start getting ideas in their head about the sort of person they think I am. I just like to get to the point, and I don't care what anybody says.

I'm in the eleventh grade, and there are a lot of kids in my classes whom I've never even talked to, but they all have these ideas about me and look at me with these faces. They give me stares, they stare me down to scare me. That way they can say that *I'm* afraid, when really they're just trying to hide their own fear. Especially after that school shooting, these kids started telling teachers that maybe I should be suspended for a few days, because they felt threatened by me. So the school made up an excuse to suspend me. They said I was disrupting class. I think I was talking in class and the teacher told me a couple of times to be quiet. But that's no reason to get suspended for three days. When that happened, I was really upset. I was really, really mad at the students first, and then at the teachers, who pretended they were on my side and then just turned their backs on me. They pretend to be your friend, then they look for any reason to get you in trouble.

These people who are afraid of me don't even know me at all. I don't really care about anybody at school; I don't care what they think. It does make me upset when they say things out loud, but I don't think I would waste my time telling them who the real me is. I just don't think I would want to waste my time. Really, though, I'm not a threat to other people. I've only really been in two fights at school. One girl who used to be a friend started making things up about me and telling people that I'm abused at home. Then she told some other people that I'd told her I was going to do something to hurt them. The other fight was when some kid just came up to me and started insulting me. I told him to shut up and get out of my face because I didn't want to deal with him, but then he pushed me. When they start shoving me around and doing stuff like that, then I don't waste time talking, I just do it.

If anything, I'm more of a threat to myself, and that's something people make worse by saying things about me when they don't even know me. That's what I get upset about, the assumptions people make. And when I get mad, I usually end up turning violent against myself. I hurt myself. I scratch myself. I'll be sitting at home thinking of everything that's happening, and it starts building up in my head. All of a sudden I just burst, and I'll punch the wall or scratch myself with a knife until I'm bleeding, and then that's it. Then I just sit and I calm down. I throw a fit and it's over like in five seconds.

Sometimes I just want to end it all. When something really good happens in school, I don't think about it, but most other days I come home from school and I picture it in my head. I picture me holding a gun to my head, and I start thinking, What if I didn't do it, what difference would it make? I don't cry, though. The last time I remember crying was in junior high school. I can't remember why.

When I'm feeling sad or upset, I hang out with my friends for a little while after school, then I go home. Usually they get the same kind of treatment at school, too. I'm not really the kind of person who lays everything out. I talk to them about how I'm upset with something, but I think maybe it's easier for girls to talk to their friends about being sad or upset. It's like they're sad, they're normal, they're girls: it's OK for them to feel bad about something. But guys are different. We don't tell people that we're sad. We tell people that we're angry or that we don't really care. We use anger to make it look like we're not hurting.

HELPING ZACK
Max, 15, from a suburb in the Northeast

Last year, one of my friends, Zack, wanted to commit suicide. He didn't want to live anymore because his parents were being mean to him. He said he just didn't have a great life. He told his very best friend, Matt, that he wanted to commit suicide, and Matt was just like "Whoa!" Matt told me, and I said we've got to tell other people and help him. Matt told three other kids that lived in his neighborhood and we all got together and went to see Zack. We just walked into his room and said, "We all know about this, but don't worry, we won't let you do anything because we're always going to be with you." And he said, "All right, you better not, because I might start thinking about it again."

So we did everything we could to have fun with him. We took him to amusement parks and paid for his tickets. As soon as it snowed, we'd go sledding with him and we'd make jumps. We made sure that he was never alone. Somebody was always with him, doing something with him, making sure that he wasn't by himself thinking about suicide.

After we'd been doing that for a while, all the kids who had helped him decided we had to go talk to his parents. We went over to his house before Zack got home, and we all said, "Do we really want to do this? It's a little freaky." Finally, Matt said, "Guys, we have to do this, we want to save Zack's life." And we all said, "All right. Let's go."

So we went in and Matt said to Zack's parents, "Can you sit down for a second?" So we all sat down and we talked. We told them what Zack had been thinking, what we had done, and what we thought they had to do to make Zack feel better. We told them, "You've got to be nicer to Zack, you've got to be nicer." Zack has two younger sisters and his parents were always nicer to the girls than to him. If his mom told one of the girls to go empty the garbage, she might say, "Oh, Mom, I don't want to." And his mom would say, "Zack, you go do it. Empty the garbage." So, when we said that to his parents, they immediately realized what they had been doing. They said, "We have been like that, haven't we?" When we were done, Zack's parents said, "Thank you for coming to see us, because if you didn't we might have lost our son."

His mom was bawling and she said, "I always wanted to be a good mother, but look what I've done!" And we said, "No, it's not your fault, it's just that Zack wasn't thinking straight." And she said, "Yes, but I made Zack think like that." And we said, "Well, now you can make things better."

Then his parents sent Zack to a psychiatrist, but he said it didn't really help. He said, "You guys helped me so much more than that psychiatrist." He's completely grown out of it now. He doesn't know how his parents found out, and we haven't told him. His parents have been nicer to him; they've really eased up. He says his life is so much better now.

After it was all over, the kids who helped Zack got together and talked about what we had done. We were thinking, "Oh, man, if we hadn't come along, what would have happened? What did we just do?" At the time, we all knew we had to do something. We knew we couldn't leave him alone. We knew we had to go to his parents. We knew we had to do this to save his life so he wouldn't kill himself. But the whole thing was pretty scary.

I don't think it's unusual for a bunch of guys to do something like that. We were all really good friends with him, so we got together and helped him out.

I'VE FELT LONELINESS AND PAIN
Rick, 18, from a city in the West

People have made fun of me since I was a little boy so by now I've become a bit of a recluse. It's been hard to talk to many people or go out and make friends. For a while I had a small group of close friends and no one else, but that close group started to dwindle as school went on. Then, one of my really old friends who had moved away came back and started showing me that I could interact with other people. Until then I was always basically alone.

When I've felt loneliness and pain, I used to deal with it by holding it in and trying to make it go away. This hasn't worked. I tried to kill myself a couple of times. I've done some other self-destructive things, like cutting up my arm.

The cutting helps for a little while. It takes my mind off the emotional pain by giving me physical pain. I know it's not healthy but there's nothing else I can do to stop the pain without getting to the point where I am completely suicidal.

The suicidal feelings come pretty often: not monthly but pretty close. I get into a low where everything is going wrong and I can't see past it. Once I tried to overdose on over-the-counter painkillers. Another time I tried to cut my wrists but I couldn't go through with it.

When I get really depressed, I call my friends. If it's really late at night, I try to wait it out and I just go somewhere, a corner or small, closed room, where I can think and be away from everything until I can call somebody. I don't like bothering people or waking them up if it's really late at night.

I just hate some things about myself, especially the fact that I'm dishonest. Sometimes I tell whopping lies to my friends and family to please them. I'll say I've done things when I haven't. For instance, I have to renew my license plates. My parents asked me to a while ago and I just told them I'd already done it. But I haven't because I don't have enough money to pay the registration fee. I lied to them because I don't want them to think I'm irresponsible or can't be out on my own. But, these little lies build up and make me feel worse and worse inside.

I think my depression is in part caused by my past. It really has a lot to do with past times when I have told lies and then everything has come crashing down on me. But it's also caused by my own mental instability. I have a lot of strange thoughts sometimes that seem absolutely crazy to me the day after I think them. Sometimes I feel like I don't exist and at other times I feel like the rest of the world doesn't exist. I sometimes see things in a completely different way from how I've seen them before, and it's like my whole reality falls apart and I have to rebuild it. It's really strange and hard to explain. It's almost like I feel I don't exist and life is just a dream.

I sometimes think my suicidal thoughts and my cutting have to do with the anger I felt toward the people who tormented me at school. A lot of the times when I'm cutting myself or causing myself pain I've just been thinking about a person who's recently hurt me or neglected me. I guess by hurting myself more, by cutting myself, I'm giving these people even more power. I'm allowing the people who hurt me verbally to also hurt me physically. I act in a sense as their tool, helping them hurt me.

So, I've been trying to react to my emotional outbursts in a more positive way. I've been trying to write poems when I feel really angry and upset. When I was working on the school newspaper I found that if I got angry with someone and I was working on a story I would pursue the story better. I'd go out and get the information, and I'd have more passion for it. I've now decided to turn to journalism when I go to college. It seems like a positive way for me to use my anger.

How Do You Tell If a Boy Is Depressed?

Boys tend to act out depression through myriad behaviors, some of which look the same as those traditionally associated with depression in women and many of which look different. Bearing in mind, too, that every depressed boy is likely to have symptoms that look different from those of the next—and that these symptoms will also vary depending on the specific age of the boy—you can detect depression in boys by watching carefully for the following:

Increased withdrawal from relationships and problems in friendships. Look for signs that the boy is spending less time than usual with friends and family. You may notice that he is becoming further disconnected from them emotionally, acting more and more like something of a loner. He may stop talking and respond to questions reluctantly. At home he may spend long amounts of time in his own room, shrinking away from interactions with other family members. At school, he may retreat from students and teachers and avoid participating in classroom discussions and activities.

Depleted mood or increased impulsiveness.   Look for signs that the boy is acting tired, dispassionate, bored, or depleted. He may stop showing interest or taking pleasure in activities he used to enjoy. Alternatively, you may notice that he is acting impulsively, unpredictably, or irrationally. He may seem more anxious or fearful than usual, perhaps reporting to you that he feels "nervous," "worried," or "tense."

Irritability or an increase in intensity or frequency of angry outbursts. Even the smallest provocation may lead the boy to become full of rage and to verbally or physically lash out at others. What may at first seem to be a boy's tendency to be "in a bad mood" may escalate into temper tantrums or frequent outbursts of anger or ongoing irritability. When a boy becomes persistently angry or "grouchy," he may very well be suffering a depression.

Increased risk taking, bravado, or acting out.   You may notice the boy acting out at school, showing up late, disrupting classes, or bullying other children. He may also take more risks or show bravado by doing things using poor judgment, such as driving a car at excessive speed or riding a skateboard down a steep hill without a helmet.

New or renewed interest in alcohol or drugs.   You may notice the boy begin to drink alcohol or take drugs, or to increase these behaviors. A boy who might have enjoyed a beer from time to time may begin binging until he is drunk. He may smoke marijuana regularly or begin experimenting with more serious drugs.

Discussion of death, dying, or suicide.   You may notice the boy initiating discussions or making casual or even joking references to death, dying, or suicide. This may be his indirect way of letting you know that he's not feeling good about himself, that he may be depressed or in danger of enacting suicide.

Increased aggression.   The boy may exude an overabundance of aggressive energy. He may act "wild," become difficult to control, pick fights, even intentionally injure others, all in an attempt to cover over sadness.

Concentration, sleep, or weight changes, or other unusual physical changes or symptoms.   The boy may find it difficult to concentrate on any one task without becoming quickly distracted or disinterested. He may have trouble falling asleep, wake up abruptly in the middle of the night, or awaken prematurely in the morning. Alternatively, you may notice that he often seems tired or sleeps too much each day. He may suffer eating or weight disorders such as anorexia, bulimia, or obesity. Also, he may report having frequent headaches, stomachaches, or other persistent physical symptoms.

Low self-esteem, harsh self-criticism, or perfectionism.   The boy may seem very unsure of himself and say things like "I'm such a jerk," or

"Nobody cares about me" and focus on his failures more than his successes. Alternatively, you may notice that the boy seeks perfection, focusing excessively on his appearance or on how well he is doing at school or in sports.

School or academic difficulties.   You may notice that the boy is having increased academic problems. His grades may plummet and he may get a poor conduct report. Look for signs that he is having difficulty concentrating on any one given task or applying himself to complete class work.

Denial of pain, denying others' help, or inability to cry.   You may notice that even when you ask the boy directly about difficult situations, he may deny he's feeling unhappy. The boy may appear unable to cry. Thus, for instance, if he is physically injured or is obviously in the middle of an emotionally traumatic experience, he may fail to shed a tear, appearing more stoic and hardened than usual. If you offer to help him, he may adamantly refuse.

Shift in sexual activity or interest level.   In the sexually mature boy, there may be either a pronounced increase or decrease in his dating behavior or sexual activity. You may notice that a boy who once spoke about going out on dates and forming relationships abruptly stops discussing these things. Alternatively, you may notice that he begins to seek out sexual encounters in an impulsive or excessive manner.

Inappropriate silliness or "clowning."   Perhaps to mask his genuine feelings of sadness, the boy may actually act silly or outrageous. He may be told that he is the class clown at school.

Obsessive overworking in school or in sports.   The boy may work obsessively on school-related assignments, spending all his free time working on homework, studying compulsively, avoiding contact with friends or family. If he is involved in athletic endeavors, you may notice him spending excessive amounts of time working out, doing aerobic exercises, or practicing at particular sports. These are attempts at distracting himself from his depressed feelings.

While it would be extremely rare for any boy who is depressed to exhibit all of these symptoms, it may also be unlikely that he'd exhibit just one. Typically, several of these symptoms will appear in a boy who is depressed. Yet because depression occurs along a continuum from mild to severe, you should not hesitate to take immediate steps to help the boy as soon as you detect *any* of the symptoms outlined above. With depression, it's better to be safe than sorry.

PART II

THE CYCLE OF RAGE AND VIOLENCE

10

TRAUMATIC VIOLENCE: LISTENING TO BOYS FROM LITTLETON, COLORADO

"If everyone knows each other, and can pretty much get along, then maybe these things wouldn't happen."
—Sean Graves, 16, Littleton, Colorado

"If I could say anything when people stare, I suppose it would be, 'What are you looking at? . . .' I feel embarrassed. . . . Then it occurs to me that this is what happened to Dylan and Eric."
—Sean Graves, 16, Littleton, Colorado

"I played the saxophone before, and that was important to me. I can only play half the notes now, so I don't generally play it anymore."
—Richard Castaldo, 18, Littleton, Colorado

THE BOYS I MET WITH EARLY IN 2000 IN LITTLETON, COLorado, have a lot to say to America. They have survived a trauma that they, and our nation, will not forget. Many were shot at directly; others cowered under auditorium or library seats, hiding from the snipers. Several were gunned down and left paralyzed, and are now in wheelchairs. Others were able to flee the gunfire but then went home to see the tragedy repeated endlessly on virtually every major national television network. All of them lost cherished friends and loved ones.

All remain emotionally scarred. Said eighteen-year-old Andrew Fraser: "I don't know if it can be repaired."

Both during the shooting that took place in April 1999 and right up until today, the boys of Columbine have been shocked into reexamining many of their assumptions about human nature. Their faith has been severely tested. These are courageous boys. But they are also boys desperate to understand why the shooting took place.

"I don't know where the devil comes from," Sean Graves said, shifting his body to get more comfortable in his wheelchair. "Maybe it's around us, or maybe it can be inside of us."

Some of the boys told me they finally were no longer afraid to go to school—although for a time the fear that the tragedy could replay itself was there. Others said they still have nightmares, that although the high school has been refurbished and student spirit has begun to return, they constantly feel terrified that something terrible could happen again. "It can get better," said an astute eleven-year-old, Brian Barenberg, "but I don't think it can ever go away completely."

The children of Littleton, Colorado, have of course been severely traumatized. Young Brian Barenberg is right—it probably will *not* ever go away completely. The young people, the community that goes through something like this is never quite the same. But the boys I spoke with spoke eloquently of their deep sadness and anxiety, their utter confusion during and after the incident, their paranoia about reprisal, their shock that fate chose *them* to educate a nation about violence.

"I'm pretty sure it could happen again," said sixteen-year-old John Bujaci, who spent several terrifying minutes trapped in an elevator during the shooting.

Andrew Fraser told us that it is still hard for him to return to a school where he was nearly killed: "It's been so bad some days that I'll actually call my parents and say, 'I can't be here anymore. I can't take this.' "

While a few of the boys spoke about the need for tightened gun control and more school security, most suggested that the merciless shootings probably had much more to do with how Eric Harris and Dylan Klebold were treated both at home and at school. Although the facts are still not clear to anyone, some boys surmised that the killers may have been disconnected from their parents and may not have received the loving supervision that would have caught the boys' pathology before it was too late. Most of the boys I talked with cast a critical eye on a peer culture that never welcomed Eric or Dylan, a culture (similar to cultures elsewhere for boys) of teasing, bullying, and hazing, a culture that increases emotional disconnection. Most of the boys I talked with felt this had become too much for two boys who simply never found a place among their peers.

When asked what advice they had for fellow students at other schools across the country, the boys emphasized that students should stop the teasing or bullying, that they had better make good friends and keep them. "Maybe a couple of times I used to bully some kids," John Bujaci said bravely. "I haven't bullied anybody since the shooting, though. I try to be nicer to people, even if I don't like them."

Sadly, many of the boys I spoke with did not seem to have had the chance yet to grieve fully over the trauma and loss they had experienced. While many had received counseling at school, at church, or privately, and though all of them spoke about the thoughtful steps Columbine High School has taken to secure the building and crack down on teasing and bullying, I sensed that many of the boys were eager for more opportunities to talk, to find deeper meaning or lessons to learn for the future about people and behavior—to talk through their reactions to the experience, express their fears and anxieties and cry it all out, or as much as possible, in the arms of their friends and loved ones.

Several boys remarked about how quickly things seemed to go back to normal, with "normal" being the expectation that they would steel themselves against their emotions, put the past behind them, "get on with it," and revert to life at school, where the teasing and peer harassment—despite the school's efforts and good intentions—would return. "The first two weeks after the shooting occurred, Columbine was one big family, one big group hug the whole time," said Andrew Fraser. "But after a couple of months of being back in school, everybody just kind of recirculated and spread right back into their old cliques. . . . I feel angry a lot of times because even after all that happened at our school, I still see stuff in the halls, a lot of poking fun behind people's backs."

Many of the boys we spoke with said how meaningful it was to be able to go to the slain students' funerals, because these services were some of their only chances to let down their guard and share how traumatized, how sad and afraid they truly are. "If you are around a bunch of people who are hurting just like you are, it's easier to show your feelings and deal with them," explained fifteen-year-old Dennis Majewski.

Yet the boys stressed that as completely acceptable as it was to emote at a memorial service or at a wake, back at school, life simply must go on, the tears must be held back, the sadness, as per usual, must be banished from public view. Despite being severely disabled by the shooting, Sean Graves told us, "I just pretend it never happened because no one really talks about it at school. They probably talk about it with each other, but not to me."

These brave boys have a lot to teach us about the kind of society we have become. They are clear, as we must be, that what they have experienced is not limited to Littleton, Colorado, but is endemic to America. For the tragedy they endured to have any positive meaning, we must listen to exactly what these boys are telling us. They describe a nation in which the media need to be more aware of the impact they have on the people involved in a tragedy; in helping a community to heal from a tragedy. They speak of a high school culture in which the pressure to be a "jock" can be so intense and the hazing so bad that violence is the only natural result. But the boys of Littleton, Colorado, speak about forgiveness, too. "As hard as it is, I can say that I do forgive them," Andrew Fraser said of the late Dylan Klebold and Eric Harris. "But they're not people I plan to meet with up in heaven."

RETRACING THE PATH

Andrew Fraser, 18, from Littleton, Colorado

My number-one favorite weekend activity is snowboarding, for sure. I've been doing it for about four or five years now, and it just gets better. I have a season pass at a place right in the heart of Sunny County, so it's close but a bit of a drive. That's the biggest activity I do with all of my friends, and we try to hit it up at least once a weekend. I enjoy it for the freedom, getting away from parents and rules and everything. You're kind of out on your own, just on the mountain with nature, so you don't have to really worry about anything else. Relaxing, yet at the same time it's a good adrenaline rush.

I'm eighteen and I will be graduating this year from Columbine High School. I'm kind of weighing my options right now, but I'm hoping to go to college in-state, somewhere that I can finish class and go hit the slopes for a couple of runs before I go to bed. I'll take it easy at first, and then maybe transfer somewhere else after a year or two.

At school right now my favorite class is psychology, the study of human behavior and why we think about and perform things the way we do, stuff like that. It's not just another subject that you're kind of dragging through to get it checked off the schedule. And one thing I'm especially interested in learning about is dreams and dream analysis, and whether it's just a whole jumble of mixed thoughts from the day, or whether dreams actually have significance as to something in your life.

I've had a lot of dreams that seem like they actually mean something, but I don't know if they really do. One was just a really brief and strange dream: I was driving a car somewhere, and there was a girl riding with me in the passenger seat. When I looked over at her, it was Rachel Scott, a girl who had been killed in the shooting last year. She was sitting there just smiling at me, and it was strange because it was really vivid yet so simple. I mean, she was in my dream, and it was like she was speaking to me through her eyes with some kind of reassurance. *Stop worrying about me. I'm OK. I'm actually happy.* Mostly the dream was saying that everything was actually okay, and for me to quit worrying about Rachel and everyone else who'd died, because they were in good hands.

That dream was emotional for me. I woke up literally in tears, just from sadness. It seems like it wouldn't mean anything, but I woke up crying. It was strange how powerful it was and how it affected me. I mean, I was far from being real close friends with Rachel, but she stood as a symbol of peace in my dream: the person who never caused any harm and was always a real fun, nice person to be around. I'm sure she knows how many people are still thinking about her and hurting really badly. I wish she didn't have to be sacrificed for the actions of others, those jocks and other people who never really took into consideration Eric's and Dylan's feelings.

I'm intrigued to figure out whether a dream like that really means anything, whether it's a higher sign or whether it's just, like I said, a mix of jumbled memories that somehow happened to pop up in my head that night. It was strange to wake up from that particular dream. I had absolutely no concept of time at all: like I had slept through the entire night and I was practically getting up to go to school, but I had only been sleeping for about an hour or so.

I've had other dreams related to the school shooting that were more about bomb situations and stuff like that. Most of them are hard to recall and don't really make much sense. In one of them, I had been at a local church with a whole congregation of kids. We heard an explosion go off, in the midst of everyone talking. Everything was kind of silent, and we all looked in the direction of where it had happened. There was a kid who stood up, and I think he was from my school, although I can't remember what he looked like. He just said, "Sorry, guys, that was me." He walked out of the room holding himself: he was bleeding out of his side.

I hope these dreams are not severe post-traumatic stress disorder or anything like that. I think part of it is worry, or just a recollection: stuff that troubled me coming back, not necessarily to haunt me, but more to disturb me.

When the shooting began, I was in concert choir with about 110 other kids, in the vocal music room. One student had left the room to get a drink, and he came back in the door with a really panicked look on his face. He said, "Mr. Andres, there are guys downstairs with guns. They are shooting." You just don't hear something like that in school, or just about anywhere that you are, so no one really took it seriously at all. We all thought it was some kind of joke.

Seconds later, we heard loud gunshots and screams through the soundproof doors. Through the glass window we could see a stampede of kids just flooding through the halls and pushing each other out of the way, just in a pure state of panic, running in every direction. Our choir teacher told everybody to get down on the ground, but that only lasted for about two seconds because we heard the shots getting closer, from right around the corner.

Mr. Andres said, "All right, get out of here!" and we ran. We ran across the hall and through the auditorium and got down on the floor. When we heard echoes of gunshots through the doors we ran again, because we thought someone was already in there shooting at us. When I left the auditorium, I saw the most vivid scene that I remember: on the way to the front entrance of the school there are two sections of double doors that are normally opened, but they had been closed, and there was a bullet hole that had gone all the way through one of them. Another one had stopped about halfway, so it was just a lump in the metal, and there was also a hole through the glass panel. I stopped to look through, and the whole hallway on the other side was filled with smoke. And I remember smelling really heavy gunpowder, then shaking and turning the other way to run out the front exit.

I ran with a group of kids all the way out to Taconda Park, where we tried to collect our thoughts and figure out what the heck had just happened. The feeling was like nothing I've ever felt before. It was just a pure state of panic and confusion. I remember reading about the shootings in Springfield, Oregon, and how some of the students had actually tackled the kid and taken him down to save the day. You think, "Wow, man, that's heroic. I wish I could do something like that," you know? I would like to have been a hero like that, but when it pops up on you that quick, your only instinct is to save your own life. That's one of the things I still carry with me a lot, the survivor guilt, wishing I could have done more to help out other kids instead of just running for myself. But when it started happening, I forgot about anyone else around me and suddenly had pure tunnel vision. I only thought about myself and my own life and just getting myself out of there, as opposed to worrying about anyone else. I just forgot about my best friends and said, "I need to get myself out of here."

In a state of panic like that, I feel that what 95 percent of the kids did was fend for themselves. But that's going to live with me for a while, just wishing that I had done a few things differently to help out other kids, or even that I could have been at the right place at the right time to stop one of the gunmen. Looking back, I almost wish I had sacrificed myself to stop them or to save as many other kids as I could. But at the time, I wasn't thinking along those heroic lines at all. I was pretty much just concerned for myself.

It's hard to give reassurance to other kids about something like school violence, since it's been proven that it can pop up anywhere and everywhere that you wouldn't expect it to, including in the middle of church. So, as far as dealing with violence and struggles with other kids, my advice is to try to keep your head up. I mean, obviously you're not going to be able to pick out all of the people who are potential suspects, so there is not really anything you can do to completely reassure yourself that nothing is going to happen. I don't really worry about it anymore myself, now that it's already been an experience for me. The odds aren't very likely for it to happen twice.

To deal with the shooting and everything after it, the best help I've found so far is my friends. I've talked to a few different counselors and my parents, but the conversation seems a lot shallower with them. I can't say exactly what I want to say because they'll tell me that they know how I'm feeling, they know what it's like. But they don't completely know; they're not exactly on the same track as me. With friends and other people who experienced the exact same thing, you can talk and say whatever. You know they're all living with the exact same thing and experiencing the same emotions about it. So the best thing that I've found to cope is just being open with it and trying not to keep it boxed in. Just saying whatever is on your mind to your friends.

Tragedies like this affect different people in different ways and at different stages, but a lot of times I will walk through the school hallways and feel like I am the only one who even remembers that it happened. It just seems like not a whole lot has really changed. There are still kids that are picked on and made fun of—people have stone emotions, like they have forgotten what happened already. For me, it's just really small details that I experience every day, like seeing a kid's face in the hall that reminds me of someone who died, or walking down the same hall that I had been running down before, literally retracing the path I had taken to escape the school. Small things occasionally catch my eye and shoot me back into the past, like looking at a door or a wall being repaired now but which I can remember with bullet holes.

EVERYONE STILL REMEMBERS
Brian Barenberg, 11, from Littleton, Colorado

When I was in first and second grades, there was this kid who always would make fun of me. He would just call me names, and I ignored him a lot of the time. I got really good at ignoring people. He was just mean, and I think it was because his parents were divorced and his dad was lazy and kind of mean, and he only got to see his mom like once a year. I think he was mad at that, so he took that out by being mean to me. I ignored him and told him to stop, but that didn't help. I told my mom, and the teachers knew about it, and we even both went to go see this counselor together. The counselor talked to us and suggested that he should try not to be mean for a week, and that then we would get to play a game. Well, we played the game and then it went back to normal, with him being mean. I never saw the counselor again. I kept complaining to my teacher and my mom. He got in trouble a lot, but it didn't really stop until his mom decided to move back here. Sometimes I think he was so sad, that's why he was so bad all the time.

What got me through being bullied was the fact of going home every day. My parents supported me by talking to me about it. I really like my dad, but he's at work most of the day. He likes to build things with wood, and a lot of times I just come down there and talk to him as he's making things. My mom is there to take care of me, and I really like her. We watch football on the TV together, and she sings to me sometimes. I like that.

I didn't really know anybody there at Columbine, but my brother, who's two years older than me, knew Patrick Ireland. Patrick got shot twice in the head, I think. When the shooting happened, we were kept at school and we didn't know why we couldn't go home. I don't think the teachers knew why either. We got to watch part of a Wallace and Gromit show. Finally around three o'clock, they said that there had been a shooting at Columbine, but they didn't really describe it. At first they thought that like twenty-five people were dead, and our parents had to come and pick us up because they didn't know where the shooters were. So my mom finally picked me up, and we went home and watched it on the news to see what was happening.

I had been mostly mad at first because I couldn't go home. Then I was confused because I didn't know why Eric and Dylan did it. I only kind of understand now. The gym teacher talked about it when some kids started yelling at each other in class. He said that the boys had had a lot of anger because lots of people didn't like them, and that's probably why they did it. He said we don't want to make people angry.

Another reason I was mad after the shooting is that me and my brother and some of my friends had liked to play guns, but that wasn't a very good thing to do at the time. We would have teams with three kids on each, and there is a tree house that one team defends and the other team tries to get in. It's like playing paintball, just with squirt guns. It's fun because you've got to hide and climb around. I like to do both of those.

Because of what happened, it didn't feel good to play with guns anymore, but it also made me mad that I couldn't do something I liked. Well, I could do it, but I didn't really feel like it anymore, because of what happened and the people who were injured and the people who died. It didn't feel right. I wanted to play, but I didn't want to play. It was confusing, but we decided on our own not to play anymore.

I was mad at the boys for not only hurting people but also for making everyone else around so sad. Everybody was really worried after the shooting, and I didn't like it. We talked about it a lot in school, about what our feelings were and the different ways that violence can happen. A lot of people said that they were sad and that they didn't know why. They also started this no-bullying program, with slips that you got if you were bullying somebody. Plus we got two cops for our school.

I think that a lot of people here aren't as afraid now, because it's already happened and they don't think it will happen again. I felt safer because it has changed a lot of people. They were a lot nicer, like they wouldn't make fun of people as much. But not all of the bullying went away, and it's pretty much gone back to normal by now. Some kids just really don't like some other kids and think that they're stupid, and so they make fun of them. And if some kids are kind of overweight or they're not really good at sports, they make fun of them.

I felt sorry for the people who knew the kids who were in there. Some people still have feelings about it, but most of it has gone away. Everyone still remembers it, though. It can get better, but I don't think it can ever go away completely. When we go to church, sometimes I pray that nothing will happen to the people that I love, because I would be really worried about that.

Sometimes I get really angry and I feel like I would want to hurt somebody. Like even if our team is losing really bad and the other team are being bad winners, yelling, "Yeah, we're so great." But I know I wouldn't hurt anyone, and I would tell other kids who feel angry like that to try not to get so worked up. The only way to be happy is to have good friends. Having people who like you can make a big difference in how you feel.

LOVE
Sean Graves, 16, Littleton Colorado

I live with both of my parents. I have a younger brother, Seth, who is thirteen. My parents work at Lockheed Martin, an astronomics company. Lockheed helped build the Mars lander that disappeared recently. My father is a computer security specialist. I don't know exactly what he does. And my mother is a secretary. I like space, but I'm more into electronics. I love computers, anything technological. I've been into electronics since I was a kid, that and cooking. My mom's a pretty good cook, but I'm not crazy about some of the stuff she comes up with, like leftovers, for example. When I cook, I always just make it up as I go along. I never follow recipes. I may look at a recipe, but I don't measure. I just dump it all in. I go by the feel of it.

If I was to list what I physically can't do now that I could do before, it would be a long list. But what I *can* do is get around. Learning to walk again is hard, because after the shooting, I was left with no strength in my legs. It was like being a newborn. The doctors immediately had me up in leg braces. I started off with zero skills and zero strength, but then I learned to crawl. I can crawl around the house a little bit now and go down stairs. The stairs are tricky. It takes a lot of strength, strength I didn't know I had, but I'm getting there. My upper body isn't affected. It's basically just my legs. I do have sensation in them. I can pretty much make my legs do what I want them to do, but they're weak. In the beginning, everything was weak, my feet, my legs, but now I'm getting strength back. I'm slowly, gradually getting my walking skills back.

I could cry. Like everybody, I could get real upset and say I can't believe this happened. There is always one bad day about every week, but I'm learning. If I start the day off on a bad foot, I think about all the good there is in my life and how I can overcome a bad thing. I try to make the best of what I've got. On the bad days, I want to avoid everybody. I wake up with the idea that people stare at me all of the time. If I could say anything when people stare, I suppose, it would be "What are you looking at?" I don't really know, though. It depends.

I feel embarrassed to be stared at, and I feel put on the spot. Then it occurs to me that this is what happened to Dylan and Eric. This is what everyone says drove them. I thought, Now all I need is the teasing, and Dylan and Eric's history will be repeating itself with me. I stop and tell myself, "This person is staring at me because they're curious about what's happened to me and how I'm dealing with it." There is a way in which my experience now of going to school and having kids stare at me reminds me of the same kind of teasing and bullying that Dylan and Eric got and that drove them to such a place of anger and rage. When I'm trying to walk, at times I get really angry because my right ankle will hurt and I get really ticked off at all that's happened, but I use that anger positively. I tell myself, *I'll show them!* Every time I try to walk, I am one step closer to being completely back on my feet.

When the shootings first took place, I didn't know what was going on. A huge group of us were eating lunch. The group was so big we needed extra chairs. We had sixteen people sitting around a table, but Dan, Lance, and I got up and went outside. The three of us left lunch early for some reason. We never do. The cafeteria door opens onto the rear of the commons. We were going up the hill when we saw the two kids with guns. At that point, we stopped. We were trying to figure out what was going on, and then I remembered a senior game that was being played at the time called Annihilation. None of us had ever seen it, but we knew it involved paintball guns.

In Annihilation, people shoot each other with paintballs in the parking lot. So we all figured these guys were using better-looking paintball guns than the little plastic gizmos that other people had been using. Then—I think it was Harris—the shorter one unloaded about ten rounds at the school from the hill. We were shocked. But I figured, maybe they were cap guns. Then they started shooting everyone. Suddenly, I was the last one standing out of the three of us. Dan got shot—I don't know where but he hit the ground. And Lance was shot in the foot and was also on the ground. Every one of us still thought they were shooting paintball guns, but we thought they were frozen paintballs because blood was starting to stain our clothes. I was grazed on the neck. I looked back to find the paintball but didn't see anything. As I turned my head back, shots sprayed across my gut. I was hit three times. At that point, I knew I had to get out of there. I turned and started running. I thought to myself, Why am I running from paintballs? I felt like a wuss for leaving my friends behind. I figured, If my friends can take it, so can I.

There was a six-foot chain fence that I had to get around to get back into the school. To tell you the truth, I don't know how the last bullet hit me. It looks like it hit the top of my backpack, nicked my spine, and then exited through my hip. It was the first shot that really hurt. I felt shock waves, like someone had knocked the wind out of me. I fell in the middle of the cafeteria doorway. Shock set in and I couldn't feel anything. A teacher started pulling me into the school. The lunch lady stopped her, because you're not supposed to move someone with a neck injury. I don't know if I was bleeding a lot. I assume so, but I couldn't really see. I kept thinking that I felt bad about leaving my friends behind. When I couldn't feel my leg, I thought I'd been shot in the back with a tranquilizer, so I was cussing up a storm. I wanted someone to

pull the tranquilizer out. I thought, "It's a tranquilizer! I hope you people suspend these two morons. This is crap. This isn't Annihilation. This
is stupid."

I didn't know about Dan. I never really talked to Lance about it, but
he was shot in the face with a shotgun. I didn't realize what was going
on. I was in shock.

Why do I think the shootings happened? I don't know. I think Dylan and
Eric were so overwhelmed with hatred toward people who teased them
for being different that they opened themselves up to the devil and allowed the devil to take over. I don't know where the devil comes from.
Maybe it's around us, or maybe it can be inside of us. It's like the two
little guys on your shoulder. One is a good conscience, and the other is
the part of us that could be full of hatred, or could do bad things. Which
one do you listen to? Maybe if we all treat each other well, and don't
make fun of somebody who was smaller or wimpier, then people would
listen to the good guy on their shoulder, instead of the bad one; but if we
beat up, tease, bully, hate, or abuse people who are different, for one
reason or another, they may be tempted to start listening to the bad guy,
the devil.

I think it could happen again. It could happen anywhere. There's
always somebody in the group, in any group, who's capable of doing
something.

If I had to suggest a solution, I would like to see people not treating
everybody so differently. If you see that somebody needs help, I'd
rather get the person help before he breaks down or does something to
hurt himself or anyone else. Instead of teasing or harassing a guy who's
weaker or smaller, people should try to understand that person and be
there for him and put themselves in the other guy's position.

There is pressure on guys to act tough, to be cool and fit in. I don't
know from personal experience, but I assume that if a guy shows emotion, he's accused of being gay. If you show emotion, you're being more
feminine. I don't think that's right. Some people like to talk things out and
others like to beat up on somebody rather than talk about it. To be honest,
I'm probably somewhere in between. I'll talk it out, but I still want to
punch a guy if he's said something that makes me angry. But I know it's
probably best to talk it out. Sometimes when my emotions get strong, I
might feel like lashing out instead of talking, but I'll catch myself and ask

myself, "What am I doing?" I tell myself that whatever it is, it's not that big of a deal. It's not worth getting hurt over or hurting someone else.

Dylan and Eric, not being tough or cool, were probably the sort of guys that people would call "wusses" or "gay." But rather than harass a guy who's different, whether he's black, gay, overweight, or whatever, you should get to know him first. A first impression is going to last, so it never hurts to go up and say hello or think about what it's like to be in that person's position, how it feels to be outnumbered and not know what to do because he's just trying to fit in as best as he can.

One day I'll forgive Eric and Dylan for what they did, but not now. In a way, I'm angry: they set out to hurt people. But then I think of the bigger picture—maybe it was just our time to learn a lesson. It's not that I believe in destiny, but I figure, why make this a total tragedy? It already is a tragedy to those who were lost.

I lost a friend in the shooting, Dan Rohrbough. I miss him. We used to hang out a lot at school. It is difficult at times to try and move forward with people who have all been through this in different ways. Other times, I don't really think about it and we're all just friends.

When I'm feeling down or lonely or angry, I turn to my parents or my friends for help. I can turn to both my parents, but when I'm feeling bad I mainly talk to my father, because he's been in a similar position. He understands.

When I was in the hospital, I wanted to leave and I couldn't. I was ticked off. My father sat down next to me on my bed and told me a story about when he had to go to war in Korea. He wanted to leave, too, but he stayed for an entire year. He could relate to being in a place where you don't want to be. My father was in the military police in Korea. He drove the general's car. He thought he'd stay in America and do his training here, but instead, they shipped him off to Korea. Being in a wheelchair feels like that, too; I'm in a place that I just want to get out of.

I pray every night before I go to bed. I pray that God will look after my family, and I thank him for all of the movement and strength that I've gotten back and hope that I'll continue to progress. During the night I don't often dream about being shot. I mostly have dreams of getting better. I'll dream that I'm walking or running and then I'll wake up, start to climb out of bed, and all at once remember, "Oh yeah, I forgot." I kind of laugh about it sometimes. I'll wake up needing to use the bathroom, begin to climb out of bed, and just as I'm about to fall on the floor, think, "Oh yeah, oh God." So I climb back in my wheelchair, go to the bathroom, and get back into bed.

The shootings have taught me not to take anything for granted. I focus on what I have rather than on what I lost. There are times I wondered what would have happened if I'd permanently lost all feeling and movement below the waist instead of being weak temporarily. Or what if my neck had been hit and I was completely paralyzed and in a power chair, not really able to do anything?

I'd tell guys who are nervous about going to school because of what happened at Littleton that as you get to know people, try not to be on somebody's bad side. If everyone knows each other, and can pretty much get along, then maybe these things wouldn't happen.

I try not to think about the shootings. I don't really get scared any-more. I just pretend it never happened because no one really talks about it at school. They probably talk about it with each other, but not to me. It's true that if you're a guy, some people figure, "Oh, he's a guy, he doesn't want to talk about it," but it depends. I don't think anyone knows what to say, so unless I bring it up, the subject doesn't come up. Some people at school have questions. And I don't mind that. They should know what it was like.

My number-one dream for the future is to be able to walk normally again. I also want to help people. That's what I've gotten out of this so far. If Eric and Dylan were in this room right now and I could say anything to them, I'd say, "You need help," because they really did need help. If I could go back to any point in time, instead of going back to find them with a fully loaded gun and killing them, I'd go back to when they most needed help, and somehow get it to them. That way, no one is lost. I'm pretty sure they're in hell now, but if I could have stopped it, I would rather have seen them getting along with people and not being so hateful.

I hope to fully recover, but I might as well learn from this experi-ence, so in the future, when I see somebody in a wheelchair, I won't stop to think only of how sorry I feel for that person. I'll remember how I survived, and I'll honor him, too. I'll see the person as courageous for not giving up.

If I could change anything in the world, I'd stop people from hating each other. I'd make love the law of the land instead of hate. But I don't know how to enforce that.

JUST BY CHANCE
John Bujaci, 16, Littleton, Colorado

I've been a student at Columbine for two years. The day of the shooting, I was in the cafeteria with a group of friends. We were sitting right next to where they had the two propane tanks. When it happened, at first we noticed a lot of people standing up to look out the window. Somebody said there was a fight or something, and I was like "Okay." But then we heard some firing of some sort. We thought maybe it was cap guns or something like that, a senior prank. And then the teacher came in screaming for us to get down. So everyone got down to the ground and stayed there for a while. Then someone screamed, "Everyone get out! They're coming in!" There was a mad rush for the door and the stairs. I got out pretty fast and ran toward the stairs and didn't look back. I was thinking about hopping over the railing, but people pushed me out of the way, they were so scared. I noticed a lot of people running into the elevator, so I went in. I just wanted to get out of the school.

The elevator was really slow, and at the time I wanted it to go fast. Kids were panicking, trying to get out, but it was pretty quiet inside. Some people were huddled really close together toward the back, trying to hide. The elevator took us up right next to the library, and Eric and Dylan had just gone past there, so we were glad then that the elevator had gone up so slowly. But when they saw the elevator doors open, they started shooting at us. One kid almost got shot as he was stepping out. So we got back into the elevator and went back down again.

When the doors to the elevator opened downstairs, Mr. Andres, one of the music directors, was standing at the door to the auditorium. He pulled us all in and we stayed there for about fifteen minutes. At that point there was a lot of confusion and I was just wishing I was somewhere else. People still thought it was just a stupid senior prank, because it was almost surreal. We weren't really sure what it was. All we heard was the noise.

I wasn't as traumatized as some other people. I wasn't trapped in there as long as some of my friends. One friend was in the science room for about three hours. He said that after a while that he got used to the sirens, and then when they finally shut them off, it was really eerie to not have them there. Some of my friends were shot, and one kid I knew a long time ago, Dan Rohrbough, died. One of my best friends, Sean

Graves, was injured. From what I could tell, at first he was really angry, and then he started to feel better. I don't really talk to him about it. It can be hard for guys to talk about that kind of stuff together. You've got a lot to live up to; you've always got to prove yourself.

Sometimes it's a good thing not to talk about your emotions too much, because then you can help other people out better. It can be bad, though, when the pressure builds up too much in you and you're about ready to snap. Then you could do something you shouldn't have done. I think that might be what happened with Dylan and Eric. From what I've heard, they didn't really fit in and people made fun of them. If people are bullied they should deal with it by ignoring it, but if it's constant, you need to let someone know, some staff member at school or wherever. A guy might bully other kids to show people that he is a guy, to prove that he's strong. So he beats up on other guys or he calls them a wimp, or he pushes them around. He makes himself feel more confident. Sometimes this causes the guy who is being teased or bullied to strike back. I would like to know why Eric and Dylan did what they did, why they thought people should suffer.

Sometimes it feels like everything's gone back to normal, until something else happens and the media just show up at our school. I sort of knew Littleton was going to be in the news, but after a while I was getting kind of tired of seeing ourselves on TV. They just wanted to get a story. They interviewed one of my friends and they changed their question into his answer and distorted what he really said. It made him sound like he was the bad guy, and that screwed his life over: the FBI took his hard drive off his computer and stuff like that. I don't really like the media. I think it would be better if, instead of sending in five hundred media people when something bad happens like this, they sent in five hundred psychologists and priests and people who are there to help you.

There are probably some people here who still need a little bit more help getting through what happened. They should turn to family, friends, people they know. Friends have helped me the most. The experience has made me more aware of what's going on, like what's happening around me and what other kids are doing. There is a lesson to "do unto others as you would have done unto you." Maybe a couple of times I used to bully some kids, like the ones who act like they are better than me. Mostly there would be fights that started off with something really small or stupid, but as time went on, we got more angry at each other and the conflict escalated. I haven't bullied anybody since the shooting, though. I try to be nicer to people, even if I don't like them.

It is kind of terrifying that something like that could happen, but I'm pretty sure it could happen again. To prevent that, I would raise the age for firearms and put laws on semiautomatic weapons. I would make more exits in the schools so it's easier to get out. It has become strict at my school now, and sometimes it's good but sometimes it's not. They put little signs on the doors saying that if you go through here, or if you prop it up for people to come in, you can get suspended. They also have a police officer in the main office now, but he just sits there and watches people walk in and out. It's really not hard to bring weapons inside. But tightening security is not the best solution anyway. I feel that if we all get the message to look after the people who don't get that much attention, then maybe this won't happen again.

What happened at Columbine was just by chance. You go to school and nothing could happen, or you go to school and something could happen. You don't know. You just have to take your risks, and there is no way to change that risk. It can either happen or not happen. It comes down to keeping guns out of people's hands, and stopping the bullying and teasing.

SHOCK
Dennis Majewski, 15, Littleton, Colorado

The worst moment in my life so far was the whole Columbine thing. When it happened I was at school, and nobody would tell us what was going on. They just locked down the school and we couldn't go outside. We didn't know what was going on, so we all had a bunch of stuff going through our minds. We didn't know what was going on.

My mom works at the parish that is attached to my school, and she went with the pastor to where all of the parents were waiting for their kids. I got home and I was alone. I heard some stuff on the radio on the way, but I still didn't know what was going on. When I checked my messages, I had a ton of them from everywhere, mostly from my relatives on the East Coast. And I still didn't know what was going on. So I turned on the TV, and it was all over the news.

From playing soccer and other sports, I had a bunch of friends and acquaintances at Columbine. I was wondering about them, worried that they might be hurt. One kid on my soccer team, I wasn't sure whether he went to Columbine or Chatfield. I was hoping it was Chatfield, but I wasn't sure. He ended up getting killed.

That evening we had a prayer service and retreat at church that had already been scheduled. I went because I still didn't know many facts; I didn't know if any of my friends got hurt. My mom was there, and she told me that one of my friends, a friend of the family who lives down the street from us, had been shot and was in the hospital. We didn't know if he had been killed or just hurt. It turns out he was the kid who crawled out the window.

At first, I was just shocked. I didn't know what to think. I said to my mom, "If you hear anything else, just come back and tell me again, and I will wait." So I stayed at church, so she would know where I was. It ended up really helping, because all my friends were there for me. They understood that I was hurting, so I could just cry and let my feelings out. We broke up into small groups and talked about what was on our mind; that's where I let everything go.

In the days after that, there were all sorts of memorials and funerals. My sister ran in a race that was a fund-raiser for the victims' families, and she raised about five thousand dollars. I was pallbearer at my friend's funeral. His father was the coach of our soccer team, and the whole team served as pallbearers. It was hard, but it was nice to have that private chance to come together and say good-bye to him. Everything was happening so quickly with the media, but they wouldn't allow any cameras at the funeral.

Usually you don't cry out in public if you're a guy. You might see girls crying at school because they broke up with a guy or something like that, but you don't see guys doing that at all. If you're a guy, you just don't feel right crying. I am sure that everybody would be nice to you and help you through it, but you just can't do it. It's a pride thing.

Columbine changed all that in some ways. It definitely brought the community closer together. For example, our soccer team really came close together this year, because we did a lot of stuff together. It was really good just being with everybody and seeing that they were hurting, too; knowing that I wasn't alone, that everybody was kind of going through the same thing. If you are around a bunch of people who are hurting just like you are, it's easier to show your feelings and deal with them. So when this terrible thing happened in Littleton, and there were other guys feeling that same sadness, it was okay to show people how you were feeling. Girls are much more comfortable, I think, about being open. Guys can sit around with a close friend and talk about anything, but girls can talk to pretty much anybody about anything.

I'm trying to move on from it now, and I'm not really feeling those feelings anymore. I'm still sad about it but it's not like I'm going to cry over it again, unless something happens. It's hard to live with but I have to do it, so I might as well do it to the best of my ability. I would definitely take it back if I could, but I can't go back in time so I may as well live through it. I'm not trying to forget about it, but just to stop thinking about it all of the time. I've been putting it in the back of my mind. It's still there, but not as much. Every once in a while I'll still talk to my friends about it, like if something comes up on the news about it. We all try to be helpful to each other.

My dad used to be a teacher at Columbine, so he knew a ton of people there. He knew Dave Sanders, the teacher who died, and a whole bunch of other teachers who were there. The principal, Mr. DeAngelis, is a really good friend of the family. And my mom was pretty close there, too, because of my dad; she knew everybody. So it really affected the whole family, and dealing with it brought us closer. We talk to each other more, and we're more careful to make sure we communicate with each other, to remain connected.

I have a bunch of friends who are freshmen now at Columbine, and they tell me that if you say anything wrong, like make fun of someone, they can report you and get you suspended. The school has really cracked down on teasing, and it's harsh but I don't blame them at all for what they're trying to do. They don't want it to happen again. Because the teasing was definitely part of what made Eric and Dylan do it. They were made fun of, and they didn't have any other way to take out their anger. This was the only way they thought they could get it done, by taking other people's lives. It's almost like just a couple of dumb kids who didn't know what they were doing. They were just angry and they didn't know how to let their feelings go.

I heard from the media that Eric and Dylan weren't very close with their parents at all. They were making the bombs in their rooms and their garages, and their parents didn't even know about it. So how can you take out your anger in any safe way? You can't tell your parents about it, because they don't care. At least, that's what the media made it sound like. I'm not sure if that's what it was like or what.

Guys should stay close to their families, be nicer to people in general, not make fun of people. Treat everyone as equals. Don't think they are lower than you because you play sports, or because you're strong, or fast. Some guys are sort of afraid of their own anger in a way now, because of what happened. They think they might be able to do the same thing themselves, or at least have the same feelings as Eric and Dylan. I would say to them, Tell somebody if you feel like this at all. You have to talk to somebody. Talking about it is important, and if you can't talk to your parents about it, like these kids couldn't, go to a friend or a counselor or a teacher. But Eric and Dylan weren't close to their parents at all, so where else could they have gone?

These days I go to church every Sunday and try to go to youth group as much as I can. A lot of the kids in youth group go to Columbine, and they help me understand the situation better. Religion has really helped me a lot during this situation. We pray through things together.

When I pray, I thank God that I'm still here, that it didn't happen at my school, that I wasn't there that day. I pray that my friend has gone to heaven and that he will be all right, and that his family will be all right in dealing with this. I pray that everything can kind of be back to normal and that all of the media would leave, so we could deal with it ourselves. I pray that all of my friends and family will be all right and that I can stay close with them, that we can overcome whatever comes our way.

A LOT DIFFERENT THAN I THOUGHT
Richard Castaldo, 18, from Littleton, Colorado

On the day of the shooting, I was eating lunch with Rachel Scott. I can remember somebody coming in and shouting that there was a bomb. Right then the bomb went off, but it didn't do anything. But then after that, there was shooting. I didn't have time to run or duck or anything. It was just so sudden.

I remember lying there for twenty or thirty minutes before someone came to take me to the ambulance. I was lying there hoping somebody would come over and make me better. I just tried raising my hand. The SWAT team came first, and they sent me to the police car, which took me over to the paramedics.

I don't exactly remember the surgery. I remember my dad being there in the critical care unit afterward, but I don't know how long I had actually been in surgery. They hardly said anything in CCU about my condition. I think they just said I was doing all right. I didn't even really know what had happened, exactly. I just knew that I felt pretty bad, but I wasn't really exactly sure what it was.

When I was in the multitrauma unit, someone told me it had been a shooting, and it was hard to believe at first. It was a weird feeling. Being shot was a lot different than I thought it would be. The first couple of seconds, it seemed like my whole body froze, like I couldn't move anything. I was in shock, or something like that.

I didn't really know everything that went on until about two or three weeks later. I want to say my dad told me, but I'm not completely sure. I was like "What? There was a shooting?" I couldn't understand how anybody could conceive it. I tried to figure out exactly why they would do something like that. I didn't even know their names before. I saw them in the hall a few times, and that was it, basically. If I had one wish right now, it would be to know what could provoke people to do something like that.

Columbine High School was pretty normal before all this happened. I think everybody pretty much knew each other. Eric and Dylan just got lost in a sea of people. All I know about them is what other people have said. I guess they were extremely good friends and had shared all their feelings between each other and never told anybody else about it. They got isolated, and I would say they must have been pretty angry. "Pretty angry" is probably an understatement. You'd have to be pretty angry over a long time to do something like that. But nobody else knew because they must have been hiding their actual feelings.

I think the argument that Eric and Dylan were angry because they were being bullied and being teased makes a little bit of sense, but it's not the whole story. I think they wanted to be like that. If they decided not to be bullied and teased, they could not have been bullied and teased. They would have found a way out of it, but I don't think they wanted to find a way out of it. Or their way out of it was to go insane and kill a bunch of people. I don't know. I think to do something like that, they must have been out of their minds. Why else would they want to do it? They probably decided they wanted to do it a long time ago, and so they just let all that anger and stuff build up inside of them. I think if you have it in your head to kill a bunch of people, there's really nothing that can stop you.

At the hospital, there was a pretty big outpouring of emotion. I was able to be more open with my parents. We have a close relationship, and of course they were both upset about what happened. It seems to be a little easier now for me to tell them I love them.

I'm not sure if I've talked about my feelings as much with my friends. I mean, I never actually cried in front of them or anything like that. I probably could if I wanted to, but it's a harder thing for guys to do, even when tragedy happens. In our society, you're not really supposed to do that.

Physically, I can pretty much do everything I could before. I'm basically independent, although I'm still doing more rehabilitation with my hands and stuff. I played the saxophone before, and that was important to me. I can only play half the notes now, so I don't generally play it anymore. They said it should come back pretty much all the way, like after maybe a year or two. I'm playing the tuba right now in concert bands. It only has three valves on it.

I don't waste my time thinking about Eric and Dylan. I figure they're being taken care of by someone else. And if I put too much thought into it, I'd probably be depressed. I just try to focus on being independent and think about the future more than the past.

I don't know if religion is a thing for me anymore. I think I'm getting kind of scared of God lately. He doesn't quite make any sense. With all those other shootings, it makes me wonder if there is a God. How can there be the kind of God we usually learn about who lets these kinds of things happen?

What's helped a lot is that I have a really supportive family. My mother and my father, and all my aunts and uncles, too. It makes a big difference. My mom and dad have been divorced since I was pretty young, like four or five. Before all this happened, I was living with my mom in Littleton and I'd go see my dad in Virginia for vacations, maybe a couple of months out of the year. Then after all this happened, he bought a house here, too. He has been here a lot, and that's helped out a lot.

School is going pretty good. It helps to get some normalcy back. The other kids are pretty helpful, really. There is some bullying and teasing again and I'd say it's mostly guys who do it. They'll pick someone who looks different from them, or has different stuff than they do.

I would tell guys who are worried about the same thing happening in their own school to get by as best as they can, and not be worried. I think putting your thoughts down on paper helps a little bit, too. I used to write in a journal but haven't in a while. I guess I probably should.

I Don't Think We Can Ever Really Forget
Chris Hoffner, 11, Littleton, Colorado

I go to elementary school in Littleton, and when the shooting at Columbine happened our teachers didn't tell us what was going on. They just told us that we had to stay away from the windows. Everybody thought that it was just a police chase or something. Our parents all knew what was happening, and they were all in a line outside waiting to pick us up. At the front office they had to sign a checklist and then one of the cafeteria ladies would go get us from our class so we could go home. It was strange and confusing. Eventually, I heard somebody say they found out that a girl had been shot around Columbine or something. Nobody really knew the real story about what was happening, so we were all wondering if it was just a rumor. It was hard to believe. But on the ride home from school, my dad told me what had happened. And then we turned on the TV, and it was all over the news.

I remember feeling sad, thinking of why a person would do that. I was kind of scared, wondering if something like that would happen at my school or when I became a high school student at Columbine. After what happened, everybody has been careful. At our school now, you can't just walk in and tell the office that you're going to go to your son's class. You have to sign yourself in and get a visitor card. And every time the aide sees you do something wrong, like throw something at somebody or call them a name, they'll write you up. And if you get a certain amount of those, you don't get to do special activities and things.

I think Eric and Dylan were angry at not being popular. I can understand a bit what that feels like. You have a little group of friends, and there's always a big group of other people walking around and making fun of you. Some of my friends will call me bad names sometimes, and I just tell them to stop and walk away from them. They're just saying stuff, and if I just walk away, they'll leave it alone. Or if they don't, then I just ignore the person and go do something else without them. Sometimes I might feel like I want to yell at them, but I did that once and then they just teased me more because they knew they were getting to me. And that's what they want.

There are some kids that really get picked on a lot. A group of three or four or five might just decide to do it, and they just keep doing it. Guys will hassle and hit other guys just to look cool and tough. It makes them feel big and important. It would be better if people could be popular and cool for what they like to do, not just how tough they seem.

Guys think they can deal with things by themselves but it's different with girls. Girls go tell somebody what's happening. Plus, they don't tease each other as much.

When the shooting happened, everyone in town was calling each other. Patrick Ireland lived on my street and my mom gave his mom her cell phone, so they could call around to figure out where he was. They didn't know that he was still in the school.

People were upset and sad for a long time afterward. In my family, my mom would be gone for a while sometimes, helping out and visiting people. My dad stayed home from work for a couple of days because he wanted to stay home with me and my sisters, so we could be together.

Even now, I get upset when I think about it. I cried when it first happened, and sometimes I still do. I don't usually talk with my friends about it. It was so sad, they don't want to have to keep bringing it back up and reliving it all over again.

But I don't think we can ever really forget about it.

11

THE COLUMBINE SYNDROME:

FEAR OF VIOLENCE

"I don't want to be that type of kid who comes to school and just takes out a gun and starts shooting."

—Bobby, 12, from a city in the West

"The other day I walked into school and a girl was carrying balloons and one of them popped. Everyone in the whole school got really terrified."

—Errol, 17, from a suburb in the West

"I think there are people at my school who have the potential for doing something similar."

—Jules, 17, from a suburb in the South

"People were coming up to me and begging me not to kill them. I felt like telling them: 'Cut it out; I'm not going to do anything.' "

—Cody, 14, from a suburb in New England

"You can't say 'them' or 'you.' You have to say 'us.' "

—Jimmy, 16, from a small town in the West

VIOLENCE HAS MADE AMERICA MORE AFRAID OF BOYS. IT has also made boys more afraid of *being male*. Though it has been understood for decades that the perpetrators of most violent crimes in our nation are male, the recent spate of school shootings—culminating in the heinous massacre of teachers and students in Littleton, Colorado—has made us ever more frightened and confused about the threat of extreme violence and its connection, in particular, with boys. Adolescent boys, boys just like the ones who contributed to this book, are the ones pulling the triggers and injuring, sometimes killing their peers and teachers. What many people do not realize—and what the media following Columbine have failed to portray—is that most of the *victims* of teenage violence, indeed the vast majority, are also boys.

The impact of these terrifying crimes has been immense. It has led to the "Columbine Syndrome": students, parents, and teachers across our nation are absolutely terrified about which boys among them are violent, about who the next perpetrators might be, and about who their victims will be. Paranoia is rampant. Schoolchildren and the adults around them are constantly canvassing the student body and worrying, often inappropriately, that some students may be murderous. Across America boys are being subjected to written testing programs that purport to predict violence, the installation of intrusive gun detectors in the entrances to their schools, and alarmist lockdown or so-called Columbine drills, all of which are meant to increase safety but actually exacerbate boys' confusion and anxiety. Grady, age seventeen, from a school in the South, says, "When a kid's wearing a trench coat and he's going for something in his jacket, you learn from watching the news that more than likely he might have a gun."

The consequence is that boys themselves are becoming increasingly afraid. They are frightened not only of being victimized by the rage and violence of other boys, but also of being accused, or falsely accused, of having the disposition it takes to snap into hyperviolent action and embark upon a murderous rampage. Boys fear that despite their true nature, they will automatically be seen as somehow toxic, dangerous, and culpable because they are boys. As one young preadolescent boy said, "I think women like small kids. Girls like newborn babies. They don't like big people. We bigger guys scare everybody and then we get blamed even when we've done nothing wrong."

Boys are also afraid of the violence they may feel inside themselves and of whether it is safe to talk about it. As they internalize this fear of being misunderstood—and of being charged with having a violent temperament they genuinely do not have—boys themselves are beginning to worry if maybe, just maybe the demon is within. They fear that lurking underneath their conscious understanding of themselves there might be an uncontrollable urge to commit depraved acts of violence. The Columbine syndrome means that America's boys today are as confused about violence as they are afraid of it. *They fear each other and they fear their own selves.*

While the statistics indicate that teenage boys not only commit a considerable percentage of the nation's violent crimes but also become the frequent victims of those crimes, in reality there does not seem to be some inherent biological factor that makes boys more violent than their female counterparts. Violence committed by and acted out upon boys seems to stem, more often than not, from what we teach (or don't teach) boys about the behavior we expect from them. It comes from society's set of rules about masculinity, the Boy Code, which says, "To be a man, you must show your strength and your power. You must show that you can hold your own if challenged by another male. You can show your rage, but you must not show any other emotions. You must protect your honor and fight off shame at all costs."

Think of it yourself. When a boy becomes slightly angry as a means of expressing his pain, there will be mixed emotions. Some of us may show some fear, but if the anger is under control, we're unlikely to respond in a drastic manner. As long as it is "within bounds," society tends to approve of, if not encourage, aggression by and among boys. Violence in boys is widely (although, as I've said, incorrectly) seen as inevitable, if not biologically preordained. As long as nobody is seriously hurt and no lethal weapons are employed—especially within the framework of sports and games—aggression and violence are widely accepted and even encouraged in boys. Society is complicit: winning a game, or even a fight, helps many boys gain respect.

The corollary to this message is that soft, gentle, nonviolent boys are considered feminine and therefore losers. While we often pay lip service to helping boys "put feelings into words" and even create multimillion-dollar educational programs to address this, boys will tell you that if you're "a big guy" and start to express your vulnerable emotions too openly, people crawl back in fear. Imagine the boy who misses a goal and bursts into tears on the soccer field. He is not considered masculine. Peers call him a "girl," "sissy," or "fag." Parents cringe. It is precisely in this environment that even the most hearty boy soon learns to avoid showing his pain in public. He may want to cry, he may wish he could speak about his fear, sadness, or shame, but he holds it back. He resists. Instead, he displays anger, aggression, and violence.

Perhaps it should not shock us, then, that what we hear from the boys in these pages is that while they overwhelmingly condemn extreme violence, and to a large extent do not engage in it, they can understand and empathize with the boys who hit, hurt, and even kill. They tell us more about what the teasing and razzing "can do to your head," how alone and isolated they can become, and how rage is indeed often the only sanctioned emotion that doesn't produce further ridicule. We are all afraid of boys and violence, but boys, it turns out, are the most fearful. Gun detectors, violence-screening tools, armed guards, and "zero tolerance" only goad our sons into the very aggression we, and they, are afraid of. By expecting boys to be angry, rambunctious, and dangerous, we push them to fulfill these prophecies. This is the essence, I believe, of the Columbine Syndrome. By living in fear and expecting danger, that's exactly what we produce.

To compound the risk to all of us, society is now giving boys another complex and confusing message. It is what I call the "no black shirts" response. Because the Columbine killers were outcast boys, spiteful, nonconforming boys who wore dark clothing and were estranged from their peers, society has now rushed to the conclusion that adolescent boys who seem "different"—especially those who seem quiet, distant, and in pain—are the likely perpetrators of the next ghastly Columbine-like crime. Sadly, what the huge majority of outcast boys need most—in fact, what many so-called popular boys, boys on the "inside" often desperately need as well—is not to have their pain suppressed and disregarded, but rather to have it listened to and understood.

Boys in pain require immediate intervention. As soon as we detect that a boy is experiencing emotional distress, we need to stop what we're doing, turn toward him, and hear him out. Whether he is wearing a black hood or a Brooks Brothers sweater, whether he is well liked or an outcast, he needs us to come toward him, embrace and affirm him, and assuage his hurt feelings before they push him to the edge. Boys are simply not inherently violent or dangerous, and the emotional distress they may feel, in the first instance, does not make them any more so. But if we continue to give boys the message that expressing their distress is forbidden, that we will ignore their vulnerable feelings when we see them, and that we actually expect them to act out angrily and violently, we should not be surprised that the world becomes, for all of us, a mighty frightful place.

The solution, I believe, is for society to commit to a whole new way of seeing boys and violence. First, we need to decide, unequivocally, that as much as we will not exalt boys who fight, we will also not punish or ostracize those who show their vulnerability. By defending and actually providing positive reinforcement to boys who openly exhibit their moments of fear, longing, anxiety, and despair, by telling these boys and men that they are fully "masculine" no matter what emotions they share with us, we can help them avoid the repression and resistance that may make them bottle up their emotions and then spill them out in irrational acts. Second, because society may not change overnight, we need to be on the lookout for the signs of sadness and depression that in boys and men so often seem harder to see, or more difficult to believe and accept. In *Real Boys* and in this book (on pages 167–69), I outline these many signs. If we are attentive to them, and if we help boys overcome the pain and disaffection that gives rise to them, much of the aggression and violence we now see will evaporate or be directed toward safe, appropriate channels.

Finally, we must simply decide that most boys, as angry or aggressive as they may become, are highly unlikely to become dangerous in any way. The boys' voices in this chapter offer overwhelming proof that most of our sons have a nonviolent nature and that, in reality, their greater struggle is with sadness and the fear of violence rather than with violence itself. Perhaps if we listen to how boys fear violence, and read these stories with a new empathy, we may be able to reach across the boundaries of that fear and create a new dialogue of peace. For boys and for all of us, the only cure for the Columbine Syndrome is to develop safe spaces that will create genuine security.

IT COULD HAPPEN ANYWHERE
Grady, 17, from a suburb in the South

My cousin is a freshman at my high school, and he saw this kid wearing a trench coat with his hands in his pockets. My cousin got scared when he saw that, because it looked like the kid was going for something in his pocket. When a kid's wearing a trench coat and he's going for something in his jacket, you learn from watching the news that more than likely he might have a gun. I think about what happened at Columbine and other schools sometimes, but I try not to worry about it.

There's a difference between a fistfight between two kids and drawing a nine-millimeter out and shooting people down. The difference is sense, common sense. Fistfights are spontaneous things, squabbles in school, nothing to get upset about. Kids are going to fight. I used to fight with my brother. To kill someone, though, takes a deranged mind of some sort. I just don't comprehend how someone could actually pull out a gun and start laying people down. It's more than just rage. You can get angry, and then there's something else that pushes you over the edge to act on that anger. There's probably a certain incident in their life that turned them on a different path, that hardened them. Like being abused or something. There's got to be an element added that pushes someone over the edge from anger to violence toward someone.

I think that what happened in Columbine could happen anywhere. If it could happen in a suburban, little Midwestern town, why couldn't it happen here in the city? A bunch of things cause that sort of violence, like loneliness, frustration from getting picked on, being an outcast.

I've been teased before, too, but I don't have the capacity to kill someone. I'm too sensitive a person. All my relatives go hunting, but I can't even bring myself to kill an animal. I think that's why those boys killed themselves after they were done. They just couldn't handle what they did. I think they chose death instead of having to live with it.

People I'm acquainted with will say stuff about wanting to do the same sort of thing. "I'm going to go get my gun, I'm just going to shoot this girl," stuff like that. It bothers me a little bit, but I try not to think about it. I've never seen a weapon at school, but I know people who have access to them, who have brought them in before. Switchblades, bowie knives, rifles, handguns. Most of the guys here hunt. I have access to guns, too. My uncle, he's a big hunter.

I think metal detectors are a good idea, but that isn't going to stop something from happening. There will always be outcasts and people teasing them. Since they pulled it off at Columbine, people will always try to do the same thing themselves. If everyone keeps things bottled up inside, someone's going to snap one day.

No One Is Perfect
Ricardo, 11, from a suburb in the Northeast

I would never be angry enough to kill anybody. If I were that angry, I would have to be prepared to die myself. Because if you shoot somebody, you don't know if you're going to die, too. Suppose the person you want to kill is standing on the Great Wall of China. You might try to jump at them, but they could move out of the way. Then you're going to fall straight down, and you probably won't make it. You probably won't walk anymore.

Sometimes I think shooters just do it for attention. It's not right to kill somebody who didn't do anything to you. You should only kill them for a good reason. Before you kill them, they have to almost kill you, and you still have to have a good reason. And if you do want to kill them, you have to be prepared to die yourself. Suppose you shoot at a person you want to kill and you miss, they might come back at you and kill you. You can shoot a guy in the leg, and he still won't die. Or let's say you're trying to hit somebody with a car you're driving. He might jump off a bridge and land in the water and swim. And your car might go in the water; it might blow up, or start sinking, and you might suffocate because the doors are hard to open. If you have a knife and stab somebody in the neck but don't kill him, you don't know what might happen. One day, that guy might get you back.

I have some friends that get really angry, but I don't think they would try to kill anybody. They might get mad, but I would tell them to get over it because it's not worth it. You might think you're tough, but there is always someone better than you. There is always someone stronger, someone faster, someone smarter. No one is perfect in this world.

I COULDN'T BELIEVE WHAT HAPPENED
Greg, 18, from a suburb in the West

I couldn't believe what happened at Columbine; it was a really big shock. A lot of kids at my school went to counselors in tears, very emotional. I still don't see the reason in their actions. Everybody blames TV. There was a court case where a young boy shot his younger sister because he was watching *Beavis and Butt-head,* and they blamed it on the show. But I can't see how that works, because if the media and TV affect a kid that much, then there have to be some parental problems. If they're getting that much influence from TV and not from their parents, then there's something wrong there; the parents are not doing their job. And I guess I would say that was the problem at Columbine. I'm surprised, though, that there was so little parental guidance that they were able to go around and put the whole thing together.

William Butler Yeats wrote a poem, "The Second Coming," that I studied in my English class. I can't remember the entire thing, but the first two lines are "Turning and turning in the widening gyre / The falcon cannot hear the falconer." In my class presentation, I likened the falcon to the children of our society today, and the falconer to the parents. Kids can't hear their parents. They don't get as much guidance as children have had before from parents, and I see that as a big problem. Nowadays the children and the parents are getting so separated. Even in this technological age, we need to keep that connection. With Columbine, I think it was a combination of not being accepted at school and a lack of parental guidance. Had there been more parental guidance, more love, more contact, they probably wouldn't have done what they did.

There are things in this world that I would be willing to stand up and fight for. To be free, to be able not to live in fear. To just be able to do what you want within reason, and have fun, have a good life, and stand up and fight for your goals and what you believe in. Freedom is very important to me, maybe because my mom and a lot of the programs at school have given me a lot of space. My mom gives me a lot of responsibility. A couple of days ago she got back from spending a week in Pennsylvania and New York, and she had left me alone. She has trusted me like that for four years now, since I was thirteen. I think that if you've taught your children well enough, you can give them that trust without being afraid that they'll abuse it.

I CAN UNDERSTAND

Vincent, 18, from a suburb in the West

I can understand some of the pressures facing the kids who did the shooting at Columbine. Just going to high school every day and being taunted by everyone and being shunned because they didn't conform . . . that would create awesome pressure in most people. I could see how in an extreme case it could get to the point where a student might snap. I don't in the least condone their actions but I do appreciate the pressures they might have been under. I've faced experiences that might have been similar to theirs and many days at school I wished certain people dead. But that doesn't mean I would ever want to kill or hurt them. What I really wanted, of course, was for these people to be less cruel and more kind.

When I was in high school, I wasn't a member of any clique. I tried to be friends with everyone. And it worked while I was with people.

People from different cliques would act friendly with one another when I was there—but once I left the divisions would come back. It's nice to be in a clique and feel like you belong but there are advantages to not being in any clique. For instance, you can be flexible and free to be friends with whomever you want.

I think the high school cliques had a lot to do with what happened at Columbine. The two boys who killed all those people were ridiculed by everybody. They were different. They were in a group by them-selves. So all of the other groups would make fun of them because they were different.

After Columbine I didn't worry that the same thing could happen at my school. Some kids at school acted up after the killings. But I'd been with the same group of students since kindergarten and I knew them very well. Everyone at my school had at least one good friend and was in some group or another. I don't think anyone was as isolated as the Columbine shooters were.

WATCH OUT, HE'S GOING TO SHOOT EVERYONE
Cody, 14, from a suburb in New England

What I hate about this school is that I'm being picked on in the halls and just about everywhere else. They shove me into the lockers, take my pens and fling them and break them. And last year somebody started a rumor, right after the Columbine thing, that I was going to do the same thing and kill everyone in the school.

Before that, a kid named Mark had tried to beat me up. He had pushed me into the walls, kicked me, punched me and all that kind of stuff. But I had shoved him out of the way, and told the principal's of-fice. I got him in trouble, and he resented that.

Mark is one of the so-called popular kids. He's smaller than me, and I really could have beaten him in a fight, beaten him into the ground. I wanted to fight him back. Every part of me screamed to beat his face in. But (a) that wouldn't be good; (b) the right thing to do was tell the of-fice; and (c) once I beat him, his twenty cronies would have come and beat me.

Mr. Jackson once in a while would bring in newspapers and have us read up on current events. In class one day Mark stood up and said, "Everybody, hey, come look at this. I bet Cody wrote it." On a scrap of one of the newspapers, someone had written, "On March 15th everyone will feel my pain."

They called me down to the office during last period. I was going to go down earlier anyway and say, "Look, there's this rumor going around that I wrote a threatening note. If it reaches you, it wasn't me."

But I didn't get that chance. Somebody else had already reported it to the office and blamed me. People were coming up to me and begging me not to kill them. I felt like telling them, "Cut it out; I'm not going to do anything." There was a big investigation. Parents were calling, demanding that state troopers be present on March 15.

The kid who did write it really didn't mean anything by it. He and I were actually on good terms, and I kind of like him.

Eventually he came forward, with a little coaxing, and admitted it. It was the other kid, Mark, who's got a vendetta against me now.

I felt like the school administration was supposed to be on my side, yet they were prosecuting me. Because people were scared, they needed someone to blame so they could say, "It's under control, we have the kid and it's being dealt with." At first, they were questioning me just to get to the bottom of it. By the second day, they believed that I was responsible. By the third day, they started to believe me and hunt for the right people. By the end of the third day it was over.

We had a big assembly, and the kid who wrote it apologized. I really didn't feel like it was his fault. If it had been me, I probably couldn't have come forward like he did, and I just can't pin any blame on him at all.

Nobody could prove anything against Mark. Everybody said, "Oh, I heard from Mark that it was Cody." But the office didn't do anything. All they cared about was who had written it. I've still got people coming up to me in the hall and saying "Watch out, he's going to shoot everyone."

Most of my teachers believed it, too. For example, my science teacher told us to decorate a folder and I drew aliens fighting on it or something. And she went to the office, saying, "Look, look, he drew violent drawings." Never mind that Evan tortures his gerbils and plots means of mass slaughter. Never mind that. "You drew an alien killing somebody, so it's got to be you." They were convinced I was the guy.

My mom was really, really angry with the faculty for believing it about me, and for letting it go on so long. My mom was a good support. She's really good about believing what I say.

That was last year. In the summer I didn't see anybody I knew from school. I didn't care if I ever saw anybody again, except my friends. My friends were good when this happened. Actually, three of them went to the office and signed letters saying they knew I wouldn't do it.

My friends are not very popular. Some aren't very physically fit, and we get picked on a lot. I don't see why this doesn't go on in other grades. Maybe by this time, kids have seen R-rated movies and they think, "Oh, cool, there's somebody blowing another kid up." Maybe they do it to boost their own self-esteem.

Last year the attitude of the school was "If somebody comes up with the intention of hurting you, you can't hit back or we'll expel you." This year, what's better is that you can use self-defense methods. The guidance counselor said, "I know that last year we told you that if you fight back, you'll be expelled, but this year, you can fight back."

I started martial arts last summer after the whole incident, the attacks and the shooting spree and that stuff. It was actually my mom's idea. I didn't really have much interest in martial arts at all, but I went along with it because of these kids who were attacking me and really being jerks. She thought it would boost my self-esteem. I thought that if somebody comes and wants to hit me, I'll be able to defend myself instead of scrambling for the nearest tree or teacher or whatever.

It's more effective if you're able to do something physical. If you hurt him bad enough, nobody's ever going to pick on you again—"Hey, look what Cody did to Ryan; don't mess with him." And a fight buys you some time to run off. My biggest fear is that I'll panic. Like, "Why is he doing this? Why is he coming after me? How am I going to take those twenty kids once I beat him? How will the administration take it?"

Now it's not so much fights, but constant annoying things that make my life miserable at school. Like pushing me into walls, knocking my books out of my hands, taking my writing things and breaking them. It's terrible. One example, I got an A-plus on a report and some kid took it and ripped it up. I gathered the pieces and put them in my folder. I tried telling the guidance counselor and the assistant principal, but I haven't gotten terribly great results. They say, "Get your pen back and then come tell us if it happens again."

How I cope is that I do what I can. I try to live with the feelings and the shame and humiliation or whatever. I tell who I can, if I think they might be able to do something. I buy new pencils.

People still come up to me and say, "Please don't kill me." Not seriously, but just to be jerks. I look back on the beating incident and think that I really should have just hit the guy. If I had used violence, he would have had his fight. He would have been content or discontent, and he probably wouldn't have said what he said about me.

I think the people who actually make plans to blow up their school are people who are in my position, only worse. The Columbine High School kids, people said that they did it because they were miserable and people were picking on them and they just couldn't take it anymore. So they decided to "cleanse the world" of those type of people. And there's also the Hitler obsession. They said that they were obsessed with Hitler and the Holocaust and stuff. In sixth grade I had done a report on the Holocaust. I chose something that I knew absolutely nothing about, with no motives or anything. But I chose it, so that didn't help me. Somebody else came forward and said, "Cody did a report on the Holocaust. He chose to do a report on the Holocaust in sixth grade."

I almost wish they'd just walk up and hit me instead of making my life miserable in little bits. It's just little things that add up to a lot. But when I try to tell teachers, I hear myself say it, and it's like, "I'm complaining about that? The littlest thing." I feel like I am griping about the smallest thing. I tried to make it very clear to the guidance counselor that it was constant, and that I wouldn't complain about just one small thing. Again, I felt like, Why am I complaining about this? Is there anybody who's not going to think that I'm just silly?

THE WILLINGNESS TO DO IT
Jules, 17, from a suburb in the South

I have a theory about Columbine. I think the kids who did the shooting were just attention-starved, and they wanted to do something that would get them in the spotlight of the media. Their original plan was to bomb the school and do the shooting and then escape. They were supposed to get away with it. Now, granted, they were a big media spectacle after they were dead, but I don't think that was part of the original plan.

I think once they got inside and started shooting, it just got out of control, and they didn't know what to do with it. And so they just had to keep going and going and pushing it further and further and further until the point where they couldn't take it themselves, and they wound up committing suicide in the school. I think there are people at my school who have the potential for doing something similar.

But every person has some problem or another, trouble with a past girlfriend or boyfriend, or whatever they happen to have going on. There's just a certain point at which people crack, and you can never tell when it's going to happen. It could be the most popular, the most trendy, the most beautiful, perfect person in the school, and they just completely go nuts.

So why are we violent? Violence comes from a basic instinct. It can come from the suggestions of friends. It can come, in small part, from the suggestions of television. The instinct is always there. The key is the willingness to do it. If you have that willingness, any small thing can set you off.

I think it's pretty easy to get a gun if you want one. If I wanted one, I could get it. I would have to do a little bit of research and it would take time. I'd have to figure out the people I'd need to talk to, both in school and out of school. I'd have to find out how to get a fake ID, how to have my background faked so that I could pass the three-day waiting period and background check required for handgun purchases. I could also just find someone and pay them for their gun. None of my friends have handguns, although one friend who has a house up in Virginia has a rifle for hunting. His dad keeps it locked when they are not using it for hunting. So if I wanted a gun, I could get one.

I don't think people do things that they have no conscious awareness of. I also don't think things happen purely by accident. You have to go outside and stand in the rain before you can be struck by lightning.

THE RUMOR
Terry, 17, from a small town in the Midwest

With all these school shootings that do go on, I think I can see how the boys feel, but I don't understand why they take their actions so far. Just being in a certain clique, being with your friends and making sure they like you and stuff, can be stressful. If you know that every day you are going to be made fun of, you might get pushed over the edge. Then there's school, and maybe home life, like making sure your parents are proud of you. I understand how the stress of everyday life can get to you.

I try not to get upset by the little things that happen, like how the people at school will just cut you off in the hallway in between classes.

I don't know if it's on purpose or not, but it seems to me that it happens a lot. It's not a big deal, but it makes me wonder: "Why did you do that? What is the purpose of it?" But I just try to go on, because it's not worth getting in trouble over. It's not worth getting in a fight and being suspended for two days, and missing homework, and tests. I just go on about my business.

The fights I've seen at school have mostly been over girls. Like if one girl is going out with this guy, and another guy likes her, too, that can lead to fights. They usually start out making fun of each other, calling each other names and stuff like that. Then a push usually happens, maybe two or three punches are thrown, and it's broken up by teachers.

Our school is generally pretty good, but last year there was a rumor for a while that a kid was going to bring a gun to school and shoot some people. I was scared because I'm black. I guess he had been in jail before, and the rumor was that he was going to come and shoot his dad, who was a teacher at our school, as well as a couple of the black people who he thought had gotten him in trouble. A lot of people that could drive went home, and some kids called their parents and got picked up. Even our radio station here announced that there was somebody with a gun in our school or something like that. There was no real threat, but a rumor just got started and it really scared a lot of people.

Maybe it's just me, but I don't think there's anything that is worth taking a gun and shooting somebody over. If you just stand up for yourself and let a bully know that you are not going to take it, then he is not going to pick on you. First tell him to stop, and if he doesn't, then do it back to him: if he makes fun of you, make fun of him. Make him feel how you are feeling—that usually makes him quiet. It has worked in my case.

THE BALLOONS
Errol, 17, from a suburb in the West

The shootings have affected people tremendously. It's just amazing. The other day I walked into school and a girl was carrying balloons, and one of them popped. Everyone in the whole school got really terrified. I honestly don't think things will ever be the same.

The first few weeks after Columbine I was pretty scared. The day after it happened our school closed and I can't even remember what I did that day. The weeks after that I went to school because I felt I needed to go, because if I didn't go then this was going to keep haunting me. There were times when everyone was afraid to come to school. The incident had such a big impact. Some kids I know weren't allowed to go to school the whole week after it happened. Their parents were terrified. We still get a lot of threats at school, bomb threats or threats over the Internet. The authorities got nervous because they knew they could never have predicted the incident. After all, no one who knew Eric and Dylan said they thought they would ever do something like that. It was only recently that school began to feel normal for me again.

My accounting teacher got really upset about it. She just started crying in class and saying that she hated kids with guns. A kid at a school her husband taught at had committed suicide with a gun.

12

ABUSE

"If you see it coming, just walk out of the room or walk out of the house or go somewhere, go to a friend's house, go for a walk, take your dog for a run, whatever. Just try to get away from that situation before it actually explodes."

—Paul, 18, from a suburb in the West

"Maybe sometimes people just shouldn't be forgiven for what they do."

—Gary, 16, from a city in the Northeast

W HILE BOYS' DANGEROUS, HURTFUL BEHAVIOR IS IN-creasingly featured in headlines across the country, as a nation we've given far less attention to boys' own experience of being abused, witnessing abuse (of a parent, a sibling), and living day to day with the menace of serious verbal and physical violence at home. Fortunately, we have recently begun to do more to understand the plight of abused girls and women, trying to give them shelter from further emotional and bodily harm. But as caring a society as we are, responding to abuse in boys is even more difficult—not just because it's hard for us to think and talk about the ways boys or girls are mistreated, but because many boys are even more reluctant than girls to report that the abuse is even happening. A further complication is that boys sometimes retaliate by hitting back—and feel an additional load of shame because of this.

I think of our recent talk with fifteen-year-old Shane, from Pennsylvania, who spent the first years of his life traveling from apartment to apartment with his mother and her troubled boyfriend. Shane spoke to us cheerfully for more than forty-five minutes about the different activ-

ities he is involved in, what music he likes, and who his friends are before slipping into the conversation subtly, in the most cursory way, that
Nat, his mother's former boyfriend, frequently beat him. "He would hit
me with sticks and hangers. Some were plastic and some were metal,"
Shane explained, smiling anxiously. "The plastic ones hurt worse than
the metal ones," he added casually, as though he were comparing con-
struction materials at a hardware store.

When we consider the layers of shame that boys like Shane are almost certain to encounter, it is no wonder that they are reticent in telling
us exactly what life at home is like for them. First, there is the shameful
feeling of betrayal and self-blame that every child experiences when
one of the very people who is supposed to love and care for him loses
control, lashes out violently, and actually inflicts injury upon the child.
"What did I do wrong to make him hit me?" he must ask himself. "Am
I a good son?" Confused, contrite, and terrified, he feels utterly humiliated, devastated that such a close loved one could find so much "fault"
in a child's disposition and actions.

Boys also experience another layer of shame because of the silence
they're expected to maintain, even as major damage is being done to
their bodies and souls. This force of repression tamps the feelings down
even further, so that when they do come out it is often with greater violence. Since the Boy Code makes it clear that "big boys are not supposed to cry," boys respond dutifully by keeping absolutely quiet about
the abuse they're encountering at home, often doing whatever it takes to
hide the emotional and physical pain. But this is a secret that eats away
at a boy's self-esteem and his sense of well-being. Too often boys feel
they must silence the truth and bury the pain, creating a wellspring of
repressed anger that someday may come bursting forth in a rampage of
abuse or violence toward themselves or others.

Added to this is often a third layer of shame over the fact that the
boy has been goaded to hit back at the abuser. To *become* like the
abuser, so he feels.

The mask of masculinity, and society's expectation that boys will
stay quiet about their anguish, not only prods them to hide this unfortunately growing phenomenon of abuse but reinforces boys' own denial
about what is happening to them. Boys will often make believe a violent
incident never happened or they will force themselves to forget it.

Mickey, seventeen years old, from a city in the South, told us,

"Maybe a year ago my father was drunk and slammed my brother's head up against the bookshelf. I was in the apartment but didn't see it. I heard him yelling, and then I heard my brother screaming, then crying . . . [But] I don't really care to know what happened."

Add to this emotional repression the message from the boy culture that boys should act tough, be a "real man," and fight back measure for measure, and the boy becomes not only isolated, shamed, unhappy, and upset, but also very confused. Here is a boy's parent or caretaker to whom he is supposed to be respectful—he's certainly not supposed to take him on in a physical fight—yet who is injuring the boy blow after blow. It's a horrible double bind, a psychological catch-22 that pushes more than one boy over the edge.

Take sixteen-year-old Robert from New Jersey, who felt goaded by his father and a male code of honor to fight, and to take the abuse: "My dad and I got into a bad fight. The argument got worse. He pretty much challenged me to get up and fight him. It was a hard position to be in for an adolescent like me. He punched me hard and my face was fractured and caved in. I was bleeding a lot. He told me to go clean myself up."

But what doesn't get cleaned up so easily is the devastating and dangerous rumination of a boy being abused: shame, secrecy, a sense that he is all alone, a feeling that he has become a vessel of bitterness and anger that may sometimes become too difficult to contain. To spill the beans is to be less than a "real boy"; to fight back is to take on the personality of your aggressor; to grit your teeth and bear such abuse is to accumulate the hurt and rage, which can be controlled for only so long.

I believe the boys whose stories you will read will not only tug at your heart strings but possibly prod you, and all of us, into taking steps toward bringing this hidden pandemic into the light, where we can begin to conquer it—much as we have begun to do so for victimized girls. If we take the right steps and intervene early enough, we can also diminish the ways that boys victimize girls, and men victimize women, through acts of verbal, sexual, and physical abuse. As the voices of these boys reflect, boys in America are eager to stop the cycle of abuse, which is too often repeated within our families. They've felt the sting of the punches, the searing pain of having to keep it all secret. Now they're ready to talk, share their stories, and put an end to the suffering. So let us listen carefully, give them our love and affection, and offer them the sanctuary they so desperately need.

I JUST CAN'T STAND REALLY HURTING
SOMEONE BAD

Paul, 18, from a suburb in the West

My father was abusive. When he was angry he'd just start ranting and raving, cussing like a storm and going out of control. Sometimes he'd resort to physical violence on me or my sister or my mom. He'd use a belt on me or my sister. He used to hit my mom, and with her it wasn't planned but something he would suddenly do when he got frustrated. He would grab her and she would get scared. I was never that worried about her—I always had confidence my mom could take care of herself. She could say, "I don't need this anymore," and stop whatever he was doing. I was so happy when she got the divorce—happy for her to be out of the relationship.

Sometimes my father would get angry and frustrated about work. Other times it was because no one at the house would be quiet. My sister and I played around a lot and we were often really noisy. We ran around the house having fun. It would make him really angry.

At first when my dad hit me, I'd get really scared. But when I turned twelve and then became a teenager, I was big enough to get away from him or even retaliate. And a couple of times I did retaliate. I hurt him back: I'd hit him in the chest. He acted like it hurt him badly. Maybe it was because of his stomach cancer. So, when I retaliated after that, I'd try not to hit him in the stomach because it hurt him too much. I just can't stand really hurting someone bad.

My father started abusing my family before I was born. The problem goes back to his father: he was the same way and abused him. I didn't know my grandfather (he died when I was four). I'm trying to break the chain. I don't want to be like my father to my son.

Because he is my father, I have had to accept my dad for the way he is. I don't want to lose him. I don't approve of the things that he does, or did. But, no matter what, I have never wanted him dead.

When he started getting older, I believe my father started to recognize that he was doing something wrong and I think he started trying to fix himself. He's changed a lot since the divorce. I went for a weekend and he seemed like a different person. It was the first time I'd seen him for two years. But I haven't spent enough time with him to see how he might cope today with anger or with frustrating situations.

When I was young I used to let my anger out in front of everyone at home, just like my father did. Back then, I didn't realize how bad the things he did were, so I imitated him. But I don't want to be like him anymore. These days, when I get angry, I usually try to walk it off and concentrate on something else for the time being, to take my mind off what's bothering me. I do sometimes get violent but I don't show it in front of people. I'll just hold it in and then let it out somewhere where there's no one about. I don't like people seeing me like that. It's not something I want to project about myself. I went off recently to the locker room, when no one was there, and just hit a locker.

Usually I try to talk out my anger. I spend a lot of time at church with the pastor or with my friends, talking about my father. I also try to have a good relationship with God. When I think of God, I imagine him as my father. I've always depended on love from my Heavenly Father, especially in the times when I wasn't getting much love from my biological father.

It's hard to deal with an abusive parent. I think the best thing to do is to let it happen, but if you can, try to avoid it. If you see it coming, just walk out of the room or walk out of the house or go somewhere, go to a friend's house, go for a walk, take your dog for a run, whatever. Just try to get away from that situation before it actually explodes. I used to just try to walk out of the house and find some peace.

When I have a son, I hope he's just like me. I want a kid that I can go around with, play and have fun with, and teach everything that I've learned throughout my life. I want my son to be able to show his feelings and his sadness. I want to have that sort of special connection with somebody else besides my wife and my mother and my sister and my father, one so strong that the other person would be someone special to me for the rest of my life.

My dream is to become content with what I'm doing with my life. I want to work in medicine and I'm thinking of becoming an anesthesiologist. I love the thought of being able to lessen or even eliminate other people's pain. It's just like helping them through problems with their family in their lives.

I REMEMBER

Shane, 15, from a city in the Northeast

I love to ride on my skateboard. I love going downhill, but I can't really do any tricks.

I live at home with my dad. My mom and my dad never married. My mom actually wanted to marry my dad but back then she was getting welfare. When you're on welfare, if you're living with someone, the government won't pay. My dad wasn't making a big salary. So if they got married, she would have lost the welfare money. So they never got married. They just lived with each other until around 1990. Then my father moved away. I wanted to be with him, but my mom took me with her.

It was summertime and my mom and I moved into a new house. We had two TVs, normal furniture, and a refrigerator. There wasn't much food in the fridge, though we had enough food to survive. But we couldn't pay the rent so we got kicked out. We moved to a house down the road. The landlady there wasn't very nice because we still couldn't pay the rent. I remember I used to play by myself in the backyard behind that house. I didn't really know anybody. So I would just stay in the yard and play with my little toys. I was lonely.

That summer my mother started dating. She and her younger sister would wander around the clubs. One time she went to a disco and met this jerk named Nat. She married the guy that same year. Nat never paid rent, he just kind of moved around from one apartment to the next.

Sometimes I have painful memories of my childhood. I remember a *lot* of things, too. Like the Berlin Wall. I remember when it came down. I don't remember what it meant, but I remember it happening. I remember that when I was younger, when the child support ran out, my father would actually have to give my mom money to pay for milk and stuff like that because Nat just stopped paying.

Nat wasn't very smart and didn't seem too together. He was a real wacko. He used to abuse me. He would hit me with sticks and hangers. Some of the hangers were plastic and some were metal. The plastic ones hurt the most.

Nat and my mom had my sister in 1991. The four of us moved from place to place. He and my mom used to argue a lot. And he would make my sister cry all the time. Nat didn't have it all upstairs. There was something mental about him that just wasn't right.

In 1992, I moved away to live with my father. Then about four years later, my mom and Nat just took off. They always had problems. She must have left with him in the middle of the night. I don't know exactly . . . that was a long time ago.

Actually, I remember a couple of times when I was younger, I would come home from school and my mother was nowhere to be found. I didn't have the key so I used to have to wait at a neighbor's house. I would just think to myself, "Where is she?" She wasn't even working, she was getting the welfare money, but she couldn't be there. I just waited there, like she told me to, in front of the building. And she would never come. And I was only like six years old. It was very lonely and I was afraid.

After a few years, Nat left my mom. She's kind of been living at his mother's house ever since. But the mother-in-law subsequently died, so my mom just stayed there with some other relatives. For a while she was getting alimony from Nat. But then he moved, and now they can't trace him. So my mom has to get temporary jobs so she can afford to buy food. She's not very smart. I mean, she tries her best, but she's not really "there" all the time. I mean, I can't really have intellectual conversations with her because she doesn't have all that much to talk about. Sometimes I wish I could be closer to her.

When I was younger it was hard for me to make friends because I have always been kind of nerdy. I used to get bullied a lot. When people bullied me, sometimes I would have to fight, but I would run away when I could. I don't consider myself a fighter. I don't like to fight and am not going to get into one unless I get really pissed off, and then only as a last resort. I guess you could say that I'm a gentle person.

Nowadays I don't ever see Nat. He doesn't even come around, not even on holidays, to see how we are. My sister doesn't even see him, and I don't think he should be a part of her life. If I saw Nat now, I would tell him what I told him back then, that he's a deadbeat, that he's not even a real father to my sister, that he's never been there for her at all.

My advice to other kids is to stay in school and find extracurricular activities. Try not to be in the house that much.

HE PUNCHED ME HARD

Gary, 16, from a city in the Northeast

Over the summer, my dad and I got in a bad fight. My mom had gone to a horse show with my little sister. While they were gone, I went out for a ten-mile bike ride with friends and then Dad was supposed to take me out for dinner. When I got back I just said to him, "So, are we going out to dinner or not?" And he said, "No." So I said, "Well, you sort of said we were, so I was planning on it." It didn't really matter that much to me, but he got really mad and started insulting me, saying that I was fat and things like that.

The argument got worse. We were just yelling back and forth and he was insulting me pretty bad. Finally, he pretty much challenged me to get up and fight him, so I did. It was a hard position to be in for an adolescent like me. I hit him first, so I feel like I forced him to hit me back. He punched me hard and my face was fractured and caved in. I was bleeding a lot. He stopped punching me when he saw I was bleeding. But he was still pissed for a few seconds. And then I think he got scared or upset, because he told me to go clean myself up. I just went upstairs to my room and locked the door. I felt very angry at my father. I also felt ashamed, because he beat me. I should have beaten him up.

When my mom got home, my dad said, "I hit Gary. He's hurt." Mom ran upstairs, ran into my room, looked at me, and starting calling my father a bunch of swears. I was still bleeding, but I wasn't crying. What good would crying do? She was bullshit at my father. She took my side and tried to comfort me. She took me to the hospital right away. I had to stay in the hospital so they could do surgery on my face. The police came to our house that night and arrested my dad; it was two in the morning and he was asleep. He didn't put up any fight. He had to spend time in jail. Fortunately, this all happened during the summer so kids at school didn't really know about it.

I resent that my father hit me. Our relationship had been pretty good before the fight. Every once in a while we'd get into a verbal argument, but not usually too bad. I know my dad regrets what he did, but our relationship is much more on edge now than it was. I'm a gullible and forgiving kid, but maybe sometimes people just shouldn't be forgiven for what they do.

MY FATHER HAD BEEN DRINKING
Mickey, 17, from a city in the South

Maybe a year ago, my father was drunk and slammed my brother's head up against the bookshelf. I was in the apartment with them, but I didn't see it. I heard him yelling, and then I heard my brother screaming, then crying. That's the only time he ever touched any of us, and I don't really care to know what happened. All I know was that my father had been drinking.

Our parents divorced when I was two and my brother, Ron, was four. We live with our mother and stepdad, but we see our father every few weeks. I was always the son that followed in his father's footsteps. He was an athlete, I was an athlete; my brother wasn't. My father connected with me through sports. We would enjoy sitting down and watching a football game together, but Ron didn't. I feel guilty about it, because I've been able to have that kind of relationship with our father and my brother hasn't.

Neither of us was ever hurt except for that one time. He still drinks every once in a while, but he's giving it up. I see him every other weekend, and he doesn't drink when I'm around. But even though I can vent to him, I still don't feel like I can go to him with important things. His drinking just kind of rips us apart.

A few weeks ago I made a very bad decision when I was upset. My girlfriend and I had just broken up, and I found out that she was hooking up with this guy that had been trying to come between us ever since we started going out. That really made me mad, and I got pretty messed up on alcohol with three friends. We were all drunk, and we went to throw oranges and eggs at this guy's truck. But we didn't feel like that was enough, so we went back with a few cinder blocks and a screwdriver. That night we did three thousand dollars' worth of damage to his truck.

The next day I felt horrible about it, but it was too late. It's something that I'm not proud of, and I wish I hadn't done it. Messing up his truck is the one thing in my life that I wish I could take back, but I can't. If I don't touch another drop of alcohol ever again, it'll be too soon.

That night I didn't think I needed to talk to anyone about how upset I was feeling. I thought I could handle it on my own, but I couldn't. If I knew anyone else in that sort of situation or feeling that upset, I would tell them to talk to somebody before they take any action. Separate yourself from the crowd and just think about what happened and why you're feeling the way you're feeling. No matter how bad it hurts, find someone to talk to.

There's pressure on us as guys to handle things on our own, but it all just balls up inside you, and eventually it'll explode. It exploded for me that night, and now all four of us are getting jobs to pay back the damages. Thank God they're not going to press charges.

I've always stood up for my own and wouldn't let anybody push me around. If you let them push you around, then they think they can do it any time they want to. When I have an issue with someone, or something is bothering me, I carry it with me until I deal with it. It's just how I am. I have a strong sense of justice, of what's right and what's wrong.

Male pride gets us in a lot of trouble sometimes. See, in a typical fight somebody insults you, then you respond, then he pushes you. Now, if you don't push back you'll get made fun of for God knows how long; people will call you a "wuss" or a "sissy." And that hurts anybody's pride, so you push back. In some ways it's better to get beat up to protect your pride than to take a punch and walk away. You show that you know how to fight and that you won't take it, so you won't end up getting teased. Of course, you still have to suffer the consequences of getting in a fight. You just have to decide which is more important: keeping your pride or staying out of trouble. Life is often very unfair.

PART III

Boys Reaching Out and Connecting

13

LOVE FOR MOTHER

"A mother's love transcends all things, even time, in its limitlessness and boundlessness. It is the most blind, most faithful form of love. Or, so it is with my mother."
> —Gregory, 18, from a small town in the South

"I've always been able to go to her."
> —Peter, 12, from a suburb in New England

"She tells me not to hide anything from her, and I feel comfortable talking about everything."
> —John, 15, from a suburb in New England

BOYS OF ALL AGES, FROM EARLY CHILDHOOD THROUGH adolescence and on into adulthood, yearn for their mother's love, and benefit enormously when their mothers provide it. In their own way and on their own terms, they want to remain closely connected to their moms and to the realm of love and authenticity that a mother creates for them. In *Real Boys,* I suggested that a mother cannot love her son too much, nor too long. Increasingly, boys are discovering that they can embrace their mothers fearlessly, that a mother's love can have a positive effect in helping them grow into happy, healthy, masculine men. Many boys I spoke with described their mother's love as a deep, incredibly sustaining aspect of their lives, perhaps the deepest of all.

But in the public sphere, boys are still sometimes punished for conveying open affection for their moms. "I think most boys are close to their mothers," says thirteen-year-old Troy from a suburb in New England, "but a lot may not want to say it. I don't know why." As males living in a society that is still somewhat confused about what it wants from boys and young men, they frequently will be taunted and teased for breaking that aspect of the Boy Code that says, in essence, "Stay away from your mom; avoid any context in which you will appear dependent on her; make yourself 'masculine' by removing yourself from any person, situation, or behavior that seems 'feminine.' " Society still shames boys who appear to be dependent on their mothers. In turn, openly nurturing moms continue to be admonished for "suffocating" or "feminizing" their sons. No wonder boys are perplexed about their natural love for their mothers.

Yet today's boy is prepared to resist the old-fashioned idea that he should completely separate from his mother and her "feminine" surroundings. He rejects the traditional Boy Code rule that leaning on his mother for comfort and affection is unmanly. "As long as you know you are a good person, who cares what they think about you?" says Troy. "If you want to be close to your mom, that's fine."

Just the other day I observed a fifteen-year-old boy as he ran over to give his mother a big hug after he kicked the winning goal in his school's championship soccer game. The other team razzed him mercilessly, almost bringing him to tears, until finally, after waiting much too long, his coach stepped in. When I later asked the coach why he had hesitated to intervene, all he could muster was "I agree, what those kids did by teasing him was wrong."

"It sure did seem wrong," I said.

"But maybe it was bad judgment on Rick's part," the coach added, squirming in his seat. "Being so gushy with his mother. Jeez, did everyone have to see that sort of romance in public?"

"That's not romance, Coach," I found myself responding. "That's love, real love, unconditional, self-esteem-enhancing love. A few more kisses like that from moms and maybe fewer of your players would be suspended for fighting or drinking. Maybe we'd have fewer boys with guns at school."

Many mothers provide boys with a warm, loving, accepting environment, a comfort zone in which they can relax, enjoy an affectionate and affirming squeeze, and receive encouragement for being their real selves. As a society, perhaps one thing we haven't recognized is that this deep, connected, nonjudgmental love—whether it comes from a mom, a dad, a coach, a teacher, or just a friend—provides so much to boys whose confidence and ease of mind become shaken up in the "outside" world, a world in which their masculinity and innate goodness are constantly challenged.

Love Is Patient, Love Is Kind
Gregory, 18, from a small town in the South

Lifting the wrinkled note from the bottom of the box, I had little idea either of the message written upon the paper, already becoming yellowed by time, or of the memories it would awaken in me by reading it again. Signed with a kiss, the note told me to "Stay tough and always keep my smile." I immediately recognized the large, neat print as my mother's and realized that she had written it for me several years earlier, while I was depressed. As I reread her words, I was washed over with love.

I Corinthians 13:4–7 states that "Love is patient, love is kind." Love does not envy, it does not boast, it is not proud. It is not rude, it is not self-seeking, it is not easily angered, it keeps no record of wrongs. Love does not delight in evil but rejoices in the truth. It always protects, always trusts, always hopes, always perseveres.

I cannot help but think that when this popular biblical passage was written, the author had his mother in mind. For the love a mother has for her son is the paragon of this particular emotion. A mother's love transcends all things, even time, in its limitlessness and boundlessness. It is the most blind, most faithful form of love. Or, so it is with my mother.

The earliest memory I have of my mother is her flinging her body across mine, attempting to save me from my father's unchecked brutality. Though I was merely a toddler then, wisps of memories still greet me in my dreams in which I see her again, shielding her child, taking another double beating to save her son from that fate. How she would lie to my father, attributing my accidental breaking of a household item to her own clumsiness, sparing me from a severe beating. Later on, when we had escaped the irascible man, she began working fourteen-hour days, sacrificing her young-adult life to provide for me.

Eventually, in my teenage years, my mother would become a beacon and a buoy, lifting my head above the cold, teeming waters of depression and providing a light with which to guide myself back to land and safety.

My mother and I share one of the strongest friendships I have encountered. It is a friendship fortified not just by time, but by the glue of shared tribulation. By having me when she was only sixteen, the two of us almost grew up together, much like best friends. Like her love for me, this friendship knows no boundary. There isn't any feat that she and I wouldn't attempt for one another. No obstacle seems too great. Through the years, she has proven her devotion to me over and over again. I wish I could say that I've always risen to the occasion for her, that I've been there for her like she has been for me. Sadly, though, I cannot, and this weighs heavily on my conscience.

Now, two years after my battle with depression, I have almost totally come to terms with it. But there are a few memories that I cannot release; memories of words I spoke and actions I took which now I pay for dearly. These memories, all of them, concern my mother. Painfully, I recall the numerous times I told my mother I hated her, the days I refused to get out of bed or eat a morsel of food, the many nights I blasted my stereo in my room, barricading the door. That it ever soothed me to inflict pain on my mother's psyche now floods my being with indescribable shame and a yearning for repentance.

These memories sting so brutally, for now I realize that, contrary to my thinking back then, I was never truly alone in my depression. During those extremely long and difficult six months, someone was there by my side feeling the amount of profound pain that I felt. Someone was there to pick up the burden of my cross, carrying it faithfully until I could regain enough strength to carry it myself. Someone was there to shovel coal on my inner flame, keep it burning brightly when I hadn't the will to do so myself. Someone was there to lift me up when I fell down, make me feel loved even when I replied with bitterness and resentment. This person, my mother, never gave up on me, even when I wanted nothing more than to give up on myself. That it took me almost two years to grasp this fills me with grief, and knowing that I'll never be able to repay her for the strength she gave me makes me even sadder still.

If a law listing the responsibilities of a mother were ever to be promulgated, upon reading it one would be sure to find that my mother has far surpassed the call of duty. For I am all but sure that this law would not include sitting up with a child, holding him while he suffers through a case of delirium tremens. I am all but positive it would not require exchanging a hug for a spit in the face. But my mother has done this and more. With me, she has traveled to hell and back, battling insurmountable demons within me. She has thrown her body over mine so that I would not have to face the sting of countless injustices, even as she cooked me dinner, washed my clothes, and toiled hours and hours to raise the funds we needed to cover the monthly rent.

I have made my mother sound like Christ, because to me that's what she is; she is my Savior. I know that without her I would not be writing this today, for I would be dead, if not physically then spiritually.

Recently I was asked to name the aspect of my family life which I treasured most. Quickly, I thought of the blessing I have found in my little sister, how much I enjoy playing with her, reading to her, taking in her laughter. I thought about the priceless memories I share with my favorite cousin. I thought of my grandmother's unbeatable apple pie. But these sentiments, though wrapped tightly in a silken handkerchief and stored within the deepest chamber of my heart, are transcended by what I value more than anything else in this life: my late-night conversations with my mom. Oh, the countless nights that my mother, weary from her daily household chores, has sat up with me, offering me advice for my trivial pubescent dilemmas, giving me words of wisdom attained from her own experiences in life but always leaving a clear opening for me to make my own decisions. She has even offered her counsel to many of my friends, saving them more than once from an enormous amount of trouble. Somehow, in the end, she always ends up being right. Yet when I bring her achievements to light for her and show her just how good a person she truly is, she looks back at me lovingly, smiles broadly, and says: "This is just my job."

I THINK YOU SHOULD BE CLOSE

Troy, 13, from a suburb in New England

I think most boys are close to their mothers, but a lot may not want to say it. I don't know why. A lot of kids pretend not to have a good relationship with their parents, and some kids even disrespect their mother to try to be cool or something. But who really cares? As long as you know you are a good person, who cares what other people think about you? If you want to be close to your mom, that's fine.

Sometimes I feel nervous about my schoolwork, doing well on tests, or if I have any papers. Just simple things. I must have gotten it from my mother, because she is really a worrier and so am I. We talk a lot about it, like if I'm feeling bad and my mom can tell. She always asks me if I'm not feeling right, and we talk about it a little bit. She just talks me through it and tells me to stop worrying and stuff. She just helps me through it.

I try not to talk about deep things with my mom, but I think you can. She's like a regular person. It's like talking to your dad, same thing. Now that I'm growing up, my mom talks to me about issues like girls and sex and drugs. Well, she mostly talks to me about girls, kidding around a lot about girls and how she doesn't want me to go out with them and everything. She's like, "You better not go out with girls." She's just being protective, and she's mostly joking.

I look up to my mom. She is a caring person. There was a lady at her office who was divorced and had two kids in college, and she didn't have a lot of money. And when she was leaving the office, a bunch of the people there decided to give her some money, and my mom was one of them. My mom is also a hard worker. I admire her personality. She knows how to laugh at herself sometimes. We like to just relax, watch TV, go to the movies, just talk.

When I'm moody, I feel kind of depressed and I get mad easily. Like last night, I was just totally out of it. I wasn't being myself. My sister did something and I got really mad at her, just for a simple thing. I also might get upset about school, like if someone bothered me or made fun of me. So then I will act out in the classroom or say something, or lose my temper at sports and talk back to the umpire, or get really frustrated with homework and stuff. I'm just not myself.

The moodiness is like a depression. I hide it in a ball because I don't really want it. I don't want to tell anyone or share with my parents. And I think that makes me more depressed, because I'm keeping it inside. The sadness does eventually go away, though.

If I talked a little more I think it would solve the problem more easily, but I think I feel embarrassed. Mostly I think I'm a good person, but there are times when I get disappointed in myself, and that's when I start to feel depressed. But everyone should understand that they are human and that they're going to make mistakes.

Last night was really the first time I felt deeply depressed, and I'm going to start trying to tell my parents. I may get in trouble, but, hey, it's going to happen. I know they are understanding, so I don't know why I didn't tell them last night. I mean, my mom knew anyway and asked what's wrong. I had tried to avoid it, to hide it, but I guess it didn't work that well. She knew that it was there. If I went to talk to one of them about my depression, it would probably be my mom, because I think she is less strict than my dad is. I would go to her first.

She Can Understand

Cedric, 14, from New York City

Sometimes school frustrates me, like being in class and getting a lot of work. Then after school I'm home alone for like three hours by myself, and being bored can make me angry. I do my homework, check my e-mail, watch TV, but it does get lonely, not being able to talk to somebody. Usually I'll call my mother and ask how she's doing, how her day is going. But some days I don't call her, and then she knows that I'm bored so she calls me herself. "Cedric, how you doing?" She brings a smile to my face.

I go to her about everything. Some people are scared to go to their mothers with some things, but I can tell my mother anything and she won't get mad. She'll talk to me about it, just tell me the consequences and rewards. Some days, when I'm moping around the house, she notices and asks what's wrong. If I don't feel like telling her right then, I'll write parts of it down to highlight what I'm feeling, so she can understand what's going on.

I don't always tell her everything about my troubles because I don't want her to feel ashamed or sad, like it's her fault if I'm failing in a class or something. I want her to be happy, because she gave me my happiness. I'm not an adult yet, but I'm old enough to care for myself more, so now is my time to show her how I appreciate her bringing me up to be responsible. I want to give back to her and to do good. She taught me when I was young what was good and bad, so when I do good, she knows that it got through to me.

GRATEFUL

John, 13, from a suburb in New England

I'm in seventh grade and I'm really into computers. When I'm not doing schoolwork, I like to do PowerPoint presentations just for fun. I do them with my friends. We put jokes in them and make them funny. I also really like working on *The Inkspot,* our school newspaper just for kids. And, I work on a game page.

My mom is a kindergarten teacher. She's a very nice woman. We get on very well and we don't get in a lot of fights. I can talk to her about personal stuff and about problems. We've talked about drugs, and about what to do if nothing is going right at school, and about tests and grades and how they can be hard. She tells me not to hide anything from her and I feel comfortable talking about everything. I don't lie to my parents. If I had a really bad grade, I could definitely talk to my mom about it. She'd understand. She's much happier if I talk to her than if I lie to her about it and she later finds out from my teacher.

When my mom isn't working, she likes to write. And she has lots of friends that actually live on our street. She spends a lot of time going out with them. But she also spends a lot of time with me and we have fun. I like it when we get in the car together, listen to the radio and sing. We crank up a good R&B or alternative rock song and we sing out loud. I used to do all the high parts, but now my voice is beginning to change, I'm beginning to do the low parts.

I feel really sorry for kids who are abused or neglected by their parents. I think kids who are having problems should first just give their parents another chance. They should try to work on the relationship. The problem is that kids who have really bad parents often don't themselves know the difference between right and wrong, and it's really hard for them to know what to do. When we see news of a murder or another terrible crime, my parents always say it happened because the criminals did not have good parents and they weren't taught the difference between right and wrong. So the best thing for those kids to do is to immediately seek help. Talk to a teacher, a guidance counselor, to other kids in school. You just have to tell someone even if your parents threaten you.

A guy came to our school to talk about child abuse, and I learned a lot from him. He had one of the worst cases of abuse ever in California.

I learned from him to be grateful about my parents and my home and the way I grew up. I like school a lot and I'm really grateful I have great parents like I do.

I'VE ALWAYS BEEN ABLE TO GO TO HER

Peter, 12, from a suburb in New England

I think I go to my mom to talk to about stuff more, probably just because she's around more than my dad, because she's always home. She asks me how my day was, and we usually talk after school for a little while. Sometimes if I worry about something, or if I'm not sure if I'm going to do as well as I think, I'll go to my mom to talk about it.

My dad likes us to use psychology when I approach him for anything. So I always have to say, "Is this a good time to talk to you?" or something like that. I've learned to be pretty good at that, because my dad can be really crabby after work and approaching him then is not the smartest idea.

One year, I didn't make a basketball team and my mom and dad were away in Pennsylvania. The mother of the friend I was staying with called my mom, and I talked to her on the phone, and she came back the next day. My mom had really wanted to be home for me. Now whenever I have a tournament, she is afraid to leave in case that were to happen again, because she wasn't there the one time it did. She did that with my sister, too, when she had a big problem and called my mom in the middle of the night. My mom drove back six hours the next day to surprise her. She's always supportive and tries to tell us that it's going to be OK, or tells a story about when it happened to her and how it turned out OK. Most often I would be comfortable showing my mom all of the feelings I have, if I'm really upset about something. That's happened once or twice before and I've always been able to go to her.

A TIGHT RELATIONSHIP WITH MY MOM

Adrian, 12, from a city in New England

I moved around a lot when I was young. I was born in the city and lived here for three years. Then I moved to a suburb and was there for two years, then to another suburb for three years, then to another one for a year, and then I came back to the city and have lived here ever since.

I live with my mom. My dad lives right down the street. My parents split up when I was about three. Before that, I remember certain things, like that I would be with my dad when my mom wasn't around, and with my mom when my dad wasn't around. But I never really saw them argue. My father remarried last April.

I have a tight relationship with my mom. I talk to her about anything and she talks to me about anything, back and forth. When I was little, I would tell her exactly everything, but now, I have certain things I don't want to talk to her about and I go talk to my father because it is more of a guy thing. I talk to my dad about certain things, and I talk to both of them about certain things, and I tell my mom some things I won't tell my dad. Either way, I get input from both of them.

As I began to get older, my mom and I would sit talking and all of a sudden it would get quiet and I would be thinking, "I want to bring this up." Then I would realize, "This is my mom. She probably wouldn't understand." Later I found out that she does understand, because she grew up with two brothers. My mom was a tomboy, so everything I am going through she understands. She understands puberty. She understands girls. She understands the attitude that I will get sometimes. She understands why I get mad and when I get sad. She just knows me. Basically, everything I do around my mother, she will understand. If she doesn't, she will ask me.

For example, I will be around my friends and get into a little horseplay. When we get home she'll say, "Why do you horseplay like that? It's dangerous." And I'll say, "This is just fun." She understands. That is just me, and she is cool with it.

I can see how everything I have learned and all my choices are from the input from my mom. Some are from my dad, but most of them are from my mom. Basically everything I do is from her influence.

She doesn't want me to lose my temper. She doesn't want me to fight. I just will do it sometimes. I lose my cool and blow my top. But she won't get mad about it, because she knows who I am and the way I think and she goes by that. A situation that I am in, she knows my reaction to it. She will let me have my reaction, but she will give me some advice so the outcome won't be as bad. For example, if I want to fight somebody, she will give me a way to get out of it. Then if I still end up fighting the person, I won't get in as much trouble. My mother trusts me to make the right decision. The first time I mess up, she says, "All right,

I am going to forgive you this time, but just don't do it again." That's what has happened. I never did it twice, so that's why we have that trust.

My dad was never really around and he used to lie to me a lot. So my mom basically became my mom and my dad. I was fine with that. I don't hate my father. I talk to him a lot on the phone and I go over to his house. Certain things I don't even tell him. If I were to get in trouble at school, I wouldn't tell him because he has never been there for me and I wouldn't want him to give me a lecture since he was never around. It's like, "I get in trouble and you want to be around me now and you are going to give me a lecture? What happens when I did good and you weren't there to talk to me?" That's why I talk to my mother. She has been there, whether I have done good or bad.

14

THE DAD CONNECTION

"I like the way he talks to me and the way I can talk to him."
—Marcus, 11, from a suburb in southern New England

B OYS TALK A LOT ABOUT THEIR DADS. THEY TALK ABOUT
how much they love them, how much they enjoy spending time
with them, how much they look up to them. They make it clear that fathers—though sometimes flawed—are central figures, not only in shaping their moral lives by teaching, advising, and providing discipline to
their sons, but by also nurturing them with love and caring and by doing
things with them throughout their childhood and adolescence. Fathers
connect with their sons through a wide range of activities. Though some
dads get close with their sons through hugging and kissing and quiet
talks together, many others find it more comfortable to engage in some
shared activity: fishing, hiking, wrestling, golfing, cooking, watching
movies.

Nurturing fathers are *not* "male mothers." They demonstrate their
affection in many different ways—ways that our boys appear to appreciate as an important complement to their mothers' love. "It's easy to
talk with him even if I'm really sad," says fifteen-year-old Tim about his
dad. "He always tries to make jokes or say other things that cheer me up
and make me feel better. He makes me feel better after I do something
stupid because he tells me about the mistakes he's made and the stupid
things he's done."

The voices you will hear in this chapter show how important it is for
us to recognize that a father's caring expression need not necessarily di-

rectly mirror a mother's style of communicating and connecting with her son. Boys seem to crave, absorb, and use to their advantage their fathers' unique way of conveying friendship and love.

Yet as close to their dads as many of the boys I spoke to seemed to feel, many of them, especially as they grew into older adolescence and into young adulthood, had much to say about how painful it was not to be able to feel even closer. Many felt a looming sense of separation, a wall between themselves and their fathers. Other boys to whom I spoke shared how angry they were that their fathers were not around more often. Still others felt profoundly betrayed, livid, or simply numb because their fathers had quit their lives entirely. There was a clear theme of yearning for more, a kind of "father hunger" that pervaded many of the interviews I conducted. Some of these stories reflect good, thoughtful boys with caring decent fathers who don't quite yet know how to meet their boys' natural need for attention, affection, and love. Other stories involve fathers whose actions deeply hurt their sons.

But as unforgivable as some fathers' actions may seem, most of them beg a new interpretation. For the painful dilemmas they raise— ones that have profound consequences for our culture and its survival— need to be understood from the perspective of empathy rather than of blame.

Many men who are fathering today, struggling to do the best job they know how, grew up in an environment in which the Boy Code was strongly enforced, a world in which male affection, especially among boys and their primary male caretakers, was frowned upon and rarely demonstrated. Too few role models of the "new dad" were extant. Therefore, many men have had to reinvent themselves as fathers. Some succeed superbly. Others, according to our boys, fail to meet their sons' needs adequately.

After living for seventeen years without his biological father, Juan struggles to imagine how he would respond if they were reunited: "If I saw him now, I'd tell him that I have been working since I was fourteen. I don't need you. You can come if you want to. You can be my friend. You are not going to be my father." While there are too many stories like Juan's, I believe that in most cases boys are telling us that even the fathers who fail are less likely to be "deadbeat dads" than "deadpan dads," men who are depressed and cut off from their feelings because of their own early upbringings, often at the hands of their own harsh, distant fathers. At seventeen, Kevin sees his father repeating a family pattern: "My father's dad was very competitive with him, he wasn't nice, they didn't communicate. But instead of overcompensating, my father is like his own father. He's not very communicative. I don't care if he coaches my soccer team for nine years in a row; I would rather he just talked to me once in a while."

Once, during one of my speaking engagements, "How to Parent Boys," one brave man raised his hand. His was not so much a question as a somewhat self-condemning plea.

"Hearing you speak, I begin to feel I'm not such a good dad," he said.

"Well, blame and shame are the problem, not the solution," I responded sympathetically, "so let's see if we can get by that self-criticism and to an issue you've had the courage to bring up."

"It happens when we're on the street together," Roger explained. "My son Harlan wants me to hold his hand, and I shy away or whisper to him that real men and 'big boys' don't do that. I tell him people might get the wrong idea."

It became clear that this shame about the public expression of affection came from Roger's own upbringing. He had a father "who loved me" but "didn't like to show it much." I thanked Roger for his openness and courage, and put the following proposition before him: "You very much want Harlan to grow up to be both healthy and masculine, don't you?"

In response, Roger nodded his head enthusiastically.

"And you see yourself as a reservoir of some of that masculinity," I continued. "So how does a reservoir deliver its contents to its thirsty users?"

"You mean like through a connection, a pipeline?" A broad smile began to play across his face. "So, if I hold out my hand and grab on to his, I'm connecting our masculinity, letting it flow between us!"

As I nodded in assent, I couldn't help but notice the tears forming in Roger's eyes. I had a clear suspicion that two generations—or more—of fathering and being loved as a boy by a male role model were changing before me.

Fortunately, the tide seems to be turning. Many of the voices you will encounter in this chapter are from boys who speak about having been hurt or disappointed by their own dads. They show an insight, a forgiveness, a yearning to change this process when they finally "step up to the plate" to take on their fatherly responsibilities. These stories poignantly describe a variety of father-son relationships with vastly different levels of closeness and connection: sometimes there is an open pipeline that flows with love and respect; sometimes there is a blocked conduit; and sometimes there is a disconnected coupling that requires a great deal of repair.

SIMILAR TO MY DAD

Tim, 13, from a suburb in southern New England

I go to my dad's showroom on Saturdays. He watches me when I do my homework and then he corrects it. I like taking drives with him— once we drove all the way to Florida! We can really talk about things on long drives. It's easy to talk with him even if I'm really sad: he always tries to make jokes or say other things that cheer me up and make me feel better. He makes me feel better after I do something stupid because he tells me about the mistakes he's made and the stupid things he's done.

I've had some hard things happen to me. When I was seven or eight, I was in Vermont with some of my cousins in their cottage in the mountains. My grandfather told us about the dangerous things in the woods, the bears and snakes, and how we had to be careful of them. One day my cousin Adam and I went off into the woods and we got lost. We couldn't find our way home and it was starting to get a little bit dark. I started to think I'd never get back and never see my mom or my dad ever again. But finally I saw a tiny bit of light off in one direction. Adam was crying and I was still really scared. Then the light got a bit stronger and we realized we were definitely going in the right direction. Finally we saw the house and realized we were home again.

I also had a really hard time when my grandfather was ill. He'd had a stroke in 1995 but he recovered pretty well. Then, suddenly, he was diagnosed with prostate cancer and that just totally disabled him. He lost the use of his legs. I even had to help him go to the bathroom. One time he was coming out of the bathroom and he was about to sit himself down in his wheelchair. He'd forgotten to put the brake on, so when he tried to sit down, all of a sudden the wheelchair shot forward and he hit the ground hard. It was just terrible. I was too small to pick him up and I didn't know the address of the house so I couldn't call 911. So I called my dad and asked him to call 911 and then fire trucks and paramedics and police arrived to help my grandfather back up.

It was so hard when he died. He was in the hospital, and my parents had a telephone call around 2:00 A.M. to go in and see him, and I knew then and there that he was about to die. He died the day after Christmas and everyone was crying. I tried to talk to my mom about it and she really didn't feel like talking. It was hard for her to talk without crying. So I kept telling her it was all going to be all right and that I would take care of her.

I take after both my parents, but I guess I'm kind of similar to my dad. We both really like golf, especially miniature golf. We played a really good game on Myrtle Beach. It was really competitive and we each won about the same number of holes. When we play golf we like to talk about the news and current events. I have strong views on issues like the death penalty. I'm against it because it's not right.

I worry about my dad when he comes home late from work. Once he actually fell asleep at work and didn't come home until midnight. My mom was scared, thinking he'd been in a car accident. I also get worried when he travels a lot. Recently he went to China on a business trip. He goes to a lot of shows. What gets me nervous are the plane trips. I get really nervous on planes. With all the news about crashes like the Alaska Airlines crash, it's hard not to get nervous.

My mom misses him a lot when he goes. The China trip lasted for two weeks and that was pretty tough on her. I miss him a lot, too.

THE SMART ONE
David, 16, from New York City

My father is the smart one. He dropped out of school but he's smart at least. He was born in the 1950s so he's kind of old. He grew up in the fifties and sixties, with Kennedy, the Cold War, Vietnam. In the seventies, they had gonorrhea, and then HIV and stuff, so he's been through a lot of the history we see today.

My dad is a nice guy and a hard worker. Sometimes he gets up at four in the morning to pick up cans and bottles in the street. When he gets back, he cleans them up and then goes back out to Pathmark to turn them in to get the money. Drug dealers used to come up to my dad and ask him to make deliveries for them. But my dad didn't want to do that. Collecting cans and bottles is better than selling drugs.

Each morning after my father comes back from Pathmark, he takes a shower, gets ready for work, and then comes to my bed to say good-bye on his way out to work at around 7:20 A.M. He doesn't exactly wake me up—he just says 'bye. Then I go back to sleep. I have a radio alarm to get me up.

My dad has to take two trains to go to his job, where he works through a job placement program as a janitor. He doesn't come home at the same time each night. Sometimes he only has light work, so he gets home early. Other times, he has a heavy workload. Yesterday, he had to do a lot of pipework because there was a flood in the basement. He had to clean up a lot. He said he wanted to quit after that day because they forgot to bring the guys to get the pipes cleaned. Once another place offered him a job, somewhere in the city health department, working part-time. The pay would be okay, but he wouldn't get full benefits.

My dad and I talk to each other a little about what's going on and stuff. I don't get to talk to him a lot. I mean, I talk to him, but he doesn't play any games with me like he used to. He tells me to do good in school. If I don't do good in school, I get punished—no TV, no nothing.

I don't have any plans for the future, really. Sometimes I think I want to be a psychologist, but I don't feel like going to college. Some-day, I'll have a family, but not anytime soon, because you need money to have a family. I don't know if it would be fun to be a father. You have the parents screaming at their kids. It has to be really stressful, but it must have its moments.

If I had the money now and could buy the things I wanted, I would get computer stuff, like a regular computer with at least the Internet on it. I'd like one of those mini-computers, a palm pilot. I'd like a gold chain, you know, nothing big, and I'd give it to my father.

SOFTER

Marcus, 11, from a suburb in southern New England

I've played the cello for about six years. I perform classical pieces by composers like Bach and Mozart. I'm finishing up a Vivaldi piece right now. Other guys don't say too much about my cello playing. Some-times, they compliment me after performances. A few guys asked me to play in a concert. We started a little group together recently.

I live with both of my parents. I have a sister, Andrea, who's in fourth grade. She's nine now. So I'm the oldest in the family. I also have a dog and a goldfish who's been with me for seven years.

My dad is Indian and he grew up in New Delhi. My mom is Danish. My mom stays home and my dad works. My mom sings opera. She has a nice voice. She likes cooking and to go biking sometimes. I see her in the morning before I go to school and then after school. My mom's pretty nice but she yells a lot. If I do bad on a test, my mom will go nuts, really nuts. My dad won't be as angry. He will ask me why I didn't do as well. He'll ask me what went wrong and how I might have studied better. Sometimes he'll help me with my homework, especially when I have a big exam or review. We have a TV room in our house with big, loafy—soft and comfy—couches that I like to study on. My dad will come in there and quiz me sometimes.

My dad is softer. Maybe it's because he doesn't see me as much. He's a businessman and he travels everywhere. He's always gone. When my dad's away, Mom is in charge, and I just do my thing, my homework and stuff. I miss my dad when he goes away but he calls every night. He'll talk to me and then to Andrea. Sometimes he's home on school nights. I see him a lot on weekends. On the weekends, we like to be together as a family. I feel close to my dad when he's around. I can talk to him about things. I like my dad a lot. He's a good guy. I like the way he talks to me and the way I can talk to him. When I'm having an argument or need to talk about private things, he un-derstands. If kids at school are making fun of me, he will try to com-fort me. He'll tell me stories from his past, about things that have happened to him, to make me feel better. Like once when my dad was in college, he and his friends made a huge snowball and rolled it into the street. The cops came after them. Another time, he dared his friend to jump into the snow naked and then he gave him a dollar for it. My dad would tell me these stories for fun and to show that he didn't have a perfect childhood. My dad's childhood in New Delhi was not a lot of fun. He is really smart and his parents were really strict. My dad told me that he never had even one play date when he was little—I'm seri-ous. He was always studying. His family was middle class but he was expected to work really hard. My dad knows what it's like to work hard in school because he had to work hard, too. He empathizes. I think he got teased when he was little, too. He was one of the best students all through school, so there was always a lot of pressure on him. All of his friends made fun of him. They would tell him not to take himself too seriously. They were probably jealous or something. Now, when I do well in school and play the cello, maybe kids make fun of me for the same reason.

My dad and I play sports together. He also reads to me. Like right now I'm reading *The Hobbit* just for fun. My dad likes to read it to me because he likes the story, too. In *The Hobbit,* the main character, Bilbo, goes on adventures with these dwarfs to find the gold. At the end, there is a big battle with four or five armies, and they have to kill a dragon. It's a good book. The chapters are long so my dad will read about a chapter and a half a night. He'll read to me while I'm in bed. Sometimes, I doze off while he's reading. Other times, I am just listening or half-listening. When he reads, he doesn't do different voices for the different characters or anything, but it's OK. My dad speaks with a sort of Indian-English accent, almost in between the two. Some words he pronounces differently. He has a light accent.

I'm really close to him. I love him a lot. We just fit together. My dad is probably the person in my life who I look up to most. I'd like to be like him someday but I don't want to be a businessman. I'd like to be a natural scientist and work with volcanoes and stuff like that. But I'd like to be the type of person my dad is someday. I like the way he handles matters nicely. He is very smart and he's funny sometimes. He knows what he is doing.

HE IS AFRAID

Kevin, 17, from a city in the Northwest

I have an OK relationship with my parents. My mom's mother was a terrible alcoholic, and died when she was in college, and so my mother was extremely distanced from her mother, had no relationship with her. She has been deathly scared that I wouldn't have a relationship with her or my father, so she kind of overcompensated for both of them. At the same time, my father's dad was very competitive with him, he wasn't nice, they didn't communicate. But instead of overcompensating, my father is like his own father. He's not very communicative. I don't care if he coaches my soccer team for nine years in a row; I would rather he just talked to me once in a while. But he has never talked to a male figure in the way that I would talk to my mother, for example, or my friends. It's very hard and disappointing for me. Our relationship is just like a casual friendship. I play tennis with him.

In part, I think he is afraid it is kind of fruity: two guys taking a walk and just talking is kind of touchy-feely. My father is very homophobic, and even though he knows that I am not gay, that I am interested in girls, he has this thing. Old preppy, East Coast things, like the pink monogrammed shirt. My mom got me one for Christmas, and it's like a little joke. But he said, "That's kind of gay, don't you think?" And it was like "Dad, why are you so homophobic?" He answered, "I'm not, it's just kind of gay. People will think you are gay." "Well, why do you care? I am not gay, but if I wore a pink shirt and some guy on the street thinks I am gay, what do you care?" "They will think you're gay and you're my son." And then he realized what he was saying and he stopped right there. But he has that masculinity complex for me, maybe because he sees that I don't really have it for myself. I am very comfortable with who I am, and he thinks that only gay guys are comfortable with themselves, not caught up in proving their masculinity. He doesn't want to be ashamed of himself and he doesn't want to be ashamed of me. I am much closer to my mother.

I am trying to open a line of communication before it's too late, but I don't know what it would do. All I know is that early communication and understanding are crucial. If fathers can understand the whole masculinity complex, that proving ground, it would help them understand their sons so much better. I want to tell my father to talk to me: "Tell me what you are feeling, tell me what your worries are, tell me about your concerns. Let's go at it."

It would help, too, if we could eliminate that proving ground, the competition to be most masculine. I am very sure of myself and I used to be afraid that other people wouldn't know that. But I've found that being sure of myself makes me happy, and other people see I am happy and then associate that with being sure of myself. I see some people struggle and cause problems because they aren't sure of themselves and they want others to think that they are. What I would change is to make people more sure of themselves. When you are sure of who you are and what you are, others will be able to see that reflection.

I Would Have Missed My Father

Juan, 17, from a city in the Northeast

I don't really care about not having a father. I would have missed my father if I would have needed him. If I saw him now, I'd tell him that I have been working since I was fourteen. I don't need you. You can come if you want to. You can be my friend. You are not going to be my father. I am seventeen now and you have never been there for me. You could be my friend. If he came to me now, would I forgive him? I just don't know. If he comes later when I am a professional, will he want me to take care of him because he is old?

Then I'd ask him, Why do you come now? Why didn't you come before? One day about two or three years ago, he called me at home and said, "Oh yes, I'm calling because I want to see you."

I told him, "I don't want to see you."

I am mad at my father. I told him, "I don't want to see you. You want to see me, but I don't want to see you." And then he is all the way in the Dominican Republic and all that. "Oh yes," he told me, "but you've got to understand that—"

"I don't have to understand anything. You calling me now after like fifteen years." They told me that I saw him once. And I don't think that's true, because I don't remember.

"Where have you been? Why? Why weren't you there? Was it something I did? I don't think it's something I did. I was a little kid. I'm innocent."

I don't think it was my fault. I know in my mind that he'll come if he wants to. If he doesn't come, I will learn from that. I'll learn how *my* kids would feel if they didn't have me as their father. Like, "Oh wow, I lived without a father my whole life." I wouldn't want my kids to be raised saying that. I would want to be there for them.

I would love to be a father. Right now my sister has a new baby named Kimberly. She loves me. Every time she sees me she is like "Oh, yes!" And I just picture myself having my own daughter. It's great. I love her.

If I had kids I would look forward to spending time with them. I would teach them about life, read to them, play Nintendo, bring them to the movies. Doing things like that together would be good. Because kids, you need to be there for them. You've got to, you are their first teacher. They don't learn everything in school. It's your job to teach them, too. That's the way I think of it. I would love to be a father.

My advice to other kids from a family where there is just one parent is just try to live life as it is. Don't go back, don't ever go back. Always go forward. And just try your best. I mean, you are going to think about it, but don't stress yourself. If he is coming, he's coming. If he's not, he's not.

If it was my choice, I would really want to see him. See him in person. I am curious. What does he look like? Do I look like him? Does he work? Sometimes I wonder, Why weren't you there for me?

MACHO
Ralph, 17, from a suburb in the West

Parents are very important and I have a good relationship with mine. They each help me in different ways. I connect with my mother emotionally and I connect with my father through sports. They're both there for me and together they're a good balance.

I can talk to my mom. She knows that I get angry at myself and tries calling me on it, saying things like "Oh, it's all right. Try to be easier on yourself." My mom really tries to sympathize with me. My mom was a perfectionist when she was a kid but she grew out of it as she got older. She's hoping that I'll grow out of it, too.

My relationship with my dad is pretty good. When my dad is home, he cracks the whip and tells us what to do. I don't really talk to him because he's really the manly type. He tries to be macho and not talk. I've never really had a good talk with him unless it was about football or baseball. He's into sports. Sports are it for him. I have never seen him emotional. He never shows that side. Maybe at a funeral, but otherwise he's just happy or angry. He never really cries. I've never really seen my dad cry before. I cry all the time, so he must cry sometimes. I try not to cry in front of other people, but I have before. I try not to because a lot of guys think that if you cry, you're being a baby or a wuss.

So I can cry and I do cry if I have to, but I generally try to hide in front of other people, like schoolmates, for example. But not in front of my mom. Crying in front of my mom is OK; it's a safe place. With friends it's not so safe. And it's not safe to cry in front of my dad. He gives me a hard time. He'll laugh and say things like "Come on. Cheer up." He tries to be empathetic but I don't get the sense that he sympathizes. He doesn't make fun of me, but he tries to get me out of it. But he doesn't understand how bad I feel. I think he tries to be too macho. My dad never had a dad when he was growing up. He always lived with his mom. His older brothers pretty much raised him and they're the big, macho type. So I think that's how he's tried to influence me. But I don't mind. I am still who I am. I try to be friends with him. I try to be a little bit hard, to be more macho. But it's not exactly me. It's too bad that it has to be that way.

ALWAYS WORKING

Henry, 18, from a city in the Northwest

It's awkward with my father, because when I was younger he was always working, was always just leaving the house. When I think of my dad I always think of him coming in my room and saying, "Well, okay, I am going away for a couple of days, so I'll see you in three days." And I wasn't hurt by that. We had a close relationship where we would go to basketball games and stuff, but it wasn't like we had any close talks. Growing up, there were a lot of times when he wasn't even around. He was just gone. So we definitely don't discuss issues that I have now. The connection was never there and I never really wanted it to be. I thought I pretty much had it figured out myself.

I rarely talk to my parents about school, and I never, ever talk with them about my problems. Oh God, there have been times when I've just hated them. I mean, I never wanted to kill them, but there are so many times when I literally just completely hated them, hated their guts. I mean, they just killed me. My dad is really mellow but sometimes he would just explode. He is just like me, where he will control himself for so long, but then if he gets mad he erupts. It's like an earthquake-type thing. He just freaks out. And then my mom continuously nags, and I get so angry. Like recently, I come in frustrated with school or just kind of sad, and I will kind of snap at them; I won't be really respectful toward them. Then they will explode and tell me I am being disrespectful, and they will scream at me and all this stuff. But besides that, it's not like I come in and want to have big talks with them. So it's kind of a weird situation, because they do want to have those sort of friendly talks, but I just don't. I've always had a weird feeling being around them. I just feel uncomfortable.

I REALLY LIKE HIM

Chip, 12, from a city in the West

I can talk to my dad about any problems at school. He is a really good listener. I would imagine I am a good listener, too, but only when I want to be a good listener. When there is something interesting, I listen very well. My friends come to me with their problems sometimes, and they tell me things about their girlfriends and what is going on with them.

I look up to my dad. I sometimes go on bike rides with him and sometimes he helps with my homework. We mostly do family things. I think he works really, really hard, and I think he's a great man. He has a good way of dealing with people. He is smart, and he has an excellent sense of humor. I think that's what I admire most about him. When I grow up I would like to be a combination of a great actor and my dad's personality. I really like him.

15

FRIENDSHIPS AND
ROMANCES WITH GIRLS

"I think girls would agree that they want more give from guys."
—Jesse, 17, from a suburb in New England

"Guys take on a new persona to impress girls."
—Max, 17, from a city in the South

*"If I'm interested in a girl I'll talk to her, but sex or romance is not
the only thing I'm aiming for. Of course, it does happen sometimes
to me where I see a really cute girl, and I just want to kiss her!"*
—Aaron, 16, from a city in New England

CONTRARY TO CONVENTIONAL WISDOM, MANY BOYS DUR-
ing adolescence rely upon girls as their primary source of platonic
friendship and social support. In and out of school, girls often provide
boys with a special kind of nonsexual companionship, one that enables
them to relax, be themselves, and find support when they feel vulnerable
or exposed. When they feel ashamed to turn to their parents and male
friends for support, female peers are frequently there to listen, understand, and help them stay the course. Boys feel at ease in sharing their
fears, sadness, and disappointments with close female peers. They go to
these special female friends to talk about difficulties about doing well at
school, about their conflicts with parents and siblings. They discuss their
anxieties about getting a job or going to college after high school; they
talk about dating, love, and sexuality, and about their feelings of isolation

and loneliness. Boys told me that they count on these friendships to boost them up as they face the tough challenges of young adulthood.

Some boys told us that they were able to nourish their close friendships with girls openly, without worrying about what others would say or do. Others explained that they felt they had to keep these friendships secret. Several remarked that their parents misunderstood the nature of these friendships or that they were teased or bullied by peers when most of their friends were girls or if they had not "scored" with one of them.

As much as we give adolescent boys a mixed message about girls— try to conquer them sexually, but don't be their friends; act warmly and lovingly toward them within a sexual relationship, but don't seek out their warmth and love in nonsexual friendships—many boys seem to be saying, "Leave us alone. We love being friends with girls. Girls are important to us." Simply put, as much as some boys, in order to seem traditionally masculine and be considered popular among their peers, may seem to want to close the door on girls, in reality, most of them are eager to open that door and cultivate girls as friends. Boys want to let girls in. They want female buddies.

Naturally, some girls may be afraid of reaching out to boys in a platonic way. They may fear that the boys will attempt to sexualize the relationship or that they won't be interested in friendship at all. One hopes that girls will be able to move beyond those fears, because probably most boys actually do not feel interested in rushing into sex. So many of them are yearning to be liked, understood, and nurtured by close female friends.

As they grow into young men and seek out romantic relationships with girls, teenage boys are often encouraged to connect to girls through sex. Bravado and boasting about their sexual conquests is commonplace. But underneath the braggadocio, boys are confused about girls. Often they can't discern whether a girl is sending the message that she is interested in a friendship or a romantic relationship. In addition, boys are confused about how to form a successful romantic relationship. Although sex remains a strong, driving force, boys also want to know how to navigate issues of closeness. Because of the restrictive Boy Code, which discourages the expression of emotion and vulnerability, some boys may be uncertain about the ways of achieving a balanced intimacy with members of the opposite sex.

Many of the boys I spoke to openly stated that they have trouble decoding the subtle messages their girlfriends sometimes send them. One day everything seems smooth in the relationship. The next day their girl-friends are distant, angry, or want to break up. One day a girl will claim that she wants a sensitive, understanding boyfriend, and the next day she will be going out with the football team's quarterback. It seems that the rules are always changing. Boys seem to be aware that they might be missing the nuances in their romantic relationships, that girls are much more attuned to shifts in feeling and to people's different needs and emotions. But boys hope that girls could be more clear about what they want. Some boys told me that girls want their boyfriends to be able to read their minds and always know what they're feeling. When boys fail to do this, their girlfriends break off the relationship with them without explanation or notice. These breakups are devastating, and this devastation reveals just how much boys truly care about and need romantic relationships.

Several boys told me that their girlfriends complain that they do all the giving and that their boyfriends aren't attuned to the day-to-day details of the relationship. Jesse, a seventeen-year-old who attends a New England boarding school, described an incident with his girlfriend: "I wouldn't call her very often. We each went home almost every weekend during the year. I wouldn't call her much over the weekend. She'd say, 'Jesse, why don't you ever call me?' I'm like 'Well, it's only two days!' That was the wrong thing to say because to her it was a big deal. To me it wasn't. I didn't miss her that much in just two days. We'd see each other Friday night, and then on Sunday night. But girls tend to be need-ier in terms of contact or acknowledgment or recognition. And she wasn't getting enough of that from me."

The reality is that young males have been tethered by the Boy Code for centuries. For years, they have been scorned if they revealed their true need and dependence upon girls. Only now are they acquiring the tools they need to reveal their genuine yearnings and achieve the intimacy with girls that they truly desire. As the voices in this chapter will tell you, though boys sometimes stumble, they want to have both friendships and romantic relationships with girls that have closeness and meaning.

IF YOU'RE JUST NICE, IT WILL COME TO YOU
Aaron, 16, from a city in New England

I'm different from most boys because I'm not hormone crazy. With most boys between the ages of thirteen and sixty-five, I would say it's basically girls, girls, girls. All they want is to have sex and stuff like that. When they see a girl, the first thing they see is her body, and if her body is nice, that's *all* they see. And they'll do anything to get with that girl, they'll do anything to be her boyfriend. Then they'll do anything to try to have sex, even if it includes trying to put on the impression that they actually care.

It's not like that with me, though. I can sit down and have a conversation with a really cute girl and not mention sex at all. It's like I just chill. If I'm interested in a girl I'll talk to her, but sex or romance is not the only thing I'm aiming for. Of course, it does happen sometimes to me where I see a really cute girl, and I just want to kiss her! But I calm myself down; that's just something I learned. Like I said before, I have to block certain things out, I have to take control.

In my family I've really turned to two people in the last few years, and not the people you would expect: my fifteen-year-old brother and my ten-year-old sister. My little sister is really neat, so it's especially easy to talk to her, and that has helped me understand girls a lot better than most guys do. From spending time with her and talking to her, I kind of know what girls want and can pretty much tell what goes on with them. I look at it as a kind of science project, where I come up with a hypothesis about certain girls, gather some information, maybe talk to them or just watch them. And then I kind of analyze that data. For instance, I'll notice that a certain girl doesn't like to be hugged or touched, or she doesn't like certain types of jokes, or she doesn't like it when guys look at her body. And then I'll come up with a conclusion and I'll use that to act respectful toward her and treat her in a way that makes her comfortable. That makes it a lot easier to become friends, and when you have friends who are girls, you start to realize that girls are people, too.

A lot of my guy friends are really nice but they don't know how to block out their hormones. They haven't been able to learn how to handle it like I have. Maybe they didn't have any girls around them that they could get used to, like I have my little sister. They just can't figure out why I'm able to have conversations with all these cute girls that they can't even talk to. So they see me as having a lot of game. Sometimes, though, when I'm talking with a girl, she or her friends will say, "Are you gay?" I answer back, "No, I'm not gay. I like girls." And then they wonder what's wrong with me. They say, "Why are you so nice to girls, then? Why aren't you flirting with us?"

A lot of times girls come to school with skimpy clothes on, and they have all sorts of moves to make us look at them. I've seen a lot of girls move in ways that I could not imagine, but I've learned how to control myself and not let it get to me. Then they wonder, "Why is his jaw not on the ground? What's wrong with him?" They do stuff to attract us, and the fact that a lot of sixteen-year-old males are out of control anyway just adds to it. And that causes a whole big mess.

Girls definitely play a role, but you have to know how to deal with it. My first instruction to boys out there would be to calm down. In other words, stop and think. Look at that girl you noticed because she had a dope body, and look at her overall. Look at her personality and instead of saying all these crazy lines, just say hi and try to find out what she's like. Also, I'd tell people that sex is not everything, because you can have a baby come out of that. Most people I know cannot afford a baby at this time. And finally, if you're just nice, it will come to you, everything will fall into place.

THE BREAKUP

Jesse, 17, from a suburb in New England

Just before my girlfriend and I started going out, she had broken up with another guy. She wasn't ready for a deep commitment. So, we started going out and then she immediately broke it off. But then a mutual friend told me that she still liked me. I didn't know what was going on. So I asked my dorm parent to explain girls to me in twenty words or less. He said, "Stay flexible." Later that week she said, "Will you go out with me?" I said, yeah, and we did, and I was glad because, in the beginning, it was a great relationship.

That "stay flexible" advice is very important. In the big things, like what girls want from a relationship, you have to hear them out. And in little things, too, like if they want to see a particular movie. If you don't want to see that one, just say OK anyway. Be ready to change.

I think girls would agree that they want more give from guys. From the girls I've spoken to about relationships, one of their biggest complaints is that they're doing all the giving and the guy is doing all the taking.

Girls also tend to be better able to understand social situations. Girls can look at someone and tell what they're feeling. They have more social intuitiveness, more than we clueless guys do. I think that makes them more aware of what's happening in a relationship than we are.

My girlfriend went away that summer and I spent a lot of time thinking about our relationship. I realized that the relationship was not working; it wasn't what I wanted to be happening. I wasn't enjoying the relationship anymore, and she wasn't either. I realized that she had always been more worried about commitment than I was. I didn't think it was a problem, because I didn't want her to see anyone else, and I wasn't planning to see anyone else. I wanted to stay with her. But she worried that we were growing apart, and that's why she became more affectionate toward me.

So, as I thought about our relationship, I realized that I hadn't really seen what I was doing. She obviously saw it and she let me know. But I still didn't understand it.

For example, I wouldn't call her very often. We each went home almost every weekend during the year. I wouldn't call her much over the weekend. She'd say "Jesse, why don't you ever call me?" I'm like, "Well, it's only two days!" That was the wrong thing to say, because to her it was a big deal. To me it wasn't. I didn't miss her that much in just two days. We'd see each other Friday night, and then on Sunday night. But girls tend to be needier in terms of contact or acknowledgment or recognition. And she wasn't getting enough of that from me.

We broke up at the beginning of this school year. The breakup itself was not that bad. I had made the decision to break up with her and said, "I don't think we should go out with each other anymore." And she just said, "OK." I've never dumped anyone before. I was hoping for some tears or something, and all I got was "OK." She told me that she was planning to break up with me, too. So it ended up being mutual.

I haven't had a girlfriend since then. Maybe some part of me doesn't want a relationship right now because I'm afraid it's going to happen again. I guess the only way to find out would be to try to get seriously emotionally involved with someone again, but I don't know if I want to do that if it means a risk of hurting them. I haven't made a resolution never to date again, but I am hesitant to get emotionally involved right now.

HANGING OUT WITH GIRLS
Max, 17, from a city in the South

If a guy wants to get involved with a hot girl in class who is academically average, he might act like the disinterested anti-intellectual to impress her. Guys take on a new persona to impress girls. It's the same at any school. Even at a boys-only boarding school, there is a pressure to impress other guys by not acting smart. But I think it happens more in a coed environment. It's hard to tell if girls do the same thing. I don't know where it comes from. I think with guys it's sexual attraction, or maybe it's peer pressure.

I was talking to some guys about hanging out with girls as friends because it's a new thing for me. At boarding school we used to have the girls bussed in. It's humorous, but sometimes the comments can be pretty harsh, like "The meat is rolling in." In a setting like that, your only approach is to try to get some kind of relationship going quickly. In public school there's a lot more friendly interaction between girls and guys. It's hard to explain to my friends at boarding school what that's like. They don't understand or they don't believe it, and it's hard to explain to them. There's a part of me that likes meeting girls that way. And some girls I think are interesting, but I wouldn't want more than just a friendship with them.

It's different having friends who are girls. You can sit down and chat with them. You can't sit down and chat with a guy. There is some tension when I'm chatting with girls, but after a while it goes away. With guys you always need to make wisecrack comments, and lambast this or that. I know it's a stereotype, but girls are more sensitive. They have more feelings, whereas guys will joke with each other nonstop. With girls it seems more emotional. You're dealing with somebody who's softer and more emotional, more chitchatty.

Sometimes I can't figure out girls. They'll have things on their mind and expect you to know what it is, but guys don't pick up on those things and become confused. When you can't read their mood, I think they have a problem with that. Some girls seem to understand and they seem to put up with it, but they'll complain later or confront you. Other girls cut you off and move on, go somewhere else. If I could give advice to guys, I would tell them to communicate better to girls, that sometimes we just don't get it, and it's not because we're being mean or negative. Girls are always fishing around for it, but it would be nice if they helped us out a bit. I guess girls feel like guys don't care, or that we don't understand them. The fundamental shortcoming in relationships must be interaction.

Guys have always been behind girls in emotional development. In grade school, girls would approach boys with less fear. Boys seem to have more fear of being rejected by girls, but as you develop, guys are supposed to take charge of situations. It's an interesting conflict.

A VERY, VERY HARD TIME
Ben, 17, from a suburb in New England

The thing that is always bubbling in my mind, as I'm sure it is for most other guys my age, is, of course, relationships: girls and stuff. About a month ago, I came out of a one-year relationship, and I'm having a very, very hard time dealing with it.

I got dumped. I think she got a little scared. The whole thing was up and down for a long time, and it was complicated. But I know she still has feelings for me.

If I had to use one word to describe Sara, I would say crazy. She is energetic and outgoing. She and I do a lot of the same stuff; we love doing theater. She is very funny, and likes to have an audience.

That contrasts a bit with me. I think of myself as more reserved and shy, although other people tell me that's not true. I think that is a self-image I have left over from middle school, when I was really quiet.

I had been in a relationship with another girl before Sara. Then I went on the Boston-to-New York AIDS ride in October. The girl cheated on me with another guy while I was on the ride, and then dumped me when I came back. I guess she had been interested in him for a while, and took the opportunity of me being gone to jump on it.

That was pretty traumatic. I was in the process of getting over it, when Sara and I got together. She and I had been close friends for five or six months. We were good buddies, and we liked to hang out. When I got dumped by my previous girlfriend, Sara and I kind of fell for each other over the course of a month or two. The relationship officially started Friday, November 13.

We started spending all of our time together, flirting, tickling, and all of that stuff. One day we went up to a classroom at the top of this building that is legendary at our school. It has a little skylight. People like having classes in there. And it's a fun place to go and hang out when there is free time. So, Sara and I were sitting up there one afternoon not doing anything. We were chatting. She tickled me. I tickled her back. We kissed. It was cute.

In the couple of weeks leading up to that, we had been going to the movies and going out to dinner. After we kissed at school, we stopped going out to dinner; we would just spend evenings sitting around watching TV, eating at home, kissing, fooling around.

Over winter break, we spent the whole time together. It was wonderful. It went on in a fairy-tale-perfect way for a couple of months. No arguments. No disagreements. A good physical relationship, but no sex.

Thanks to the miracle of modern technology, we communicated over the Internet all the time. It is actually a lot easier to bring up things if you're just seeing a person's words appear on a screen, and not talking to them on the phone. That's how a lot of people first get to know another person, and then they talk to them in school. It is so much easier. You don't have to deal with the emotional impact of what you say. You just type it and the words appear. It is nice and clean.

We talked about sex over the Internet. We would joke around about it. We would say, "Hey, wouldn't it be neat if we could do this? Wouldn't it be neat if we could do that?" Then we would stop and one of us would write, "Do you think we are actually going to do that?" Then the other one would say, "Only if we're both comfortable with it." We'd both say "I am comfortable if you are comfortable." We would go back and forth like that.

After about three months we did have sex—which was me losing my virginity. You hear all sorts of horror stories about that, but I thought it went pretty well. No hitches, no arguments, no huge mess. No embarrassment, fumbling, or anything like that, which is something that you hear about.

Having sex didn't change things much. It was fun. It was nice. After that first time, we did it relatively regularly. It was a big part of the relationship, but it didn't really change the focus. In fact, there was a feeling of relief. I felt like "I don't have to worry about this anymore." One of my best friends is a year younger than I am and lost his virginity the year before I did. As soon as he did, I felt pressure not to be the last one. I thought, "How did he do that? He's a dropout and a druggie. Why can't I do it?" We have another friend who is eighteen and a half now, and he is still a virgin. That pisses the hell out of him. We're careful not to talk about sex around him because that frustrates him.

As soon as Sara and I started going out, everybody at school knew about it. They all thought, "That's really strange." Nobody saw it coming. They were surprised that it happened, because they were used to us spending a lot of time together as good friends. Then, after everyone got used to it, they were saying, "That is really cute."

Sara did not like being cutesy and clichéd. Even so, we would walk around holding hands; we would hug and give each other a quick kiss before we would go off to class. She had no difficulty with public displays of affection. She just didn't want to be cute about it.

My parents knew about our relationship. It's kind of hard to hide from your parents when you're spending all your time with somebody. Besides, my parents have always been incredibly open with me about stuff like that. I have known all about safe sex, drugs, and alcohol from a very young age. They always said, "You make your own choices, you make your own mistakes. This is what we can tell you. Please be wise." I think that contributed a lot to my decision to do no drugs and use no alcohol whatsoever.

Part of who Sara is, is that she pokes fun at people. Just friendly little jabs that most people don't even think about twice. But because I was going out with her, I didn't expect them to be directed at me. I didn't learn early enough just to let them go. Instead, I would make a big deal about it. I'd say, "Don't say that. It upsets me. You're poking fun at me."

After a few weeks of my being like that, she decided to take a break. I was out with my friends on a Friday night when I picked up a voice mail from her on my cell phone. It said, "I need to talk to you right away. Give me a call unless it's too late, then call me in the morning." That, of course, ruined the rest of my night with my friends, because I was worrying about what she was going to say.

I called her in the morning. She said, "I need a break. Just one week. Let's try being friends." She didn't want a break from me, she just wanted a break from going out with me. She wanted to reestablish our friendship. I was upset about it, but I thought if we could just have fun, that would be good.

Sometime later, Sara and I made up. We went through eight more months of ups and downs. Then, a couple of weeks ago, she decided she was having a bad day, and she was going to ignore me. I got really upset.

I don't know what possessed me to do it, but I grabbed a leather-working tool and gave myself a scratch on the wrist.

I don't even know where the idea came from. It was right before a theater performance. She was stage managing, and I was running the lighting board. I thought: either you can go back down and sit at the light board and wait for ten minutes for the show to start, or you can go into the bathroom and cut yourself.

I chose B. I don't know why, but I did. It just sort of happened. I wasn't trying to hurt myself. It was just a scratch. I think it probably was directed at Sara. I think I was trying to show her how incredibly upset I was. It was a minor cut, but I hadn't cleaned it, so it had a little bit of blood on it. Sara saw it, and she freaked out. She thought, rightly so, that it was because of her actions that I had cut myself.

I think I scared the shit out of her. She said that. I couldn't find any way to get it across to her how upset I was, because when she doesn't want to listen, she just won't listen. That was the only way I could get it across.

Sara took me home and made me call my parents. The next day, she broke up with me.

She hasn't spoken to me for three weeks. This is quite a blow for me in a bunch of ways. First of all, we had been completely attached to each other. We could finish sentences for each other. We liked the same things. We liked the same food. We told the same jokes. We were practically one person for the better part of a year. To suddenly have no connection with her now is devastating. Add to all that a sudden lack of sex; it is really terrible.

Also, Sara's family had kind of become my family. I stayed with them a lot in the spring and the summer, because my parents were getting separated. They had been having problems for as long as I can remember, with screaming arguments and all that. In a way, Sara's family became my surrogate family. They kind of adopted me. I hung around with her dad and helped him with chores. That was a wonderful thing to me, to have a regular old normal family.

Then I lost that.

Sara is only the second girl I have ever gone out with, and certainly the only girl I have ever really loved. It is an incredibly strange concept, thinking about going out with somebody else, not Sara. Not having that same life. Not going and having dinner with her family every other night. Not driving around in her little red sports car. Not spending my time with her. Not telling those jokes. Not playing with her dog.

She is a year ahead of me, so she is a senior now. We both figured we would be going out until she graduated, and then, of course, we would have to part ways. I knew there was that time limit on it, but I could never really envision an end to it. If I could, I envisioned something a little more peaceful than this.

SOMEONE ELSE

Lonnie, 18, from a suburb in the West

Loneliness really gets to me. It's one of the bigger things in my life, for some reason.

At the beginning of this year I was lonely because I've never had a girlfriend, and I've always liked and admired women. I've always had these really huge crushes that I could almost call love; maybe not so intense as love but close. But they never synthesized. I waited too long for them to ask me out, and I never had the guts to go up and ask them.

But I have a girlfriend now. I sat down and said, "Will you go out with me?" She said to wait a minute, and then she came back and she said yes.

Things are not really much different. There's less loneliness, but I don't know . . . there wasn't too much change, so I guess loneliness was only an imagined enemy of mine. More like a yearning—it was wanting someone else.

YOU CAN TALK DEEP WITH THEM

Dwayne, 17, from a city in the Northeast

I live at home with my mom and four sisters. It's fun being the only boy at home. I love my sisters. We have a good relationship. You feel this certain thing with girls, a confidence. When you have five females living in your house, you get to know things that other guys do not know about females. You get to know secrets, things like that.

If you have sisters, they can give you advice and tell you what to do. They can explain to you what girls do not like for a guy to do—like holler at them, scream out their names. They tell you to be respectful, have manners, things like that. You can talk deep with them; you practice talking deep with your sisters so you have a better chance of talking deep with a *female*. You share with them.

For boys who don't have any sisters, I wouldn't say they lose out. I can't just generalize like that. But when you don't have any sisters, you might become narrow-minded. If the parent is very strict and he doesn't want the guy doing any dishes or anything like that, you could become narrow-minded in thinking that the man is the head of the house. That's a disadvantage because then, when they go up to females, the female is like, especially in the nineties, "Uh-uh, I'm not going to cook for you, we're going to share fifty-fifty." That's a disadvantage right there.

Having experience with girls, having sisters, prepares you for a society where, as a guy, you're expected to be egalitarian and share with women. Today it's fifty-fifty all the way. It's not like the women clean the house anymore. Women get more respect because they work. With my sisters at home, everything that we do, like chores for instance, everything is fifty-fifty. When my sister does the bathroom, I do the kitchen. When she does the kitchen, I do the bathroom. And so on.

All my friends are girls. It's so funny because they feel comfortable with me. It's not like "Oh, you're a guy, I can't say such-and-such about this guy I like." I guess if you practice with your sisters, you are able to speak better to females and have a better bond with them.

One of my best friends is Rosa, and the other one is Mercedes. I have a lot of respect and love for them. They are unique people. They're very different from me; that's why I hang out with them. Opposites attract me. I don't think you should hang out with a person that's just like you. That would get boring.

Rosa is my partner in crime. She has so much talent. She's independent and strong and creative. I'm some of those things, but I see things in her that I want to attain. She's my love. I love her to death. Mercedes is also a strong person, a lovely, sincere person. She has everything that I want to strive toward. She shows me, she teaches me. Sometimes I have an attitude and get real nasty, and she's like, "Don't do that, don't do this!"

Rosa and I can exchange advice. Right now, for example, she likes this guy who works at a pharmacy, so she's asking me, "Dwayne, what should I do? What should I do?"

I'm like, "Girl, just go up to him and ask him his name." Guys are not going to get a big head if you go ask them their name, it's just gonna be like, "Oh, is she interested, or is she not?" You gotta be straightforward.

Yesterday Rosa called me at 9:30 P.M., and she's like "Dwayne, Dwayne, guess what? I talked to him. I feel so good about myself."

I can relate better with girls. I don't think guys are as straightforward. I'm a straightforward person, I like to be upfront. I like to say,
"Look, this is what I like, this is what I feel." But guys always want to
hide things and pretend. I'm not down with that. I like to know what's
going on.

When guys are with me, I think they feel scared or threatened. They
come up to me and ask me, "Why are you always hanging out with
girls?"

I am like "Why not?"

All of the girls that I hang out with are attractive. I'm sorry to say,
they are all very attractive. So maybe the guys like these girls. Maybe
they want to be in my position. They want to be close to this girl or that
one. That's why they feel threatened. I'm just doing what I want to do;
it's not like I'm trying to provoke them or anything like that. Maybe
they're jealous.

If you ever sit down and listen to guys' conversations, most of the
ones that I've listened to are all full of it. For instance, they're talking
about a girl, the problem with being a virgin or something like that.
They always want to say, "Oh, I'm not a virgin," or "I want to get with
her" and things like that. But they're just not being straight with themselves. They're so wrapped up in trying to be cool and popular, and
worry about what everybody else thinks that they don't take care of
what they really want to do. I think it's very sad that people go through
life not doing what they want to do because they're worried about what
everybody else is gonna say about them. Life is too short to be thinking
about what people are going to say about you.

JULIA

Evan, 18, from a suburb in southern New England

One of many special people in my life stands out more than the most.
She is there through thick and thin, rain or shine, heaven or hell. She
will always be there. Her name is Julia. She is in her junior year of high
school and, at the age of sixteen, has put me in the line of success.
Whether it was just listening, giving me advice, forcing me to do the
right thing, she's always there.

I remember it like it was yesterday. Summer of 1997, going into my
freshman year of high school. I met the only girl I have ever truly loved

and wanted to be with. It was the best time of my life up to this point. It all started on a beautiful summer afternoon . . .

It was just Julia and I, at her house. It was about noon, and we were going out with some friends for the day. Julia and I had become great friends over our last year in middle school.

Well, she had to take a shower and I think she was a little nervous because of my presence. So I told her to trust me. She did and she got into the shower. I thought about joining her but I didn't. I had grown to like Julia in a friend *and* a girlfriend kind of way. But in no way did I express myself to her. I didn't want to lose her friendship.

I heard the shower shut off. But I just continued to sit on the little green love seat. She opened the bathroom door, and I looked over my right shoulder. It was at that point that I saw the most beautiful sight ever. She stepped out into a spotlight coming from the sun shining through the window. She was brushing her beautiful blond hair. She looked like an angel sent from God just for me. At this point I was stunned. I just stared at her. I had my right hand on the top of the seat, and she walked over and held out her left hand and placed it on mine. She said, "I knew I could trust you." It was at this point that I felt something come over me. I grabbed her hand, pulled her ever so slow and gentle over the top of the seat onto me. I looked into her beautiful blue eyes and I brought my lips close to hers, and began to kiss. After we kissed she got up and I grabbed her hand and looked up and said, "Did that just happen or was I dreaming?" She bent over and kissed me and said, "What do you think?"

That was the beginning of a beautiful thing. That summer Julia and I grew on each other. We spent a lot of time together and found out what love is really about.

I treated her like a man is supposed to, with respect, love, dignity, and everything she needed. She and I became one. I was going through some rough times with my mom, and Julia was there to support me through everything. It was indeed love. When we weren't together we were still connected at the heart. I would have done anything for her, like a real man. Even as much as taking a bullet for her love and life.

As our love grew, we realized how much we were meant for each other. There was just one problem. No one knew about our love. I told my best friends (three people) and she told her best friend. That was it. My friends told me there was something wrong. I didn't care as long as Julia and I knew that we loved each other.

Everything was going good. School started and Julia and I were still together. We would spend all kinds of time together, after school and on weekends. We got a job together, we would go out and eat together, and we would go on walks, anything to be together.

Then there were complications. Everyone at school started talking about Julia and me spending so much time together. Julia and I started to argue a lot. Everything went downhill. Before we knew it, we weren't even talking to each other. For two months we did not say a word to each other. Then finally Julia wrote me a letter that explained her feelings and sorrow.

From this day forward, Julia and I will always be one in some way or another. We are still friends. Maybe we will never be as close as we used to be but we will always be together in our memories. Who knows, maybe we will get back together someday? You never know—God works in mysterious ways.

Ever since the summer of our last year in middle school, Julia and I have become "like peas and carrots." We can talk to each other about anything and everything. We will always be friends, for ever and on.

Over our three-year friendship, we have been through the worst and yet managed to still be there for each other. For this I love Julia and always will until the end of time. (This is someone who nobody can ever take away!)

It's Going to Happen Soon

Sam, 12, from a city in the Northwest

My problem right now is that I am trying to get a girlfriend, which is kind of hard in an all-boys school. That's what I've been thinking about lately, and I think it's going to happen soon because I know some girls I really like. There's not a lot of pressure to have a girlfriend, but I would like to do it anyway, pressure or no pressure. It seems like so much fun to have a girlfriend, to pick someone up on dates and everything.

I've been watching a lot of movies and TV shows that show good relationships, and it looks like a lot of fun. Of course, I am not actually sure because I haven't tried it yet. I did have one girlfriend, but she lived in New York and I live on the West Coast. So that didn't really work out. It was a lot of fun, though. She convinced me to try my first cappuccino.

I would like to find a girlfriend who is pretty. But unlike most people, I am also really into personality. I am looking for a good sense of humor, someone who is really funny and knows what to say. So I am going mainly for personality. But if she is ugly it would be really hard. I think it would be fun to go out on dates, take her out to movies or to the beach, anywhere. I usually like being around girls more than guys anyway. I think it is much easier to talk to girls about problems. They listen better and seem to have a better sense of humor.

16

HAVING MALE BUDDIES

"Eric and I are close buddies, and I definitely think it's important to be able to really trust someone and talk to them, to be able to work stuff out with them."

—Pierre, 17, from a suburb in the Northwest

BOYS RECEIVE MIXED MESSAGES ABOUT WHAT THEIR friendships with other boys should be like. At one end of the spectrum, they observe media images celebrating boys having good buddies. On the other end, they see the fear in other people's eyes when two guys appear to be getting a little bit too "mushy" or too close. Thus, many boys feel conflicted about friendships, which range from intensely close and caring ones—sometimes their most important relationships during adolescence—to those that may be severely restricted, competitive, confrontational, or unfulfilling. Some of the boys to whom we spoke, when asked if they had a "best friend," named a male buddy. Others claimed they couldn't completely "be themselves" around other boys and that they therefore chose a female companion as a best friend. Some said that they had no best friend at all.

Boys who become close with other boys sometimes do so outside the pressured environment of school. At school, weighty expectations are heaped upon boys, especially those who are preadolescent or in early adolescence. They're expected to pursue girls and young women, to succeed athletically, to put each other down, and to hold their own when confronted. They feel tremendous pressure to convey their masculinity and establish the respect and admiration of their peers, especially among their male peers. It is when what I have termed the Impossible Test of Masculinity is probably at its peak, with boys being terrified of becoming humiliated and losing face.

"The pressure to be manly has always been there," explains sixteen-year-old James. "Life would probably be easier if I didn't have to be that way. . . . At times it stops me from being able to show how I feel, especially around my guy friends."

In such a rigid and constantly demanding social milieu, too often boys find it difficult to be honest about their feelings of friendship with other guys, to openly show their compassion and empathy toward male friends, and to connect with other boys in deep and meaningful ways. One boy explained how even his friendship with his brother was compromised by the antifriend boy culture: "He is the nicest person when it's just me and him. But then, when he is with his friends, or his girl-friend, he goes from this nice guy I thought I could talk to, I thought I could trust, to this person who doesn't care about me. He doesn't care what I'm thinking, he doesn't care what I have to say. I think he makes this change because he is afraid he won't seem cool if he is seen talk-ing to his little brother, like I might say something stupid to embar-rass him."

But beyond school and other restrictive settings that are encased by peer pressure and surrounded by shame, many boys do find one or more male friends whom they genuinely trust and in whom they confide. "Over the summer," Graham says about his friend Colin, "we will see each other six days out of the week. And we can each tell the other *everything*." Such a friendship that takes place mostly away from the larger peer group may provide an anchor for boys who generally feel completely isolated and are constantly anxious about how they are being perceived. The special friend, many boys explained, is someone with whom they can "be themselves" without the fear of shame or em-barrassment. That special friend is someone who has few preconceived notions or strict expectations, someone with whom a boy can feel free to say and do what he wants, share his secrets, expose his vulnerable feelings, open up about trouble at home, about conflicts with girls, about issues at school. With such a buddy, boys told us, you no longer need to feel all alone. You can feel good about yourself. You can feel protected.

CLOSE BUDDIES

Pierre, 17, from a suburb in the Northwest

I have one really close friend in school who I hang out with most of the time named Eric. Eric and I started an Internet music business together. It's funny; at my school I saw a memo once, a list of the students the administration wanted to approach to do a special survey. At the end of the list it said, "Pierre or Eric," so I guess we have affected each other quite a bit if we're interchangeable in the eyes of the administration!

Eric and I are close buddies, and I definitely think it's important to be able to really trust someone and talk to them, to be able to work stuff out with them. But I think it's also important that you don't get caught up too much with having that one person and shut yourself off from everyone else. If you get everything from one person, you are not really going to know how to relate to others. And that's really not what you want.

Eric and I communicate really well. And I have another close friend, Kurt, who I went to elementary school with. I can really, really feel open with him. We know each other's lives very intimately just because we have known each other since we were in kindergarten, and we can really talk freely and openly. I think that's really something a lot of people are lacking, especially guys. They really can't express their feelings. But I think I lucked out growing up. With my mom it was all about feelings, which is good.

I don't think a lot of guys have the skills to express their feelings. And people push guys to be separate and shut down. Of course, the media definitely have something to do with that. I hate to bring up the whole Columbine thing, but in the news you've seen every reporter asking, "Could this happen here, could this happen there?" Especially recently, teenagers have really been like the devil. I don't know if it's because I look different from the status quo, but I will see people grab their purses closer or cross the road when they see me and my friends walking on the street, just because they are afraid of teenagers.

A lot of guys are unwittingly taught by their parents not to express themselves and to buy the whole American hero thing. The all-American football player who gets hurt and doesn't say it, and then goes out for the team, and makes the touchdown. I think that has really percolated down through generations, and so people feel that they have to be like that. If you look at all the real role models, who do you have? You have war heroes who got shot fifteen times and dragged everybody back to the line. You have football heroes and basketball heroes. You don't really have any poets or anyone representing other perspectives or ways to live.

SOMEONE IN YOUR LIFE YOU CAN FALL BACK ON
James, 16, from a suburb in the West

Friendships are important. When a friend gets in trouble with his mom, I try to help him out. Or if a friend is mad at someone, I'll try to calm him down. If he is having trouble in school, does bad on a test, you try to help him out. I will try to sympathize with my guy friends but still try to be kind of macho about it.

I want to succeed so bad that when I don't, it becomes too much. Too much of that could get a guy really down. Like my friend Denny, for example, he gets really down. He seems depressed. I feel sorry for him. He's harder on himself than I am on myself. Thinking you're not as good as everybody else can lead to depression. Some guys who get picked on or who are perfectionists can feel so depressed that they might get suicidal. We learned in health class how the suicide rates are high, especially among teenagers and especially among guys.

I have a couple of friends who are girls but not nearly as many as guys. There isn't really a difference in the way I am with my friends who are girls than with my guy friends. I try to laugh a lot with both but maybe I laugh a little bit more with my friends who are girls.

I try to be more macho with the guys in front of a girl. When you're just alone with a girl as a friend, you drop the macho act. A lot of people say that girls are more sympathetic. Girls like to be talked to and I can do that when other guys aren't around.

Some men accept trying to be macho and that's what they will become. The pressure to be manly has always been there. I don't think it's going to change in the future. I consider myself kind of macho. It will always be one small side of me.

Life would probably be easier if I didn't have to be that way, but life would be a lot easier if you didn't have to do a lot of stuff. It's another thing you have to be able to do, like being motivated. There are a lot of things you have to be. If you're going to grow up and be a man, being macho is part of the deal. It's always been there. At times it stops me from being able to show how I feel, especially around my guy friends.

If I had to give advice to another guy growing up, I'd tell him to strive to be successful but don't be hard on yourself. Always make sure there's someone in your life you can fall back on, so in hard times you'll have a shoulder to cry on, and have as many friends as you possibly can.

MY BEST FRIEND

Nick, 12, from a suburb in New England

I have a group of friends. Sam is my best friend. We went to nursery and elementary school together, through third grade. Then he moved into another district, but now in middle school we're back together, and although I have three other friends, he's my best one.

Over the summer we had nothing to do, so Sam and I rode our bikes everywhere. When you get your car, you like it so much because you have your freedom. You can go wherever you want, when you want. We had something like that on our bikes. We rode at least five to ten miles a day. We rode to my friend's house, from this side of town to that side of town. We rode everywhere, and that was fun. Then school started and it got cold; now we usually hang out and watch TV and have parties and stuff.

To make friends like Sam, you have to be outgoing and be able to talk. You have to be able to go up to anybody at a table, even if he's not your friend, and have a conversation with him. You could start a conversation with anybody just being able to go up and say, "Hey, dude." Say something. Even sports is an okay way to start a conversation. "Did you see the game last night?" "No." "It was good." Although I don't really like to talk about sports, if I start it with that, then the conversation will move on. Then later I can talk about stuff that interests me more.

MOST GUYS NEED SOMEONE

Graham, 17, from a suburb in the West

If I'm ever really upset I talk to my best friend Colin. It's so important to have a best friend. One of my good friends doesn't have one and he just shuts down if you ask him how things are going with his girlfriend.

I can remember the first day I met Colin. We were in fourth grade and it was right after winter break. He had been moving around a lot because his dad was in the navy. And we have been friends ever since. We were in the Boy Scouts together. And we do literally everything together. Over the summer we will see each other six days out of the week. And we can each tell the other everything. I talked with him when I was really being teased and when some of the guys used to say I was gay. He could relate to that: he's really into theater and, despite the fact that he has a girlfriend, too, he was teased for a while about his sexuality. I have no shame with Colin; I can literally tell him anything and he can tell me as well.

Most guys find it hard to talk about their feelings. I have a big group of friends and we're all pretty comfortable with one another, we all like each other. But we never talk about our feelings unless something is *really* up.

Most guys need someone to talk to about personal stuff, and they don't have anyone to talk to. Perhaps it's because their dads raised them not to need anyone else's help, and because of that they don't realize they need help even if they do. Many guys don't ask for help: they repress their anger and repress their feelings so much they can end up losing it and acting out. Some guys get in lots of fights. It's like when a guy's girlfriend breaks up with him and he's really upset. If he can't talk to anyone, it's likely he'll act out and do something like get in a fight with the ex-girlfriend's new boyfriend.

Just last week one of my friends came to me and was so upset about something that he started crying. He has really liked this girl since June and he thought he was in love with her. She showed some interest and they dated for a while, but now they've stopped dating and he's really upset. She's been toying with him. And now they've broken up, she feels she can't act the same way with him that she does with her other guy friends. For instance, she won't hug him anymore, in case it's misinterpreted, but she hugs her casual male friends. That makes it even tougher for him. He's very upset. I just tried to be a good listener.

Guys need to be able to say, "I've got a problem. I can't handle this myself. I need to get it off my chest." And I honestly think that there would be less fighting, less jealousy, and less anger if guys had somebody to talk to about the problems that weigh on their minds.

I would say that about 80 percent of boys go into grade school with high self-esteem, and 20 percent go into middle school with high self-esteem. And after high school, only one to 5 percent of high school boys have high self-esteem. And I think the time between sixth grade and senior year is a really hard time to be a guy. Seventh and eighth grades are among the worst. Everyone harasses everybody. I got pushed around by the older kids, teased about being small and immature. One of my friends is really skinny and in those years all his jock friends used to tease him. In seventh and eighth grades, people love to pick on you about your physical appearance, your financial status, your age, your race and sexuality!

I think a lot of the problems guys have go back to prehistory, the caveman days. The men always went off on hunting trips together, and were in charge of feeding and caring for the family. The men always had to be on guard to protect women and children and they could not open up and bond like the women. The result of all this history is that if a man tries to open up and bond with anyone, it seems like he's acting in a feminine way. And society disapproves of that.

We would live in a better society if guys could share their feelings more easily. But guys still hear mixed messages from our society. On the one hand they hear that it's OK now to talk about their feelings, but on the other hand they still hear that they have to be tough and that only girls get emotional. My friend who talked to me and cried about his girlfriend was on the football team. His teammates would laugh at him if he tried to talk to them about that sort of stuff. But the fact is that most of them have had similar experiences. And, most of them know how hard it is to feel emotional pain and not talk about it. Some of my friends are like me, and believe guys should talk about their pain and that sharing doesn't make anyone less of a man. But we get mixed messages on this from our parents, our friends, and from society in general.

When I try to have deep conversations with my guy friends, I start off talking about sports, girls, or whatever they like to talk about. It's only once you talk for a while about this stuff and gain their confidence and trust that you can move on to more personal territory. Once you gain their trust, then you can start to say, Well, how are you and your girlfriend doing? How are you doing? And once you can get them to talk about stuff like that, I think you've really accomplished something. You've developed a rapport with them, gotten them to begin opening up.

A COUPLE OF FRIENDS

Scotty, 16, from a small town in the South

I have a couple of friends I can talk to and they help me through stuff. Like fights with my dad, or this one time last year when I had a girlfriend break up with me, and then my grandpa died, and my parents were on me again about grades. I was real close to my grandfather. We would talk, and he would show me how to make stuff. He came down with lung cancer all of a sudden, and he died within a month. Oh, it hurt pretty bad. I was shocked, and my friends helped me get through that time. I'm lucky to have them.

My brother Grant is actually an all right guy and he tries to give me some advice. We'll talk about things like troubles with our dad or problems with girls, and he will actually listen and tell me his opinion and give advice. He is the nicest person when it's just me and him. But then, when he is with his friends, or his girlfriend, he goes from this nice guy I thought I could talk to, I thought I could trust, to this person who doesn't care about me. He doesn't care what I'm thinking, he doesn't care what I have to say. I think he makes this change because he is afraid he won't seem cool if he is seen talking to his little brother, like I might say something stupid to embarrass him. He worries what his friends will think of him because of something I might say!

My closest friends are girls, but I have a couple that are guys. Girls are a lot better listeners than guys are. You can be yourself when you are around them, because when you have good friends that are girls, they have accepted you for who you are. But guy friends have accepted the front that you put on, and not the real person.

17

EMOTIONAL INTENSITY: CONNECTING THROUGH SPORTS

"I like sports because you really make friends."
—Donny, 17, from a suburb in the South

SPORTS ACTIVITIES PROVIDE MANY BOYS WITH SOME OF their most emotionally intense experiences. For some, athletics are one of the few arenas in which boys feel truly masterful in gaining a sense of personal fulfillment and self-worth. The risk and competition of sports also offer the opportunity to test perseverance, strength, and stamina, to "sweat it out," to challenge physical and psychological limitations, to perform at peak. Through sports, boys learn to win and to lose, to celebrate their strengths, to face and accept their limitations and weaknesses.

Warren, fourteen, says football is a release for him: "Sometimes school frustrates me . . . when I get angry about things, I take it out on the football field." The rough-and-tumble offerings of such contact sports as football, basketball, wrestling, and rugby may allow boys like Warren to release pent-up emotional energy, feelings of fear, anxiety, humiliation, and rage.

On the playing field, boys feel more free. Surrounded by their male peers, they often sense that it's acceptable to let down their guard, to loosen the mask of masculinity, which generally suffocates their most vulnerable emotions. Boys cry on the playing field more than they do in the classroom. They also feel less constrained by the Boy Code rules that generally forbid them from showing their love. In sports, boys are able to convey a tremendous amount of affection for one another, without fearing that they will be perceived as effeminate or homosexual.

Games won and lost—and injuries incurred along the way—leave lasting impressions on many boys, some positive and some negative. Boys speak frequently of that one big game during which their own strength and competence were central to the success of their team. And they never forget the mistakes they made—the strikeout, the foul, the disqualification—that caused a missed point or a lost game. Memories of important games, plays, and moves are prominent in their psyches. When boys err or are injured or removed from the game, the pain and loss they may feel is acute. But transcendence is possible. Richard, a seventeen-year-old from a suburb of Boston, remembers how defeated he felt by his hockey injury: "The first couple of weeks after the injury, I tried to deal with it by myself. I slipped into a little depression. I remember going home from school crying, because it was so horrible to me that this had happened. During that period when I couldn't play hockey . . . I really discovered who I am and what I'm all about."

Unfortunately, however, sports can sometimes become too focused on winning and shift from a healthy, confidence-building experience to one that leaves some boys feeling incompetent, rejected, and ashamed. When it comes to sports, boys like Richard not only rejoice in their every success, they also lament or obsess about their every bungle, blunder, or error. Being involved in sports has its underside: there is the pressure to "kill" one's opponents, to win at all costs, and to ostracize team members who are less strong or less able. Many boys attempt to resist this negative pull, yet others surrender to it.

The coach has significant influence. While some are supportive, loving mentors who help mold team spirit, others become drill masters, encouraging boys to be ruthless warriors on the court or in the field. This sort of coach becomes an almost-despised figure who can turn healthy competition into sheer aggression, play into combat. Sheer competition among boys rarely builds character and does little to bring them closer. But when we keep sports in its proper perspective as a chance to come together for joyful, spirited, and high-energy play, we can see that sports activity can help boys to discover new competencies. Sports can buttress their feelings of self-worth, reconnect their "voice" with the deepest stirrings of emotion in their hearts; it can widen their circle of significant relationships.

More than anything, sports create a context in which many boys develop a stronger, more confident sense of their unique identities. Listen to Thomas, sixteen, from New York: "I like school but sometimes I get frustrated. . . . What I like about sports is not thinking about anything— just doing it, not being stressed, having fun. It's a very freeing experience." For some boys such as Thomas, who struggle at home or at school, being able to do well at a sport holds incredible importance. At last, they sense that they are good at something, that people will take them seriously, that they can form relationships with teammates and coaches upon which they can count.

Other boys talk about the wonderfully positive feeling of using their bodies in a constructive and successful way that gives them a sensation of personal achievement and mastery they may not have experienced before.

Ty, thirteen, already senses how sports activity allows him to overcome the worries he's had about his body: "When I was little, I was a chubby kid. So, in fourth grade I decided, I've got to shape up, I can't go on like this. So I got into sports. I play for two ice hockey teams. I play football. I play baseball and I'm thinking about street hockey. I go to all the sports camps, and I keep myself really active."

I LOVE SPORTS

Donny, 17, from a suburb in the South

My hope is to get a college scholarship for sports. I play soccer, and I'm starting to kick for the football team next year. I'm also starting track so I can keep in shape year-round. I'm constantly trying to practice. Sports are exciting, and if you're mad or stressed, you can relieve it by playing soccer. I love sports.

My parents encouraged me to play sports and I've been playing since I was little. If I'm angry or nervous about something, I tend to just keep it in; then when I play sports, I give it the best that I've got and let all my energy fly. Sometimes if I'm nervous about something, as soon as I step into the game, my mental state changes, and I focus on the game, and tend not to worry about other stuff.

Playing sports seems to take my mind off a lot of things. I tend to think more about the game, and I feel as if the game is my game, and I can play as hard as I want, or run and kick the ball as hard as I want. I can let my aggression out without getting into trouble.

I also like sports because you really make friends. I would say soccer allows me to do that. You just go to the game and meet your friends and see everybody there. People want to see you play, and when you step on the field, you feel motivated to win the game.

A Big Part of My Life
Jonathan, 12, from a suburb in New England

Sports are a big part of life. They've something you get your energy on. I look forward to playing soccer. Sometimes it gives you a rush, if you know people are watching you and you can do something good.

You get emotional highs. And you get lows sometimes, if you're losing. Sometimes you just get overwhelmed. You play teams that are really tall, or that are really good, and you feel like you can't score, you can't do anything, you'll lose. And that's kind of hard.

When you lose a game, you kind of hang on to it until later. Then it usually drifts off because most of the time you play kids from other towns you don't know and won't see. You don't need to tell everyone.

I don't even tell many people if I win. Truthfully, not many people really care. They think you're a jerk if you're always like "I won this," or "I won that." If they're your friends, they care because it's you, but they don't really care who you beat.

I've been playing soccer since before I was in kindergarten. I had a good coach from first to fifth grades, and that helped me. I play midfield, the position in the middle, where you go up and come back. You score some goals and you defend some.

A real good player lifts his team up to the caliber. You're in with your team, and if you face a bad ref or a good opposing team, you're all facing it together, so you have a common enemy or common good. So you form friendships. You're with the people a lot, so you can't really be enemies.

In school, it's different. Most of the time you're working for yourself, to get the good grades on your own. On your team, you're all together because you're all doing the same thing, fighting for something, to score a goal or to win.

I Like Sports
Thomas, 16, from New York

I like school but sometimes I get frustrated with the amount of work. I find reading the most difficult. I hate reading. Sometimes when they give me homework and reading, I don't like to read the packets—it gets me too stressed and confused. I like sports, all sports. I play baseball, football, basketball, hockey, whatever. If I put a lot of effort into it, I could be pretty great. What I like about sports is not thinking about anything—just doing it, not being stressed, having fun. It's a very freeing experience. The things that I'm good at are more fun to get involved with than the things that are a struggle.

THE ONLY SPORT I REALLY LIKE

Carl, 17, from a suburb in the West

Rugby's the only sport I really like. There's not a team at my school, but there's a kind of private league that they announced over the intercom at school. I just wasn't sure what to expect, but I decided I'd try it, because I decided I wanted to have a sport in my life, so I went out, and I started playing and loved it. I was pretty good at it, too, so that helped. Everybody was really nice. They weren't the type of people you find in your average sport. I don't want to generalize too much, because I'm friends with some of them, but I'd say that the average person who'd be classified as a jock is probably not the nicest person. When I was a sophomore, we had a really good football team, and we had a lot of guys who were getting written up in the newspaper and stuff, and I was not welcomed by them. It didn't bother me too much, but I didn't like it. A lot of the people you find in a school-sponsored sport are almost like a clique, and in general, I don't like the way they treat other people. They like to pick on people who aren't quite as fortunate as they are, whether that's about money or physical attributes or disabilities—I don't really like that. I'm not competitive in that way.

I played sports when I was a little kid, but I had never played a school sport. I don't think I feel threatened by it, but I'm at odds with the people who play school sports because these are the exact same kids who gave me hell when I was little. We treat each other with respect now, but when I was younger, I was forced to stand up to them. In elementary school, I met a lot of kids who were the real wealthy kids, and my family was kind of rising up from maybe the lower middle class to the lower upper class. I was at odds with the wealthy kids. Some of them tried to bully me, but I didn't accept it and I fought back. I became pretty mean to them, actually. I wound up almost bullying them. It was definitely an eye for an eye. When I was younger, I was one of the smaller people, and I think that was one of the reasons I was picked on. Then suddenly I got bigger, so it was definitely sweet revenge.

The people who went out for rugby were more like people you see just walking down the street. The majority of them didn't have a school sport, and they were all different types of people. You had kids who didn't do very well in school, and you had kids who did do very well in school. You had people who were "druggies," as we'd call them, and people who weren't. I liked the mix of all the different types of people, and the way they all came together. You learned from the coach and from some of the kids who played the previous year. There was a real team spirit, and I loved that.

RED-CARDED

David, 16, from a suburb in New England

I got red-carded this year in soccer. My brother and I are on the same team. He's thin and he doesn't weigh that much. He was getting knocked around. A kid started hacking at him right in front of the parents. They're all yelling at the ref, but the ref wasn't doing anything. The kid started pushing my brother, pulling on his shirt. So I went over and said, "Get the fuck off my brother," and pulled him away. And the ref said, "Hey," and pulled out the card. He blew the whistle and I said, "Oh, no." I was out for the rest of that game and two more games.

The first game after my suspension, my dad was the assistant coach. In that game, I got the ball, the goalie slid out, and I shot under him and scored. He got his legs wrapped around mine and pulled me down. As I got up, I put my hand on his back to help me up. My dad said, "You went after the goalie," and pulled me off the field. He said, "Why did you do that?" And I said, "What are you talking about? I didn't do anything." He said, "You threw a punch at the goalie." And I said, "I didn't do anything." He thought I was going to get a red card. I blew up with him and he blew up with me. I said, "Don't even start giving me this crap." It was hard because he's my dad and my coach.

Finally, he said, "I'm taking you out." It was freezing cold, I was wet, and I didn't have anything to put on. So I said, "Can I just go home?" He said, "No, we might want to put you in later, so just sit there." I was freezing.

Later, I talked to the head coach about my dad. He said, "I know you didn't do anything on the field, and I was going to put you back in." My dad had told me that the coach had asked him to take me off the field. It turned out that the coach didn't even know what was going on.

That night I got really mad. I said, "If you don't want me to play in the games, I don't have to play anymore. Do you really not want me to play? Do you not want me to be on the team, because it seems to me like you need me. I've led the team since we started here. Do you not want me to be here?"

He said, "It's up to you." And I said, "If you're going to treat me like that and not respect what I'm doing on the field, then I don't want to play with you."

A RELEASE

Warren, 14, New York City

I'm fourteen years old and I've been playing football since I was eight or nine. I'm a big guy, so my size is perfect for football. When I was younger my friends used to say, "Warren, play football," but I would always say, "Naw, football ain't my sport." But then I played one day with them and really got into it, and as the years went by I got better and better, so I just stuck to it. My position is linebacker, and I play three times a week in a local park with other teams from my school. The good side is it's an activity for us to do instead of being in the streets, and it's a way to have fun.

On the bad side, though, it also can cause enemies. People get jealous of each other, so they try to hurt each other. If someone on one team is better than the other team, the other team will try to take that person out. My friend who's a running back had the ball once, and some guys that didn't like him tried to take his knees out. That's not competition, it's cheating. When one team is better than another team, that's it, just let it go. You don't try to hurt somebody because they're better than you.

Football can be a violent sport, but I don't mind much. I'm used to it. I like the contact. I like getting hit hard, and I like to hit, too. When I get angry about things, I take it out on the football field. But I don't want to hurt anybody, because it's not personal. Football is like a release for me.

WINNING

Jake, 16, from a suburb in southern New England

Ever since I've played Little League the word "win" has been forced into my mind. When I was eight years old, the coach would tell us at the beginning of the season that we were just out there for fun, but I knew that it wasn't true. Every day that there was a game, my day would be ruined. I was too worried to go anywhere and was constantly thinking about the game. I envied my friends who didn't play baseball and wished that I could be in their shoes. You could always see the disappointment in the eyes of the coaches—one of whom was my father—when we lost, and you could see the delight in their eyes when we won. Now don't get me wrong; I love the game of baseball and because of the coaches' winning mentality we won championships three out of the four years that I was playing. But did I love Little League? No!

After a few years passed, I found a new sport that I loved: soccer. I had played soccer since I was four years old, but I didn't love it as much as baseball until my last year of Little League. I loved it because I felt none of the pressure from the coaches. Also the game is so fast that you can't really comprehend what the coaches are saying to you. I played the sport year-round and was all set for the challenge of high school soccer. Boy, did I get a big surprise. The high school soccer coach was all about winning! He said, "We are only here for one reason, and that is to win. If you are out here to have fun then you should go home now." I had problems my first year playing for this man, and after it was over I wanted to quit. I wasn't having fun in the way that I always had, and I longed to be four years old again, when winning was not our only reason to play. But I decided to stick with soccer and just block out the coach.

There was still that winning mentality through the four years that I was playing, but I did manage to have some fun. I am a little ashamed to say that in the meantime, the mentality has rubbed off on me. Now everything to me is about winning. I believe in winning now, and I can only hope that I don't pass this trait on to my son to the extent that I had it passed on to me.

THE INJURY

Richard, 17, from a suburb in the Midwest

I have played hockey since I was five years old. I had only one mind-set: hockey. Hockey this, hockey that. I thought about hockey twenty-four/seven. I thought that the only thing was to get to the NHL. That was my only future, and I saw it so clearly.

Two years ago, I separated my shoulder in a game. Then two months later, I was playing again and I separated it worse, which put me up for three months. The day it happened, I went home and cried because I didn't know what to do. I knew it could be the end of hockey for me.

The first couple of weeks after the injury, I tried to deal with it by myself. I slipped into a little depression. Sometimes I just couldn't stay in class, and I'd get up and walk out. I remember going home from school crying, because it was so horrible to me that this had happened. I had all this pent-up frustration, and I'd go running just to tire myself out so that I could at least fall asleep, because I was so wound up. I wrote a lot of poetry during that time. I just wanted to get my feelings down on paper.

My advisor talked to me about how I'd become a stronger person and more rounded because of the experience. And that maybe I needed something like the injury to become more aware of things around me.

Then I started talking with my health teacher. She's the happiest woman alive. She helped me get through the worst time. She made me realize how good things can be without hockey. At that time, I had started teaching little kids to skate, and she helped me see how happy those kids were that I was helping them. Even if I couldn't play hockey, at least I was skating, and I was helping little kids learn.

Then I started talking with my dad. I remember he was driving me to a friend's house and he told me his story. He said that he had had trouble with alcohol in the past, and talked about all the things he had been through. He doesn't drink at all anymore; he knows that he can't. The reason he quit, he said, was because of his kids. He didn't want us to grow up having to deal with that. He said, "You can be high or get a buzz just from life and living. The sheer joy of spreading love and happiness, bringing a smile to someone's face." I thought about that a lot. I started to express myself more, about what I felt inside. I decided that I didn't want to experience what Dad had been through. That would be ridiculous.

During that period when I couldn't play hockey—when I was talking with my health teacher and my dad—I really discovered who I am and what I'm all about. I developed some great views on things around me, issues and kids today. I think I became independent in a good way. If I hadn't been injured, I might have ended up doing the same things like everyone else. It's almost like it was a message from God. I feel kind of blessed, and that I should help other people to do what's right. It made me realize there's so much in life—that life can be good, even without hockey. I became a better person, I was happy all the time. I kind of felt reborn.

My girlfriend helped me, too. She made me detach from hockey a bit, and made me realize some of the joys in life. Like being caring for one another, and loving. I had never felt that before. She made me want to be a better person.

I'm playing hockey still, but I don't have the same love for it. I still want to go to the NHL, because I think that I could get there. Maybe I'll rediscover the passion, but I won't have the tunnel vision of hockey, hockey, hockey.

A VERY PERSONAL THING

Mo, 17, from a suburb in New England

Football is a very personal thing. It's more important to me than to anybody else in school. Football has always been something that no one can really understand about me, how it takes so much emotion out of me.

In the opening football game of this season, my senior year, I dislocated my knee. I had already dislocated my left knee over the summer, then I did the same thing to my right knee in the opening game. I was bummed. But I accepted the fact that I was going to be out for X number of games. Even so, I couldn't keep up a positive attitude while I was hurt. When we lost I thought, "Maybe if I had been in there, we would have won." That's the worst feeling. I've always tried to come to every game so emotional, but it's tough to come to every game emotionally when you're sitting on the sideline. After most games, we'd all go out and do something. But when we lost, I didn't want to go out. I was too frustrated.

In our sophomore year, we went to the Super Bowl. We won 20–6. It was one of those games we can look back on and say, "Thank God we won that last home game." We won it because we made sure that we had fun, that we were out there on the football field for a reason. We didn't want to feel sorry for ourselves. We wanted to go out there and have a good time and win.

I played on the offensive line and a lot of my job was to double-team the nose guard. He'd come this way and I'd hit him. In one play near the end of the game, we were having a good time because we were basically sure we were going to win. We just wanted to score again. So we drove that nose guard fifteen yards behind the line of scrimmage. We just didn't want to stop moving. We were pumped up.

I don't think anybody can understand how much football means to me. When you're in the stands, you might say, "Going under the lights Friday night, yeah, that would be kind of cool to be out there." But if you're out there, it's not *kind* of cool. It's unbelievably cool. It's a feeling you can't have unless you play football.

18

COMING OUT AS GAY
AND SUPPORTING THOSE WHO DO

*"The Matthew Shepard case offers a lot of lessons. It teaches us
that we should all try to be open to one another, that no matter who
we are, we should be able to get along."*

—Cory, 18, from a suburb in the West

IN TRAVELING ACROSS THE COUNTRY AND TALKING WITH BOYS
about their deepest emotional experiences, fears, disappointments,
and longings, I was particularly moved to learn that many, often at a
strikingly young age, develop a clear sense of the qualities they hope to
find in a romantic partner. They spoke about the values they would like
to share with that person, and the life they would aspire to construct together. While some told me about a special girl who might fulfill these
dreams, others spoke of a special boy.

If we once lived in a society in which boys felt that being gay was
strictly forbidden and talking about it was tantamount to suicide,
slowly, many of the schools and communities in which boys are growing up appear to be teaching students that whether one is gay or straight
is simply another variable in a person's personality. Many boys felt that
someone's sexual orientation ought not to affect how they are treated by
others. Several actually chose to "come out" during our interview, dis-
closing their relationships with other boys, candidly discussing their
lives as gay adolescents. No matter what their sexuality, some spoke
simply about how much they longed for it to be okay to develop loving

friendships with other boys. "My friend Brian and I have so much fun and can be so open," explains Joseph, a high school senior who lives in a small town in the Northeast, "but then one of our other friends will come in and we can't talk about half the things we would otherwise."

Many boys such as Joseph and Brian, while they are heterosexual, long for society to provide them with the same latitude it gives girls and women. They want to form caring, affectionate, deeply loving relationships with other boys and with men. In America, homophobia is the cruelest form of the Boy Code prejudice. It restrains gay people from being completely integrated into our society. It keeps people from feeling completely good about who they are. And it also places devastating limitations on all boys and men—heterosexual and homosexual—suffocating the love and intimacy they secretly long to create in their most important friendships and relationships. Eighteen-year-old Brendan, from a small town in the South, laments: "I would like to be able to talk to another guy, especially my dad, because he has been through everything I've been through and knows more. But it's just so hard to even start the conversation."

Perhaps because of this universal longing for connection, many boys I spoke with—boys like Joseph, Brian, and Brendan, all of whom identified themselves as being straight—conveyed the abundant empathy they felt for people who were perceived as gay. They stressed how unfair it would be to mistreat or discriminate against a boy merely because of his identity. Eighteen-year-old Jackson, from a small town in New England, told us, "I could care less if a person is black or Hispanic or gay." Says sixteen-year-old Julio, who is straight but copes daily with society's racism, "I don't discriminate against *anyone*. People are all different from one another and that's not bad. If I were homosexual, I'd feel different, too. You have to always look at the other person's point of view. I try to get on with everyone and give them love."

Some boys, too, expressed their sympathy for gay men, but then stressed their heterosexuality. "I don't really have a problem with people saying they're gay . . . it's not going to make me like someone more or less," Rick told me confidently. "But," he added promptly, "I know that I am not gay."

How complicated it must be for these boys, I thought to myself. Despite how much they want it to be acceptable to become close with one another, and as mindful as they are about not wanting to mistreat or discriminate against gay people, they are still afraid they could be seen as gay—when perhaps, in fact, they are not. There are, no doubt, a fair number of psychologists who would analyze a boy's "I am not gay" declaration to be a sure sign of repressed homosexuality. But I wonder whether, rather than trying to solve that impossible conundrum, we should instead be heeding the cries of so many of the boys with whom I spoke to make same-sex love a nonissue, about which they no longer need to feel worried or ashamed. "I like it when they ask me questions," stressed Cory, who decided to tell his high school classmates that he is gay. "I like to learn about people and come to know them. So I would like them to ask me questions so that they can come to know me." Many boys across the nation—straight and gay—make clear that they yearn for a day when their fear and isolation can come to an end, when they will be completely free to share the truth about whom they care for and whom they love.

ENOUGH STRENGTH TO JUST BE WHO I AM

Cory, 18, from a suburb in the West

I am very open about who I am. I am gay. For a long time I wouldn't admit it to myself, but then I just snapped and admitted it to everyone. It was so painful to keep it a secret. But I'm lucky in that I can talk about it freely with my family. My mom's sister is a lesbian, and my mom was the only person in her family who accepted her sister. My mom is very open and supportive. My dad had a very debilitating injury at work. He fell down a flight of stairs, and for six years couldn't move his left arm. So he had a lot of time to think about things and "find himself." Since he's comfortable with who he is, he is comfortable with who I am.

When I turned seventeen, I felt enough strength to just be who I am. I was very much influenced by the Matthew Shepard murder. The first day I heard on the news that somebody had killed him because he was gay, it made me incredibly angry that anyone could truly hate another person just because of their sexuality. The news made me want to change things in our society. And it made me realize that I can't hide from my sexuality, and the possibility that people might reject me because of it. Hiding away my sexuality would just keep things the same. And so I started coming out to my friends. And eventually I wrote an article for the school newspaper stating that I was gay and that I was tired of the lack of awareness in our school. It's almost like the Shepard murder gave me a lot of inner strength. It made me not want to hide anymore.

I had a pretty supportive response to the article. One person harassed me, but only once. I didn't really let it bother me but my friend got furious and went after him. The rest of my friends all said they were really proud. All my female friends hugged me at least once that day. One of my gay friends said it was really courageous of me to write the article, and a couple of straight guys told me they really respected me. One of my teachers told me that my coming out was really helpful and important. Last year I was the "only" gay student at my high school. This year there are at least twenty or thirty openly gay students.

I guess I was able to really change things for the better. The other gay and lesbian students saw, when I came out, that someone could do it without getting hurt or killed or facing any really bad repercussions. I guess that I've helped a lot of people be more open about themselves.

A lot of people I know are surprised that I don't "act gay." When I came out, it really opened their minds about gay people and helped them realize that not all gay people act like the stereotypes. It also really opened their minds when they realized that someone they liked, a friend, could be gay.

I wish people would more often just come out and ask other people about their sexuality. I wish more people would just ask me point-blank. In my last two jobs, the people I've worked with assumed I'm straight. One of my coworkers tried to hook me up on a blind date with a woman. It really irritates me that they don't even seem to consider the possibility that I might be more interested in a man.

I like being open around people and I like it when they ask me questions. I'm always happy to answer questions about my sexuality. I like to learn about people and come to know them. So I would like them to ask me questions so that they can come to know me. It's very different if people are prying and asking questions just to be rude. It's usually obvious if they are, because their questions are stated in a negative way. But when they ask positive questions it's affirming, as it tells me they're interested in who I am as a person.

The Matthew Shepard case offers a lot of lessons. It teaches us that we should all try to be open to one another, that no matter who we are, we should be able to get along. I'd like us to appreciate America as a melting pot, in which different, diverse groups live alongside one another. America is an integration of all the cultures of the world. But we don't often see it as that. We see it as I am who I am and I'm not going to change, and anyone who is not like me should change for me. And that's wrong.

If I knew someone who was gay and just beginning to deal with it in high school, I would tell him above everything else to be true to himself. If you have to hide it because you feel you're in danger, seek out someone who you know can help you, someone who will support you. If your parents are very religious and don't condone homosexuality, find a friend or a counselor who does. Don't pretend to be who you're not. Don't try to fake being straight. Be honest with yourself. When people aren't honest with themselves, that's when they start getting hurt.

A LOT OF GOOD
Bradley, 17, from a suburb in the Northeast

In middle school, when I was being called things like "fag" in the halls, I don't think I considered that I could possibly be gay. Eighth grade, in particular, was complete hell for me. Everyday I was poked, prodded, jabbed, punched, and called every politically incorrect name in the book. It was a horrible year.

I used to think that being gay had to be just awful. I had an image that you couldn't be gay unless you were an adult. Then I saw some gay high school students and I thought, "Wow! There are gay high school students. I didn't know there were gay high school students." About that time I realized, "I could actually be gay." And I realized it wasn't a horrible thing.

I'm confident that if I were to tell my parents I am gay, they would support me. I have gay relatives, and my parents are very supportive of them. Many of the people my mom knew in high school are gay. So I'm sure they would be right there behind me, marching in gay pride marches, and all sorts of things. It's all I can do now to stop them from breaking into anti-Vietnam protests and singing "How many roads must a man walk down?" I'm not sure if I want to give them the satisfaction.

The real problem is bringing it up with them. Do I bring it up with my mom and my dad or with my mom, my dad, and my brother? There's no good time to say, "Mom, Dad, I'm gay."

Then they'll ask, "When did you know?" And I'd have to say, "Since freshman year." They're going to say, "You're a senior. Why did you wait so long to tell us?" Then there will have to be a continuing conversation and discussion about it. I don't know how comfortable I feel talking with my parents about my sexuality, beyond the fact that I'm gay, and that I've known for a long time. And telling them that I'm comfortable with it, not to worry. I think they deserve a discussion, but it's something I dread.

So, it's very hard. Sometime I will tell them. I'm thinking maybe when I'm in college, over the phone.

The problem is that I can't really have an honest and open relationship with my parents when I'm keeping a life secret from them. When you're hiding something from parents, like you're gay, it becomes much easier to lie about other things. So, if I get a bad grade on a test, I tend not to tell them for a while.

Every year I think, "This year it's going to happen." There's a gay pride week in the city near where I live, with gay events every night. Last year, I was thinking, "I want to go to all of them." I could have said to my parents, I'm going here one night and maybe there another night, and make up two events. But I couldn't go out three nights in a row; it would sound too weird. The only way I could do it was to tell my parents the truth. But I didn't.

The other issue is my brother. He's eleven, in middle school. If it had been me, and the other kids in school found out that I had a gay brother, I would have been teased relentlessly. And if I had a gay brother and I heard people bad-mouthing gay people, I would have felt conflicted about whether I should save myself or defend my brother. I don't want to put him in that situation.

There's also no telling what my brother's been exposed to at school. Maybe he doesn't have the same mind-set that I do about gay people, even though my parents have brought him up to be open and accepting. Maybe he will feel a distance from me. When you're that young, and something that had been constant dramatically changes—like your brother turns out to be gay—it could be traumatic.

Even at school, it's been difficult. At first, I was really mortified about telling people, even in this accepting school environment. I felt weird saying it. "I am gay." The word "gay" was a strange word and I had trouble saying it. I had to write one person a note to tell her. Her response was "I never thought about it, but now that you mention it . . ." And I thought, "What's that supposed to mean?"

I hooked up with somebody at school, and that person, much to my annoyance, told some people who told some people who told some people. Eventually I opened up more. Now most of the campus knows or has some idea or doesn't care. They just hear someone's name. "He's gay." "Oh, isn't that nice." Now I'm in the closet, but the closet doors are open. Anyone who wants to look in, I'm there. I'll say, "Hi."

The friend that I spend the most time with, Peter, doesn't know I'm gay. I don't want the friendship we have now to change. We're great friends and we go to the movies, and I'm worried that if I were to tell him, it would change everything. It's probably an irrational fear—he is not homophobic. But I worry.

I may be underestimating both Peter and my parents. It is, at times, a good question that I ponder: How much do they really not know? I wonder if my parents think it's odd that I'm a senior and I haven't had a girlfriend in the four years that I've been in high school.

Naturally, when you discover your sexuality, you want to explore it—especially when you have enough testosterone running through your system to kill a large animal. There is someone at school who I had known through various activities and I had a huge crush on him. And, it turns out, he had a thing for me. We hooked up several times.

The first time we went into the woods so he could smoke a cigarette. He showed me a treehouse there and he asked if I wanted to kiss, and I said, "Sure." We kissed and he wanted to go further. I was pretty naive and I thought to myself, "You can't do that. We're not even supposed to kiss. We're supposed to go out on dates."

I felt like our relationship was a bridge, and it helped me become gay. He helped me figure out what to do. I had dreams of us being boyfriends and it just didn't happen. I realize now that he just thought of it as hooking up, which is how I would come to think of it eventually.

In high school, if you're a guy looking for another guy, it's really hard to find someone. Last year I was on the way to a party with several people and we were walking along the street and two guys came up to the guy I was walking with and punched him in the face. Random act of violence. My friend was badly hurt. His nose was bleeding and he had a black eye, and his lip had been jammed onto one of his teeth. The guys said, "Not funny now, is it?" and walked off.

I don't think it was gay-bashing. But at the same time, there is all this violence and hatred coming out. Some people have compared the gay movement to the civil rights movement, bringing an issue that was difficult into the light.

The road ahead for gay people is much better now than it was ten years ago. There are places you don't want to go and things you don't want to do, and you have to be careful, but I think things are going to get better. Hopefully, someday you'll be able to marry if you're gay in America. The future can be very bright. But I'm being optimistic today—you could ask me tomorrow and I could say, "Oh, everything's going to shit."

One thing I have learned, from my own experiences, is "That which doesn't kill you makes you stronger." Suffering can make for a lot of good. A lot of good art and good poetry, great writing, comes from people who face great adversity. If you're gay, it's almost a plus, because you're bound to face adversity.

The Golden Rule, "Do unto others as you would have them do unto you," has been forgotten by a lot of people. In my worst days, I have never forgotten that. I never wished any harm on the people who bullied me. Well, maybe I wished they would step on a thumbtack, but I never wished them any real harm. People have to learn to love themselves and through that love, to love others.

LIFE IS ABOUT BEING DIFFERENT

Eric, 11, from a city in the Northwest

The people I look up to the most are probably the people where my dad works. He is a cook at a nearby museum. There are a lot of cool guys there who are always telling me jokes. They are older, and they are not nerds and they are not jerks. They are nice guys, and they are funny, and they are cool, and they are weird. There are kids with funny hairstyles, and a lot of ear piercings.

There are tons of gay people where my dad works and they are really nice, and I just wish that everyone would stop being mean to gay people. Everyone here at school is calling people gay and queers, and they don't even know any gay people. They will say, "I saw one on TV," or something stupid like that. Like, "Oh, I saw one on a billboard." And they don't even know what gay people do, and how nice they are. I don't think people should be so mean to them, because gay people are cool.

I think some people are mean to gay people because they are different. Some folks just can't get the fact that life is about being different.

A lot of people's lives are just like a straight line. Mine is swervy. I mean, I bet some of the kids are even thinking about high school now, and it's only sixth grade. Come on, really! We don't have to think about high school *already*. A lot of people out there get up at six, eat breakfast, take a shower, get dressed, go to work at nine, have lunch, coffee, work till five, come home. I think that's a pretty boring life. I don't like the weather people because they are always predicting stuff, and they are usually wrong, too. The future should come as it is, and I'm going to just play it by ear. In the future, I am just going to be whatever happens.

PART IV

DEALING WITH LOSS, LONELINESS, AND SHAME

19

PUMPING AND CRUNCHING: BODY
IMAGE AND THE MEDIA

*"A guy is supposed to be strong, tall, and fast and have the quali-
ties of an ideal athlete. At the same time he's supposed to be smart.
He's expected to be nearly perfect."*

—Chandler, 14, from a suburb in the Northwest

ALL HUMAN BEINGS FOCUS ON THEIR BODIES AS A PRI-
mary source of identity and self-confidence. One of Freud's earliest teachings was that the first ego, or secure sense of self, was the
"body ego." Boys are now suffering significantly in the arena of body
ego. For decades, the gender straitjackets in which we have placed
males required them to act indifferently about their bodies and their
looks—boys or men who spent more than a moment worrying about
their appearance were perceived as less "masculine." But as society
loosens the rules and "allows" boys to pay attention to their looks, a
new arsenal of exploitative media images has come forth to present an
image of the "perfect" man. In popular magazines, billboard advertise-
ments, even in video games and dolls, the "alpha male" is portrayed as
having biceps that seem to grow year by year. Just as images of the
"perfect" woman have plagued girls' and women's sense of self for
years, images of the perfect man are now beginning to adversely affect
our boys' sense of "acceptable" body type and self-worth.

As the voices in this chapter reflect, boys are feeling an increasing
pressure to develop their bodies into the "right" size and shape—not

only to improve their own self-views but to win the admiration of peers and potential mates as well. Sports, and some coaches, have compounded this trend by encouraging football and baseball players to become gigantic. Wrestlers are pushed to starve themselves into a lower weight class, and then binge just before the match. The rates of bulimia and anorexia—once thought to be almost completely "female" illnesses—are markedly on the rise in the general population of America's boys and men.

As we've learned from girls, this phenomenon of distorted body image is hugely connected with inappropriate feelings of self-loathing, depression, and, in extreme circumstances, self-destructive impulses and suicide.

David is a popular seventeen-year-old in a suburb of Houston whose Chinese-American parents co-own a successful accounting firm. Good-looking, well-built, with short-cropped black hair, David has performed fairly well in most sports at his school, but he has never quite excelled. More than anything, he has always hoped that the other guys would see him as athletic, to view him as a "winner" they would want to befriend. For years, David felt he wasn't meeting his objectives. But then, in his junior year, he discovered the varsity wrestling team. In wrestling, he found a chance not only to succeed at a sport but to establish himself as popular in a school of nearly 1,500 students. But winning the friendship of his peers and doing well at a sport came with a huge price. To compete within a lower weight class, David spends hours of each day running and weight lifting. For days at a time, David gives up both food and liquids. At his two o'clock interview with us, already focusing on his wrestling meet later that afternoon, David was fasting. For the preceding forty-eight hours, he had not consumed a morsel of nourishment, not even a drop of water. "I'm obsessive," he told us. "I'll admit that."

"What do you mean?"

"Every day, every waking hour," David continued, his eyes darting about nervously, "I'm thinking, Man, am I 'in weight'?"

"Are you worried that it might not be healthy?"

"I *know* it's not healthy for me," he added emphatically, grinning anxiously. "I feel like crap right now. But that's what you've got to do to win. That's what you've got to do."

David's lament—that of an adolescent boy obsessing over his

weight—is not as uncommon as you might think. Today's boys and young men spend an increasing amount of time worrying about the way they look, dwelling on whether they are too fat, too thin, too small, too big. While they are sometimes hesitant to discuss it (note how David feels he must "admit" his behavior to us), prepubescent and adolescent boys focus on the size and shape of their bodies, constantly fearing they will be teased or bullied because they don't meet the standard. Now more than ever before, our boys frequently feel ashamed of how they look.

Consider the testimony of seventeen-year-old Dylan, from a suburb of Chicago. "I'm very self-conscious about my body," he offers, flipping back his long, blond hair and looking at us with intense brown eyes. "I'm afraid that I might look unattractive. I weigh 120 pounds, or something like that. This summer it started happening. Over the Christmas holiday, I was [down to] about 112. I felt like I had to be skinnier to be attractive. I worked out like crazy and didn't eat. Most of it was running and push-ups, just stuff you do about weight."

"Has anybody been helping you with this?" we inquired.

"I'm fine," Dylan told us. "I don't need help with this kind of thing. It's just a thing. I've dealt with it, I'm pretty much over it, I think. I've conquered that beast . . . at least chained it up."

Though statistics for eating disorders are now on the rise for boys, there is no major campaign to help them avoid believing in these destructive distortions. We have not yet found a shame-free way to intervene and help stop boys and young men from using unhealthy steroids, wasting pounds through skipped meals or induced vomiting, and overexercising to the point of exhaustion. Too often this growing nightmare of boys' distorted and confused body image and quickly eroding self-esteem remains unnoticed—until the appearance of serious psychological and physical symptoms.

As we listen to these boys who are striving to look good, who feel like outcasts because their biceps are not large enough, who feel too fat or short to find love, we must listen carefully, recognizing the echoes of girls' struggles about the body-self. We must offer our young male friends the message that they are just fine, that we admire and love them as they genuinely are, that they can be successful. They can be real and masculine boys without changing a thing. We must help them break through the mask of masculinity, the veil of shame and secrecy, letting

America know that body-image illnesses are not the exclusive province of girls anymore. As caretakers we must become aware of the signs and symptoms of this esteem-eroding body distortion before it is too late.

THESE GREAT BODIES

Samuel, 18, from a suburb in the West

I'm a gymnast, which is really fun. My friend Matt got into it last year, and he helped start coed gymnastics at our school. It's extremely hard. Your actual performance time is only about two and a half minutes, but you prepare for two months before that. Those two and a half minutes are nonstop and by the end you're out of breath, especially the guys. All of us do conditioning and at the end we're still all out of breath. It's a combination of the adrenaline and just the stuff that we do.

I don't get nervous for the state competitions, but I do get nervous when we're performing in front of our school. I know everybody at school and I'm going to have to talk to them, but most of those people at State I'm never going to see again. We still take some flack, mostly from people on the football team, but it really doesn't matter to us because from our standpoint, gymnastics is probably the hardest sport. Not only do you have to have strength, but you have to have balance and coordination, and you have to be able to put them all together to make a two-and-a-half-minute routine look perfect.

I have a membership to a spa, where I work out and run to keep in shape. You want to be this perfect person and have the perfect figure. Men are supposed to be strong, tough, and have these great bodies. You see it in the movies and the magazines, and I know it affects people. It affects me. I have to keep in shape. I have to keep doing this or that. But I don't think that's necessarily a bad thing. You can take it with a grain of salt and not overdo it.

I think that if a guy is comfortable with himself, it's fine. I mean if a guy can say, "Okay, I'm happy with how I look. I could look better, but I'm fine this way," then it's good. But if you're not happy with how you look and you have no confidence and you have no will, no drive to look better, then you're just on a downhill slide. You just continue going downhill physically, mentally. I've known a couple guys like that. When that happens, you have to find something you like to do and just continue doing it: "Well, let's not just sit here and concentrate on that. Let's do something about it." And as long as you have some confidence in yourself, whether it's mental or physical, you can improve in all areas.

That's how I got into working out and sports and gymnastics. I had been on the edge emotionally for a while, too, when I didn't feel good about myself. I thought I was fat. I didn't feel comfortable with the way I looked, with the way I felt. I'm sure I wasn't really fat, but I felt like it. I think if I had fallen off the edge, it would have become a complete depression. I would have lost motivation in school, I would have stopped doing any activities, I would have just sat around and become a couch potato and watched TV and done basically nothing.

I looked at the people around me, like my friends Matt and Bruce, and saw that they were able to do all these things. Matt is very athletic and great at all these sports, and Bruce is like top in the class and he's Mr. Smart. It was like I couldn't keep up with them. So I've got double goals: I have to be able to do everything that Matt can do physically and go beyond that, and do everything that Bruce can do mentally and then go beyond that.

There are probably some guys in school who use steroids. There are some sophomores that are bigger than I would expect they could be, even if they've been working out forever. When creatine first came out about three years ago, I thought it was a great thing, but since it was new I didn't try it. I decided to see if it stayed around for a while and was still safe. I've started using creatine now myself, mainly because I don't have enough time to work out. I would love to work out six days a week, but with all my homework and gymnastics, I'm lucky if I get into the gym two or three times a week. I try to work out two hours every time I go, but if I could I would work out two and a half, three hours.

Creatine helps me get stronger with the little workout that I'm doing, and that's something I need for gymnastics. I found that I wasn't strong enough, not as strong as I want to be to do gymnastics. We don't specifically have a weight, but we all try to keep each other going and push each other to keep in shape. The girls don't need any motivation for that—they do that on their own—and for the most part, neither do we.

Any diet that my mom has been on, I pretty much go on it, too, since it's just the two of us at home. She's found a couple that really work, like this one where you try to cut sugar almost completely out of your diet. It's hard for the first week, but after that, if somebody says,

"Let's go get a candy bar," it doesn't sound so great. One guy on our squad just stopped eating altogether, but he said it didn't work so well.

I guess it is kind of the jock thing to focus on looking good and pumping up. There are some athletes who concentrate on sports and nothing else. Yet if they would stop and think, they'd realize that when they get out of high school or college, they're not even going to be playing sports anymore, and then what are they going to turn to? Maybe some of them can become models, but even with that, once you pass a certain age you're out. I'd rather take the best of both worlds. I'll work out and try to look good, but I'm also going to concentrate on other things—on academics and careers—and just basically prepare myself for a life of my own.

I Had to Be Skinnier

Dylan, 17, from a suburb of Chicago

If I get in shape, if I develop a more attractive body, I'd be more popular. It's like the way life is around here, what society shows you. It's a problem to be naturally skinny like me. You're not as athletic or muscular or attractive; you're not as good as the other kids are.

Everything in movies, TV, and especially the girl magazines tell you what your body should be like. Magazines like *YM* and stuff are biased and unrealistic, and they make girls expect guys to be a certain way. Girls definitely influence the way guys try to look, and they want us to be buff, wear certain clothes, and have a certain haircut. It's the girl magazines that make them want us to be a certain way: we are supposed to work out, get a good job, get a certain car, and have the right look.

A lot of guys worry about their bodies and working out. I think I did the opposite of what everybody else does, though. Instead of working out, I tried to get smaller. Because there's so much pressure on guys to be muscular and strong, I tended to go exactly the other way, to avoid that competition. Last summer I decided I had to be skinnier in order to be attractive. I worked out like crazy and didn't eat. I did some weights and a lot of running and push-ups. I ate only one small meal each day. I would not eat breakfast and there was no snacking after dinner. I would look at the music scene and celebrities and friends, and I didn't want to get pudgy. I wanted to be attractive. Eventually I got down to about 112 pounds.

I still skip breakfast and lunch each day, and I go through phases where I won't eat at all for a day or so. I don't talk to anyone about it, not even my parents. I'm fine, I don't need help with this kind of thing. It's just a thing, and I've dealt with it. I'm pretty much over it, I think. I've conquered that beast, so to speak, or at least chained it up.

WRESTLING

Dev, 17, from a suburb in the South

I've been wrestling for two years. This is my second year and though I'm average in wrestling, I love it. Wrestling is such an individual sport. You and the other guy are on the mat, and you can't blame anybody else for your mistakes. It's something that you go out and do yourself. And if you win then you look good. It's not like you can blame it on the whole team because their left guard was blocked. When you wrestle, if you lose, you just have to say, "He won because he was the better man." You're more self-reliant and responsible for your own wins or losses.

Cutting weight is probably the hardest part of all, but then there's going to practice every day. We wrestle two and a half hours every day and, afterward, I'm really tired. The other day I lost seven pounds of water weight. I read in a book once that one day of practice in wrestling will equal the amount of calories a normal person will burn in three days.

To wrestle, you have to be physically and mentally strong. Day in and day out you have to give it everything you've got. It's not something many people can take. A lot of guys who can't make it are just not mentally strong enough. There are always guys who will join and just drop out the first week because it's a lot of physical and mental pain. It takes discipline, stamina, and physical energy.

There are a lot of strong guys out there who quit. They don't quit because they're afraid of getting beat—because you're willing to get beat if you're mentally strong.

I'm in the 45-weight class, which means that my weight can't go above 145 or below 120. Naturally my weight is 155, so I'm constantly battling to keep off those ten pounds. For instance, today I have to lose two pounds of water weight by four-thirty. I think I lost a pound in my sleep, and I've got to lose two more pounds before this afternoon. Normally, to lose weight, I just put on sweats and wrestle. Sometimes I put on plastics and wrestle. Plastics are made to help you sweat. They sell them at sporting good stores. Mostly, though, what I do is take a garbage bag, make three holes, and stick myself through. They really make you sweat. The worst part of it is not eating. That's hard.

As of now I haven't had a drink in twenty-four hours. I haven't eaten in forty-eight hours. One time I lost twelve pounds in a day. The other day I sat up from my desk and had a blood rush. I almost blacked out. But usually in class you just kind of sit there. You try not to do too much. The worst is when you have to take a test the same day you're trying to cut weight. But as long as you get your sleep, you're pretty much OK. Sometimes I want to sleep, and I haven't eaten all day so I eat ice cubes. Just enough to have your tongue not stick to the roof of your mouth.

We're not that extreme at my school. I don't think any of my friends do Ex-Lax or induce vomiting. The worst thing I've ever done is for two days, I stopped eating. Last year three college wrestlers died from cutting weight.

I don't worry at all whether what I'm doing is risky or not. The thought doesn't even cross my mind. I mean, twelve pounds may sound like a lot, but your body can take more than most people realize. I know one guy who is losing fifteen pounds every match. That might be dangerous. But could it cause something like dying? I could see passing out, but not dying.

My parents worry a bit when I try to cut weight. We argue a lot about it. They just have a cranky attitude. I get mixed messages. For instance, I got yelled at today for spitting in class; I spit into a cup to take all the water from my system. So on the one hand, I'm supposed to do well at school in my classwork and not spit during class. But then on the other hand, I'm supposed to do well in wrestling, lose weight, and perform well. But how can I do that and do well in school if I'm starving all day? That's when my teacher tells me to move to a higher weight class. She doesn't understand that everybody's cutting weight, so if I moved up to fifty-two, that means I'm going to be wrestling a guy who's actually 160. If one person does it, everybody has to do it.

My hunger passes from hour to hour. I get hungry for ten minutes at a time, but then it goes away. If you can drink orange juice then you're like basically satisfying your thirst and taste. I don't like drinking water when I'm cutting weight. I like drinking something that has sugar in it. To get enough energy right before I wrestle, I eat like three Power Bars and I drink two gallons of water. One of my guys will have a gallon of water sitting next to the scale, and then when he weighs in, he guzzles the whole thing. It's really funny, actually. We never talk about the guys who died in college. But I do think about it occasionally. I was watching ESPN and they were talking about how they moved up the class by seven pounds so more kids wouldn't die. I just kept thinking that if they did that, 145 plus 7 would be 152, and I know that would be a really difficult class for me.

Wednesdays are probably the worst day for me. On Wednesdays I start cutting weight, and we've got tests on Fridays and by then I'm feeling that I just can't take this anymore. I can't get through the rest of the week, and there's so much pressure and responsibility on me. It seems there's so much to do and sometimes I don't want to do it. Like screw it. Especially Wednesdays, because you know, you're only halfway through.

I've seriously contemplated quitting wrestling. But then I tell myself that this, too, shall pass. And what doesn't kill you is going to make you stronger. You know the harder your obstacles, the stronger you'll become. I guess I'm a Darwinist. If I'm the strongest, I'll survive. I'm also afraid of being normal or of being a kid who goes home to play a little tennis for four hours before bed. I can't imagine a life that has no meaning, no purpose. And also, when I'm feeling this way, I can look back on myself when the season is over and say, I went all the way through this, and I didn't give up.

I guess I just can't stand weakness. Like all those guys who quit. When I see them in the hallways I can't help thinking that they did the worst thing possible. They quit. A lot of kids from middle school who I grew up with just seem to fall back, one after another, from freshman to sophomore. I was the biggest loser freshman year. I think that's the reason why I'm still afraid, because I was a loser. I tried out for wrestling freshman year, and I quit the first day. All I was ever good for was academics. I was never an athlete at all until sophomore year.

I was fat. I weighed more than I weigh now. Kids constantly made fun of me. Then I got fed up and started exercising, running. Then I got really skinny. And then I became really small.

I do think guys, like girls, really do care about how they look. I don't want to be fat again, so I exercise a lot. I spend at least four hours a day exercising. I would have to say that most of my friends are worried about being too fat and about being too thin. The thin guys should take creatine to build up, and the fat guys should stay off the steaks.

There's this huge, three-hundred-pound guy who looks like a whale. We make fun of him all the time. He's got to want to be thin. Steroids are available but nobody really takes them. There was this senior who graduated last year. I hear he took steroids. He was pretty big, pretty bulked up. Guys use a lot of creatine also. It makes your muscles pop out. You look more powerful. You look better.

Guys are always trying to prove themselves by scoring with girls, or winning athletically. In weigh-ins, you're in your underwear and looking at the other guys. It's all joking, but it's like, I have a bigger dick than you. That's definitely something. It's even down to that level. I think that's the quintessential level. How big your dick is and how many girls you get on the weekends. I want to be healthy in mind and body. Some would say that what I'm doing now with my body is not healthy. I disagree, because now that I have higher self-esteem, I can achieve more.

I realize I do put a lot of pressure on myself. My parents tell me to go to sleep because I study too late. They're a bit worried that I've gone too far. When I lose at wrestling I get depressed. I just sit there and think. If I lose because the other guy is better than me, then I just blow it off. And I realize he's better than me. If I lose because I quit, that's the worst feeling ever.

I'm not sure if my dad was athletic during high school. I'm not really close with my dad. I'm really close with my mom. If I'm going to talk to somebody, it's going to be Mom. It's not that he's hard to talk to. We get into a lot of intellectual conversations. But if I ever have feelings or emotions I want to talk about, it's always with my mom. It feels awkward having conversations with my dad about emotions and feelings. I know he wants me to talk about emotions with him, but it's awkward for me. I guess I feel I get more sympathy from my mom than my dad. My dad's a bit harsher. He tells me stuff that I don't want to hear. For example, if I'm cutting weight, and I tell him I don't want to cut weight anymore, he'll probably say that I'm not allowed to quit. I am afraid that I will let him down, at some level.

THE REVOLUTION COMES FROM WITHIN
Louis, 16, from a suburb in the South

The fact is that people on TV are typically beautiful people. That's just because people don't want to look at fat, ugly people. I really don't know why that is. I guess it's just part of our human nature and our breeding.

The standard of beauty for men is set in stone—it's the six-one Ken, with flowing brown hair, chiseled chin, and plastic smile. That's truly the American image in all the men's magazines. It has been for quite some time. It's just part of our conditioning. Sometimes the media try to mix it up a bit and throw in some other people, but that's just due to complaints. I don't think that's real effective. Some people want to live up to those images, trying to impress women and trying to impress friends.

I think that's a personal fault of people, to allow themselves to be manipulated in such a way that says they have to look a certain way. The media just set the standard, and that kind of gives American boys—I don't want to say something to live up to—it gives them that one extreme.

The revolution comes from within. The only true way to the greater good is through ourselves. We just can't blame anymore, because we've learned that gets us nowhere. We can't blame and we can't scapegoat. We have to do it for ourselves. We can't say, "Pop culture is doing this to us." We're *letting* pop culture do this to us. The media have been telling us how we're supposed to look for quite a while. That's more or less inevitable.

It's not a real personal thing for me. I don't really care about what people think. I've just learned in the last few years that all that image stuff is really not important. Above all, you just have to be happy with yourself. That philosophy is preached to us and preached to us, but I know from experience that the only way to learn that is to learn yourself. For some people, there are a series of experiences and lifestyle changes that ultimately lead to self-fulfillment and happiness, but a lot of people won't reach that. I think that I'm well on my way, and I just have to keep making and meeting my own goals to reach that plateau of happiness.

BECAUSE THEY'RE BIG

Warren, 14, from New York City

Sometimes it's hard for guys who are overweight, but not for me. I'm social, so I can make friends easily. My first time coming to school, I didn't know nobody, but after the first week I had a lot of friends, because of my personality. I'm a good person to know.

Some people think that because they're big they can't do anything, they've got to just stay home. It really brings their self-esteem down. I have a friend who thought that because he was big he couldn't make any friends, couldn't have girls, couldn't do anything. So he went to school, and then he went home, and that's it: he didn't hang out or nothing, because he just felt like nobody wanted to be around him. He was thinking, "Why should I be here?" He wanted to isolate himself. Because his self-esteem was low. After I introduced him to a couple of my friends, he started to realize that people wanted to talk to him.

My advice for big guys is to go ahead and have fun, do exactly what you want. Don't let weight bring you down. Just go have fun, because if you let it bring you down, you get more depressed, start thinking things, and then you'll just be stressed out. Go to the movies, play sports, just do whatever you can.

WEARING TIGHTS

Roland, 17, from a city in the Northeast

I've been dancing since I was six years old. I've always liked to dance at parties and everything. In elementary school and at junior high I joined a community dance group. It wasn't ballet or modern dance, just a community dance program. Then I took a modern dance class later in junior high school. It has beautiful choreography. With modern, you put your spirit into it. It's like you're flowing through the dance. You do different things with your arms. You're organized and steady. You're synchronized with everybody else. In high school, I began taking tap, then hip-hop. With hip-hop, you're doing a lot of jumping around, lots of pumping. You do anything you want with your arms and legs. Hip-hop is energy. Later I did a little bit of classical. But I never did ballet, not yet. I don't want to do that. I'm not ready for the tights.

I'm not ashamed of my body. I think my body is fine. But I feel embarrassed, especially in front of guys, to dance in tights. I don't like the negative energy that I'm gonna get back. And I've seen shows that guys have done in tights and the other guys just act ridiculous toward them. I was thinking: "Why are you laughing at him? He's doing something that you can never possibly do, so you shouldn't be laughing at him!" I mean, it takes a lot to get up there, first of all, and dance in front of a lot of people; and second, to be dancing in tights and being probably the only guy up there. I was really upset and that kind of pushed me away from getting up there and dancing in tights. With the negative feedback they were giving, I was just like "No, I'm not getting up there."

It's easy to dance in front of strangers, but it's hard to dance in front of your friends. It's such a nerve-racking experience. If I were running the ballet class, and a boy in the class didn't want to put on his tights, I would tell him, "I've been there, it's okay to feel embarrassed."

I am worried about my upper body and arms. I want to look nice with my muscles and things like that. Most of the guys do. A young person like me, I'm really not that toned. I don't feel insecure but I feel like I'm kind of skinny. I want to be more bulked up, not to impress anybody, but just for me. Just to feel good about myself. But I think for a lot of guys it's mostly for the look, so they can impress girls and other guys.

I think boys and men are concerned about their bodies and the way they look. One time I went to this audition at a nearby high school and this guy—it was so funny because he had tights, and he put socks in his tights to make it look bigger, and I was like "Why are you doing that?" And he was like "Because it's not big enough!" And it was so funny, but I was like, who cares? The thing about him, he wasn't insecure about dancing, but he didn't like the way he looked in his tights.

The other guys think that girls are the only ones who can dance and girls are the only ones who are supposed to be wearing tights. They don't know that guys can do it, too. You can do whatever you want! I think that guys are insecure about themselves, basically. They don't know what they are or what they want. Whenever you're judging somebody, I think that you are insecure about yourself. Because you wouldn't be judging other people if you didn't think there was something wrong with yourself.

Maybe they're insecure about their body, maybe they're insecure that they can't dance. It could be a lot of things. Their bodies, their personality. Do people like them? How well are they liked? Things like that can make you act stupid, really. If you don't know where you stand among your peers, you can act stupid. I think it's mostly boys, because girls, they have this freedom, that's why I admire them so much. Girls have this freedom to be like "Yeah, I can do whatever I want." I'm not saying that all girls are secure. But most guys have a problem with being insecure, that's what I'm saying.

BEING SHORT

Dennis, 17, from a suburb in the West

Sometimes things get hard because I've always been teased about my height. I'm five-five and that's seven inches below the norm for my age. And so all through elementary school and all through middle school I was the shortest guy in the class. I was the shrimp. People said, "Hey, Smurf, come over here!" And it really bothered me for a lot of years, up until about seventh grade. One day I was sitting down talking to my dad about it, and I was really angry and stressed out about it. It was just really getting to me.

And my dad said, "Look, the only reason people do that is to get a response out of you. If you just ignore it or go along with it, they'll realize it's pointless to continue. You may develop a nickname from it. I'm called Lucky the Leprechaun because I'm a short guy. People sometimes call out 'Hey, Shorty' when they see me. It just doesn't bother me anymore. I have incorporated it into who I am. I have accepted the fact that there's nothing I can really do to change these people, so I might as well live with it. I mean, if you can't beat them, join them. When in Rome, do as the Romans do."

I was hurt when I was younger when people called me "Shorty." So I found friends that didn't care. Friends who wouldn't make comments when I went up and talked to them. So I'd ask them if they cared about it. And they would answer, "Why would we care that you're shorter than we are? It's no big deal."

People sometimes think guys don't care about their appearance and their body. But it's not true. If you're fat, when people look at you they're going to picture you as a fat kid. They're not going to say, "Oh, he's a cool guy." Each time I have moved, the kids in school all look at me and the first thing they think is "He's a short guy. He's not supposed to be here. He must be like a smart kid that's three grades ahead of what he's supposed to be, because he's too short to be in fifth grade. So he must be a second grader who skipped grades." Once you get to know people, these impressions wear down. There's one guy here who's built like a truck and at first glance the girls think he's real attractive. But once they get to know him, they discover how weird he is. They always decide he's a little too strange for their taste.

When you first meet someone, judging them by physical appearance is the best way to start, because it's the only basis you have to go on before you get to know them. If you meet a really built guy who's friends with a fat kid, you might find out the really built guy is a jerk and the fat kid is really a nice guy. Physical appearance is really important at first glance, but after a while the real person shows through underneath.

Once you get past that, it's smooth sailing. Once people get to know you, it really doesn't matter anymore what you look like, because they see you as a friend. They see you pretty much for who you are. If someone is going to stay away from you because they don't like who you are, then they're going to stay away from you because they don't like who you are. They're not going to stay away from you anymore because you're the short kid.

Girls put pressure on guys to have a well-built, muscular appearance. Girls right now are looking for the big, muscular guys that walk around in muscle-beach shirts. I don't let it bother me. It doesn't matter to me. I don't play any real heavy upper-body sports, so I don't feel the need to bulk up. I do track and cross-country, which requires a lot of lower body. If I did bulk up my upper body I wouldn't be able to run as well. I'd rather be lean and fast than be real built and heavy. I can deal with having the girls not look at me at first because I'm not the most attractive guy on earth. Not that I am insecure about my looks—I'm pretty confident about them. I think it all works out in the end. You're going to find somebody in the end who really doesn't care about your muscles and likes you for yourself. But I do think the pressures on guys to look good and be a certain way are building. I think we're slowly turning into a female-dominated society and the pressures on guys will get worse than on girls.

I think my life has been about overcoming obstacles. I've had to deal with moving many times and always starting over again. Having people teasing me about my height and stuff like that. Making new friends, then having to abandon everything and start over again. Having to maintain my center, being who I am, and not trying to be someone

I'm not. Overcoming these obstacles has built me up mentally to the point where I can take anything that people throw at me. If someone challenges me to do something, I'm going to do it. Even if I fail, I'm going to go do it. And it's not going to bother me if I fail because I'm going to know I tried. I went out there, I tried, I didn't do it; so what? No big loss.

20

THE STING OF
DIVORCE

"I don't know why they got divorced. They were a happy couple."
—Garcia, 12, from a city in the Northeast

"I felt like someone had put a hundred daggers in my heart. I never before knew what divorce really meant or what went with it. . . . My dad moved out less than a month later."
—Bruce, 14, from a suburb in northern New England

"It's such an emptiness, such a hole in your very soul which can't be filled; at times you will be doing some routine mechanical thing, like homework, and you'll think, 'Oh, I don't know how to do this, I'll just ask my dad . . .' and things trail off as you realize that you don't have a dad who will be coming home that evening."
—Chip, 15, from a small town in New England

WHILE MANY OF US MAY ALREADY KNOW THAT BETWEEN 40 and 50 percent of marriages in the United States will end in divorce—and that over 65 percent of children born in the last three years of the twentieth century will reach eighteen not living with both of their biological parents—the boys whose voices speak from these pages highlight the complexities and pain of these circumstances.

For many years, America underestimated the effects of divorce on girls because young women tended to be "good" about divorce—they cooperated and did not complain. Over the years, however, studies have shown that divorce actually has had devastating long-term effects on girls, damage that we missed because of girls' outwardly calm and compliant behavior.

With boys, we've observed how divorce seems to increase their outward misbehavior. We've noticed that these boys seem to fail classes, skip school, start fights, and take drugs more often than those who have not experienced their parents' divorcing. Sometimes these boys' acting up may occur and be responded to before anyone even realizes that there is parental trouble at home. Perhaps because most boys of divorce may have channeled their suffering into action-based conduct—by rebelling or being so-called bad boys—we've tended to address their behavior with swift disciplinary solutions rather than with the empathic and psychologically oriented ones they truly require. Often we may have punished or ignored their acts of defiance rather than addressing the underlying emotional pain. By failing to understand and appreciate the acute suffering boys are all but certain to face before, during, and following their parents' separation or divorce, we have made much the same kind of well-intentioned mistake as we did with girls.

In my experience, when boys speak of divorce, too often they speak of losing their fathers. It is so frequently the case that it's the fathers who leave the home when a divorce occurs; many of them leave the emotional lives of their children as well. For boys, this separation and loss intensifies all the repercussions of the Boy Code, deepening their sense of isolation, loneliness, and disconnectedness to the world. A boy may feel he has to toughen up even more in order to hide the pain and shame of such a horrific loss. This toughening process is deepened when a boy is led to believe that he is now the "little man of the family," responsible for his mother and siblings.

The single-parent arrangements that flow from divorce often wreak special havoc on boys. Though I firmly believe (and many studies show) that single mothers can raise happy, healthy sons, society places impossible demands upon these moms, often questioning their ability to keep up with the requirements of the job. Society also telegraphs the message to mothers that if they remain too closely tied to their sons, they will somehow scar them emotionally. This forces single mothers and their sons—who have already suffered a sense of loss—to separate further, leaving these boys feeling deeply confused about which if any parent they can continue to hold close. "I used to be much closer to her," seventeen-year-old Joel, from New England, says about his mother, who recently divorced his dad. He adds sadly: "I just don't try to tell her stuff anymore. There's no point. Why would I want to make somebody a part of my life who doesn't want to be there?"

Angry and disappointed by their loss and frightened about facing life without their dads, these boys may don the mask of masculinity and try to tough things out on their own. But as strong and determined as he may be, deep down a boy may come to feel intensely unhappy, ashamed, alone. Victor, a seventeen-year-old living in New York City, told me, "I know other kids have a father who lives at home with them. . . . There was one time in junior high school when I started crying because my father wasn't there. I just remember sitting in the classroom and crying because he couldn't be with me. I mean, I saw all these kids with their fathers."

Tony, a sixteen-year-old from a city in the Northeast, whose father left the family when he was a toddler, also illustrates this vacillation between the mask and the pain. "I don't know how I'm supposed to approach a guy to talk about things like feelings. My dad is supposed to be the guy I'm to be comfortable talking to, the only guy, and he's not there. So I have to deal with things myself. Even my mom taught me that: since I don't have a father I've got to be tougher than most kids who do have a father. But some things you can't go on dealing with by yourself, you need somebody to talk to."

Some boys are simply unable to wear the mask because nothing can diminish the pain of their parents' separation. Chris, a fifteen-year-old from New England, said his parents' divorce left him with "a feeling of indescribable loneliness." He felt as though he was "left behind," with "such an emptiness, such a hole in your very soul which can't be filled."

NOT SIMPLE BY ANY MEANS

Chip, 15, from a small town in New England

There are some things in life that we just don't want to deal with, accept, or even acknowledge as existing.

Almost a month ago—and it seems like a lot less—I found out that my parents would be getting a divorce. That sounds simple, sounds common, sounds like something that would be accepted and possibly even expected, as one-half of all marriages end in divorce.

It doesn't matter what it sounds like! If it sounds simple, then believe me when I tell you that it is not. If it sounds common, then believe me that I have never had anything remotely close to this happen in my family. If it sounds like something acceptable, then, by God, believe me when I say it is not. As for being expected, there was no hint, no warning, no smoke before everything went up in flames. It was sudden, harsh, cold, and impersonal; and worst of all, it was my family that it was happening to.

The divorce process is not simple by any means. Trust me, I've done my homework, I've done research, and I've found out everything that is supposed to happen. I've been blessed with a very caring girlfriend who went through the same process when she was five. Although her circumstances were vastly different from mine, she has helped me tremendously by telling me what is supposed to happen, and what I'm going to feel like as it is happening. That's the worst part of a divorce, by the way—it's the *not knowing,* the feeling that you're being left behind, that the divorce is not a subject to be discussed, that it's just something which is supposed to happen on its own. It's a feeling of indescribable loneliness.

It's such an emptiness, such a hole in your very soul which can't be filled; at times you will be doing some routine mechanical thing, like homework, and you'll think, "Oh, I don't know how to do this, I'll just ask my dad . . ." and things trail off as you realize that you don't have a dad who will be coming home that evening. You have a dad who lives down the street, or in the next town, or around the world; it doesn't matter. The important thing is that you have a dad who doesn't live at home. This is the hardest part, recognizing the change in the normal routine. Recognizing and realizing that from now on you will be split between two parents, or will not see one except on weekends, or will not see one again. I don't know which of these things is worse.

Although statistically half of all marriages end in divorce, that doesn't mean anything. Saying that is like saying, "You have a one in five thousand chance of having a fatal accident while driving." That means that one of those other five thousand people driving home *will* have a wreck, not you. Numbers, statistics, percentages, while they never lie, make lousy condolences and even worse reminders. I never thought at all, ever, not once, that something like this would happen in my family.

There is no history of divorce on either side of my family, and I've checked. Both sets of grandparents have very detailed genealogy records dating back literally hundreds of years, and nowhere in either one will you find a dashed line, which represents a divorce. This is something completely new, completely wrong that is happening to my family. This was never supposed to happen to the little kid with the funny mom and the really tall dad. This was not supposed to happen!

As for this being acceptable, allow me to quote with great emphasis that bald guy from *Apollo 13*: "Failure is not, *ever,* an option!" This is giving up, this is quitting, and this is failure on the grandest scale. That is divorce, simply and bluntly. Quitting. What a disgusting, dishonorable, and altogether deplorable act.

Talking or thinking about or even feeling all that the word "divorce" encompasses is difficult. In fact, this is the most difficult thing that has ever happened in my fifteen years of life. I have overcome many obstacles in my hopes of one day walking on the ocean floor, once diving deeper than all the safe limits to save a friend. I have jumped off cliffs with nothing but a thin rope dangling in the air to hold me to this earth. I have done things that other men only imagine. Yet dealing with my parents' divorce is more difficult, more challenging, and more taxing on me mentally and physically than all of these feats combined.

The only advice I can offer to anyone else going through this is the advice which my girlfriend gave me: "Hang in there, baby. Hang in there."

THE REAL WORLD
Victor, 17, from New York City

I'm close to my mom and love her a lot. But she is often in a bad mood.

My mom didn't have love when my father was around. To tell you the truth, I don't know my father. I have never seen him. He didn't pay attention to my mom, and he didn't take care of us. My little brother and I, we don't have the same fathers. After my mother had me with my father, she got together with my stepfather and had my brother. Then my stepfather just got up and walked out. He didn't care anymore. And now my brother hardly sees him anymore. His father doesn't come home either.

I have only seen one picture of my father. I don't care about him anymore. I have lived my whole life without him, and I don't think I need him now. And I don't think I will ever need him.

I know other kids have a father who lives at home with them. For me, not having my father is not that depressing because I just don't really think about it. I don't really know what goes down, I just live life as it is and accept the real world. But sometimes it is hard.

There was one time in junior high school when I started crying because my father wasn't there. I just remember sitting in the classroom and crying because he couldn't be with me. I mean, I saw all these kids with their fathers. I don't know. I guess my grandfather has been my father. He has almost always been there. But he is very, very strict. He has cooled down now because he is old. But, boy, he has raised his kids using power.

I want to live somewhere else now. I want to move right now. It's not cool where I live. When you are walking in our kitchen, mice will just pass you by. They just jump right in front of you. I'm like "Oh my God."

At home you have to worry about putting out mice traps, even though you know the mice are going to come right back even if you catch some. Last night I caught two. And they were making so much noise because they were trapped, and they were trying to get out. I had to get up at midnight to get one and then at two in the morning to get the other. I was so tired. I was so afraid, even though they were stuck to the trap. I took a broom and a dustpan, and I just took them out to the hallway, and they landed upside down. Then they started moving. I looked at the mice and was like "You are on your own now." I just closed the door and went back to sleep. But I don't like being around mice. I hate them. They are the nastiest creatures I have ever known.

Sometimes when the going gets rough, I think I want to see my father. I don't want to see him when he's dead in a casket. I want to see him alive. I guess I'm ambivalent. Part of me wants to see him, and part of me is really angry. It's hard to figure out. If I could see him now I would say, "You should have been there for me. You should have been like every regular dad taking their kids to school, and helping them with their homework, and doing that."

I'd tell him that my mother raised me, my brother, and my sister. And I'd tell him that my mother has done a very good job.

In the Picture Again

Rodney, 18, from a city in the Northeast

My dad is in the picture again. We're working on our relationship, but we have never been close. I don't know why. We were just never that close.

When I was younger I stayed with my dad only for a little while. When you're little, you don't know what to do. He always wanted me to play sports, and do things like auto mechanic stuff. I was never really into that. He's a very old-fashioned man. He's sixty-five; he's very old. He always thought guys should not clean the dishes. So he thought that *he* should not clean the house. He thought he should just sit and watch TV, or work. And have the women cook for him.

My mother used to get frustrated. She was like "No, you need to get up and clean." I'm glad she made me do that because I don't have to depend on anybody to cook or clean or do my laundry or things like that. I'm glad that she got me out of that thing that my dad almost got me into.

I go visit my dad every Sunday. We're working on it little by little. I do feel that it has improved a lot because now I actually do talk to him. Before it used to be just going over there and getting some money and that's it. But now I do talk to him, and he is taking an interest in my life and the things I do.

I think that deep down he loves me a lot. He knows what he did wrong and I think he knows that it's time to make up. I would never say that I don't like my father; I would just say that I didn't really get to know him.

I am going to be in a talent show at our high school soon. I hope my dad would like to see me perform in it. But he's never come before. My mother's always there. But Dad, no. I would like for him to come.

Mixed Around

Joel, 17, from a suburb in New England

My parents got separated five years ago. It sucked. It was bad for all three of us. There was a lot of fighting building up to it. I didn't actually see it coming, but when my father told me that my mother had asked him to leave the house, I wasn't surprised. It was good to get them apart because when they were together, all they would do is fight.

When they separated, we didn't come together. We used to be a five-person unit, and then it all got mixed around. My younger brother and I have gotten tighter and tighter as the years go by. But my older brother definitely focused on the fact that he was going to be leaving to go to college. When he finally went to college, it was like "All right. See you." We don't see each other much anymore.

There was a lot of side-taking, when my parents split up. The separation did affect me—what happens in the past affects the present. I had a lot of stress, and I was trying to keep the two separate so that I could deal with school. I think I did a pretty good job with that. I was just stressed out most of the time, which was no fun.

Now, we see my dad twice a week for dinner, and my little brother sleeps over there on the weekends. We're both supposed to sleep over there every other weekend, but I usually go to a friend's house. My dad's apartment is pretty small and there's only his bed and the couch, which pulls out into a bed. But we don't even use that anymore because it's so uncomfortable. So somebody can sleep on the couch and someone can sleep on the floor. If I have to go there and sleep on a dirty floor—I don't think so.

I keep my dad more informed than my mother, though. I get the feeling that he cares and listens more when I tell him things. With my mother—when she does even bother to ask—it's more like she's just asking because she feels she's supposed to. My mother, in my opinion, is a confused person.

I used to be much closer to her. She focused a lot of her attention on my older brother when he was around and getting him into college. Then, as soon as he went off to college, my little brother was getting in a lot of trouble at school. She started focusing a lot of energy on him. As soon as he would get home, helping him with everything. She never leaves him alone. When she does ask me something, she's really just waiting for me to finish so she can start talking to my brother again. So, I never really got a turn. But that's all right with me. I could either let that hurt me or just accept it and not let it bother me.

I just don't try to tell her stuff anymore. There's no point. Why would I want to make somebody a part of my life who doesn't want to be there? Besides, she's not interested in most of the things that I'm interested in. It's not like we could ever have really good conversations about theater, music, and writing, art in general.

When my parents separated I became a different person. I became expressionless. Just as a defense. I tried to live outside of school as much as I could. I didn't have many friends at that point in my life. I didn't talk much at all. I never smiled or frowned. I always had a blank expression.

Then I came to this school my freshman year. I really didn't know how to smile when I got here. I didn't understand smiling. It would be something I'd have to do consciously. It didn't feel right. The response to smile didn't come. I might get the emotion, but it never got to the mouth. I went to camp after my freshman year and I got the award for biggest smile, because I never smiled.

Now I smile. I've learned to enjoy life as much as possible. Up until this year, I felt a lot of depression and I think it's closely related to stress. Last year I was having trouble with classes and I had a lot of other problems. I got really depressed, to the point that I would just come home and sit and not know what to do with myself.

I told my mother I wanted to see a psychologist because I was worried about myself. But by the time I did go to see one, I felt like I didn't need to anymore. Things just got better.

IT WAS RAINING THAT NIGHT
Lionel, 11, from a suburb in New England

When I was about six, there was a time when we didn't have food. When I was born, I lived with my mother and my father. We all lived together. But then they got divorced, and I just lived with my mother. She had trouble at work or something, and we had to move back to the foster home she lived in when she was younger. My sister was born there. Then the lady who ran the home said there were too many people in the house and wanted us to leave. We didn't have anywhere to go.

It was strange because it was like a movie. It was raining that night, and we were walking and walking and we were lost and we finally found a shelter. We were there for only one night, then we stayed with my sister's father's cousins until my mother could get enough money. I still went to school, and she worked more than one job so that she could get money to get an apartment.

My mother says that she's regretful that I remember that stuff. I'm glad my brother and sister don't remember it. But I've never really cried about it or anything. It just makes me think about how it makes me a strong person.

There was a time when my father wasn't in my life much and I felt a lot of grief because I had seen so many boys with their fathers. I would cry sometimes. Sometimes I could just be perfectly fine and then it would come into my mind how I hadn't seen him in a while, and I would start crying, and my mother would talk to me. One time I called my grandmother and she told me that I just had to keep going. I couldn't sit and wait to see if my dad was going to come back into my life. I had to keep going and let him catch up.

Recently, my dad's been seeing me about once every other month. I would like to see him more. He likes to sit down and talk to me about things like sex and drugs. My father was into drugs before I was born. So he has the perspective of going through that and he tells me, "It's nothing you want to go through." My mother also has had friends who have done drugs. She focused a lot on telling me about peer pressure; that's her main concern. I always tell her I'm not going to do drugs and cigarettes and I'm not going to have sex until I'm married.

I think I have an advantage because some kids, if their parents are together, they bring one point of view. But I can get a man's point of view and a woman's point of view. So, as I grow, I have more knowledge.

A Hundred Daggers
Bruce, 14, from a suburb in northern New England

When I was eleven, my parents got divorced and life as I knew it was turned upside down. It all started on an October night when I was reading to my mom. I came across the word "summer," and so I asked my mom the question that popped up in my head: Were my grandma and grandpa on my father's side coming up from Florida this summer? It was probably one of the worst things I ever asked in my life, due to the answer I received. My mom did not say anything at first and tried to change the subject, but I wouldn't give up, and finally my mother said, "Well, they might come up and stay somewhere else, but they're not staying here." I still did not understand. She finally just came out with it. "Bruce, your father and I are getting a divorce."

I felt like someone had put a hundred daggers in my heart. I never before knew what divorce really meant or what went with it. I was too young and too ignorant to really know anything about it. Even though I knew kids whose parents were divorced, I did not know what to do next.

My dad moved out less than a month later and at first I stayed with my mother. Every night when I came home from school we fought and tried to hurt each other verbally. These arguments really affected my little brother—he was too young to understand what was going on, but he recognized the tension between us, which caused him agony. I admit that a good amount of it was my fault; I started fights and did things out of spite. But I also believe that a good amount of it was my mother's fault. Her attitude changed because of the divorce, and she seemed to be a totally different person. She seemed meaner, with less patience and flexibility. Everything was her way or the highway. It was only until much later in my life, about four years after the divorce, that she became more flexible, easygoing, and able to come to agreements about doing things differently.

Two months after their separation, I started staying with my dad a few nights each week. My mother and I couldn't deal with each other and she was starting to push me out of the house.

By this time, I was living with my dad full-time. I was having a really good time living with him, but it was putting a major stress on his job. He has to do a lot of traveling to see his clients, and having me there made it difficult for him because he couldn't leave me alone in the evenings.

Less than a year after moving in with my father, he got remarried to a woman I did not like. We moved into her house in a different city and then my dad's company relocated, so his new commute meant that he was gone two or three nights each week. This meant that my stepmom, Barb, took on the responsibility of taking care of me. A person who I had never spent more than two days alone with was now my primary supervisor.

There were a lot of things to cause stress in that house: my troubles fitting in at a new school, my stepbrother's laziness, my stepmother's dissatisfaction with her job, and my father's absences. Whenever he came home, we would argue about what was going on. He never wanted to listen to my side; it didn't really matter to him. That whole year we were at each other's throats. It tore the whole family apart and pushed everybody further away from each other.

I'm not at public school anymore, nor do I live with my father and stepmother anymore. I am now at a private school for learning disabled students, which has been very beneficial to me. However, I feel that I am not a part of any family. My dad still has custody of me, but I spend 90 percent of my summertime and vacations with my mom. My mother is good to me now and tries to make me feel that I have a family there, but it has yet to feel complete. Every time she doesn't want to deal with something, she says that it is my father's responsibility, but he's usually not responsible enough to take care of it. I want my mother to take over custody, but she wants to wait another six months before making a decision. Once again, I feel that I am so close to having a family, but yet so far away.

Every time I think about this, it crushes me with great pain. Everybody has problems, including kids. Even though we don't have to pay the bills or the mortgage, we still have problems and stress just like everyone else. I don't think problems should be made light of just because of age. A child's problems may not seem as important as an adult's, but they are important to the child.

21

ADDICTIONS: DRUGS, ALCOHOL, AND THE MEDIA

"Sometimes it's the kids who are the most popular or well thought of who are the most insecure underneath."

—Rubin, 13, from a suburb in the Northeast

"It's like a row of stairs and you just go from one to another; you just get bored of one drug and you move on to the next. It's this process where you go deeper and deeper."

—Adam, 18, from a suburb in the Northwest

"There are some people I've met on-line who are on the Internet for twelve hours a day, like the Internet is their whole life."

—Bradley, 18, from a suburb in the Northeast

UNABLE TO FIND FRIENDS WITH WHOM THEY CAN TRULY be themselves and desperate to fit in among their peers, a majority of America's boys experiment with drugs and alcohol, many slipping precipitously toward addiction. Still others fill the social and emotional void with their fascination with television (more than 80 percent of boys tune in every day), the Internet, video games, and the whole gamut of electronic media. There's a broad dilemma of disconnection that is infecting our culture, with many boys spending many of their free hours engaging in these isolating, repetitive behaviors rather than building and deepening their relationships with friends, family, and adult mentors.

The boys I spoke with who use drugs and alcohol suffer varying levels of dependency and addiction. Some drink lightly or smoke marijuana from time to time. Others consume huge amounts of alcohol, smoke pot daily, and abuse a wide range of hallucinogens, prescription sedatives and antidepressants, and narcotics. For some boys, taking drugs seems a passing flirtation with escapism. For others it entails a relentless, grinding descent toward total disaffection, depression, even death. Whether it is smoking pot to get stoned, binging wildly on bourbon, or simply diverting themselves with electronic media, these boys are numbing themselves as a way to end their loneliness and hopelessness. Many of them speak of a painful sense that no one really knows or understands who they really are, that no one cares about their true, inner lives, that they may never find friends with whom they can connect in a genuine, loving way. Addiction crosses all racial and class boundaries. The boy who is about to drop out of high school is just as susceptible as the president of his class or the captain of the hockey team.

The confusion boys feel is made all the worse by how common addiction is, and by how well accepted it is among peers. "I guess I fit in best with the potheads," José told us, with a hint of resignation. "Sometimes I want to smoke pot. . . . But I don't consider myself a pothead." Once he was almost caught by his father and it made him wonder about others who get addicted to it. "You think to yourself," he said sadly, "I don't want to end up a pothead." One friend "used to smoke pot and now he does acid." He concluded, "It all starts with other kids saying, 'Hey, you want to try?' "

But when boys speak about addiction, they speak not only of peers but of parents, too. Although current research shows that parents, much more than peers, hold sway over teenagers' ability to steer clear of addiction, Steve, a seventeen-year-old from a suburb in New England, told us something we heard over and over again: some parents just don't want to listen. "We just don't talk about the things that make my parents uncomfortable. They say they want to hear it, because they want to know what I'm doing. But they don't *really* want to hear it. If they hear it, then I end up in trouble."

This presents a conundrum of disconnected communication: adults are willing to listen, but they're quick to shame and punish. While boys understand the importance of their parents setting limits, they yearn to be able to talk about their use of drugs and alcohol without facing lectures and angry reproaches. The so-called just-say-no approach doesn't seem to sit well with most boys. They are quick to observe the many adults around them who are saying yes. They perceive the hypocrisy and then they rebel by taking their own risks. They long to be able to go to a loving adult, one they can trust and with whom they can feel comfortable, and say things like "I tried pot last night. I was scared and didn't really like it. I want to make sure I don't get addicted to it." Or "My friends drink all the time and I feel left out. What should I do?" Or "I love the feeling of getting high. Should I be worried? What should I do?" These are questions adolescent boys really have. If we are not prepared to answer them honestly and directly, without being punitive and judgmental, who will be there to answer them?

Boys also struggle with the permissive messages they hear from both peers and adults who see so-called experimentation as part of an adolescent's learning process and a "normal" exercise of boyhood bravado. Ernie expresses his sense that some drugs are not always "bad." "My own philosophy is that they serve as a catalyst for things happening." But as we talked, he began to speak about his fear of addiction. "I am under control," he said, his anxiety beginning to show through. "I wish I hadn't started so early."

Other boys seemed to understand that the experimentation heralded by young men like Ernie may go beyond normal adolescent trials and become a form of dangerous bravado. Many worry that they're playing with a fire that may turn out not to be so easy to extinguish. Writes seventeen-year-old Jasper in his essay that appears below, "Coming down off the high that narcotics can deliver, I went tailspinning into the murky, dank bowels of life, a place from which very few ever return."

Many boys spoke about parents who were conflicted because they too use, or once used, drugs or alcohol. Several told us that their parents "didn't mind" their dependencies, ignoring it as "child's play," a boy sowing his wild oats. Steve explained that his friend Keith's parents told their fourteen-year-old son, "If you want to have the kids over here to smoke pot or drink, it's OK."

A positive component one could extract from the approach Keith's parents took is that they were reaching out, in an honest, caring way, to create a safe, controlled environment in which their sons could try drinking and drugs. But what seems missing from that picture are the long, open talks that could help boys like Keith and Steve to understand the major hazards inherent in the behavior. A glass of wine or a puff of marijuana are probably not the primary risk. The danger, and the tragedy, is that boys repeatedly use these substances to anesthetize themselves against the symptoms of emotional suffering, including those of actual clinical depression, that should and must be addressed. This is when boys become seriously addicted, alienating themselves from friends and family. They then spin out of control. "Turning to drugs and alcohol to solve your problems just prolongs them," says eighteen-year-old Adam from the Northwest, who began drinking hard alcohol at age twelve. "The pain is still there afterward, and you still have to deal with it."

Drugs, alcohol, the compulsive consumption of video games, TV, and the Internet all take the place of real relationships, soothing a boy's loneliness and self-doubt. Yearning to connect, but perhaps too frightened to unmask his true self, seventeen-year-old Ben, from suburban New England, explains, "Thanks to the miracle of modern technology, we communicate over the Internet all the time. It is actually a lot easier to bring up things if you're just seeing a person's words appear on a screen, and not talking to them on the phone. . . . It is so much easier. You just type it and the words appear. It is nice and clean. You don't have to deal with the emotional impact of what you say."

Compulsive behaviors offer only a temporary form of anesthesia. Boys are looking to their friends and families for honesty about addiction and the painful feelings and experiences that lead up to it. They know that while drugs and alcohol, video games, TV, and Internet sites may present serious health risks, they are not the issue. The real problem is when boys feel that they must rely on these outlets because there is no one there for them, that without such things they cannot cope, cannot continue.

CLOUD NUMBER NINE
Jasper, 17, from a small town in the South

I will never forget seeing Hope for the first time. The memory still plays vividly upon my brain and heart. She was Aphrodite springing from the froth of the sea. My young, immature heart leapt, right then, straight out of my chest into the palm of her hand. Hope was new to the area and I offered my friendship. At amazing speed, she and I became close friends, then boyfriend and girlfriend. Looking back with hindsight at the night that she agreed to be my girl, I laugh at how good it felt as she responded to my flirtations. That first night with her, I had gotten no sleep. I still greeted the next day with joy.

As I prepared for school, I do not believe that my feet tread the floor once. If anyone has ever truly floated on cloud number nine, I did that morning. I couldn't wait to get to school and walk down the hall with her, our arms interlocked. I couldn't wait to show everyone that Hope and I were together, that the beautiful new girl was taken, by me.

After nine months of bliss together, Hope came to my home one night and told me that she was seeing somebody else. I was absolutely devastated. Once she had betrayed me, the relationship was over. The mere notion of not having her in my life crushed my spirit. I was convinced that without her, life would be nothing more than a never-ending abyss of hatred and despair, devoid of sunshine. I couldn't take the thought that my life would go back to normal, back to what it had been without her.

Days went by during which I never rose from bed. Hope had been the fuel that ran my engine, and without her, I hadn't the energy, or the will, to do even the smallest tasks. Everything became futile and pointless. I didn't understand the point of taking a shower, when a day later I would only have to take another one; the same way with shaving. Why eat, when hunger would soon come again, and the whole process would have to be done over? With each day, I sank deeper into despair and slough.

No longer able to live in the brutal real world, I soon brought marijuana and alcohol into the picture; then I added speed. Narcotics gave me power. With them, I could manipulate reality. I could travel to foreign lands. I could escape the horror that my real life had become. When I heard my mother crying in bed at night, I knew that drugs, my new best friend, were causing the tears. I felt powerful, for I knew that by using drugs, I was hurting someone as much as I had been hurt.

This power to hurt became addictive. I became a masterful artisan in the craft, even as I crushed my loved ones and strangers alike. One night, around this period, I was at a party where I was so high on cocaine, marijuana, and liquor that I didn't even know my own name. Someone who I was unfamiliar with approached me and asked me for a stick of gum. Becoming enraged at his audacity—how dare he talk to me without my consent—I beat him into unconsciousness with a broomstick. I hurt him for no other reason except to inflict pain. My friends, seeing this unchecked rage burning so passionately within my bosom, became frightened and stopped coming around. I was alone.

At first being alone did not bother me, for I was too strung out to comprehend the meaning of the word, the pain that "alone" can inflict. But, coming down off the high that narcotics can deliver, I went tailspinning into the murky, dank bowels of life, a place from which very few ever return. Stumbling in the door early that morning, I was surprised to see my mother still up, sitting on the couch. The sun's rays had just begun to puncture the darkness of the eastern sky, and though hard to distinguish with merely the dim track lighting of the den as light, I could tell that her eyes were bloodshot and swollen, her cheeks puffy. Upon seeing me, she grabbed and pulled me to her bosom, squeezing me so tightly that I was convinced that I would soon enter her being. She held me there for what seemed like an eternity, crying and petting me.

Her words I will never forget, for they made me realize just how far I had strayed from the beaten path. She asked me, "What happened to my honor student: the tall, thin, handsome young man who loved sports, books, and his family; who considered me his best friend and always turned to me in time of need? What happened to him? What happened to the young man who, although he had suffered many hardships in his life, was making amazing progress, and was in the process of transforming into a man with learning, with probity? He's gone, and I know that in my heart he'll probably never come back. I blame myself, because I left you when you needed me the most. Because of me, you've never been able to be a child. I'm sorry that I failed you in being a mother. With your sister, I promise that I'll do better."

Her speech brought forth in me a fount of tears; tears that had been pent up for sixteen years; tears of frustration, anger, loneliness, and fright. In an instant, I realized that I had inflicted irreparable damage on my mother's psyche, and that although she had returned to me several years after her departure, I had never forgiven her and had deep down always hated her, making me no better than my father. I had let down the only person that I had striven my entire life not to let down. I could not withstand the guilt that came with being in her presence, and pushing her away, I ran to my room, slammed the door, and locked it.

Through tear-filled, bloodshot eyes I looked in the mirror. What I saw disgusted me. The reflection I encountered was that of a drug addict, an alcoholic, a loser. Once a well-dressed, neatly groomed person, I now re-sembled a madman. My face was scruffy, my hair uncouth, and my clothes dirty, ragged, and vomit stained. Stepping back to get a full look, I saw a shell of my former self. My face was thin, gaunt, and jaundiced. My eyes were so deeply sunk into my skull that their colors were undis-tinguishable, and were underlined with deep, black pouches. I was so thin that every bone jutted from my sallow skin, as though I was merely a skeleton. I was not me any longer, and I had no idea how to get me back.

THEIR WHOLE LIFE

Bradley, 18, from a suburb in the Northeast

On the average, I spend about two hours an evening on the Internet, a fair amount. It's had a positive impact on my life, because the concept of the Internet is free information in a forum that is accessible to any-one. There are some flaws in it, but I don't think you can regulate or control it because the concept behind it is free trade of information. I think it could happen that the Internet becomes just another form of the media, and it is probably sort of happening already. But one advantage over something like television is that any person can make their own web page; if you have a computer you can make your own web page. Because of that, there is more open-endedness to it, more opportunity for people to be self-expressive and not follow what society says.

If the Internet is used the wrong way, I think some problems can be caused. One thing with the Internet is you have anonymity. No one knows who you are so you can essentially say whatever you want with-out consequences. It gives people the power to say things that they wouldn't have the guts to say face-to-face, and therefore they could be more destructive or make mistakes. People might say things just be-cause no one will know that they've said it.

Also, some people might not develop healthy social habits. I mean to a certain extent they have a human connection, but they don't have that face-to-face human connection. There are some people I've met on-line who are on the Internet for twelve hours a day, like the Internet is their whole life. That seems wasteful, because there is so much more to life. The Internet is an awesome tool and it can be fun in it's own right, but there is just so much more that someone could be doing.

I Can't Really Win

Steve, 17, from a suburb in New England

My relationship with my parents is really good. We talk a lot about every-thing: politics, books, whatever. But there are certain things that fall into the "don't talk about it" category, like anything to do with parties.

My mom will say, "So, you went to a party. What happens at these parties?" And I say, "It's a party." It feels like she knows what happens at parties and thinks that I don't. She'll say, "We should really be hon-est about this." And I feel we should talk about it, but I know it's a mis-take because we've tried to talk about the subject before. She'll say, "It's good you're being honest with us. I'd much rather have an open di-alogue and I don't condone what goes on, but if you're going to do it, it's much better that you can be open about it." But then she wants to re-strict the parties I go to. So, we just don't talk about the things that make my parents uncomfortable. They say they want to hear it, because they want to know what I'm doing. But they don't really want to hear it. If they hear it, then I end up in trouble.

The problem is that I am doing stuff on the weekends that my par-ents wouldn't want me to do. I know if I went to this kid's party and his parents weren't there, there would be a lot of drinking and drugs. I have friends whose parents won't even ask if the parents are going to be home, they just don't want to know. They'll say, "All right, we'll drop you off," or "Here's the car, go ahead." But my parents always ask, "Are the parents going to be home?" And "When are you going to get home? Who's going to be there?" My parents are a bit anal about it, particu-larly my mother, because she never did any of that in high school and doesn't get it.

My mom and I had a confrontation the other day. I was upset be-cause I went to a kid's party two weeks ago and his parents were there, but they are the type of parents who will deliberately look the other way. They say, "You have this furnished basement and we'll be upstairs and have fun!" and then they leave for the night. So, kids are running around outside and getting drunk and that kind of thing. And his parents don't care. They don't even talk about it with him. He's not supposed to do this stuff, but it's reached a point where it's so blatantly obvious— they're not stupid people, they can't just have missed it—they just choose to look the other way, which I feel like is pretty irresponsible.

This kid had had another party a while back that I couldn't go to, but my mom had heard about it. So I told my mom I was going to this party. I said, "I'm going to Brian's party and his parents will be there." My mom said, "Yeah, right. As if that means anything." I didn't try to deny it or cover it up. I just said, "Yeah, pretty much." And she said, "All right. Whatever." She didn't say yes or no. So I went. She knew that I went. I stayed the night and came back and we didn't talk about it.

Then we're eating dinner the other night and she said, "So I heard about Brian's party," and did the raised-eyebrow thing. That pissed me off. I said, "What's your implication? If you're implying something, get it out on the table. Don't do this raised-eyebrow crap."

She said, "I just heard it was a pretty racy party."

I said, "Oh, for God's sake. That's such a ridiculous statement."

And she said, "Why is that a ridiculous statement?"

So I said, "First of all, that you used the word 'racy.' And second of all, you knew this was going to happen."

The way she presented it was as if to say, "I'm hip. I know what's going on." But she really didn't, so we got into an argument about it. She said, "I feel like I didn't entirely know what was going on," and "I'm upset because I don't think you should be over there. I know his parents don't care and they're irresponsible."

I was thinking, "Wait a minute. You realize this happens every weekend, everywhere." I assumed that she knew this and trusted me to handle myself and not do dumb stuff. But then it came out that she really didn't trust me, and that she really had no idea what was going on. And I felt troubled by this because we'd had conversations previously where I basically said, "Yes, I've been doing this for two years," and "It happens."

So I said, "Wow, you really just don't understand." And she was like "What don't I understand? Tell me what I don't understand." But I said, "I'm not going to tell you that because the last time I told you I got in trouble." I would like it if we could talk about these things. I really don't like lying to my parents.

My best friend's parents do the freedom thing pretty well. He's a very good student, he's very smart and he does very well in school. As long as he does his schoolwork and doesn't screw up the rest of his life, he has a lot of freedom. "If you want to smoke pot or if you want to go drinking, if you want to have kids over here and go drinking, then we'll let you do that." But if he ever got into serious trouble, got arrested or something, or compromised himself academically, his parents would kill him. They were really hard on him about homework, much harder than my parents were; my parents are hard on me about drinking or partying or any social life in general. They are polar opposites.

His mom said to me, "I don't entirely understand your mom's thinking on this. We feel that if Keith wants to have a couple kids over whom we know, who are close friends, and you guys want to smoke pot or something, that's okay. We know you guys are going to do it, and we would much rather have you do it here, where it's controlled, and not do it stupidly than have you running off to someone's party or going to Motel 6 and partying. We feel there's a lot more risk in that." There's real honesty there, which I feel I don't have with my parents, and which I kind of envy. My mom says, "No. None of it. Ever." And "If it's in my house, I'll kill you." And "If you do it anywhere else, then I'll kill you."

I think I'm more logical than my mom and she's more emotional than I am, but I still have a big chunk of emotion. And that's part of our problem because my logic is generally beaten by her emotion. I'll be saying, "I've completely beaten you, you don't have a leg to stand on." And she'll say, "I don't care, I'm your mother, you still lost." So I can't really win.

DRINKING

Adam, 18, from a suburb in the Northwest

When I was in sixth grade I matured quickly. With sports it was awesome because I was the biggest one, and I didn't really have problems with being teased because I had facial hair within a year.

I had my first drink when I was twelve, at my brother's college graduation party. Ever since then I get nervous because I find myself being led around by a devil and am afraid he is going to take over. It's like in cartoons, with the good angel on one shoulder and the bad devil on the other. When I have the option to do something bad or something good, it's like a constant argument between the two. Listening to that devil is exciting, thrilling; it's what I have been doing for a long time. I know it's bad for me, but it's what I want to do. And so I tell myself to do it a small amount, keep it under control, but the problem is it's hard to keep those things in control.

By seventh grade I was drinking regularly, a continual process of becoming more and more into it, and by eighth grade I was drinking every weekend. I drank hard alcohol a lot, never really beer. In some ways I thought it was exciting to be drinking a lot. I didn't think it was that big a thing, especially since I was so young. I wasn't worried about being an alcoholic.

I'm the youngest of four brothers, and they are all gone now. It's very lonely, I guess. Before my older brothers left, life was awesome. I would get tickled a lot at home, and I loved it. It was better with them around because not all of the attention was on me.

Just after my brothers left, my parents got separated. They didn't divorce, and they got back together about three years later, but it was tough to deal with. They thought that I was getting in trouble because of them, and they kept telling me, "Oh, it's not you. It's just that you're mad at us and are rebelling against us." I cared about them but none of the drinking or smoking had anything to do with them.

I had urges to do that by myself, I guess. I had seen my brothers drinking before, and my dad would drink wine during dinner or after, and so I felt like I wanted to try it. And when I did try it, it sparked this thing inside of me and I realized how much I liked it and how much I wanted to do it. I liked the thrill of drinking. Someone once said that my dad and I were basically twins, in that we were both thrill seekers and risk takers. My parents have always told me to channel that thrill seeking into something more positive, and I guess if I had the option to, I would. But you can only skydive so often; it's not nearly as accessible as alcohol. So on the weekend I became prone to just go drinking.

I've felt depressed so many times. It's hard to be steady because there are so many things in life going up and down—your friends, how school is going, your parents, getting into trouble, your social situation. The depression comes in cycles of a couple of days. In that mind-set, I've thought about suicide before, but never seriously. I've thought about it maybe twenty or thirty times, but just randomly, kind of daydreaming. I've never thought about planning it, though. Some good thing will happen—I will have a good weekend or something—and then I'll be really happy for the rest of the week. But it's hard to keep up because there are so many things to take care of, so many responsibilities with school, with all the sports. There is so much constant pressure to achieve. It's like being enclosed in a room, with such a repetitious life of playing sports, school, and just hours and hours of studying. And you get so lonely in there, and you get depressed just sitting at your desk until all hours of the night, studying and reading books.

I wouldn't say that I started drinking to mask my pain, but that's what my parents thought. It's kind of hard for me to tell if I was masking, because I was blocking it out so much that I wasn't really examining myself. I just wanted to put all those feelings in a room and close the door. I didn't set fire to the room with all this stuff in it, though. I didn't burn the house down, but I definitely kept the door shut. Going into that room is painful, and I just didn't feel like putting myself through all this mental trauma. If it's a problem that needs to be dealt with, of course I will deal with it, but if it's a simple thing, if it's something that can be blocked out and I won't suffer for it, then I would just as soon block it out. It's easier.

The pain that I think guys deal with is a private thing. Girls are always talking about pain with each other and the terrible things that happen to them, but guys deal with it privately. At least, the pain I deal with is mostly inside. Maybe a random two or three times in my life, I have talked to my friends about the really serious problems I've had. They want to help you with it, but it's just an awkward situation. It's touchy-feely. Not like they are too macho to do it, but it's a thing that you just don't do. It's understood that it would be going out of the boundaries, like stepping into some area where people don't really want to go. Something that just doesn't feel right.

With the help of Alcoholics Anonymous and a counselor, I have realized that I can take control, that I have to deal with myself and not let other people take care of me. I have realized that I have to tame myself and decide what my actions really are going to be. It's good to talk to someone who knows what you are going through, who has gone through it themselves, and who knows the type of person you are.

The most amazing thing that I learned was how when people stop one thing, they will start up another. I understood how one thing leads to the next. It's like a row of stairs and you just go from one to another; you just get bored with one drug and you move on to the next. It's this process where you go deeper and deeper.

In middle school I was drinking and we were doing anything for the crazy thrill. But then I looked at myself and I thought, "That's terrible. If I keep doing that I will end up killing myself. I will get bored of everything and I will try the strongest drug and finally kill myself." I realized I needed to limit what I do, because maxing out on everything is just terrible.

Turning to drugs and alcohol to solve your problems just prolongs them. It's something to heal it just for the moment, a temporary relief from the pain. The pain is still there afterward, and you still have to deal with it. It's just for that couple of hours, or that night, when you don't have to deal with it. To deal with a problem you have to talk about it.

I Don't Do It, Period

Emmanuel, 17, from a suburb in the West

My stance on drugs and alcohol is just, I don't do it, period. My friends have loosened me up, because some of them do it (not drugs so much, but alcohol). Previously, before I'd met them, I was really hard-lined. I didn't want to have anything to do with it, and I didn't want anybody else to have anything to do with it.

Now I've loosened up, so my friends can do it if they want to, but I just don't. It's still not for me, but I feel less judgmental.

I feel good to be able to say that to this day I've never smoked a cigarette or had any sort of drug, and the only alcohol I've ever had is some wine at a special event with my family or something. I just feel like it's wrong. It's an escape from the real world.

But in the real world we have real problems, which you should deal with rather than try to escape.

A Major Problem

Malcolm, 17, from a suburb in New England

Last year, when I was a junior, our school baseball team traveled to Cooperstown to see the Hall of Fame. We were caught drinking by our coach and the state athletic association, whose penalty is two weeks or two games, whichever is more severe. Since there was only one week left in the baseball season, we had to miss that and also the first football game in the fall.

It was an especially big deal because I had just been elected my class president when it happened. I gave an apology speech to the class because the school administration said that, as the representative of my class, I shouldn't have done what I did. Then I had to write a letter to the parents. I did what I was asked to do, because I had to, but I didn't necessarily agree with it.

Probably 80 to 90 percent of the students in the class use alcohol, 60 or so percent on a regular basis. The people involved all talked about why we did it, and the best answer I could think of was that drinking is something we do almost every weekend anyway. If I had thought I would get caught, I knew the consequences and I would not have done it. But you never think you're going to get caught.

The incident has changed my relationship with the baseball coach. He knew that we drank alcohol, but he didn't think we would throw it in his face. He told us that people had worked very hard to put this trip together, and that we had put a serious damper on it. I know that I hurt the coach a lot. The day before the trip he had spoken to the entire team about not drinking. What we did so obviously showed a lack of respect.

The problem is that as soon as someone tells you not to do something, you're going to want to do it. That is the attitude that teenagers have toward authority. Drinking is something that we can do to rebel. And if you walk into any high school in the country, they'll say that alcohol is a major problem. It's the way teenagers operate. People drink and they don't realize their limits. Kids are not like older adult people with all their ideas and ideals all shaped. They're shaping and changing.

Drinking brings together a mixed group of people. There will be people who you don't necessarily hang out with all the time, but if someone is having a party, everyone will be there. People will intermingle among cliques. It's not like they'll give up their whole persona, but they will tolerate different people in order to be where there is a party—not because of alcohol, but because that is where the social scene takes place.

My parents have been understanding because they know that underage drinking might be wrong, but it's real. I had a conversation with someone about how I'll deal with alcohol and my children. In one sense you have to be a good parent and punish them at times, to teach them lessons. But in another sense, you know that they're going to go out and do it anyway, no matter what you do. So it's the old catch-22. If you teach them about alcohol, a lot of people say you're encouraging them, but I don't. I think that I'd rather teach my children about alcohol than have to go to a hospital and see them hurt.

After the incident in Cooperstown, I was grounded for a month or so, until the last day of school, and awhile after that. My parents were most mad that I risked so much. They were also mad that they had driven me up to Cooperstown with the beer actually in our car. They were really upset about why I would put everything on the line. Like, "Was it worth it?"

It wasn't worth it. But I did it. It's over and it wasn't worth it. What can I do now?

NOW I AM CLEAN

Paul, 16, from a city in the Northeast

When I was about twelve years old, about three years after my parents were divorced, my mom started hanging out with a guy I really didn't like. I harassed him quite a bit and my mother asked me to leave the house. I think she thought this would get me to behave better.

But I was too deep in my own self-pity that I didn't care about getting better. I couldn't believe my mom kicked me out over her boyfriend. By this point I was willing to do anything anyone dared me to do. So when kids in the cool group introduced me to smoking pot, I figured, "Why not?" I figured nothing else could go wrong for me at this point.

Boy, was I wrong. To support my new habit I began stealing money from my family and soon enough my grandfather also got sick of my antics and started getting violent. I walked down the street to the nearest pay phone and called my dad to see if I could live with him. He came up to get me that night and all I had were my clothes. So I moved back in with my dad.

In eighth grade, for some reason, everything went wrong again, and I stole about three ounces of my dad's marijuana. When he went to North Carolina on a business meeting, I got into the liquor cabinet and crashed my dad's Cadillac. He sent me back to my mother's house in New Hampshire, which lasted for about a year.

She couldn't take it because she was always worrying about where I was or what I was doing. One night I came home at eleven when I was supposed to have been home after school. When I got home she asked if I would like to go rent a movie. So I got in the car, not noticing all of my belongings stuffed in the backseat of the car. She dropped me off at my dad's and threw all of my stuff on the lawn and told me that from here on in, I would be living with him. This was just as much of a surprise to my dad as it was to me. We got along for about six months.

Then, with help from a few friends and some stupid choices, I dis-covered acid, PCP, and crystal meth. Now, instead of yelling and slam-ming doors, my father and I got into full-blown fistfights, and eventually he got sick of this. The police got involved when I was arrested for pos-session of marijuana. I went to various lock-ups and youth centers, then went to a shelter. I resided there for about a year and it gave me time to think about what I've done to myself and my family and to clear my head of all the substances I had put in there. I realized I had to slow down and mature a bit. Also I had to realize the importance of family.

As of now I am clean except for occasionally smoking pot and still being hooked on cigarettes. But I'm passing all of my classes. Best of all, I've got my whole family back.

ALONE

Kirk, 18, from a suburb in the Northwest

I'm not very happy. I was recently accepted into college, and now I have just started to slack off. It's been hell for four years, but I'm almost through. At least school is better than it was last year, when I was sure I wasn't going to get into college. I'm pushing myself for two more months, and then it's done.

My friends and I do a lot of drugs. We get high on everything. We drink a lot and smoke weed. Drugs that I've seen at my school are Ec-stasy, cocaine, mushrooms, alcohol, and pot. I've done Ecstasy, but I don't do it now. I smoke pot and drink.

I'm addicted to pot and I have my share of problems with it. Some-times I think it bums me out. I always want to smoke and when I try to quit, I can't. I start to wonder what my life would be like without it.

We all experiment. We limit it to coke and Ecstasy. Everyone knows that people start with pot, then you drink, which leads to other drugs. Ecstasy is the drug of our generation. The grossest thing about it is that the next day I feel retarded. My body feels like a piece of shit. When I'm on Ecstasy, I don't talk and I'm not myself. That's what I noticed the last time I was on it. I have one friend that we call the "Gnome," be-cause when she does drugs, she puts on her hood and hides under the blankets. She just watches things without expression. Then one time, I was called the "Guy Gnome" because I was doing the same thing. That was the last time I did Ecstasy, and I noticed that I hated it.

I don't like really hard drugs. All I do now is drink, smoke weed, and take mushrooms—pretty normal. Every year I drop acid or something.

I don't really know who I am when I'm alone at night. It's a confusing time for me right now. The real me is sensitive and confused, and trying to get through this harsh time. I think I am going to be seen as the kid who has everything except brains. He has accomplished everything and is leading a good life. At the same time, he's not happy with things. He's depressed sometimes. There is definitely always something going on inside. I'm confused, I'm not happy.

I think it's hard growing up in the year 2000. It's definitely hard for a guy. Going through high school is tough. I have pressures in sports, school, life all rolled into one. My parents pressure me to do well in school, do well in sports, and I pressure myself to do well in life. My sister got like a 4.0 GPA and 1450 on her SATs. She didn't party at all in high school. We are exact opposites. It's so hard to live up to her that I never really tried.

I was always a huge athlete but not great in school—learning disabilities. I'm documented. Slow processing, poor concentration, but I don't have dyslexia or anything. I definitely do have some minor disability. It's hard sometimes, especially here in school. I've got something the other kids don't, and they have something I don't have. I blame it on an accident I had. I almost drowned as a child, as a baby. I was at the bottom of our pool for two minutes before my mom found me and gave me CPR. The doctors said nothing happened, but I personally disagree. I think I was damaged.

Everyone tells me I'm smart, but I don't believe them. I used to get down on myself a lot. As much as my parents would say to me "Don't ever let anyone say you're stupid," it only made me start to think that I was stupid. I told them that if they were trying to help, it wasn't working. I remember being teased back then, too, and getting upset about being made fun of. I was always a really good athlete and good with the girls. But kids knew where and how to attack me. They all knew that I wasn't the smartest kid in class.

I worry about life a lot. I feel like everything is going to work out for everybody except me, that I'll be left behind in the dust.

But I think everything will come together. I'll be on my own, learning to live.

22

LOSS: COPING WITH INJURY, ILLNESS, AND DEATH

"I may have appeared OK, but inside I was still hurting"
—Charles, 13, from a town in northern New England

THOUGH LOSS IS AN INEVITABLE PART OF LIFE, MANY OF the boys we interviewed seemed to have experienced more than their fair share, and at far too early an age. It is difficult to know the reasons behind this apparently increased incidence. Maybe it's the reality of coming from ever more disintegrated families, a reflection of these boys' bravado-based injuries, their susceptibility to suicide and homicide. It may also be that they simply felt safe enough, in the context of a "real boy" interview, to be candid about their greatest sources of sadness and disappointment.

I am impressed that one of the few contexts in which boys tell me that they feel it's OK to express vulnerable emotions—to cry openly without fear of being shamed—is at a time of serious loss, injury, or death, a moment of tragedy when the Boy Code rules are momentarily suspended. At a funeral, a car accident scene, a hospice for the terminally ill, boys are given a small window of opportunity to grieve, a temporary shame-free zone in which it is acceptable to remove the mask of masculinity and cry. But boys break free of the Code only momentarily—following a spate of onetime tears, they are still expected to block the complex and longer process of true mourning: talking through the loss, crying over and over again, gradually letting go of the sadness. Instead, a boy must get it over with and then "suck it up," hide the inner pain gnawing away and try to be there for others. A boy is not supposed to fall apart.

Many boys still feel the need to move quickly away from their sadness and loss. They speak of the gender-specific burden society has created: to do versus to feel, to be mad rather than sad, to get over depression that is only worsened by the stoicism we so unfairly require them to maintain. Seventeen-year-old Travis, from a suburb in southern New England, whose father died of cancer, still remembers the "close times together." But he found that the loss left him feeling simply "angry." Andy, fourteen, from a suburb in New England, talked about his mother's pain following the sudden death of her companion, Dan: "I know it's hard for her." But, said Andy, "I don't want to get upset in front of her because I don't want to make her any more upset. I can't stand to see her upset. I can't stand it. She cries and cries."

Victor, seventeen, from New York City, told us about his reticence to talk with his friend Michael, who had just lost both his parents to AIDS. There is a shame boys feel that makes them uncomfortable doing what in their hearts they long to do. It would, of course, be different if Victor were female: "Michael probably doesn't feel comfortable talking about it with me. . . . What if he starts crying? . . . Like if he were a girl he would probably go to his closest friends and talk about it."

Boys such as Victor and Michael routinely suppress the feelings surrounding life's toughest challenges—moving away from friends, being rejected by peers, romantic breakups, becoming ill, suffering physical injuries and disabilities. Ron, seventeen, from a suburb in the West, was already trying to convince us that the military life of continual uprooting could be easily absorbed by a child. But as he began to reminisce, the deeper feelings surfaced: "The hardest thing about military life is constant moving . . . when you're ten, twelve it's more difficult." Ron told us that in keeping up his correspondence with friends in other ports, "your hands get tired easily." While he was trying to convince us—and himself—that he was "happier moving around," Ron stumbled onto what I believe were the more deeply buried, painful memories. "Granted, there is a major downside," he said, "that feeling of being completely torn away from everything you know each time you leave." The pain of loss, even for our all-too-stalwart sons, inevitably seeps through.

Life is full of losses big and small, many of them unexpected. Witness the voices in this chapter and you will discover that long before they find themselves in desperate straits, boys long to be able to tell us: "I'm really hurting. I need your help. Would you please hold me close?"

MY DAD

Travis, 17, from a suburb in southern New England

My dad was diagnosed with leukemia in 1996. That day totally changed my life. For the following year I barely got to see my dad, because when I went to school it was pretty early and he'd sleep in. Then when I got home either he'd be in bed for the rest of the day or he'd be at work and get home late. I hated the fact of not being able to see him that much. This made me very angry. Just the fact that he was sicker than a dog and lying in bed all day.

He also changed a lot about himself. He went on a diet of veggies and fish. No milk products. He'd take a load of supplements. Every morning he'd make carrot juice in our juicer. He'd take enemas. And he also started Chi Quong. You know, like meditating. Started believing in the process of *chi*. I had so much hope. I knew that Dad was going to be OK.

When he was diagnosed the doctors said he was going to die in two months. So two years later Dad goes back to them and they were so amazed.

The years of his sickness went in a pattern. The first year was nasty. He'd always be in bed. The second year was so awesome. It seemed like he wasn't sick. Then the third year was back to the bed.

The good thing about the sickness is that Dad and I got real close. We spent a lot of time together. Like fishing was one of the biggest things we've ever done together. We also did projects. And then I bought a rocket. In the middle of the third year of his sickness we launched it. It was the last exciting thing we did together—that's why I'm big on rockets. I have three now. Every time I launch one it makes me think of Dad being right next to me. Looking up at it with a cheerful face.

Then the last two weeks came. Dad was acting very strange. One day my cousin picked me up from school and told me he had passed on.

I Don't Ask Him

Victor, 17, from New York City

I live on the fourth floor of a brick apartment building that has six stories. The elevator is very old and is always getting messed up. There are three rooms: a kitchen, a bathroom, and a living room. And there are three bedrooms: my mother's room, my brother's room, and my room. Me and my friend Michael share my room. They threw him out of the house where he was living before. He came to my house because his parents died. I don't like to talk about this, but his parents died of AIDS. Both of them.

It's very hard for Michael. And now ever since that time, he went into drugs. He is twenty-one. And my grandmother, ever since that time happened, she treats him like her son. She stays at my house a lot and she tells him, whenever you want to eat, just come by, just come home. And right now he is living with us. He eats at my house, he sleeps. I have a good time with him. He is cool. How are you just going to throw him out like that, understanding what he has been through?

I feel close to him. It's hard for him. I know it's hard. His parents died when he was about sixteen years old. They died about a year apart. His father died first, then it was his mother. And the sad part about it was that he thought his mother was going to survive. Like the doctors were telling him, "She is doing great. She's improving." And he was telling me one day, "She is doing good. She is probably going to stay around." The next thing you know, she just died. It's a pretty sad story.

I treat Michael like my brother. That's just how it is. I tell him, "You stay at my house as long as you want." I am pretty caring. That's one good thing about me.

When he first moved in my grandmother told him, "This is your house. You can do anything you want. This is your house here, this is where you are going to live." He started crying. Every day as we are leaving the house, right at the door, my grandmother always stops and says a blessing. She did that for Michael. Nobody did that for him before, and she did it. And he started crying. And he came and hugged her, and it was pretty nice.

Michael and I have become pretty close. We play together. I like to bother him. When he is sleeping I throw things at him, like a pillow. I'm like "Hey, fuck you!" Things like that.

Then he will be like "What's up, sucker?"

Right now he has to loosen up more. He's still uptight around our house. Sometimes I will test him. He'll be watching something on television and I just change the channel. And he won't do anything. Why? Because it's my house. And I tell him, "You don't have to be like that. This is your house, too. You could tell me to stop. You can tell me, 'Yo, Vic, what are you doing? I'm watching this.' "

It's been about five years since he lost both parents. But he doesn't talk to me about them. And I don't ask him about it. I don't know how he would react to it if I asked him. It's a big deal, losing both your parents. Like if he were a girl he would probably go to his closest friends and talk about it. He probably doesn't feel comfortable talking about it with me. I don't think I could ask him, and I know he feels bad about it. Just imagine losing both parents, then being thrown out of the house.

I want to get to know him better. Like I want to get to the point where I could tell him anything. Like "How does it feel not to have your parents around?" I would love to hear what he would tell me. Maybe I could help in some way. But I don't think I could ask him. What if he doesn't like it and starts crying? I probably want my grandmother to ask him. She will feel better talking to him about it. My grandmother is more experienced. She is old. He could probably see her as his mother, and he could talk to her about what he's feeling.

EVEN THOUGH I DON'T SAY IT

Charles, 13, from a town in northern New England

I live in a small rural village with my grandmother and two aunts. I am sure you are wondering why I don't live with my mom and dad.

Well, it all started when I was about eight months old. My mom died in a car crash. My dad took care of me for a while. That came to an end when I was about two years old. My dad was not physically able to take care of me. So my grandparents adopted me.

I was lucky enough to get adopted by my biological grandparents, so I know my family tree. For years it didn't faze me that I never knew my mom or my dad very well. As I continued to get older, my wonder grew more intense. Even though I don't say it, I have always wondered what it would be like to live with them. Even though I have a family who loves me dearly, sometimes I wish I could experience life with a mom and dad.

When I was around ten, my grandfather died. This was the first death of someone who was close to me. Don't get me wrong—I do miss my mom—but I never really knew her. I knew my grandfather very well. He would spoil me, take me to the park, and he even said that when I turned twelve he would take me golfing for my very first time. This is why it was so tough for me to move along emotionally. I may have appeared okay, but inside I was still hurting.

When I was going into the sixth grade, I had open heart surgery. This was a tough time for me. The fear of not knowing if I'd live to see the next day was growing stronger each passing day. It was then that I said to myself, If I make it through this, I will look for my dad when I get older.

Well, here I am today, a healthy thirteen-year-old boy playing sports and living a happy life. I have my grandmother and two aunts to thank. They have helped me get through my life by answering all my questions and just being there.

SOMEPLACE NEW

Ron, 17, from a suburb in the West

I think I'll probably wind up at a university on an ROTC scholarship. That means that my college will be free, but when I'm finished I'll have to do six years in the navy. I don't mind at all because my ambition is to be a career naval officer, working in the navy for twenty-plus years. It's basically the only life I know. Both of my parents were naval officers. I'm used to going from one place to the next.

Some people don't want to follow in their parents' footsteps, but it doesn't bother me. However, when I was really young, I did not want to be in the military, and I didn't want anything to do with military service. I wanted to be in business. But as I got older I started to realize that I knew nothing about business and that my parents, being career military officers, would not be able to help me if I chose a business career. I started looking again at the option of a military career, and I began to appreciate the things that my parents like about it. My parents have made some strong friendships over their years in the service.

The hardest thing about military life is the constant moving. It's hard to move every few years and live somewhere completely new, starting all over again so many times. It was much easier for me when we moved out West to this town because I'd lived here before (between ages seven and ten) and I knew the place. I already had a pretty good base of friends when I moved back here, and it was easy for me to just fall right back in with them. Of course for adults it's a little bit easier to maintain communication between friends over long distances. But when you're ten, twelve, thirteen, it's a little more difficult because you're not experienced writing letters and your hands get tired easily.

People who live in the same place their whole lives have a singular view of life. They maintain the same set of friends their whole life. While there's a lot to be said for that, I am much happier moving around. Granted, there is a major downside, that feeling of being completely torn away from everything that you know each time you pick up and leave a place. But if you're used to moving, you gain the ability to go someplace foreign to you and build yourself a new friend base, making new acquaintances, new friendships, and business relationships. And once you go someplace new, you learn how to maintain the friendships you left behind.

I MISS DAN SO MUCH

Andy, 14, from a suburb in New England

When I was four years old my parents were divorced. At the time I was too small to realize what was going on. I cried, but I didn't know what I was crying about. Now my dad has been going out with another woman for ten years, and they are engaged. My mother went out with a couple of people, and then she went out with someone named Dan for three and a half years. He was probably the greatest guy I've ever met, and he died just after Thanksgiving last year.

Dan was a great athlete. He could beat anyone. But there is a kind of heart attack that athletes get for some reason, and there is nothing they can do. Snap, like that.

My mom is not always happy, but when she was with Dan, she was. Her face just lit up. That's what I wanted for her, and I was so excited for him to be my stepfather. I loved him, but I never actually said it. I wish I could go back and say "I love you." He taught me a lot. He was the funniest guy. He used to run. He grew up in Brooklyn and his mom's name was Estelle. He used to say, "Boy, if your mom was Estelle, you were so lucky. She would whip you into shape." He was the best story-teller.

I think that even if their mothers aren't divorced, most boys feel that they have to protect them. And my mother is so upset because she and Dan were in love. Real love, like the thing you see in the movies. They were going to get married. When I see my mother in pain, I want to do something, and I can't take her pain away.

Lots of people think that some boys are very insensitive, and that they act stupid and cocky. But the truth is that all boys have feelings. They just don't like to show it because they want to keep their manly lit-tle thing going on. People don't realize that maybe boys act like that, but they are not really mean, or uncaring, as you might think.

When Dan died, it was a shock. He was played racquetball every day. He won tournaments and beat twenty-year-olds. He was the best at every sport: baseball, basketball, tennis, football, and everything. The week before, he had played racquetball for two hours and he was fine. But that week he played and five minutes later he sat down and couldn't breathe very well. Then he was gone.

My mom was away on business so I found out before she did. They called her and said he had a heart attack. She asked, "What hospital?" and my aunt paused, so that's when my mom knew. My dad told me at school. He took me out of school and I thought it was my grandparents or something. I never thought of Dan.

I have never been so upset in my life. I have never lost anyone be-fore, and I miss Dan so much. He was at our house most of the time. He had said that my mom was the first person that he always felt really loved him. My mom said that is something that she feels happy that we got to give to him. My mom was the love of his life.

My mom is working now, but she is not doing very well. I know it's hard for her. I don't want to get upset in front of her because I don't want to make her any more upset. I can't stand to see her upset. I can't stand it. She cries, and cries.

If you sit by yourself you think about it too much. Lately I can't re-ally get my mind off the subject anyway, because even when I am think-ing about something else I tie Dan in with it somehow. Like I will be playing golf and I will say, "Golf, Dan would be playing golf." And I think about Dan's golfing.

When he died, we had a meeting at school with counselors and all of the girls to say what they all thought about stuff. We all talked, and I talked about Dan. This girl was crying, and her parents were crying, everybody was crying. They think I am a good speaker but I think it's just because I know what to say. Lots of people trip up on words. They don't know what to say. They can't express their feelings. I am pretty good at expressing my feelings. I think everybody has strong feelings, but they just don't know how to say it. It never gets out, so you never really know. You don't see that side of them because they don't know how to say it in words.

I have tried in my life to be more understanding and not think about looking like a real tough guy. If a girl is talking about something, I won't say, "Oh, that's stupid." I try to listen. I speak my mind, and people appreciate that. I try to help people, and I like to talk to people.

It's worse to try to pretend you're not upset about something when you are. I think that in some cases the image is stupid of guys not opening themselves up. It's not true. Guys don't have to be like that. I am happy that people feel comfortable talking to me and I like being able to express my feelings.

CANCER

Jim, early twenties, looking back on his nineteenth year, from a city in the Mid-Atlantic states

"Right this way."

"Have a seat."

"Put this on."

"Roll-up your sleeve."

"Squeeze your fist!"

"Sign here."

"And here."

"Mr. and Mrs. Richter, come this way."

"'Bye. See you in a while."

"We love you!"

"Read and sign this."

"Now, we are going to take you . . ."

Voices, voices, and more voices. In addition to all of those sounds, I vividly recall a gray, slippery, tile floor. I remember cement walls with few hangings which accentuated those same voices. A chair, a table, a sink, and a stool filled the sterile square space. A bed on wheels arrives. I assume it is for me. I am still not sure why I am here.

All of a sudden my bad dream seemed to be a reality. A kid from the suburbs isn't supposed to be here.

Why am I here? I am overcome by confusion. Too many voices and sounds. Too many unanswered questions. I go with the flow. I assume my parents are in the know. I trust them. Who else would I rely on? I am only nineteen. They know best. That is what parents are for.

Awake for the first time in days, it seems I am met with the same confusion and similar noises. Only now I see my parents and some unfamiliar people in light blue scrubs. My throat is parched and I am unable to speak, although people are relentlessly asking me questions. I nod in response to "Are you in pain?"

I am given instructions that would bewilder a Nobel prize winner.

"Do this."

"Don't do that."

"Push this if you are in pain."

"Push this for assistance."

"This tube drains this."

"This one checks that."

Who knows what they are telling me? I once again have to rely on my parents. I hope they understand what is going on.

After what seems to be a weeklong rest, I am awakened to the familiar voices of my friends. It is Wednesday, of course. Everyone in the small room is standing and watching *Beverly Hills 90210* on television. I can talk. I can express my displeasure with the pain. I can converse with my parents and ask them questions. Some answers still elude us all.

My friends and family allow me to feel somewhat normal, although I still feel helpless. My friends have never seen me so vulnerable. Is this normal? I can't imagine it is.

The waking minutes feel like hours. My body doesn't feel the pain while sleeping but automatically senses it while conscious. I am not permitted to eat solid foods. Someone must have told me that at some point.

I watch television and visit with friends and family until I can no longer keep my eyelids open. I fall asleep still not fully aware of my surroundings and my circumstances.

My first experience in the hospital has come too early. I am not ready for the mass confusion, frustration, and clearly not the illness that follows. My unwavering optimism and indestructibility shatter during that stay in the tall brick building with square, sterile rooms. At age nineteen my body, depleted by illness, threatens my life.

Why now?

Why me?

What does this mean?

What is cancer?

All of these questions flash in and out of my mind. Unfortunately no answers follow. Simply contemplation. Contemplation that lasts and never seems to reveal simple resolutions.

Most nineteen-year-olds don't encounter these situations. Do they? I can't imagine going through this again.

More important, I can't imagine going through such an ordeal without my parents. Who else would make sure I receive my medicine on time? Who else would decipher all of the voices I am hearing? Who would figure out all of the insurance problems? Who would inform all of my relatives and give them updates?

Without my parents it would have been easy to give up. It would have been easy to fall through the cracks. Depression would have taken over. I may have become a victim.

Luckily they were there. From the first empty, tile-filled room; to the small, crowded stall with people barking instructions; to the private upstairs bedroom with the television and a view of Camden Yards. They were there every step of the way.

Thank God.

PAIN

Ray, 15, from a suburb in New England

I've missed you Mema
Each and every day,
I regret not staying in touch with Pepa
For now he is so very far away,
I wish you could understand the pain through the years,

The rivers full of tears,
Dad, I don't know what to say,
But I think about you everyday,
The time will come,
When we will become one,
Again!

PART V

BOYS IN THE WORLD

23

OVERCOMING HATRED, RACISM, AND POVERTY: JUSTICE AND ACTION TALK

"No man is an island unto himself."
—Ben, 17, from a small town in the South

N O MAN IS AN ISLAND UNTO HIMSELF," BEN TOLD ME, OB-
viously taken by the words from John Donne's sermon "For
Whom the Bell Tolls." Wise and insightful beyond his seventeen years,
Ben responded passionately to the deep meaning of the phrase, seeing
its relevance to the serious problems of racial hatred that divide his
small rural town in the South. "It's usually a black person and a white
person," Ben explained, as he began to describe the violent brawls that
frequently broke out at his school. "But it's not necessarily one race's
fault," he added with sensitivity and understanding. The "root of the
problem," Ben said, "is ignorance."

From the inner cities to the suburbs to rural farming towns like
Ben's, many boys are keenly in touch with the hatred and bigotry in
America. They are profoundly aware of the poverty, which destroys people's dreams, and of the injustices and misfortune that fate can thrust
upon any human being at any time, regardless of that person's race,
class, sex, religion, or sexual orientation. Many of the boys with whom I
met are working to speak out against injustice and create new voices of
fairness and hope. This is the "action talk" that allows them to transcend

the mask of masculinity and make their feelings heard. Traveling across the country, I encountered boys who were actively fighting racism, poverty, and homophobia; boys who were establishing peer counseling groups, antibullying programs, and suicide prevention services at their schools; boys who were walking for breast cancer and biking cross-country for AIDS; and one boy who participated in dangerous search-and-rescue missions to help save people who are lost or in jeopardy.

Beginning decades ago with Carol Gilligan's groundbreaking research at Harvard that showed how important it is for girls to express their voices, research has indicated that many girls show a propensity toward empathy and care, while in many boys one encounters urges toward justice and fairness. My own work confirms a portion of these findings: boys care deeply about moral and ethical questions and feel compelled to inveigh against injustice. But I have also found that boys especially want to reach out, take action, and connect with other people to end the wrongs they see around them. As he considers how racism might be eliminated in his small town, Ben suggests, "You can't just rely on yourself to do something. . . . Everyone should try to seek a connection and a relationship with other people. . . . That's the water I guess that surrounds the island."

Yet boys like Ben encounter two hurdles that frequently hold them back: a Boy Code that still forces them to act "macho" in order to prove their superiority and hold their ground (or otherwise lose face), and an ongoing prejudice against boys themselves, whom many in society still see as essentially thoughtless, violent, and dangerous. Thus Ben, who works hard to teach his peers that "people shouldn't judge based on stereotypes," is only too well aware that "it's usually the boys who fight one another . . . because when you're a guy you've got to stand your ground . . . act masculine and not look weak." But Ben helps us go beyond the stereotype and grasp the truth that many boys—far from being the instigators of society's harshness and hatred—are actually caring people who derive tremendous personal satisfaction from reaching out and helping others. Ben told me that he and his friends volunteer at a local housing project for the elderly who have lost their family members. On one recent occasion, Ben remembered, "We sang for them, cooked for them, helped lift their spirits. . . . It made me feel good."

He is not alone. Boys across the country are taking action to care for others. For sixteen-year-old Bart, from a suburb in the West, this means speaking out on the need for tolerance. Believing we have to change people "one at a time," Bart derides our adult society—and rightfully so—for creating what he calls "the toxic ideals [of] scapegoating and prejudice." He sees hatred as the source of much of the vicious bullying that pervades our schools. As I listened to Bart's list of oppressed minorities and absorbed his passion to eliminate hatred and prejudice, it occurred to me that even as they work to make life better for others, boys like Bart and Ben are still struggling with our narrow vision of them as boys, a vision that too often deems *them* toxic and forces them into a narrow conception of what a boy should be.

"People in this world don't pay much attention to seventeen-year-old Hispanic males," explained Ramon, a young man from a city in the Northeast. "I think that the people who have all the power don't want to listen to me in case I say something that threatens them."

And what, I asked, was Ramon's "revolutionary ideology"?

"I want my kids to have a better life than I did. I'd like them to grow up in a more compassionate society," Ramon writes poems set to music, trying to create more justice in this world.

Seventeen-year-old Ethan, from the West, echoed Ramon's cry: "It would be better if everyone was just treated the same regardless of their race or their sexuality and we could just get over this sort of thing."

Yet if boys are asking for an end to racism and hatred, they are also asking for us to see *them* in a new light: as compassionate rather than cool, as loving rather than hateful, as sweet and gentle rather than violent. Warren, a warm, intelligent high school student who lives in New York City, understands the complexities of race, age, and gender. At fourteen, he knows that being African American *and* a boy makes him particularly vulnerable to other people's fear and prejudice: "I can't pin it all on race," he says thoughtfully. Realizing that even other African Americans may perceive him as dangerous, Warren tells his story: "I was in front of my building one day, and a black lady was walking by with a shopping cart. She crossed to the other side of the street just to pass my building, and then crossed back. Is she scared I'm a robber or something? People act a certain way when they think I'm a bad person."

But Warren thinks well of himself. "If you get to know me," he says with confidence, "you'll know I'm a good person." He sees knowledge as the antidote to hatred: "If I could, I would just tell them to spend the day with me, chill with me and see how I act. Don't think of me as a bad person just because you see me for five seconds. Hang with me today, and get to know me. I'm a cool person."

In this chapter you will have the opportunity to "hang" with boys like Ben, Antonio, and Warren, boys who are eager to speak out against injustice and take action to effect change. It is difficult not to admire their courage, for here are sensitive and generous boys who are bravely defying a society that still prejudges them as surly, hateful, and dangerous. These are boys who, rather than placing themselves alone on an island, are busy building bridges of love and tolerance, helping us connect to them from the mainland.

AMAZING TRANSFORMATIONS

John, 17, from a city in the Northeast

There's a lot of freedom in the camp I go to in the summer. The focus of the camp is building trust, and I've learned a lot about myself there. In comparison to school, it's more accepting of differences in people. It is really open and accepting of everybody, and people feel very comfortable with who they are. Every night we all walk down to the chapel in the center of town a half mile away. There's always a different topic being discussed, like nonviolence, sexuality, gender. It's a place where people get to share things about who they are and get things off their chest.

The first summer I was there, I was eleven and going into seventh grade. All through middle school, there was a lot of homophobic language. We didn't know any homosexual people, and we weren't really being malicious, but we perpetuated a lot of bad language and stereotypes. When I first got to camp, I made some comments about people using the kind of language we used in middle school. And the guy I was with brought me over to the person I was talking about and told him what I had said. The guy was surprised. He challenged me, "So, what do you mean by that?" And I said, "Wow, I didn't even think about that before I said it. What *am* I saying? What do I mean?" That was a big wake-up call for me. I realized the camp just wouldn't allow the kind of behavior that was tolerated in middle school.

When I was in middle school, I used to get picked on a lot for being Korean. That was what people did. It was never really malicious, it was just part of the culture. I never realized how degrading it was until I went to camp and had this experience.

I can still see the behavior today. When I play sports, some of the guys are really competitive, and I find it annoying. I like to think of myself as breaking out of that mold. I don't want to be like that at all.

I've always been helped a lot by the Landmark Program. It breaks down reality as you know it and gives you new ways of understanding what human beings are and what they're doing. If I hadn't found this program, I think I would have been completely lost.

The program made me realize there is a clear difference between what I thought I wanted to do, and what I actually am here to do. I've always been interested in helping other people. I define it by saying, "In my life, I want to cause amazing transformations for people." And I've learned a lot of new ways to coach people through difficulties.

I got one of my friends to make a commitment to stop smoking. She didn't tell me that she smoked when we first met, because she didn't want me to think badly of her. But then I noticed her biting at her fingers, so I got her to make a commitment to stop smoking. After camp ended, I've been talking to her and calling her and writing her—just keeping in touch and coaching her through this. As much as I know, she stopped. It was amazing to help make that happen.

SEEK A CONNECTION
Ben, 17, from a small town in the South

We have racial problems in our school. That is something I really don't like. Most of the fights aren't started because someone comes up to somebody else and pushes them. They begin when someone starts confronting somebody else—it's usually between a black person and a white person but it's not necessarily all one race's fault. Usually people of each race are to blame.

I don't understand what these people have against each other. I think we need to get to the root of the problem, and that is ignorance. People need to have a better understanding of each other. If people weren't ignorant, they wouldn't associate with only their race.

In our town it's the "farmers"—white working-class people—who usually feud against the black people who live in the downtown neighborhood. I have pity on the kids who fight against each other. I think it's stupid. I wish there was something I could do, but usually the school administration takes care of everything. Sometimes I get frustrated, because I don't understand.

It's usually boys who fight one another. It's boys, I think, because when you're a guy, you've got to be macho, you've got to stand your ground. You can't be a wimp and give in, especially when it comes to other people of the same race. You think you have to be faithful to them, and stand up for your color.

I don't think people who fight based on race really have a motive. I think their hatred has been ingrained into them. It's almost like tradition—it's the way they're used to thinking. Fighting is what they think they should do. The hatred maybe starts with the parents. A lot of times I think it starts there. Or maybe someone of a different race did something hurtful to them, and they just automatically assume that's how everyone within that race behaves. People often generalize based on one bad experience.

People shouldn't judge based on stereotypes. Just because one group may act differently than another—listen to different music, wear different clothes—other people shouldn't hold these things against them. They should get to know the person. Don't judge a book by its cover. See if the other person is like you on the inside, and then you can choose whether or not to associate with him or her. And if you have a grudge against someone, even if you have a legitimate reason to be mad at someone, you shouldn't make it into a big conflict.

Maybe the reason there are these fights is that certain kids fear rejection by their own peers. They want to be a part of a group, and the group thinks that if you don't stand up and fight, whatever the conflict may be, if you give in, say you're sorry or whatever, then you've ruined the identity of your group.

On our football team, everybody really gets along well. Our team is pretty evenly balanced between white kids and black kids. But racial tensions don't really arise among the players on the team because we associate with each other. We have a lot of similarities. You are playing the same sport. You are around each other five or six times a day, five or six days a week. And that can make a difference.

If you have a conflict with somebody else, you really need to talk it out. I can usually deal with my problems myself. But if I ever have a major problem, I can go to one friend in particular. I know him and he knows me.

If more guys got the help they needed, we probably wouldn't have as many problems with fights. A lot of guys when they are upset, instead of doing what I would do, which is go to a friend, or go to my parents, or go to church and pray, instead fight, or take things out on themselves.

You can't be successful unless you have God there to support you. And even if you sit in a room by yourself, you are not *really* going to be there by yourself. And what happens to you in that room is going to affect everyone else in your life—your family, your friends. You can't just rely on yourself all the time in order to do something. You have to reach out to other people. That's the water, I guess, the water that surrounds the island.

No man should be an island unto himself, because then he is isolated. He is trying to be too self-reliant. But if he reaches out, makes friends, connects with his family, has faith, has a connection with God, that's where life begins, that is what life is about.

Everyone should try to seek a connection and a relationship with other people. Choose what you are interested in. Don't play sports just because it might make you a little more popular, because you're not going to be as happy. It's not sports alone that can give you that feeling. If you are really into music, you can go play in the band. Or if you are really good at chess, join the chess club.

It's not just about reaching out and connecting with other people, it's also about helping other people. If you do something good for someone, you make them feel good. Then you feel good about yourself. I recently went with a youth group to visit with several elderly women who had lost their families and had to live in special housing. We sang for them, cooked for them, spoke with them, and prayed with them. We really helped lift their spirits. They really enjoyed it. They smiled as we sang Baptists hymns. It made me feel good.

My advice to people is to love one another. Do unto others as you would have them do unto you.

CHILL WITH ME
Warren, 14, from New York City

Being a black guy, sometimes there is a lot of pressure on me. You've got to act a certain way to be accepted by society. A lot of times I've been hanging out with my friends, and we've been stopped and told to spread out, to leave. Once I was in front of my building, just talking to my friends, and the cops came and said, "You can't hang around these buildings." I told them, "I live right here," but they told us we couldn't hang around there. It made me feel bad, because if I can't chill in front of my own building, where can I go?

I can't pin it all on race, because some cops are black, and sometimes black people look at me as a bad person. I was in front of my building one day, and a black lady was walking by with a shopping cart. She crossed to the other side of the street just to pass my building, and then crossed back. Is she scared I'm a robber or something? People act a certain way when they think I'm a bad person.

Okay, the way I look sometimes is real thuggish. Baggy jeans, hood over my head, like that. If you get to know me, you'll know I'm a good person. But when people don't know me, they look at me and see how I dress and how I look, and they think I'm a bad person. So they're afraid of me. They probably think I'm going to rob them or try to mug them, anything bad. People are used to seeing on TV, in the news, how the thuggish black person dresses. It makes me angry, but I try to just zone it out. If I get too mad, I go on the football field and I just take it out.

You can't concentrate on racism and things like that, because it will only bring you down. If they think you're a bad person, let them think it. Just don't act out on it. Because sometimes people may think you're a bad person and you'll get so mad you'll actually do the acts they expect you to do. In my own mind, I've got things I want to say to them, but I'm never going to go to somebody in anger and express how I feel, because that would be wrong of me. It's wrong to inflict your anger on them.

If I could, I would just tell them to spend the day with me, chill with me and see how I act. Don't think of me as a bad person just because you see me for five seconds. Hang with me today and get to know me as me. I'm a cool person. If trouble comes my way I'm going to handle it, but I'm not going to go to somebody and start trouble with them.

REALITY CHECK
Abraham, 17, from a suburb in the Northeast

I'm into doing things for other people. It's almost selfish, because I get more out of it than I give. When I get that feeling of "Oh, my God, I helped someone out, I changed someone's life," I don't want to do anything else.

Two summers ago, I went to Honduras and worked for two weeks in a school and housing center for orphan girls—from first to sixth grades—called Guadalupe Center. I stayed at the orphanage while we built the foundation for a new building. My days were spent mixing cement by hand, digging a trench, then dropping rocks into the trench along with the handmade cement to form a kind of rough, "third world" foundation. We worked eight long hours a day, and then we'd go back to the orphanage and hang out with the girls.

The girls follow a strict routine. They wake up at five o'clock every morning, cook breakfast, pray, and then go to school. Their teachers, most of whom do not have a college degree, teach two grades at the same time. On the left side of the classroom is one grade, and on the right side, the other grade. School is all about memorizing facts, not about thinking. Constant repetition is the Honduran philosophy of education.

One of the girls in the sixth grade, Sara, was eighteen. She was a woman among girls. She was no taller than five feet, with long black hair, brown eyes, and dark skin. She was fully developed and looked like she was about thirty. She lived with three of the younger girls in a tiny room, the size of a small kitchen. She had only two changes of clothes. She was very shy and had no self-esteem.

School was impossible for Sara. Imagine the frustration she must have felt when she was unable to do what girls six years younger could do. She did not fit in. She felt alienated. If she had lived in an affluent American community, she would have gone to private school, or had a tutor and a psychologist, not to mention a loving family and a stable home. In Honduras, she had only herself.

Sara and I struck up a strange friendship. She was extremely immature, but somehow we formed an amazing relationship during the two weeks I was in Honduras. I came to love her, but it wasn't a sexual thing at all.

Last summer I learned that Sara could no longer stand being at the center and had left, hoping to get a job as a needle worker. She would probably make less money per month than many wealthy American teens get for their allowance. She might easily get raped and end up with a family she couldn't support. My first reaction was "Why did she do that? She should have stayed in school. Why couldn't she just tough it out?" It would have been great if she had graduated and gone on to make a good life for herself, but I realized that she wasn't going to, and she was probably going to fail. Then I thought, "If I was in that situation, I probably would have done the same thing."

Thinking about her had a huge impact on me. I realized how lucky I am to live where I do. It opened my eyes and put everything in perspective. I don't worry about as much stuff anymore. When I came back from Honduras, I spent the rest of the summer working at a swim club, where all the kids are rich suburban kids. The culture shock was bigger than anything I had experienced before. I realized that if I was to fail out of high school, there would be so many people there who would help put me back on my feet and get me started. I could go to a tutor support program. But Sara had none of that.

Although I will probably never have the opportunity to tell her, Sara has had a larger impact on my life than anyone else. She showed me, for the first time, that life is not easy for everyone. Everything is not given to everyone. For so many years, everything has been given to me when I ask. My idea of a problem has been receiving a grade of B instead of an A on Friday's math quiz. Sara opened my eyes to what real problems are: not having enough food, not receiving an adequate education, and not having a family or a support network.

Sara provided a reality check for me. She showed me how blessed my life has been. I will never forget her shy smile, the letters we exchanged, and the friendship she shared with me. Now, if I get a B on Friday's math quiz, I no longer get upset. I know that, in the scheme of the world, those sorts of problems are not important.

I REALLY CARE
Antonio, 17, from a city in the Northeast

I don't believe in violence. I would never kill anyone unless provoked to do it. The person would have to be endangering the lives of my wife or my kids. My neighborhood is divided into a lot of blocks and some blocks have a lot of power.

I've only fantasized about using a gun once but I don't think I'd have the heart to shoot anyone. I wouldn't have the heart to mug somebody, because I'd just look at their eyes, and I'd just feel what I would feel if I were them.

I don't get scared of guns, though, at least not when I can't see them. If I got scared of other kids with guns, I'd also have to fear some of the other cold realities surrounding me: crime, sexually transmitted diseases, violence at home, not getting financial aid, and not being able to go to college.

I don't fear anything. Well, the only thing I fear is being reincarnated and coming back to live the life I have today—that's the only thing I fear.

When I heard about the shooting in Littleton, Colorado, I thought it was really sick and terribly sad. But then I realized that that's what happens when people have a lot of things to say and no way to say them. When people have things to say and no one listens to them, they try to prove that they're big guys or heroes, or even villains, just to get attention. Maybe they needed love and they needed to say that to see if somebody would give it to them.

Society is tough on boys. Many people see us as worthless and they treat us like scapegoats. I think they blame us for a lot of things that happen in our society. But we can't help it if we've grown up in a really bad environment. Some boys have parents who don't love them and mistreat them. The way parents treat you is so important. The only foundation you get for life is the love of your parents. If you don't get that sort of love and nurturing, sometimes you go looking for it in drugs and violence.

I am grateful for my family and for the people who love me and I'm glad I'm succeeding at school. But there's one thing I want that I don't have. I'd like to have a voice, a powerful voice within my own community. If I could have anything I'd like to have the power to talk to my community, to tell them that you can overcome adversity. I would tell them not to trust the politicians who cut welfare money. I want everyone to have the same opportunities in life and I want everyone to get a good education. The more information people have, the easier it is for them to make the right decisions.

SEARCH AND RESCUE
Jamal, 17, from a suburb in the West

I am on a full scholarship at a private school because the tuition is more than my mom makes in a year. We live on government assistance and disability insurance, and the whole monetary issue can be kind of depressing. It can be hard at a school like this where everybody's parents have so much money. It's not so much that they look down on you, but they just make assumptions. People at my school always have what they want, like if you don't have a car they wonder why. Well, I just can't afford one.

Everyone has the thing that they are good at. If someone is really book smart and can study and do really well, they might have no friends because they just don't know how to relate to people. But some people have really good social intelligence and can play it. And I think that's where I'm strong. My teachers might not say I'm the best student, but I'm good when it comes to figuring stuff out quickly and coming back with something to say.

I enjoy people and like helping them. I volunteer at the sheriff's department doing search and rescue. I am the president of the unit and the captain of my team. When someone gets lost, we get requested by ranger stations or sheriff's departments all over the state to go and look for them. There are three different types of searches that we do. On evidence searches, you look for weapons. We also have urban searches, which are usually like kids or Alzheimer's patients who wander away and don't know where they are. And we have wilderness searches for people who go out hiking and get lost, or mountain biking and fall down, stuff like that. Recently we looked for a missing four-year-old girl who's been all over the news. The last search I went to was up in the mountains and we got to fly in a huge double-prop helicopter. It was awesome. They dropped us down and they said, "Go out." We did our area and it took us all day. The helicopter came down and picked us up and flew us back. It was awesome.

I started doing search and rescue because I am interested in the outdoors and all the training. Also helping people is a big part of it. Actually one of our unsuccessful searches was for one of my friend's grandparents. She was an Alzheimer's patient and she wound up dying because we couldn't find her. I just wouldn't want something like that to happen again. And I like problem solving, being able to look at a problem, analyze it, go through it and see what could happen, and then go and investigate.

24

MUSIC, ART, AND WRITING:
BOYS TALK THROUGH CREATIVITY

"It really helps me if I write it down, because that gets it out of my mind. I can clear it out, put it away . . . save it for later, save it for a song."

—Marc, 13, from a suburb in New England

BOYS WHO ARE ABLE TO EXPRESS THEMSELVES THROUGH music, acting, writing, drawing, or any of the other arts have the fortunate opportunity to release a myriad of emotions in a zone of safety. Although they may be laughed at and considered "feminine" when they publicly display deeper, more sensitive parts of themselves, through art they seem to feel more free and far less constrained by old Boy Code rules that equate self-expression with weakness and vulnerability. When a boy is painting a landscape, drafting a poem, or orchestrating a symphony on his laptop computer, he is able to express deep parts of his being—sadness, anger, fear, loneliness. He might write a poem to reflect a broken heart, draft a rap song to capture his outrage about poverty, splash vivid red paint on a canvas to express his fear and anguish.

"Music is the main way I express myself," explains sixteen-year-old Nicholas, from a state in the West. "It's crucial, it really is, to maintain my character, and it's really an excellent outlet for a lot of the delinquent energies I have, like anger and frustration and sadness and emotional turmoil. . . . I can express a lot through my lyrics, and when

I'm on stage I can express a lot just getting it out. When I write a song and it's about something that's just killing me, it's just angry—I sing it, and then it's just all gone, you know?" In our gender-straitjacketed society, this kind of personal, emotion-based expression is crucial to many boys.

Creative expression need not only be reserved for the talented. Any boy can keep a journal or explore emotions through color. Further, the witnessing and interpretation of art may provide just as significant a release as the act of actually creating it. Hearing a piece of music can unearth a boy's sadness. Watching a play can shed intense emotional light on a personal problem a boy might be experiencing with his father. I cannot tell you how many boys who have told me that they found themselves in fifteen-year-old Holden Caulfield from *The Catcher in the Rye*. Many said that after reading *Catcher,* they no longer felt quite so alone in the world, that they were relieved to learn that another boy had experienced the same feelings of angst and of yearning.

Sixteen-year-old Caleb, from a suburb in southern New England, explained what he learned from listening to the music of the Cure: "You have Robert Smith, this beautiful man who is very much in touch with the same sort of things you are. You don't even know this fellow but he's had the same sort of problems, and has written about them, and shared them. . . . He can just proverbially spread his wings and everything will come out of him. . . . You're not very strong if you can't be yourself because you're afraid. But if you can spread your wings and be independent and be yourself, you are strong and beautiful." For boys like Caleb, art has the power to begin healing the painful bruises left by the gender straitjacket. By experiencing expression, boys learn how to create it. By deconstructing the voices of others, boys discover their own.

Creating and interpreting artistic expression is a way by which boys reach out for a sense of authentic connection—for relationships in which they can relax and be themselves—especially with other boys. Thirteen-year-old Franklin finds his most important friendships as a drummer in a local rock group: "The band is very important to me. I can always be myself around the guys in the band, and I never have to worry about them judging me or thinking badly of me. Being in the band is like having brothers, except that you're not around them all the time." And as Nicholas explains, artistic expression can be a vital source not only of companionship but also of understanding and affirmation: "On stage playing with my band, it's just a thrill to see people clapping and having fun when they hear something they like. That means a lot to me. There's a whole lot of empathy going on when you're on stage. It's just really good to connect with people like that—that's a big part of being in a band."

For some boys, expressing themselves through music, art, and writing seems to be a matter of their very survival. I will never forget the day Andrew Glass, a forty-one-year-old father, came to see me about his twelve-year-old son, David. Mr. Glass, a tall man with curly red hair, was a very successful music engineer. He described David as a shy boy who was exhibiting quite a bit of talent in piano performance and composition. David created his own short piano pieces and performed works by Chopin, Bach, Grieg, and Beethoven with flourish. Mr. Glass wanted to ensure that he gave David the proper amount of encouragement to pursue his talent. Although he wanted his son to do well in school and sports, and to be well-rounded, Mr. Glass was concerned about whether it was OK to give David his permission to pursue music as much as his son wanted.

Then Mr. Glass told me about his own childhood. His parents were survivors of the Nazi concentration camps in Poland. Both his parents lost their entire family to the Holocaust. They came to this country penniless and emotionally devastated. In America, all their energies went into earning a living. They believed that if they acquired enough money and bought a house, nothing bad could happen to them in this country.

As a young boy, Andrew Glass loved to play the guitar. He couldn't get enough of it. At night, he would spend hours singing along with old rock albums, and at school he performed with a jazz band. His music teachers thought he was exceptionally gifted. But when he came home from school, Andrew often found that his father had put his guitar away in the closet, broken strings off the instrument, or thrown away his son's sheet music. His father was enraged that Andrew spent his time pursuing music. He believed his son Andrew would never earn a living this way, that he would never make a life for himself in America. He felt that Andrew should focus on subjects that would help him get ahead in the world.

"Sometimes, my father beat me if he found me with my guitar," Mr. Glass said. "His fear was so great that I would turn out to be penniless like he was after the war." But no matter how many times his father broke Andrew's guitar strings or threw away his music, Andrew found another way to keep enjoying the instrument. "Sometimes, I would hide my guitar in the bushes behind our house, sneak out late at night, and play my instrument in the woods where my father could not find me. It was my lifeline," he told me. "There was so much pain in my family that I was never allowed to question or talk about it with other people. Why did my parents have numbers tattooed on their arms? Why did my mother often break down sobbing? Why did other boys make fun of me because my parents had a foreign accent? Why was my family so different from everybody else's in the neighborhood? These things deeply troubled me. But music kept me alive," Mr. Glass told me. "It was my lifeline. I want to make sure my son has that lifeline, too."

Today as well, many boys experience artistic expression as a place offering emotional safety where they are acknowledged for revealing their genuine selves. "Music," says eighteen-year-old Stewart, "is my sanctuary." There are so many hurts, challenges, and pressures in the lives of boys and young men, and so few places they can go to overcome them. We help boys by encouraging them to take any opportunity they can—whether it be singing in the church choir, doing the lighting in a school play, playing guitar in a band, writing poems, sculpting clay—to use these creative activities to express their true emotions and to find their own voice.

BEAUTY

Caleb, 16, from a suburb in southern New England

Despite our attempts to fill ourselves with all these artificial, horrid things—Diet Coke, steroids, hair spray—we are all part of this world, and we have a connection to it. Beyond all of the problems we may have, we still have that simple connection with the world and its beauty. You can still connect yourself at one in the morning with the night. You just sit. . . .

Everybody always has somewhere to go. I mean, you're never completely free. I don't find security, and I don't think I'm free, I've got it all. There is always going to be an occasion where you might find that you have a weakness. And you improve and you get better and better. You just never can stand still. There is always more to learn. I think that the basis of things is to be as you are, and to accept other people as they are. You can be completely different from someone but have that one thing in common: that you accept each other as being independent people who have fun with themselves. And you might have different interests, but you share them with each other and involve yourselves in each other's interests sometimes.

I've had a lot of people who follow the same surprising pattern of sort of coming and going quickly for one reason or another, like quick angel visitations to teach me one thing or another. The first one I can really remember was a fellow named Oscar, who was a counselor at my summer camp two years ago. He was just a brilliant guy and he was someone who really supported me, and would say, "If you want to go write, you go write, that's what you do." He helped me finish what I started, and he was really proud of me for a lot of things. He was a very special person.

Even though he was like fifteen years older than me, Oscar was on my level and we could help each other out. I think I helped him just as much as he helped me. We both had the problem of being nice guys who get beat up—you know, not tough enough to be cool. We had that in common and we could talk about those kinds of things. He was a thinking person. He was a caring person. He was open and he could really appreciate a moment. He didn't get angry at things. In fact, he was very calm, and he could always just be happy and enjoy himself.

The big turning when people really started to respect me was when I started bringing my writing into school to show to people. They started realizing that I'm really doing something with all of that time I'm not out playing football. You have to show them what you do, you know? If the pastry boy brings in some really good doughnuts, the kids are going to like him more, or at least understand why he doesn't play soccer. They're going to say, "Damn, he really makes a great doughnut." And in a strange way, he'll get respect for that.

So be honest about your passions and show what they are in a candid way. You're doing something that you are passionate about and that's all that matters. Every person should know their own strengths and show them in a candid way, and not focus on their weaknesses. If you have something you want to do, you should do it. We should all be able to say, "This is what I really enjoy doing. This is what makes me feel good."

For me, the things that make me feel good, that I really enjoy doing, and that have earned me some respect are music and writing. They are really amazing things, because you are creating a physical act of beauty. You have all of this inside of you and it's not even words or music yet, it's just sort of essence, and you put it into a form that can be distributed and perceived and interpreted. And it's really fascinating. Music is special because of the emotions you can invoke. Anything, anything you want. And it doesn't even have to be real words coming out, because you can interpret the emotion just from the sound.

I work with electronic bass, alka synthesizers, drum programming, samplers, and things like that. But at the same time, I work just as much with sounds and patterns that are very ethnic or influenced by a much older sort of ethnic music. Even with a modern drum machine, it can be this whole sort of shamanistic thing, with the idea of just getting in a circle and hitting the bongos and clapping and dancing and singing. There is something about beat that, if it's just right, can really move you. I think music should be sort of a safe haven. It should be empathetic to how you are feeling and able to bring you solace.

I listen to the Cure because you have Robert Smith, this beautiful man who is very much in touch with the same sort of things you are. You don't even know this fellow but he's had the same sort of problems, and has written about them, and shared them. I think Smith is brilliant and he's a beautiful man, just because of his emotions and his freedom of expression. He is almost consummate emotion. He can just proverbially spread his wings and everything will come out of him.

If you have to band together to step on someone else's hand, then you're pretty weak. You're not very strong if you can't be yourself because you're afraid. But if you can spread your wings and be independent and be yourself, you are strong and beautiful.

Writing is hard because you never know if something is good or if it's just a waste of time. But it's really nice when people encourage you and ask to see your work as soon as it's done. My mom encourages me, but I think for a while she was kind of scared. She was worried about the tragic themes and things like that, like I had a fascination with death or something like that. It's a reasonable thing to think if you're really not sure of what someone is saying as a writer. But I had a huge influence from the Gothic literature period and the Romantic period in all forms: the stories of King Arthur, the music, the poetry. Everything from those periods is beautiful and it was just something that worked for me. I'm always going for beauty, and I think for some reason it's recognized more in the tragic. That's just the way it is. And it all depends how you conclude things, and I don't really go for the clichéd happy ending. I want it to be something beautiful. The way I feel about fiction is that it is a catalytic duty at times, because it's where you can really see everything in all it's glory. It's almost like measuring the density of something by using displacement. To see how big it really is, you take that area away. You see all of this change because of it and you realize how much of an impact it had on everything. It's very different in real life because it affects people, but when you do it in fiction, you're safe from that: you can watch and you can listen because you're not part of it. The same tragic story on the news would be miserable. It's when you're not connected to it that it can be beautiful to you.

One of my favorite books is *Interview with the Vampire* by Anne Rice. It is absolutely beautiful, for a lot of reasons. First of all, the characters are so real—it's pure emotion. And also there is the lesson or the philosophy of the book. By the end of the novel, the huge significance is that Louis realizes that despite his thinkings, despite all his attempts to search out and create beauty, there was never any better opportunity for him to accomplish that than in his mortal life. And he tries to explain this to the boy who's interviewing him, but the boy doesn't understand. He still insists his life is too difficult. Every day we all refuse to believe the fact that we really do have a lot of opportunities. You really can find beauty. That you're in the perfect state to do so. Yes, you suffer the mortal coil, but along with it you have the benefit of this ability to create and to feel.

It's all about really getting a connection with the world. And you improve and you get better and better. You just never can stand still.

GETTING IT OUT
Nicholas, 16, from a suburb in the West

I play guitar and sing in a band with a drummer and a bassist, and he sings, too. We play all originals. Music is the main way I express myself. It's crucial, it really is, to maintain my character, and it's really an excellent outlet for a lot of the delinquent energies I have, I suppose, like anger and frustration and sadness and emotional turmoil. All these things.

Music isn't for everyone, but it works for me very well. I can express a lot through my lyrics, and when I'm on stage I can express a lot, just getting it out. When I write a song and it's about something that's just killing me, it's just angry—I sing it, and then it's just all gone, you know? It's a great, great outlet. Ever since I've been a wee little lad, I've been into theater and performing in front of people. I've always just had that kind of actor's attitude, I suppose. I've never had a problem being on stage.

Pretty much anyone I meet, essentially I put on a show for them, subconsciously. It helps me make friends, I guess. It's not a departure from my personality at all. It's more like when you're racing a car and you put the nitro on—it's just that extra little boost. And it's not just when I meet new people—it's when I stand up in front of the class or when I have to read something. I think it's pretty universal for actors to have that. That energy makes you do stupid stuff in public, like run around or tackle your friend, and that's a part of my life that I'm really happy with.

On stage playing with my band, it's just a thrill to see people clapping and having fun when they hear something they like. That means a lot to me. There's a whole lot of empathy going on when you're on stage. It's just really good to relate with people like that—that's a big part of being in a band, and a big part of life.

Do What You Feel Is Comfortable

Marc, 13, from a suburb in New England

My dad has his own company and my mom works every day except for Wednesdays. But Thursday is her late day and my dad works until six-thirty, so I have the house to myself until then. I just sign up for after-school programs and they usually end at four-thirty. Then I go to Mobil, get myself a coffee and walk home. And then I watch a little TV, and then my dad will be home.

I like writing. At night, I'll jot my feelings down and if something happens, I'll write it down. I have a drawer full of lyrics that I could put into songs—sad things, good things, and how I feel if someone bullies me around. I have one song that I wrote about being who you want to be: "Don't be a Trendy / Do what you feel is comfortable." I thought that was such a great song. I was so proud of myself. It was great. . . . I was singing it to myself all day.

My mom was like "That's a nice song; who's it by?"

I'm like "I don't know," because some of the lyrics she wouldn't understand.

She would be like "Marc, you're really weird. Are these actually *your* lyrics? Do you need help or something?"

But it really helps me if I write it down, because that gets it out of my mind. I can clear it out, put it away, whatever; save it for later, save it for a song or something like that. And then I just don't think about it anymore.

MY PURPOSE HERE ON EARTH
Ramon, 17, from a city in the Northeast

People in this world don't pay much attention to people like me, to seventeen-year-old Hispanic males. The people who have power and money ignore us. They think we don't know what's going on, that we're too young and too immature to have anything to say. Well, I'm seventeen but when I'm eighteen I'll be old enough to go fight in a war. I think that the people who have all the power don't want to listen to me in case I say something that threatens them.

Well, I want my kids to have a better life than I did. I'd like them to grow up in a more compassionate society. There's no way I want them to see some of things I've seen. I've seen kids get beat up, and three-month-old babies get slapped. I've seen terrible things on the news: the police brutality, the way homeless people are treated. It makes me sick.

There are a lot of things I'd change if I was in charge. I'd like to change our budget, the way we spend our tax money. We spend way too much money on the military, sixty cents out of every dollar. That's too much, especially when we spend only one percent on welfare and 2 percent on education. I think helping those who are less fortunate and educating our youth is far more important than going out to fight wars.

That's why I think it's so important for me to speak out. I just want those people in power, the people that run the media, to understand people like me. Those people should realize what we go through, what we feel, what problems are important and how they can be fixed. I just want them to see things from a whole new perspective. When politicians talk about gun control or welfare, they gotta understand that they're not the ones living in the inner city or the places where all this violence occurs. They're not in our shoes. I want them to have the opportunity to listen to what I go through day after day.

So that's why I love to write. I write poems and then I go to the studio, where I put the words I have in my head to music. I know that some people will listen to me that way. I figure I've got a lot to say to people and I like to be heard.

When things don't work out the way you want, you've just got to relax, be patient, and look on the brighter side of life. I love being a rapper and want to have a record released in the stores. I've been recording in the professional studio with real DJs and producers for two years now. I haven't tried yet to take my work to the record companies; I just make music for my friends so they can listen to what I have to say.

You know, my poetry is so important to me. When I have things to say, I say them in my poems. It's easier that way—I can't always talk to my mom about everything. Sometimes she doesn't understand and sometimes she's old-fashioned. The people I rap with appreciate where I'm coming from. They may disagree with me but they understand what I'm talking about. I don't really have anyone I bare my soul to but I'm not lonely. My pen and paper are my shelter—they're where I go when I need to think about something and talk about it.

Music is great because it gives me a way to speak to my culture. People in the inner city like to hear about other people going through the same things they go through. It helps them relate to other people. They also love to dance and I love to watch people dance. I love to watch people listen to my words—it makes me feel important.

I want to improve things. I think that's my purpose here on earth. I see a lot of people that are just intelligent, and they don't use their minds the way they should. I think if you're gifted enough to make a change, you should make that change. Because if you don't there are a lot of people that won't.

I'm a firm believer in destiny. That's why I try to make the most of every single day that I live. I want to have beautiful memories so at the time I go, whether it's early in my life, whether in my mid-twenties or my mid-forties, I'll never regret anything I've done and I'll always be happy.

I WANT TO BE REAL
Ted, 18, from a city in the Northeast

I'm not going to say that I never cared about what people think. Of course when you are in fifth and sixth grades, you worry. Back then I was trying hard not to act the way I wanted to act, to speak the way I wanted to speak, to say the things that I liked and things like that. I was unhappy. I just couldn't be myself in school.

And I didn't like that. I'm not a fake person. I'm more happy now than I was back then trying to be somebody I wasn't. Because it really isn't worth it attempting to be somebody else.

After a while, everything changed. In the seventh grade I stopped thinking about what other people think. I realized that I was being fake. I started going to school more. I started to be more active in school things. I grew up. I started saying, "I don't care what people think. They can say whatever they want to say."

At the end of the day, you're going to do what you want to do, think what you want to think, and be who you want to be. You have to come together with yourself, and realize what you are and who you are, and say, "Look, this is what I am, this is what I can be." You have to build that self-confidence in yourself first. Then you can go to other people and say, "This is what I am, and this is how I'm gonna be—and that's it." And from then on, it will build up, you will have more confidence, and you will really feel better about yourself. Everything will fall into place. Because it has for me.

When I dance, I feel like I can do anything. When I get up on stage, it's all about having fun and being positive and being able to think that you can do what you want up there. It's just a nice feeling. Not everybody gets the chance to have that feeling about himself. To get that positive feedback from the audience. That's good. That's great. I mean, getting up there and everybody clapping and screaming your name, that's fun. I wish I could tell everybody to get up there and do it, do it because it's fun. You really feel good about yourself. It really does make you feel positive. It makes you feel strong. The music sort of gets in under your skin. Once the music gets in you, then it's over! You do what you want. You kind of forget that the audience is there. You just do it, and by the end, it's probably the best performance you can give.

SANCTUARY
Stewart, 18, from a small town in the South

I like music and I love to entertain! I've been Tevya in *Fiddler on the Roof,* and I've been in *How to Succeed,* and *Crazy for You,* and other shows. One of my favorite songs from *Fiddler on the Roof* is "If I Were a Rich Man." You know, "If I were a rich man, yadda, yadda." Yes, I love that one because having lots of money is kind of everybody's wish, their idea of true happiness. *Fiddler on the Roof* was an interesting choice of musical because here in this small Southern town, we have maybe only one or two Jewish kids in our whole school.

I think music is a good way for guys to express themselves without coming out too much and breaking the norm. In choir, it's an easy way, I guess. The guys and girls are put together and so it feels comfortable expressing yourself as a group. Maybe singing in a chorus is an outlet for some people's feelings.

If you are really, really happy—or really, really sad or angry—and you are singing about it, nobody is really going to know. Music enables you to be exuberant about your feelings without people being able to know what is inside your head. It's a secret way of being able to express yourself.

I think guys have a lot of secrets inside of them. They are sort of dishonest. They are keeping secrets about who they really are, what they want to be, what they feel, what they think is right or wrong. Instead of really coming out and saying what they think, they keep quiet and keep secrets.

I try not to have any secrets, but I'm sure I do. I don't go to anyone with them. I just keep them inside. It's sad that guys need to keep secrets.

When I look into the future, I think I want to be a teacher, a music teacher. I would like to help other people's lives, not only with music, but with their own personal situations outside of the classroom, or inside the classroom, just with their own well-being. I would like to help them express themselves through music.

I have always looked up to my music teacher through high school and he is someone who has always been there to talk to. His name is Mr. Forest. He has not only taught music, but he has taught us lessons in life—about how to act and how to be. He has had a really positive influence on everybody who has studied with him. He has always made the right choices. He would never do anything that would hurt anyone else. He looks out for the good of others. He encourages people to be themselves, at least more so than most people. He gives people the opportunity through music to express themselves.

I also get close to God through music. I like singing hymns, playing the organ, and directing the choir.

I love music and like to make others feel better through it. When I want to get away from it all, get away from all the noise and confusion, I go home and, if no one is there, I go to the piano, or to the organ, and just play whatever is there. Music, for me, is a sanctuary.

MENTORING BOYS AND CREATING SAFE SPACES: A 15-STEP PROGRAM

THEY HAVE SPOKEN AND NOW WE MUST LISTEN. America's boys need safe places where they can go to be their real selves, free of shame and the constant pressure to prove their masculinity. As I read and reread their voices, I hear them saying that they want to create a new definition of boyhood, that they are ready to launch a gender revolution that will enable them to become their true selves. They want and need our help to make it physically and emotionally safe for them to do so. They cannot, and should not, make all the necessary changes alone.

Whether you are a girlfriend, a buddy, a parent, or a teacher, there is much you can do to help improve a boy's emotional life and guide him toward becoming a "real" boy, one who does not have to wear the mask of masculinity, repress his true feelings and inner experience, or refrain from saying and doing the things that come naturally to him. You must not worry about expressing your love and attachment. No matter what your connection to him may be, you can become and remain an important mentor and ally throughout his life. You can help create the safe haven that will fully protect him from any further psychological or physical assaults. You can enable him to pursue life without facing constant fear and anxiety.

Many boys are still telling us that when they walk the streets of their neighborhoods or the hallways of their schools, they have to watch everything they do to make sure they will not be taunted or attacked. Others are afraid that if the Boy Code is not dismantled, "another

Columbine" will occur. They are saying that their ability to stay alive will actually be seriously endangered.

While there are myriad ways to effect the changes our boys most need, here are fifteen steps that you and your community can implement to help make boys' lives much more happy, meaningful, and safe:

1. Create many highly accessible safe, "shame-free" zones.   The first step in mentoring a boy is to develop safe, shame-free zones in which he can go to unwind, let loose, and be his real self. Of course, before a boy will enter such shame-free zones, he must be told that they exist and where they can be located. Such a zone can literally be a place—a family room at home, a peer-counseling center at school, a specially designated office at your place of worship. It also might simply be a regularly scheduled event or program, i.e., "Every evening at 7 P.M. we will have a half-hour shame-free family gathering." Or "Every Wednesday after school, all boys will go to their shame-free mentoring group," or "Every Tuesday evening at church is the Boys' Safe Place program." Creating these zones and programs is as important as making sure every boy gets physical exercise, eats well, and goes to school. It lets him know that whenever he feels sad, frightened, worried, or alone, he has a place to go for help.

2. Identify at least one reliable mentor upon whom a boy can rely for guidance, love, and support.   By "mentor" I do not mean only men. While research indicates that young people benefit by having at least one adult who understands and advises them, a mentor can be a person of either gender—a mom, dad, coach, buddy, or girlfriend—*anyone* who will commit to being there consistently for the boy. This must be a person who listens to him without judgment when he is afraid or in pain; cheers him on as he goes about finding his place in the world; gives him a hug when he feels disappointed in a grade or a game, heartbroken over a troubled friendship, worried or sad about a loss in his life, or disconnected from friends or family. Within every family unit, a boy should feel there is at least one mentor upon whom he can count. At school, ideally every boy should know that he has at least one such person upon whom he can regularly rely, whether it is another student his age, an older student, a teacher, counselor, administrator, or school aide. It is absolutely crucial that every boy knows exactly who his mentor is, and for that mentor to be available to him dependably.

3. Develop your sensitivity to boys' unique communication styles.
Learning to be a mentor is not a complicated process, but it is one that re-quires training. First, mentors need to learn listening skills and how to set up the shame-free zones I have previously addressed. Specifically, you must learn how to: (1) create the intimate, confidential setting that enables a boy, when he is ready, to open up and share his feelings; (2) give a boy "timed silence" so that he will not feel ashamed when he does begin to expose his inner emotional life; (3) in addition to helping him to find the words to express his inner life, try to offer the boy lots of oppor-tunities for "action talk," such as writing rap songs or playing sports; (4) listen to whatever he tells you without teasing, judging, or shaming him; and (5) give him abundant affirmation and affection, i.e., tell him the good things you notice about him and offer him lots of love and warmth.

Second, as important as learning CPR or the Heimlich maneuver, as his mentor you need to learn to recognize the signs of sadness and de-pression and, in particular, be watchful for action-based approaches boys often take to convey their deepest feelings of loneliness and melancholy. Try to be empathic and sensitive to a boy's true needs when you observe him doing such things as punching his locker, skipping a class, "checking" a fellow hockey player a little too violently, or brag-ging about how drunk or stoned he got the night before. He is probably experiencing emotional pain and other complex feelings that go far deeper than the bravado he is showing on the surface.

Finally, you need to be aware when a boy is in serious distress and requires the kind of help that goes beyond what you are trained to pro-vide. This would include situations when you detect that the boy is se-riously depressed or says or does things that lead you to believe that he may imminently harm himself or someone else. In such cases, you must provide the boy with help from a qualified psychological or psychiatric expert.

4. Talk candidly about the Boy Code and the gender straitjacket. As important as it has been to develop curricula that address how society's old-fashioned rules about girls and women have suffocated their voices and restricted them from becoming their full, powerful selves, it is criti-cal that we develop analogous curricula for boys. Instead of punishing or shaming them because they enact the Boy Code (by being tough, stoic, or aggressive) or because they resist the Code (by engaging in activities commonly seen as "girly" or "feminine"), we must talk to them directly about the ways in which their feelings and behavior may be affected by the Code. Thus, instead of saying things like "Stop being so macho" or "You're such a guy—you just don't understand" or, worse, "You act like such a girl," we might say things more like "Gosh, it really must be hard to live up to the Boy Code." We should be able to say: "If you want to become a beautician, don't let the gender straitjacket get in the way" or "I'm sorry if it's hard for you to get the tears out right now—it's not your fault, it's just the way society has taught you to mask your feelings." Or we might say: "It's normal that you feel so bad about losing that game—society is hard on boys; you did fine in that game, and I'm proud of you!" In the same way that you might impart lessons of feminism, you can help boys by teaching them what you know about how the Boy Code continues to restrict their lives.

5. Teach boys that there are many different ways to become a real man. If we would like boys to become more sensitive, open, loving souls, if we would like them to become skilled at telling us their feelings, if we would like them to become artistically expressive, compassionate to others, and savvy about how to understand the feelings of friends and loved ones, it is important that we give them lots of opportunities to explore the broad range of behaviors and experiences that can lead to healthy manhood.

Sure, the media still often portray men as big, tough, macho warriors, guys who are physically strong and emotionally detached, guys who know how to fight and win. But the media alone cannot be blamed for these stereotyped images. America's boys are telling us that the media are us, and we will not be able to change the media until we change our own attitudes and approaches. At school and at home, you can help boys feel much more relaxed about themselves—and much less afraid of getting harassed—by encouraging and affirming them when they display the kinds of behaviors *you* think are humane and desirable. If you are a girlfriend of a boy, tell him how much you love the way he plays the piano, how much you appreciate it when he asks you how you are feeling, how much you enjoy it when he is willing to discuss how things are going in your relationship. If you are a parent or teacher, you can provide the same kinds of loving support.

No matter what your relationship to the boy, you can help him to get to know men (and other boys) you feel demonstrate the kinds of attitudes and behaviors that you cherish and respect. It's wonderful to talk about a dad who cries when things get rough; a grandfather who tends a beautiful flower garden; a tenor whose arias enchant audiences across the globe; a male teacher, priest, coach, or rabbi whose loving words and inspirational guidance help heal people when they are feeling the most vulnerable. It's up to you to decide the kind of men you want the boys around you to become: you get to choose which "masculine" traits to affirm in boys and which men to hold up to them as role models.

6. Create trusting bridges.   Given the Boy Code and the tremendous pressure on boys to act traditionally "masculine" (thereby shuning *any* help from others), it is important that you make sure the shame-free zones you create for boys are fun, "cool" places to be; places that are friendly, hip, nonjudgmental, and welcoming; places that will build mutual trust and therefore become highly valued. This requires not only setting up desirable physical spaces where boys and their mentors can spend time together, it also means making it clear that boys will not get in trouble for being candid about their experiences. It's important for a boy to know that no matter what feelings or situations he shares with his mentors—unless they involve the risk of imminent harm to the boy or someone else—that he will not be teased, shunned, or punished in any way. It also requires broadcasting the message that hanging out in these safe, shame-free spaces is not just a matter of getting "extra help" when one is in crisis, but that it is a core part of developing one's social intelligence and of getting the emotional support all of us need to deal with the angst of growing up.

At school, this means that the counseling center should not be hidden behind the health office; the peer-counseling room should not also be the home economics space; and mentoring should not be relegated to a monthly elective course. It also means conveying to boys and girls alike that these zones are central to the curriculum, that they are a key component of school safety, that going to them regularly is a highly positive and constructive way to make school, and life in general, much more fun and productive for all of us. At home, it means setting aside regular segments of time—at least once a day—when the boy is given the chance to connect with you in a positive, nonthreatening way, a way that lets him know you will love him no matter what he says and no matter what his struggles may be.

7. Mentors should connect with boys through actions as well as words.
Mentoring a boy should not solely involve becoming a "counselor."
While it's critical to make yourself available to listen empathetically to
a boy's most personal thoughts and feelings, it is also vital to develop a
trusting connection that may come about by actually doing things together. This could include working together to hone the stanzas of a
poem the boy recently wrote; tossing a Frisbee together while talking
about the day's events; going to see a play and then discussing its meaning over coffee; volunteering together at a local nursing home, hospital,
soup kitchen, or urban development program; taking a hike or a drive
together. It could also simply involve putting aside an hour to help a boy
with a tricky calculus problem, a tough organic chemistry theorem, or
an impenetrable line of Shakespeare or Joyce.

8. Empower boys: train them to be mentors, too.   When I sit down to
talk with boys, I often ask them what advice they have for other boys
their age. Often the same boy who might initially have told me that he
is not teased or bullied, that he feels "fine," that he rarely becomes unhappy, lonely, or afraid, suddenly opens up and tells me all sorts of
things he notices that "other" boys experience. By removing the shame
of self-disclosure and allowing the boy to share his observations about
the feelings and issues with which "other" boys grapple, you can help
him, in this indirect way, to actually convey his own inner experience.
Additionally, you help him tap into his own skills of empathy, thereby
discovering the satisfaction that comes from reaching out and helping
others deal with life's ups and downs.

*9. No matter your age and no matter the boy's age, play and become ac-
tive with him.*   Many boys relish the opportunity to explore and express their emotions by being active, playing, or engaging in sports.
Some boys have abundant energy, and sometimes feelings of aggression, that can be channeled, in a positive way, into sports and other
forms of highly active play. Instead of waiting for boys to misbehave
and then chastising or punishing them—and instead of restraining their
activity levels arbitrarily or overprescribing medications like Ritalin—
it is far more effective to help boys find ample opportunity to exert their
energy. It doesn't matter whether you or the boy is athletic or enjoys
competitive sports. What's important is to find ways for him to play and

to make the time to play *together*. Play can include spending one-on-one time building a cabinet, taking a jog, going bowling, or attempting badminton. What's important is being active and having fun together in a noncompetitive, shame-free way. Enjoying this kind of play where the boy does not feel pressured to work or succeed at anything—and where he will not get teased or bullied for fouling a ball, striking out, missing a catch, or losing the match—is a fantastic way to help him release pent-up energy and emotion. It also provides a way to strengthen your connection to one another in a fun, low-key manner.

10. Encourage creative expression. As several of the voices that appear in this book reflect, many boys develop emotional awareness and find ways of conveying their vulnerable feelings through writing, art, and music. Encouraging a boy to become involved in this kind of creative expression—without pressuring him to become a future Hemingway, Mozart, or Picasso—is an effective way to help him experiment with expressing a broad range of feelings, including sadness, disappointment, loneliness, embarrassment, disgust, guilt, terror, and rage. You can help him feel comfortable by avoiding teasing him about his particular interests or about the quality of his products or interpretations. When you clap along with the rock song he wrote, cheer him on at a school drama show, put his drawing of your mother on the fridge, organize a neighborhood poetry slam during which he and his buddies can read their best stuff, you help him tremendously. You are not only giving the boy a huge boost in self-confidence, you are validating his decision to express himself in such a personal and colorful way. Boys also benefit a great deal when you become involved with them in artistic and creative endeavors. You can work together to create a mural, write a song, coproduce an "indie" film. You can also simply spend time together listening to a favorite album or going to a movie you've both been wanting to see.

11. Educate boys about homophobia. So many boys across America are telling us that the fear of being perceived as gay is one of the main hurdles they face in trying to be their real selves. Many link homophobia to the rampant teasing and bullying we see in our schools. Some even link it to the murderous violence we have all too often experienced over these last years.

To be a competent mentor, you must take the time to overcome any awkwardness about the topic and talk openly with him about the ways in which he, and all of us, can transcend the stereotypes and hatred that still exist in our society. Let him know that you will never tease or bully him for being his real self. Tell him it's fine if he is sweet, loving, gentle, or vulnerable, or if he chooses to participate in activities that in some cultures might have once been seen as "feminine." When he is old enough to understand, let him know, too, that you simply do not care whether he is gay or straight. Talk to him about racism and hatred. Promise him that you will stand beside him and actively work with him to educate others about race, gender, and sexuality. Most important, don't wait for a boy to become so upset about how things are going that he takes drastic measures (including suicide) to communicate his angst. Ask him questions about what things are like for him at school and with friends. Make sure he has close buddies. Inquire whether he gets teased or bullied, and whether people call him names like "faggot" or "wimp." Bottom line: be proactive in investigating how the Boy Code and homophobia are affecting the boys you love. You might not only help improve boys' lives, you might actually save them.

12. Bully-proof your neighborhood and schools.   Many boys told me about special programs within their neighborhoods and schools that are designed to educate students, parents, teachers, coaches, and other people in their communities to recognize teasing and bullying when it happens. The programs teach how to interrupt it, how to help the bully involved to understand why the behavior must stop, and, of course, how to provide the victim of the bullying with whatever support and guidance he or she requires. So long as they do not rely on harsh, so-called zero tolerance solutions that leave no room for personal growth and healing, many of these programs can be effective in curbing harassment and violence. You should do everything you can to make sure that your community develops antibullying programs such as these and to see that they address not only the immediate problem of bullying, but also the ways in which the Boy Code creates a culture in which such violence and aggression are still all too common. Also, make sure the program in your community gives students shame-free zones where they can go whenever needed to address the deeper emotional issues that affect both the perpetrators and the victims of violence.

13. Seek appropriate chances to share your own feelings and experiences.   As important as it is for a boy's mentor to listen carefully to what the boy is saying (and avoid interrupting him with the mentor's own issues or agendas), a boy may feel much safer sharing his own intimate feelings and experiences if his mentor is also open and honest about his or her own. By talking about your own vulnerabilities and conveying that you understand and empathize with the kinds of difficulties that boys often face, you will help the boy feel much more comfortable in sharing his feelings and thoughts with you.

14. Encourage spiritual connections.   So many boys told me how important it was for them to be able to relate to a spiritual presence. Many claimed this was one of the few pathways they had found to relate their deepest feelings in a safe environment. You can help boys not only by affirming their interest in connecting with a spiritual other but also by becoming actively involved with them in these pursuits. In addition to encouraging the boy to develop himself by praying, chanting, meditating, or engaging in other similar personal spiritual practices, spend time with him and openly talk about the meaning and importance of these pursuits. Go with him to his place of worship, and use these times to create another kind of shame-free zone in which the boy you are mentoring can express his fears, dreams, and longings.

15. Validate authenticity instead of traditional masculine "success."   As a boy's mentor, the biggest gift you can give him is to make him feel good about being his real self. So many of the peers and adults who surround boys pressure them into proving themselves as "little men," calling upon them to act strong, do well at sports, "score" with girls, achieve at school. Instead of adding additional pressure, you can shift the paradigm and give the boy a giant sense of relief by simply encouraging him to do what he loves doing, by talking about the things he enjoys talking about most. Validate him for being real, not for being "manly." When he tells you that he's vacillating between a career in football or one in cuisine, tell him you'll support him in whichever pursuit he finds the most fulfilling. When he risks crying in front of you, tell him how much you appreciate his honesty and courage, that this is the stuff of which heroes are made. And when he tells you that he is afraid to buck the Boy Code and deal with all the teasing and bullying that could ensue, tell him that you will always stand beside him, that being a real boy is the best and bravest thing he can possibly do.

A MERICA'S BOYS, I BELIEVE, HAVE HAD ENOUGH. THEY WANT to find people who love them just the way they are. They need to be in touch with people who will encourage them to pursue their true passions and speak openly of their vulnerabilities. They need to form meaningful friendships and relationships in which they can be openly caring, loving, and affectionate without the fear of being seen as "weak" or "feminine."

We have a great deal of power to help boys make these changes. All of us—no matter what our age, our gender, or the particular relationship we have to boys—can become their guides. By joining forces against the Boy Code, we can help boys create safe, shame-free zones to which they can go whenever they want to find people who love and understand them. We must help to create a society in which boys can attain the self-confidence and peace of mind *all* human beings naturally desire and deserve.

FOR THE BEST IN PAPERBACKS, LOOK FOR THE

In every corner of the world, on every subject under the sun, Penguin represents quality and variety—the very best in publishing today.

For complete information about books available from Penguin—including Puffins, Penguin Classics, and Compass—and how to order them, write to us at the appropriate address below. Please note that for copyright reasons the selection of books varies from country to country.

In the United Kingdom: Please write to *Dept. EP, Penguin Books Ltd, Bath Road, Harmondsworth, West Drayton, Middlesex UB7 0DA.*

In the United States: Please write to *Penguin Putnam Inc., P.O. Box 12289 Dept. B, Newark, New Jersey 07101-5289* or call 1-800-788-6262.

In Canada: Please write to *Penguin Books Canada Ltd, 10 Alcorn Avenue, Suite 300, Toronto, Ontario M4V 3B2.*

In Australia: Please write to *Penguin Books Australia Ltd, P.O. Box 257, Ringwood, Victoria 3134.*

In New Zealand: Please write to *Penguin Books (NZ) Ltd, Private Bag 102902, North Shore Mail Centre, Auckland 10.*

In India: Please write to *Penguin Books India Pvt Ltd, 11 Panchsheel Shopping Centre, Panchsheel Park, New Delhi 110 017.*

In the Netherlands: Please write to *Penguin Books Netherlands bv, Postbus 3507, NL-1001 AH Amsterdam.*

In Germany: Please write to *Penguin Books Deutschland GmbH, Metzlerstrasse 26, 60594 Frankfurt am Main.*

In Spain: Please write to *Penguin Books S. A., Bravo Murillo 19, 1° B, 28015 Madrid.*

In Italy: Please write to *Penguin Italia s.r.l., Via Benedetto Croce 2, 20094 Corsico, Milano.*

In France: Please write to *Penguin France, Le Carré Wilson, 62 rue Benjamin Baillaud, 31500 Toulouse.*

In Japan: Please write to *Penguin Books Japan Ltd, Kaneko Building, 2-3-25 Koraku, Bunkyo-Ku, Tokyo 112.*

In South Africa: Please write to *Penguin Books South Africa (Pty) Ltd, Private Bag X14, Parkview, 2122 Johannesburg.*